The Legal System

THE LEGAL SYSTEM

A Social Science Perspective

Lawrence M. Friedman

Russell Sage Foundation   New York

PUBLICATIONS OF RUSSELL SAGE FOUNDATION

Russell Sage Foundation was established in 1907 by Mrs. Russell Sage for the improvement of social and living conditions in the United States. In carrying out its purpose the Foundation conducts research under the direction of members of the staff or in close collaboration with other institutions, and supports programs designed to develop and demonstrate productive working relations between social scientists and other professional groups. As an integral part of its operation, the Foundation from time to time publishes books or pamphlets resulting from these activities. Publication under the imprint of the Foundation does not necessarily imply agreement by the Foundation, its Trustees, or its staff with the interpretations or conclusions of the authors.

For Leah

Russell Sage Foundation
230 Park Avenue, New York, N.Y. 10017

Contents

Preface

There is no shortage of introductory books about the nature, practice, or history of law. Some of these books deal with law of one country only; others claim to be more general. Lawyers quite naturally have written most of these books; they therefore reflect the lawyer's point of view. There are, of course, many valid ways to look at law. The lawyer looks at it mostly from the inside. He judges law in its own terms; he has learned certain standards against which he measures legal practices and rules. Or he writes about practical affairs: how to use the law, how to work with it. This book falls into another category. It looks at law from the outside. It tries to deal with the legal system from the viewpoint of social science. Basically, it argues that law is only one of many social systems and that other social systems in society give it meaning and effect. The book will introduce some terms and concepts to develop this viewpoint and to describe and explain legal systems in behavioral terms. The book will also set out a few simple propositions about legal behavior derived or extracted from empirical research on the legal process.

From one point of view, then, this book tries to answer the question: What does social science have to say about law? Social science has in one sense a lot to say; in another sense, surprisingly little. The "lot" is scattered among disciplines and essays. This diffusion and dispersion makes what is known seem smaller than it is. Yet, on the whole, little research bears *directly* on legal process. The body of work on the sociology of law is, with some notable exceptions, the product of very recent times. Behavioral political science is also new. A science of law and psychology is barely beginning. Economics and anthropology have made contributions; more is needed.

Clearly, all have insights to offer. The people who make, apply, or use the law are human beings. Their behavior is social behavior. Yet the study of law has proceeded in relative isolation from other studies in the social sciences. Perhaps lawyers and jurists have not been hospitable. Moreover, law in the modern world is a subject of massive bulk and fearsome technicality; it tends to frighten the outsider away.

This book is about law in general, but since each society has its own legal system, the text best fits the legal system of the United States. I am most familiar with that system, and the law of the United States has been, perhaps, studied more than any other. The social sciences, however, claim validity beyond particular culture. The text has drawn on studies of many legal systems at many points in time. No experiment or study can be rigorous, if it is not comparative across space, or time, or both.

Legal systems are large and have many dimensions. The chapters that follow reflect only some of these dimensions. No one can deal with the law as a whole in one country, let alone many countries. What I discuss here are some aspects of law which, in my judgment, add understanding to the social study of law. There are other points of view and other aspects. What is omitted is not consigned thereby to outer darkness.

Russell Sage Foundation supported work on this book with generous funding. I want to give special thanks to the Foundation and to Stanton Wheeler for constant and consistent help. I would like further to thank the administration and staff of the Law School at Stanford University and particularly Myron Jacobstein and his associates at the law library for support and cooperation; and Mrs. Joy St. John for her enormous help in preparing the manuscript. A book of this sort is greatly in debt to the scholars, living and dead, who inhabit the footnotes; they made this work possible. I wish to express particular thanks for help with this manuscript or related studies to Paul Brest, Jack Ladinsky, Richard Lempert, Stewart Macaulay, John H. Merryman, and Adam Podgórecki. I would also like to thank Jean C. Yoder of Russell Sage Foundation for the smooth and efficient way in which she guided the manuscript to publication.

Lawrence M. Friedman

Chapter I

The Legal System

The subject of this book is the legal system. Before going any further, then, something must be said about this phrase. A legal system is not a thing like a chair, a horse, or a book; it is not a well-defined concept in the social world like the Roman Catholic church or the nuclear family. In brief, there is no definition on which scholars—and the public—agree. *why?*

There are many ways, in fact, to look at law or the legal system. One way is as "the law," that is, a set of rules or norms, written or unwritten, about right and wrong behavior, duties and rights. This is a common usage of the term "law"; for example, we ask whether "the law" allows us to deduct the cost of lunch on an income tax return, or we say that it is "against the law" to drive through a stop sign or rob a bank. Legal scholars often, too, talk about law in this way. John Chipman Gray defined law as "rules which the courts . . . lay down for the determination of legal rights and duties."[1] There are many similar definitions. Although Gray mentioned only the courts, "law" may mean both the rules *and* the structures that (on paper) make or apply them.

The trouble with this view of law is that it tends to ascribe to "law" some sort of independent, meta-social life; it tends to overlook the fact that structures and rules look one way on paper, while acting quite differently in life. Almost everyone concedes that law is to some degree a social product; and that law on the books and law in action are not

---

[1] John Chipman Gray, *The Nature and Sources of the Law* (1909), p. 82.

invariably the same. Rules and structure alone do not tell us how the machine really works. These provide no way to sort out dead law from living law. They do not tell us how and why rules are made and what effect they have on people's lives.

"The law"—meaning structures and rules—is only one of three kinds of phenomena, all equally and vividly real. First, there are those social and legal forces that, in some way, press in and make "the law." Then comes "the law" itself—structures and rules. Third, there is the impact of law on behavior in the outside world. Where "the law" comes from and what it accomplishes—the first and third terms—are essential to the social study of law.

Legal scholarship has always neglected the first phenomenon, that is, the *input* side of law—a neglect as serious as neglecting food, water, and air in studying a living system. Traditionally, legal scholarship treated litigants, pressure groups, and social backgrounds cavalierly. Scholars took an *internal* view of legal development. Outside forces meant nothing in discussing how a rule of law came to be. American and British jurists wrote as if courts made the whole thing up. The leading treatise on torts in the United States states flatly that the "law of products liability began with the case of *Winterbottom* v. *Wright* [an English case of 1842]"; the courts later "whittled down the general rule" of that case, until "finally" in 1916, "the problem fell into the hands of Judge Cardozo," who "struck through the fog" in the "famous case of *MacPherson* v. *Buick Motor Co.*," a decision which "found immediate acceptance" in other courts.[2]

What is striking about this language—and it is typical—is that only the faintest mention is made of the social background. Everything is ascribed to the judges. All the praise and blame are theirs.[3] Yet doctrines do not come from thin air. Intellectual debate does not make case-law; cases are controversies, and they presuppose conflicts, not to mention people and groups who take steps to set the legal process in motion. Today, courts and legislatures in the United States are building up a body of environmental law. No one had heard of such a thing in 1950. The change would be unthinkable without a mass movement putting demands on the law. Courts could not have invented this body of law on their own. Again, since 1950, the problem of *obscenity* has

---

[2]William L. Prosser, *Handbook of the Law of Torts* (4th ed., 1971), pp. 641–643.

[3]Once in a while lawyers, who may put some ideas into the judges' heads, get some credit, too. See, for example, Benjamin Twiss, *Lawyers and the Constitution* (1942), blaming on the lawyers the laissez-faire doctrines of the late nineteenth century. In continental literature, jurists give themselves some of the credit that common-law writers give the judges.

been constantly in court—what is it, how far can government control it, what forms of license are permitted in movies, plays, and books. Is obscenity "free speech," protected by the First Amendment? The first amendment was adopted in the late eighteenth century; since then, its language has not changed. Yet, for generations, obscenity was hardly an issue at all. The literature of sex was underground. The Supreme Court did not utter a definitive word, until *Roth* v. *United States,* decided in 1957.[4]

Why did the question come to a head in that year? The *issue* in the legal sense was old; the concept of obscenity was old; the books were old; the language of the First Amendment was old; but social standards had somehow changed. Victorian morals were retreating; pornography was profitable; some people were demanding legitimation. The pressures led to action and reaction. Without it, the law of obscenity would never have awakened from its sleep. What is true of obscenity and civil rights[5] is probably true of all other legal developments. Indeed, one could write a history of law in which legal institutions played no role. Such a book would deal with litigants, social movements, and pressure groups rather than judges and courts. This approach would seem strange to some, even ridiculous; yet it might paint a truer picture of the law than the hundreds of books which omitted what this book has included.

Legal scholarship has not neglected the *outputs* of the system as thoroughly as the inputs. Rules and decisions are outputs, and most of the literature is about this subject. However, the third reality, that is, the impact of output on the world outside, is usually overlooked, assumed, or ignored. The growing literature on law and society tries to fill this gap. Much of this book will try to sum up what we know or can guess about the effect of law on society.

The basic argument of this book pivots about a few simple propositions which are closely linked with each other. The first is a proposition about legal behavior, that is, about the impact of rules, orders, and

---

[4]354 U.S. 476 (1957). This case held, basically, that the Constitution did not protect "obscenity," but that material was not obscene, unless it was "utterly without redeeming social importance." In an earlier case, *Doubleday & Co.* v. *New York,* 335 U.S. 848 (1948), New York state had convicted the publisher of publishing and selling an obscene book, which was Edmund Wilson's *Memoirs of Hecate County.* The Court divided evenly; this sustained the lower court opinion, *People* v. *Doubleday & Co.,* 297 N.Y. 687, 77 N.E. 296 (1947), which affirmed the conviction. By custom an equally divided Court writes no opinions.

[5]See, for example, Clement E. Vose, "Litigation as a Form of Pressure Group Activity," 319 *Annals* 20 (1958).

commands on conduct. The proposition is that three clusters of factors determine this impact—sanctions, social (peer group) influence, and internal values (conscience, concepts of legitimacy, etc.). However, those subject to law do not simply react; they also interact. That is, they translate their feelings, attitudes, motives, and inclinations into group action, bargaining, attempts to influence the law, and perhaps into attempts to bend or corrupt the application of law.

This interaction is part of the network of forces which at the same time is at work *creating* norms, rules, and orders in the first place—creating what we will call "legal acts." These forces are social forces; they arise out of *interests,* but individuals and groups that have interests do not necessarily turn to legal institutions to gratify their wants. An interest (a felt need or desire), then, is not the same as a *demand* on the legal system. A demand comes from a belief or desire that something can or should be done to enhance an interest. A person may feel he needs and deserves more pay for his work; but he may or may not translate that interest into a *demand* for money, either from his boss or the state (by lobbying for a higher minimum wage, for example). Thus pressure to create new law, or to preserve old law, flows out of attitudes and feelings which set up demands on a group or individual basis. The basic proposition about the nature of the legal system is that these *demands* determine its content. That is, law is not a strong independent force but responds to outside pressure in such a way as to reflect the wishes and powers of those social forces which are exerting the pressure. Just as legal behavior is a mixture of conduct based on self-interest (response to sanctions) and social and moral motives, so too the actual influence of persons and groups comes from self-interest monitored by those cultural factors which determine which interests will and which will not turn into demands.

The first part of this book will deal specifically with the *impact* of legal acts. We use the term *legal act* as a convenient umbrella-word for any relevant piece of behavior by a person with authority, acting within the legal system—judges, lawyers, legislators, officials of all sorts and conditions. When Congress passes a law, it performs a legal act. So does a judge when he renders a verdict, a policeman when he issues a ticket. Every day, every legal system produces hundreds of legal acts; these are communicated to or visited on people in society. The message is given; these people then modify or fail to modify their behavior for one reason or another, in response to the legal act. We will refer to any such response as *legal behavior.* Legal behavior can be a direct response to a legal act. (The policeman shouts "stop"; and the gunman stops. If he does not, the officer legally shoots.) It can be a delayed reaction or a diffuse response to many legal acts. To consult a lawyer about a divorce is legal behavior of this sort; so is settling a case out of court.

Chapter II will classify and discuss types of legal acts, in particular, *rules;* we will then move on to analyze and discuss the conditions under which legal acts make or do not make an impact on those to whom they are addressed (Chapters III and IV). This part of the book deals with the effect of legal acts on behavior, that is, on the life of society. But the most basic proposition underlying this book is that legal acts themselves are the product of social forces. The next part of the book examines and expands on this proposition.

It is, of course, too crude to state simply that social forces "produce" legal acts. People and groups have real, concrete interests and needs, but only some of these turn into demands on the legal system. A hungry man has real interests and needs, but if he suffers in silence, he has made no demand, and legal institutions not only *can* ignore him, they most certainly will. Culture and ideology are important intervening variables, determining when interests turn into demands. One chapter, then, will deal with *legal culture* (especially the consciousness of right) and with some attention to legal reasoning and style. The last chapter takes up the question of law and social change, looking explicitly at long-term trends.

THE LEGAL SYSTEM

The subject of this book, then, is not "the law" but the legal system. A system, essentially, is an operating unit with definite boundaries. Systems can be mechanical, organic, or social. The human body, a pinball machine, and the Roman Catholic church are all systems. David Easton has defined the *political system* as a "boundary-maintaining set of interactions imbedded in and surrounded by other social systems to the influence of which it is constantly exposed."[6] This rather heavy definition introduces some fundamental concepts. The political system is a "set of interactions"—a social system, in other words, not a structure or machine, but behavior, and behavior that interrelates with other behavior. And the system has boundaries; that is, a careful ob-

---

[6]David Easton, *A Framework for Political Analysis* (1965), p. 25; Dallin H. Oaks and Warren Lehman, *A Criminal Justice System and the Indigent* (1968), pp. 179–188, apply the language of systems-analysis to criminal justice. See also Sheldon Goldman and Thomas P. Jahnige, "Eastonian Systems Analysis and Legal Research," 2 *Rutgers-Camden L.Rev.* 285 (1970).

server can see where it begins and where it ends. He can mark it off as different from other systems. Any set of interactions can be called a system, if an observer can describe it as such, by finding real boundaries or defining some.

But what are the boundaries of the *legal* system? Can we mark the legal system off from other social systems? Can we tell, in other words, where it begins and where it ends? *Legal* means nothing more than pertaining to law; hence, to define a legal system, we need some sort of working definition of the law.

Legal philosophers[7] and social scientists[8] alike have made innumerable attempts at definition. Yet, definitions of law, however various, fall into a few natural groups, reflecting different ways of looking at law and different purposes in writing about it. The first major type is *institutional*. In many societies, there are people and institutions that, by conventional reckoning, are part of the legal system. One can build a definition around these professionals and institutions: The legal system is bounded, then, by the relevant work of lawyers, judges, police, legislators, administrators, notaries, and others.[9]

If law is what lawyers and legal institutions do, then a society without lawyers or other professionals and without legal institutions is a society without law. Many simple societies, in fact, do not have lawyers or special legal institutions. Nor would there be "law" in many subsystems in more complex societies—schools or factories or clubs. Institutions and professionals are difficult, too, to compare cross-culturally. Lawyers do different things in different societies. "Courts" exist in many societies, but what exactly is a court?

The cross-cultural problem is particularly vexing for anthropologists. Hoebel, for example, defines "law" to include the concept of a court; but then, in order to find law in simple societies, he stretches the idea of a court almost beyond recognition. The Eskimos, for example, have no obvious "courts." It sometimes happens that a killer threatens the safety of the community. A "public-spirited man" may then decide

---

[7]See, in general, Julius Stone, *Legal System and Lawyers' Reasonings* (1964), pp. 165ff.

[8]See, for example, Leopold Pospisil, *Anthropology of Law, A Comparative Theory* (1971), pp. 11–96; Jack P. Gibbs "Definitions of Law and Empirical Questions," 2 *Law and Society Rev.* 429 (1968).

[9]Of course, the word "relevant" is a necessary qualification; as Jerome Skolnick points out, lawyers, for example, do a lot of things—"eat, sleep, go to the theater, read, write, talk, make love." The sociology of law would be interested only in what they do *as lawyers*—in their professional capacity. Jerome Skolnick, "Social Research on Legality: A Reply to Auerbach," 1 *Law and Society Rev.* 105, 107 (1966).

to act. He sets about "to interview, one after the other, all the adult males of the community." If these men agree that the killer should die, the "public-spirited man" goes out and kills him. "No revenge may be taken by the murderer's relatives," because a "community 'court' has spoken." A social norm is "legal," according to Hoebel, "if its neglect or infraction is regularly met, in threat or in fact, by the application of physical force by an individual or group possessing the socially recognized privilege of so acting."[10] This presses the idea of a court or institution to the limit.

Paul Bohannon also feels that legal *institutions* are the essence of law. An institution is legal if people in a society use it to "settle disputes . . . and counteract any gross and flagrant abuses of the rules." *Law* is a body of binding obligations which have been "disengaged" from the institutions in which they arose and "re-engaged" in legal institutions. The essence of law is this "double institutionalization." Legal institutions "have some regularized way" to "interfere" with "malfunctioning" institutions, to pluck out the problem and handle it "within the framework of the legal institution."[11]

Institutional definitions of law typically look for the nature of law in its *public* character—law is bound up with government. Donald Black recently defined law as "governmental social control . . . encompassing any act by a political body that concerns the definition of social order or its defense."[12] A cluster of definitions express or imply that the *state*, pure and simple, is the source or criterion of law. The legal philosopher John Austin defined law as the command of the sovereign.[13] Oliver Wendell Holmes, Jr., defined law as "the prophecies of what the courts will do in fact."[14] There are considerable differences of opinion about what makes up a state, a government, or courts. The argument, in part, is whether "law" is universal or not. States, governments, and courts are not universal; but, as Leopold Pospisil points out, *authority* and authority structures are everywhere. Hence one might find law universal, too, even in the absence of a "state."[15] For Pospisil,

---

[10]E. Adamson Hoebel, *The Law of Primitive Man, A Study in Comparative Legal Dynamics* (1954), p. 28.

[11] Paul Bohannon, "The Differing Realms of the Law," in 67 *Am. Anthropologist*, no. 6, part 2, 33, 35 (1965).

[12]Donald Black, "The Boundaries of Legal Sociology," 81 *Yale L.J.* 1086, 1096 (1972).

[13]John Austin, *The Province of Jurisprudence Determined*, originally published in 1832 (1954).

[14]Oliver W. Holmes, Jr., "The Path of the Law," 10 *Harv. L.Rev.* 457, 461 (1897).

[15]Leopold Pospisil, *Anthropology of Law, A Comparative Theory* (1971), ch. 3. Pospisil isolates four "attributes of law" which he feels are empirically important and allow good cross-cultural comparison: authority, intention of universal application, *obligatio*,

norms are legal if they carry the threat of a *sanction*. This is an element, too, in Hoebel's definition; and Max Weber, in a well-known passage, defined law as an "order . . . externally guaranteed by the probability that coercion (physical or psychological) to bring about conformity or avenge violation will be applied by a *staff* of people holding themselves specially ready for the purpose."[16]

Other definitions, as we have mentioned, equate law with a set of *rules*. Clearly, in a sacred law system, "the law" is the body of sacred norms and nothing more. Other scholars look at law as rules or norms but not necessarily *official* ones; they stress the customary basis of law, that is, actual patterns of behavior. Michael Barkun finds law in the shared norms of a "jural community."[17] Eugen Ehrlich coined the phrase "living law" to describe actual behavior patterns in a community.[18] Bronislaw Malinowski found law in patterns of behavior enforced by "reciprocity."[19]

These definitions may, and mostly do, avoid defining law as bound up with the government or the state. So, too, do those definitions which define law in terms of the functions it performs. One function, for example, is dispute settlement. One can treat as "legal" any institution that settles disputes. Or we can call "legal" every aspect of society and every institution that exercises social control. Functional definitions are useful in comparing legal cultures.[20] Institutions with different

---

and sanction (ibid., p. 43). By "intention of universal application," he means that "authority, in making a decision, *intend*(s) it to be applied to all similar or 'identical' situations in the future" (ibid., p. 79). *Obligatio* refers to "that part of a decision which states the rights of one party to a dispute and the duties of the other" (ibid., p. 81).

[16]Max Rheinstein, ed., *Max Weber on Law in Economy and Society* (1954), p. 5; for Henri Lévy-Bruhl, "law" includes the element of "obligation"; there is no obligation without sanction, thus "one might define law as a system of sanctions," *Sociologie du Droit* (1961), pp. 21–23.

In jurisprudential literature, there is much dispute over whether or not a norm must bear this mark of Cain—the threat of sanction—in order to qualify as "legal." As Jack Gibbs has pointed out, it is easy to mistake this question, basically a question of definition, with the far more complicated question, what motivates people to follow or not follow rules? Jack P. Gibbs, "Definitions of Law and Empirical Questions," 2 *Law and Society Rev.* 429 (1968). Sanctions are positive as well as negative. A norm or rule that promises a subsidy also contains a sanction. See Chapter IV.

[17]Michael Barkun, *Law Without Sanctions* (1968), p. 92.

[18]Eugen Ehrlich, *Fundamental Principles of the Sociology of Law* (1936). Leon Petrazycki spoke of "intuitive" law, that is, legal behavior which rests on general ideas of right and wrong rather than on some specific statute or rule. Much of intuitive law, although not all, is unofficial. See Nicholas S. Timasheff, introduction to *Law and Morality: Leon Petrazycki* (1955), pp. xxviii, xxix.

[19]Bronislaw Malinowski, *Crime and Custom in Savage Society* (1926).

[20]On the importance of "functionality" in comparing legal systems, see Konrad Zweigert and Hein Kötz, *Einführung in die Rechtsvergleichung* (1971), vol. I, pp. 28–32.

names can perform the same function; and the "same" institution or role can be functionally very different in different societies. Queen Elizabeth I and Queen Elizabeth II were both queens of England and titular heads of the state, but their functions are light-years apart.

Any group, organization, or system—state or no state—can perform "legal" functions. If, like Talcott Parsons, one looks on law as a "general normative code" performing "integrative" functions,[21] then one can talk about "private" legal systems[22] or the "law" of a club or a school, meaning the ways in which clubs or schools make rules and apply them, settle disputes, or in general "integrate" themselves. Rules and processes in a school may have no official (state) character, but they will be *like* the rules of the state in their function or object, or simply in the way people go about using them. One can even talk about the "law" of a shopping center (a "community of landlord and merchant tenants") and describe how it operates.[23]

The vice of functional definitions is the same as their virtue: They are terribly broad. Who and what in the United States has the function of "settling disputes"? Courts, of course; but also policemen who break up brawls in a bar; the legislature, resolving conflicts between interest groups; dozens of agencies of government, such as the National Labor Relations Board; and also neighbors, teachers, arbitrators, marriage counselors, lawyers in their offices, clergymen, and psychiatrists, not to mention heads of families and, in other societies, heads of clans. Which of these, if any, do we want to keep out of the concept of the legal system? A parent, who settles a quarrel between two children about an ice cream cone, a coloring book, or a ball is not part of the legal system —not because his work is inherently nonlegal, but because if *his* work is "law," then the legal system has been robbed of any meaningful boundaries. For some purposes, we might want so broad a view of law —if, for example, our primary interest was the social psychology of dispute settlement wherever it occurs. Usually, however, we will want to limit ourselves to phenomena that are "legal" in some more conventional way.[24]

---

[21]Talcott Parsons, *The System of Modern Societies* (1971), p. 18.

[22]William M. Evan, "Public and Private Legal Systems," in William M. Evan, ed., *Law and Sociology* (1962), p. 165.

[23]Spencer MacCallum, "Dispute Settlement in an American Supermarket, a Preliminary View," in Paul Bohannan, ed., *Law and Warfare, Studies in the Anthropology of Conflict* (1967), pp. 291, 292.

[24]Another problem is deciding what the functions are. There is a tendency here, as in many of the definitions, to overstress the control or negative aspects even in dispute settlement. Law, especially in modern society, has a positive function: It creates opportunities and promotes desired behavior.

One last type of definition looks at law not as function or functions nor as institutions or rules but as some special kind of *process or order.* Lon Fuller speaks of law as the "enterprise of subjecting human conduct to the governance of rules."[25] Philip Selznick agrees and defines the "governance of rules" as "shorthand for a system of order that contains specialized mechanisms for certifying rules as authoritative and for safeguarding rule-making and rule-applying from the intrusion of other forms of direction and control."[26] His particular interest is in a concept of process he calls *legality.* Legality, the special subject of the serious student of law, "has to do mainly with *how* policies and rules are made and applied rather than with their content."[27] Legality is rather like the constitutional concept of due process; it can be used to measure "governance by rules" in many areas of life—in the factory, for example. Selznick is unwilling "to equate law and state"; to do so, "impoverishes sociological analysis, because the concept of law should be available for study of any setting in which human conduct is subject to explicit rule-making."[28]

There is, of course, no "true" definition of law. Definitions flow from the aim or function of the definer. Selznick's definition, for example, is frankly normative. It follows from his concern with justice in modern society, his wish to redirect legal scholarship. Definitions that equate law with rules allow legal scholarship to ignore empirical questions and justify traditional legal thought.

In this book, we want to examine how legal institutions relate to society. We want to apply to legal process techniques, findings, and attitudes of social science. For this purpose, a rough, eclectic definition of law will do. The main emphasis is on the law of urban, industrial nations. In these countries, there are social subsystems that are clearly defined by the public as part of the law. These include the courts, legislatures as lawmakers, and the system of criminal justice. Some of these plainly overlap. Less universally, but still rather clearly, one could assign to the realm of the law much of the work of administrative agencies and the private counseling of lawyers. The "legal system" would be nothing more than all these subsystems put together. One might picture the ideal definition as a large, perfect circle; the subsystems as little boxes and squares, each smaller than the circle. If we put together enough boxes of the right shape and size, we get something

---

[25]Lon L. Fuller, *The Morality of Law* (1964), p. 106.
[26]Philip Selznick, *Law, Society and Industrial Justice* (1969), p. 7.
[27]Ibid., p. 11.
[28]Ibid., p. 8.

that adds up more or less to a circle. In some places, however, the boxes do not quite fill out the circle; in others, they push slightly over the edge. Geometrically, the figure is rough and imperfect, but it is close enough to the circle for our use.

In short, we present no real definition of the "legal system." There are subsystems, most of them by common consent part of the legal system. They have in common that they are systems, that they operate with norms or rules, and that they are connected with the state or have an authority structure that can at least be analogized to the behavior of the state. Whether what a parent does to govern his children is part of the "legal system" does not matter, if what is said here applies to his little world, *mutatis mutandis.*

The lack of precise definition would, perhaps, be a serious failing, if we believed in a distinctive science of *law*. But "law" is not a science, if "science" means that principles of law can be verified experimentally, or discovered inductively, or deduced from each other as in geometry or biology. The idea of "legal science" has been strongly urged, especially by continental legal scholars.[29] We feel that there can be science *about* law but not legal science. We treat "law" and the "legal system" as parallel to such terms as "business," "China," or "the theater." All of these are or can be the *subject* of science—one speaks of business psychology, or the social anthropology of China, or the economics of the theater—but they are not sciences in themselves. To us, too, law—or at any rate, the legal system—is a subject of social science, not an independent social science, indeed not a science at all.

THE LEGAL SYSTEM AND ITS COMPONENTS

Whatever character one assigns to the legal system, it will have features common to every system or process. First, there will be *inputs*, raw materials which enter at one end of the system. A court, for example, does not begin to work, unless someone makes the effort to file a complaint and set off a lawsuit. Even earlier, some concrete act has served as a trigger: A policeman arrests a man; a landlord harasses a tenant; a man is defamed by his neighbor, injured by a speeding car, deserted by his wife. Physically, lawsuits begin with pieces of paper,

---

[29]See John H. Merryman, *The Civil Law Tradition* (1969), p. 66: "The concept of legal science rests on the assumption that the materials of the law (statutes, regulations, customary rules, etc.) are naturally occurring phenomena or data from the study of which the legal scientist can discover certain principles and relationships, just as the physical scientist discovers natural laws from the study of physical data"; see also Hans Kelsen, *Pure Theory of Law,* trans. Max Knight (2nd ed., 1967), ch. 3.

pleadings filed in court; without these no trial is possible in our society. What happens next is that the court, its staff, and the parties begin to *process* the materials put in. Judges and officials *do* something; they work on the raw materials in a systematic way. They deliberate, argue, make orders, file papers, and hold a trial. The parties and lawyers also play their parts. Next, the court produces an *output*—a verdict or decision; sometimes the court hands down a general rule as well. The court may decide for the plaintiff, or for the defendant, or reach some compromise. The result is in any event an output, even if the court simply refuses to hear the case. Moreover, the output may be ignored or not, may have a large or a small effect. Information about this effect flows back into the system. This process bears the name of *feedback*.[30] One can speak of feedback more generally to mean the way the product or output of a system turns back on and affects the system itself. A civil rights organization brings a lawsuit against a southern school district. Plaintiff wins his case. Other persons or groups hear the news and bring lawsuits against this or some other district or on some related issue. Other effects are felt by legislatures, policemen, mayors, and chairmen of agencies.

In the broad sense, inputs into the legal system are shock waves of demand, radiating out of society. In a narrower sense, the inputs are pieces of paper and bits of behavior that set legal process in motion. In many legal systems, litigants cannot approach a court informally; they must take some formal step, such as filing a pleading of a particular type. In court, these are writs, petitions, pleadings. Hundreds of rules concern the form and the matter of inputs; these rules are an indispensable part of modern Western law. The common law in particular developed much of its content out of rules about writs and forms of action. Today, procedure plays a smaller role in the law, but the rules still have major significance. They distribute power (jurisdiction) among legal institutions. They regulate the role of actors in the process. They create or lessen the dependence of laymen on lawyers. Lastly, they determine access to law and hence serve to keep intact the structure of power in society or allow change only in approved and valid ways.

The heart of the system is the way it turns input into output. The structure of the legal system is like some gigantic computer program, coded to deal with millions of problems that are fed daily into the machine. Rules of organization, jurisdiction, and procedure are part of the coding. Equally important are the substantive rules of law. They are an output of the system, but one that serves to cut future outputs to shape.

---

[30]See Easton, pp. 127–129.

why can't that it's the legal system be part of the computer?

One conventional view of the legal system—and especially of the courts—is derived from the metaphor of a huge, highly programmed machine. It looks at rules of law as a book of instructions which cover, if not all, then surely most life situations that come up for law to cope with. This view we associate especially with the late nineteenth century, but it has never died. Jurists felt that ideally law should be certain, predictable, and free from the subjective—highly programmed, in other words. Anything else was less than just. Moreover, this ideal was thought to be roughly attainable. "When an act of Congress is . . . challenged," said Justice Roberts of the United States Supreme Court, "the judicial branch of the government has only one duty,—to lay the article of the Constitution which is invoked beside the statute which is challenged and to decide whether the latter squares with the former."[31]

A judge who performed this trick honestly, laying the two texts side by side, would presumably come up with one right answer. This is the mechanical theory of law. In a factory that makes plastic toys, once one knows the machine, the raw materials, and what the machine has been taught or made to do, one predicts very well what the machine will turn out. Of course, this picture hardly fits the legal system. It ignores the element of choice—the leeways, options, and irrationalities. In the twentieth century, legal realism became a dominant school of American jurisprudence with equivalent schools in other countries. Its message was that one could not, in fact, predict output wholly from structure and rule—at least not always.[32] The realists, however, were in some ways almost as remiss as their predecessors in ignoring the input side of law. That is, they noted that the judge was not a machine; they assumed he was more like a god. The basic thrust of their work was to point out this fact and to exhort the god to behave in a more principled and socially conscious way.[33]

We can assume that the judge is not a god and not a machine, and that the *structure* of the legal system, as a whole, is neither god nor

---

[31] *U.S.* v. *Butler*, 297 U.S. 1, 62 (1936).

[32] A general survey is Wilfrid E. Rumble, Jr., *American Legal Realism, Skepticism, Reform, and the Judicial Process* (1968); Karl N. Llewellyn, "Some Realism about Realism," 44 *Harv. L. Rev.* 1222 (1931), is a fundamental statement. On Llewellyn himself, see William Twining, *Karl Llewellyn and the Realist Movement* (1973). In Germany, the "free law movement" can be considered a rough equivalent; see Klaus Riebschläger, *Die Freirechtsbewegung* (1968).

[33] Curiously, the recent attempts of social scientists to find out how judges "really" decide cases has also focused heavily on the personality and values of the judge, to the neglect of litigant pressure and outside social forces, that is, the input side of the law. See Chapter VII, pp. 170–178.

machine. The basic question remains, What is it? What difference does structure make? What difference do the legal professionals make? What independent role does the system play in bending social forces and changing society? Social forces turn into demands which flow in at one end of the system; decisions and rules flow out at the other. How much shall we attribute to the black box in the middle? How does the machine work, and what does it do? Does it act like a membrane through which forces pass without changing form? How important is it, how formative a fact that one society has a legal system of type *X* and another a system of type *Y*? What difference does it make if a system has or does not have a jury? That it elects or appoints its judges? That it has or does not have a federalist system, an adversary system, tribunals instead of courts, barristers as well as solicitors? These are questions about the role of the *structural variable.*

Structure, to be sure, is one basic and obvious element of the legal system. *Substance* (the rules) is another. When an observer tries to describe a legal system in cross section, so to speak, he is likely to speak of these two elements. The *structure* of a system is its skeletal framework; it is the permanent shape, the institutional body of the system, the tough, rigid bones that keep the process flowing within bounds. We describe the *structure* of a judicial system when we talk about the number of judges, the jurisdiction of courts, how higher courts are stacked on top of lower courts, what persons are attached to various courts, and what their roles consist of. The *substance* is composed of substantive rules and rules about how institutions should behave. H. L. A. Hart, indeed, feels that the distinctive feature of a *legal* system is this double set of rules. A legal system is the union of "primary rules" and "secondary rules." Primary rules are norms of behavior; secondary rules are norms *about* those norms—how to decide whether they are valid, how to enforce them, etc.[34] Both primary and secondary rules, of course, are outputs of a legal system. They are ways of describing the behavior of the legal system seen in cross section. Litigants behave on the basis of substance; it creates expectations to which they react.

Traditional legal scholarship was certainly familiar with structure and with the two kinds of substance, under one name or another. Yet much of this scholarship seems curiously myopic, at least to a layman. Scholars spoke, argued, and elaborated rules and structures, taking their reality for granted. They tended to ignore the difference between what the words on paper told institutions to do and what they did in fact. In the real world, some rules are not used or are misused, some

---

[34]H. L. A. Hart, *The Concept of Law* (1961), pp. 91–92.

structures do not work, others work in strange, noncanonical ways. Structure and substance are real components of a legal system, but they are at best a blueprint or a design, not a working machine. The trouble with traditional structure and substance was that they were static; they were like a still photograph of the legal system—a lifeless image and distorted at that. The picture lacked both motion and truth. The legal system, described solely in terms of formal structure and substance, is like an enchanted courtroom, petrified, immobile, under some odd, eternal spell.

What gives life and reality to the legal system is the outside, social world. The legal system is not insulated or isolated; it depends absolutely on inputs from outside. Without litigants, there would be no courts. Without issues and the will to pursue them, there would be no litigants. These social elements unfreeze the film and start the system in motion.

Social forces are constantly at work on the law—destroying here, renewing there; invigorating here, deadening there; choosing what parts of "law" will operate, which parts will not; what substitutes, detours, and bypasses will spring up; what changes will take place openly or secretly. For want of a better term, we can call some of these forces the legal *culture.* It is the element of social attitude and value. The phrase "social forces" is itself an abstraction; in any event, such forces do not work directly on the legal system. People in society have needs and make demands; these sometimes do and sometimes do not invoke legal process—depending on the culture. Whether a trade union will go on strike, start a revolution, file a lawsuit, bargain collectively, or build a political party depends on many factors. The values and attitudes held by leaders and members are among these factors, since their behavior depends on their judgment about which options are useful or correct. Legal culture refers, then, to those parts of general culture—customs, opinions, ways of doing and thinking—that bend social forces toward or away from the law and in particular ways. The term roughly describes attitudes *about* law, more or less analogous to the *political culture,* which Almond and Verba defined as the "political system as internalized in the cognitions, feelings, and evaluations of its population."[35] The basic notion is that of values and attitudes which,

---

[35]Gabriel Almond and Sidney Verba, *The Civic Culture* (1963), p. 14. The term "legal culture" can also be used in an anthropological sense—those traits of behavior and attitude that make the law of one community different from that of another, that make the law of the Eskimos different from French law, ancient Roman law, and the law of the Cambodians. The term can be used in a slightly different way to describe underlying traits of a *whole* legal system—its ruling ideas, its flavor, its style.

when translated into *demands,* start the machinery of the legal system moving or, conversely, stop it in its tracks.[36]

A legal system in actual operation is a complex organism in which structure, substance, and culture interact. To explain the background and effect of any part calls into play many elements of the system. Let us take, for an example, the incidence and reality of divorce. To begin with, it depends on rules of law. Divorce is a legal concept, and there are countries that do not allow divorce at all. Some rules about divorce, limiting the grounds, for example, will also act to deter divorce. Next, the use of divorce depends on the court *structure.* Lack of nearby courts, expensive court costs, or excessive jurisdictional complexity will discourage divorce. *Structure* and *substance* here are durable features slowly carved out of the landscape by long-run social forces. They modify current demands and are themselves the long-term residue of other social demands. *Legal culture* may also affect the rate of use, that is, attitudes toward whether it is right or wrong, useful or useless, to go to court will also enter into a decision to seek formal divorce. Some people will also be ignorant of their rights or fearful of using them. Values in the general culture will also powerfully affect the rate of use: what relatives or neighbors will think about the divorce; the effect on the children and the children's friends; religious and moral scruples. Such values in the aggregate and over the long haul are responsible for the shape and nature of the divorce laws themselves.

Legal behavior, then, cannot be understood except in context, including the cultural context. The context consists analytically of many elements which yield many sorts of behavioral propositions. First, there are general regularities of behavior—propositions about the way human beings behave, which, if valid, hold true everywhere, every time, and for all kinds of behavior—legal, economic, religious, and the like. For example, rewards and punishments affect behavior in general ways which cut across cultures and times. Second, there are more modest propositions bound to particular cultures or groups of cultures —about demands, for example, that businessmen in a business economy will make on the law. Less sweeping propositions try to explain and predict American or French legal behavior. Many kinds of propositions will be necessary to deal with the law of any society; a shipowner who lives in Greece is human and Greek and a shipowner, and behaves accordingly.

---

[36]We will discuss the legal culture further in Chapter VIII.

THE FUNCTIONS OF THE LEGAL SYSTEM

The *output* of law is simply what the legal system produces in
response to social demand. Every letter to a congressman, every writ
filed in a court, every telephone call to a policeman is a demand on the
legal system. Every decision, order, arrest, every bill passed, every
elevator inspected is an output or a response. There are millions of
demands on the legal system every day. There are also millions of
responses. However, one can also speak of output and response in very
general terms. These general outputs are the overall *functions* of law,
what society expects of the system.

The legal system is not unique in this regard. Every major subsystem in society—the army, the schools—has its function or mission. At
the most general level, the function of the legal system is to distribute
and maintain an allocation of values that society feels to be right. This
allocation, invested with a sense of rightness, is what is commonly
referred to as *justice.* Aristotle drew a famous distinction between
distributive justice and commutative justice, between the principle by
which wealth and honors are allocated among citizens and that which
pertains to individual dealings and lawsuits.[37] At the core of the concept of justice is the notion of meting out to persons and groups what
they deserve, ethically speaking—no more and no less. What this is and
how to derive it is a problem with which philosophers of law have
wrestled for centuries. We are concerned here with the idea only as a
sociological fact—as a mandate imposed by some relevant public upon
the legal system. The legal system, in other words, is supposed to
guarantee the right or proper (or, perhaps, the least obnoxious) distribution among persons and groups. In individual lawsuits and transactions, the system should apply the right or proper (or, perhaps, the least
obnoxious) rule.

Of course, "society" is an abstraction, sometimes a dangerous one.
Demands on the legal system do not come from "society" but from
specific people, groups, classes, and strata. The "legal system" is an
abstraction, too. There are different pieces of the jigsaw puzzle—courts,
legislatures, police, city councils, park boards, and administrative
agencies. In the short run at least, they respond to different demands,
perform rather different functions, and define justice in individual
ways. Hence, the legal system may seem to some (or many, or even
most) to produce injustice on the whole. Societies are stratified, and the
legal system supports the stratification. To those who find the stratifica-

---

[37]See Julius Stone, *Human Law and Human Justice* (1965), p. 14.

tion "unjust," the legal system must appear as a parent of injustice.

Another, slightly less global function is the *settlement of disputes.* Conflicts arise in every society. A basic legal function is to offer machinery and a place where people can go to resolve their conflicts and settle their disputes. Of course, the legal system has no monopoly on this function. It belongs as well to parents, teachers, clergymen, employers, and others. Moreover, some societies put more weight on this function than do others. In modern Western countries, for example, people do not generally go to court to settle petty disputes with their neighbors or to iron out disputes within the family; in many smaller and older societies precisely this was done.

Another basic function of the legal system is *social control*—essentially, the enforcement of rules of right conduct. Policemen and judges see to it that thieves are caught and sent to jail. We might call criminal justice primary social control. *Secondary social control*—teaching, admonishing, rehabilitating—is equally important. The thief who is caught and dragged before a court is not merely controlled; he is "taught a lesson." (Whether it works or not is another question.) Courts around the world act or try to act as moral teachers, reformers, and rehabilitators. We associate this function with courts in simpler societies and in the socialist countries; but in many nations, family and juvenile courts at least make a stab at secondary social control. Many agencies and boards try, or should try, to reform sinners and lift the fallen. (In Norway, for example, "temperance boards" have wide powers to help people cope with their alcohol problems.)[38] The prisoner in the dock is the immediate subject of "education," but the legal system looks beyond him. It also tries to teach, reform, and rehabilitate members of the audience, onlookers, even those who read about law in the newspapers or hear of it on the street. Indeed, this is what the deterrent value of law is all about, as we shall discuss later on.

Another function of law is to create the norms themselves, the raw materials of social control. Social forces exert pressures; these demands "make" law, but the institutions of the legal system harvest the demands, crystallize them, and turn them into rules, principles, and instructions to civil servants and the general population. In so doing, the legal system may act as an instrument of orderly change, of *social engineering*. The most obvious example is the legislative function. Courts also create rules—especially in the common-law systems, and there are dozens of boards, agencies, commissions, etc. with rule-mak-

---

[38]See Nils Christie, "Temperance Boards and Interinstitutional Dilemmas: A Case Study of a Welfare Law," 12 *Social Problems* 415 (1965).

ing power in modern government, many of them with power to direct as well as to control.

Legal institutions also serve a routine or *recording* function. They act as a storehouse or memory for the thousands upon thousands of transactions necessary or desirable in the modern world. They file and keep records; they reduce transactions to efficient routine. When people register deeds, probate a will, or file a death certificate, they make use of this function of law. It is predominantly a characteristic of modern legal systems and the legal systems of the old empires; little or none of this function goes on in tribal systems. Most of this work is in the hands of the bureaucracy, but courts or court-like institutions have a major share in some countries. Sometimes this occurs when once-contested or rarely contested matters have shrunk to mere routine—a name change, for example, a consensual divorce, the probating of a will, or the payment of a traffic fine.

The functions discussed have been simple and matter of fact. It is possible that law, legal process, and the legal system perform other less obviously instrumental functions. Law expresses and defines the norms of the community. This is not the same as the teaching and preaching function of law, since that function has an instrumental end: to change behavior. Sociologists since Émile Durkheim have been intrigued with the symbolic function of the norms of criminal law. Societies, it is said, *need* a concept of deviant behavior. Crime and punishment mark off the moral boundaries of a community. Crime must be punished not only because it is intrinsically dangerous, but also because it offends the solidarity of society—it is an attack on the "common conscience."[39] Kai Erikson feels that "interactions . . . which take place between deviant persons on the one side and official agents of the community on the other" do the "most effective job of locating and publicizing the group's outer edges." When the community calls a deviant to account, "it is making a statement about the nature and placement of its boundaries."[40]

The law, in other words, announces what the rules and standards are and affirms that society can and will punish wrongdoers—those who step over the line. The goal is not suppression for the sake of order, although probably that is the ultimate goal, but suppression for the sake of emblazoning norms upon the consciousness of society. It hardly matters, then, if a few innocent people suffer, so long as what the public

---

[39]Émile Durkheim, *The Division of Labor in Society* (1933), p. 103.

[40]Kai T. Erikson, *Wayward Puritans, a Study in the Sociology of Deviance* (1966), pp. 10–11.

sees seems like justice.[41] Still another notion that is sometimes advanced is that criminal law performs a kind of *cathartic* function. Punishment may do nothing for law and order, but it is good for society's soul. It is one way to release aggression and to satisfy in a controlled and controllable way the darker instincts of the human race. This is, of course, only a theory. It is argued on the other side that "punitive control" may actually cause or release through modelling more aggression than it quells.[42]

LAW AS AN ALLOCATIVE SYSTEM

What is this *justice* that, in the broadest sense, the legal system must produce? The concept, of course, defies definition, and it is the subject of a wide philosophical literature. For our purposes, it refers to expectations and assessments. People in a society expect the law to meet their ethical standards. They will judge it on how it performs. By "performs" we mean, how it treats people and how it distributes its benefits and costs.

Legal decisions are by their very nature economic. They allocate scarce goods and services. The legal system is in this sense a rationing system. What it does and what it is reflects the distribution of power in society—who is on top and who is on the bottom; law also sees to it that this social structure stays stable or changes only in approved and patterned ways. The system issues commands, extends benefits, and tells people what they can or cannot do; in each case, the rule of law, if followed, has made some choice about who has or keeps or gets what good. Rules of law reflect past decisions about allocations. Some conflicts or disputes occurred or threatened to occur between people or groups. Inconsistent wants were expressed. Two men fought over one piece of land. Farmers wanted high prices, consumers wanted low. The resulting legal act (rule or decision) chose among possible alternatives. Very likely it was some kind of compromise, but it was surely an allocation. Every function of the law, general or specific, is allocative. Social control—the monopoly of violence, the maintenance of law and order—is no exception. Who, for example, shall have the right to use force, and when, and why? The rules, once made and enforced, are

---

[41]Social control, too, need not be perfect. It can tolerate some errors, some slippage and cutting of corners, punish some of the innocent, let some of the guilty go—so long as order is maintained, and people do not become too dissatisfied.

[42]Albert Bandura, *Aggression: A Social Learning Analysis* (1973), pp. 225–227. The last word on the subject has not, of course, been spoken.

templates out of which other rules and decisions are cut; these, of course, perpetuate older allocations or, as we said, change them in patterned ways.

The legal system allocates directly, handing out rewards and punishments. It gives cash subsidies and puts people in jail, but these are not its only tools. There is the market itself which sets prices and disposes of goods and services through private agreements. The law sustains, defines, and limits the area in which the free market operates. It closes off certain kinds of agreement: One cannot legally sell oneself into slavery, or enter into a price-fixing agreement.[43] In free-market countries or countries with mixed economies, the law specifies which private agreements can be enforced and which cannot. The law of contract expresses some of the elementary rules; far more important, however, are more specific branches of law, such as labor law and the law of business associations. Law provides even more basic support for the market. The institution of private property rests on pillars of the law. Legal rules provide for registration of land and for gift, sale, and inheritance taxes; legal institutions control banks, banking instruments, money and credit, the operation of the stock market. The system of criminal justice protects property against embezzlement and theft. A market, or mixed, economy decentralizes many economic decisions, but the invisible hand would be paralyzed without the help of legal institutions.

Prices and markets are one way to allocate services and goods. Suppose a popular musician comes to town for one night to play in a hall that seats 1,000; however, ten times this number want to go. Obviously, tickets can be auctioned to the highest bidder, but there are other ways to ration tickets that do not depend upon money.[44] The management can fix a price and sell on the basis of first come, first served. Some people might stand in line all night in the rain to be sure of getting their tickets. Note that, just as in the "real" market, some people will be "priced out": they cannot afford the time to stand in the queue; they work at night; they live too far from the ticket office; they have small children to take care of; they are too weak and sick to wait in the cold; or the thought of a sleepless night, like a high price, convinces them they can do without the concert.

Often, when society withdraws scarce goods from the "market," they are simply handed over to this time-and-effort "market." This is

---

[43]See, in general, Lawrence M. Friedman, *Contract Law in America* (1965), pp. 15–26.

[44]See Guido Calabresi, *The Costs of Accidents* (1970), pp. 114–116.

the "market" for goods with no prices or with fixed prices and limited supplies. Court services themselves are an example. The judge's time is free to the user, but the supply of judges is limited—tragically so in most big cities in the United States. Litigants must therefore "queue"; trials are delayed for months or years. Money cannot buy a valid shortcut (except where the courts are corrupt). The queuing system, it might be added, lends itself easily to corruption—just as rich fans will try to buy tickets to the concert from scalpers. Rules that set up this sort of rationing system, explicitly or not, try to shift rights from people with money to people with patience or time. This is a common outcome of decisions to socialize goods, services, or processes. It is not the only possible result, of course. If the supply is large enough, the queue will shrink or disappear.

In a market, money talks; in a queue, patience and time. A group of other ways to allocate can be conveniently labeled as *merit*. Any agreed-on criterion can serve to define what is merit—physical beauty, strength, wisdom, virtue, or skill. Civil service jobs go to those who score highest on standardized tests; veterans earn pensions by serving. Still other criteria can be labeled *need*. People with large families and small incomes, displaced from their homes by a highway, get first place in the line for public housing. Still other criteria can be called *ascriptive*. They are based on status characteristics—birth, sex, religion, nationality, race. Rules of inheritance of property are ascriptive. So are some of the rules of citizenship. So are the many rules (now happily in retreat) that draw legal lines for or against races, religions, and nationalities in countries all over the world.

Still another way to allocate values or rights or to assign burdens is to let *chance* decide. Chance is an honest, if unpredictable judge. People in everyday life often toss a coin or throw dice, when they cannot make up their mind. Torstein Eckhoff reports that in Sweden and Finland, in the eighteenth and nineteenth century, courts used dice to decide which of two parties to the crime of murder would die and which would suffer lesser punishment. This occurred when the court could not decide which man actually struck the blow that caused death. Folk beliefs demanded that *someone* should die to atone for the victim's death, yet it was unjust to kill more than one. Chance was the criterion chosen, because there was no rational way to decide: "This way of settling the matter served to exempt the judge from taking responsibility for the fateful choice, and at the same time it made manifest that no partiality was involved."[45]

---

[45]Torstein Eckhoff, "Impartiality, Separation of Powers, and Judicial Independence," 9 *Scandinavian Studies in Law* 9, 16–17 (1965).

A *lottery* is another way to invoke the laws of chance. The lottery reduces every individual to absolute equality of opportunity. Extra investment—of money, patience, time, or labor—has no effect at all on the results, especially if each customer is restricted to a single ticket or chance. Many countries run lotteries to raise money. Other legal uses of a lottery system are less common. A recent, striking example in the United States was the draft lottery. More men were reaching draft age than the army needed. The days of the year were ranked by lottery; only those men whose birthday had a low lottery number were drafted. Any truly arbitrary decision has the same effect as a lottery. When decisions and rules are made mysterious and when processes seem arbitrary to the lay public, the public may imagine that chance is deciding its fate, not principle or reason. Without faith in authority, the formal law can look like a wheel of fortune to the average man. He will not know what to expect of the law and will avoid at all costs a process so capricious and unpredictable.

The *lottery* provides equality of opportunity but not of result. Still another way to allocate is to divide benefits or burdens equally—a straight poll tax, for example. The right to vote is another example; suffrage is divided equally among all competent adults. In theory, as we shall see, many basic civil rights have something of this quality. However, many goods cannot, practically speaking, be divided this way even if one wanted them to be.

Decisions about decisions are among the most important that any society can make. Each such decision has its reasons; each mode of allocation has advantages and disadvantages. How much to rely on markets continues to be vigorously debated—even in socialist countries. The queuing system has its own pluses and minuses. Lotteries, as Guido Calabresi has pointed out, have a real but limited value. They imply a "collective decision that although the collective deciders have no adequate reason for preferring that the activity be done by some people rather than by others . . . they expressly do not want to allow individuals to choose for themselves whether or not to do it."[46] The draft lottery probably struck many people as much fairer than any alternative. During the American Civil War, people were allowed to buy their way out of the draft; during the Vietnam war, before the lottery was used, there were tremendous local variations, and many complaints about injustice. If a person believes he has a *right* to some legal good, a lottery will strike him as grossly unfair; he will demand his due on the basis of merit or need.

When the law imposes or sustains a market or queuing system, it

---

[46]Calabresi, *supra* note 44, p. 115.

leaves decisions whether to deal, pay, or queue in private hands. The rules, including rules about jurisdiction, will tilt the likelihood of decision one way or another but leave the door open. The more the tilt, the more the decision is "preformed," that is, presented as a matter of coercion. At the far extreme are the allocative rules which leave nothing to private decision. Such are, for example, the rules of criminal law, but we will argue that the line between preformed and "private" decisions is not so sharp as appears at first glance. A person is "free" to make and break contracts. Murder is forbidden and severely punished; the potential "damages" are extraordinarily high. One *can*, however, decide to pay the price.

In every society, the legal system allows *some* scope to free choice, letting people decide who they will deal with and when to invoke the processes of law. This is true even under absolute monarchs or in totally planned societies. Every society, too, no matter how laissez-faire, makes a group of decisions collectively and tries to impose the collective will by force. Indeed, "law" means, among other things, these collective rules and decisions and the means to carry them out. The state or the collective makes these decisions by voting or by authority or command.

One special kind of rule, which we might call *constitutional*, determines the way in which decisions shall be made, but all rules of law, however arrived at, are collective, that is, they determine allocation according to some fixed, preformed scheme. This is the essence of a rule.

In other words, even when legal rules support markets and allow or foster individual choice, the rules themselves are preformed decisions more or less imposed on the population. At the present time, whether the economy or polity of a country is socialist, capitalist, or mixed, inflation of government and rules seems as inevitable as price inflation. The nineteenth-century faith in the invisible hand has dramatically weakened, but what is more important, perhaps, is simply the complexity of modern life. Society seems too interdependent to run by itself; it takes a lot of governing to keep it afloat. Stop lights and policemen are not needed on deserted roads. The alternatives to "law" —custom, habit, pressure of the peers, internalized values, free markets—do not seem efficient, or precise, or fair enough to control the behavior of masses of modern men.

Chapter II

On Legal Acts

In the first chapter, we used the term *legal act,* which we define very broadly. A legal act is any behavior by any person with authority acting within the legal system. Many legal acts are addressed to an audience and require or request someone's behavior. It is a legal act when a policeman stops a car and asks the driver to show his license. The driver is the subject of the act. The first part of this book explores the general question, Under what circumstances do legal acts lead to responses and of what sort?

Legal acts come in various forms. Some legal acts are words; others are conduct. When a policeman shoots at a rioter or gives out a ticket, he is performing a legal act. So, too, when a legislature enacts a commercial code. Verbal legal acts have special importance. They give general instructions to actors and members of the public. Nonverbal acts, by and large, happen to those who do not listen to the words. When a policeman fires his gun at a man who is running away, either the man has done something wrong, or the policeman has, or both.

There are three basic types of verbal legal acts: decisions, commands or orders, and rules. A *decision* is an authoritative statement about the legal relationships of one, two, or a number of persons in legal interaction. A decision is usually elicited as a response to a definite claim; and it does or can affect the rights and duties of the claimant, other parties, and perhaps all those similarly situated. Court *decisions* are obvious examples. Smith files a lawsuit claiming that Jones owes him money and refuses to pay. The court hears the evidence and renders a *decision* for Smith and against Jones. The decision will be followed by an *order*. The court will tell Jones what he must pay with interest. Orders are specific commands, directed to a particular person or group. They may or may not be based on more general statements of norms, that is, on *rules*.

Decisions and orders are perhaps the basic verbal output of a legal system. It is possible to imagine a legal system that produced *decisions* and, afterwards, *orders*, yet lacked (formal) *rules*. The legal systems of many small, tribal societies seem to be of this type or a variation of it. At any rate, they do not have formal, written rules. Yet these societies often have courts and judges, and the decisions made by their courts are in no way arbitrary. Anthropologists, not to mention members of these societies, have no trouble seeing regularities and patterns. Members of the society can and do talk about these patterns as rules, but the rules are not a *formal* output of the system. They exist outside the legal system as custom; and the courts-or leaders follow but do not claim to make these customary rules. Small societies the world over lack constitutions, codes, and norms set down in writing. Yet they definitely follow rules.

A *decision* is particular: *A* should prevail over *B*. A *command* is also particular: Give *A* the money or the land. A *rule* is a proposition of law couched in general terms. It can be split analytically into two parts. First, there is a statement of facts, second, a statement of legal consequences which will or may follow from those facts. Thus, in Ohio, a statute states that if a person "shall purposely and maliciously kill another," he is "guilty of murder in the second degree and shall be imprisoned for life."[2] Every doctrine, statute, rule book, code, decree, and every general, authoritative statement of law in any system is made up of propositions that can be analyzed as *rules*. Some rules are bigger and more complicated than others—whole chains of terms and propositions like immense organic molecules. Lawmakers, or revisers, may split complex rules into segments; and the segments may lie scattered about in a law book or code, like pieces of a jigsaw puzzle. The definition of murder may appear in one part of the penal code, the punishment in another. In the New York Penal Code, an elaborate section describes what facts make a person "guilty of murder"; the section declares that murder is "a class *A* felony." Another section, also quite elaborate, tells what sentences a judge may issue for people convicted of class *A* felony.[3] In our terms, the parts make up a single *rule*.

---

[1]See also the description of commercial arbitration in Robert L. Bonn, "The Predictability of Nonlegalistic Adjudication," 6 *Law and Society Rev.* 563 (1972).

[2]Ohio Rev. Code Ann. § 2901.05.

[3]N.Y. Penal Code, §§ 125.25, 70.00.

We commonly call legal propositions of all sorts "rules." Many rules, however, are only pieces or fragments of rules under our definition. For example, lawyers conventionally speak of the rule that it "is murder" to kill a man deliberately and with malice. This is true as far as it goes. To make a finished rule, one must add that the punishment for murder shall be thus-and-so. (The Ohio statute quoted did just that.) In the United States, federal labor law sets out a number of propositions about behavior which amounts to an "unfair labor practice." An employer, who will not bargain collectively with his workers, has committed an "unfair labor practice." This is only a label, like "murder" or "negligent driving"; one must read on to find out what difference the label makes and how it affects the rights and duties of labor, management, and the National Labor Relations Board.[4]

It is simply a matter of definition to insist that a rule is no rule without a statement of consequences, but the definition is not arbitrary. Why would we care *how* murder or an unfair labor practice is defined, if nothing followed from the definition? A rule without consequences is not meaningless; it may be an explanation for a rule. A complex legal system, however, must have *rules* in the sense we use the word. If the system is divided into many institutions and is built on many levels with higher and lower strata of officials, rules are essential. They carry the messages, programs, and codes from high to low— if they do nothing else. Any legal system that *works* has rules, and any one with a hierarchy or bureaucratic organization will have formal rules of one sort or another.

Many formal rules in a modern code are, to be sure, elliptical. They leave out the statement of consequences. The criminal code describing *arson* can content itself with labeling arson as a felony. What a felony is and what can happen to a felon may be defined elsewhere in the code. The Uniform Commercial Code states (Section §1–203) that every contract within the code "imposes an obligation of good faith in its performance." What fate is in store for a contract *not* performed in good faith? The section is elliptical, and indeed, the rest of the code does not spell out consequences in any detail. The clause does suggest, at least implicitly, that when a party does not act "in good faith," the courts may deny him remedies and defenses that he might otherwise have had.

To put it somewhat differently, every *rule* has two messages or objects: one of substance, one of jurisdiction. Every rule is *about* something; at the same time, it contains a direction to some public authority telling him he may do, should do, or must stop doing some act he might

---

[4]29 U.S.C.A. § 160.

otherwise do or not do. The directions may be quite explicit. For example, in Washington state, judges of the superior courts may grant a divorce "on application of the party injured," after proof of one or more of ten grounds for divorce, which include adultery, impotence, abandonment for one year, cruelty, and habitual drunkenness.[5] The grounds for divorce go to the substance of the rule; the direction to the judge is jurisdictional.

The jurisdictional side of rules is often not spelled out but simply understood. This is true of much of the criminal law. The penal codes define crimes and state punishments; typically, they do not mention in detail how the two will be made to match. A thief, however, does not go to jail by magic; public officials will have to intervene. Actually, a whole ponderous, complex system has to be set in motion. The rules of the penal code, by implication, give tickets of authority to policemen, district attorneys, judges, bailiffs, clerks, wardens, and executioners. These grants of authority, to be sure, are often spelled out elsewhere in the statutes; they need not be repeated each time the code describes a crime.

The *substance* of a rule is a message to the general public or to some specialized part of the public. The *jurisdictional* part of the rule is a message to some part of the official world. The message may be a prohibition, an authorization, or an incentive. The statute against murder is a simple prohibition, and it is addressed to the public in general. The jurisdictional part of the statute runs to actors within the legal system—specifically, those concerned with criminal law. Not every rule is addressed to a general audience. Murderers can be drawn from all walks of life; but some rules of law only affect a particular group—cab drivers, steel mill owners, merchants, drug addicts, shopkeepers, rope manufacturers. Some rules are not addressed to the lay public at all—for example, rules about the records judges must keep or civil service regulations. However, every rule has its jurisdictional side, that is, every rule contains a message, expressed or implied, for some public official or officials.[6]

The definition of a rule used here does not, of course, mean that law consists only of rules. Since every complex society has formal rules and since all formal rules contain sanctions, this definition conflicts

---

[5] Wash. Stat. Ann. § 26.08.020.

[6] The definition of a rule used here has the drawback that stateless societies without judges, lawyers, or officials would lack any "rules." Often an "official" can be found by stretching the concept somewhat. See Chapter I, pp. 6–7. And the "rules" discussed are formal rules only; every society follows rules.

with those of jurists and scholars who deny that sanctions are a necessary aspect of law. One of these is Michael Barkun, the author of *Law Without Sanctions*. For him, law is, rather, a system of "symbols"; it serves as "a representation, a model of social structure."[7] It is a normative map that members of a "jural community" hold in common.

No doubt it is useful to imagine such a map—useful in thinking about the reality of rules. It helps explain why some societies insist on making and enforcing certain rules, and why other rules are dead letters or enforceable only at great cost. For Barkun, law is more or less a dictionary of right conduct. People use dictionaries, even though no one enforces their commands. But there are many dictionaries of right conduct in society. The law is only one of them. The dictionary itself is a dictionary of right conduct, so is any and every book of etiquette, and so are the books that set out rules for playing tennis, bridge, or solitaire. Arguably, at least, what sets apart the law book as a code of rules from these other codes is the sanction—the fact that *its* propositions (and not others) carry with them the threat of official punishment or the promise of official reward.

The point, however, is partly a matter of form and of words. If a person violates the rules of etiquette—eats with his fingers, let us say —he is not immune from sanctions. If he is a child, his parents may scold or spank him. If an older person has "bad manners," friends may laugh at him. For some purposes, then, rules of etiquette are not so very different from rules of law. What they lack are official, formal sanctions. If one defines law to include only processes and rules carried on by government or analogous parts of smaller societies, then rules of etiquette are not rules of law. In any event, a theory of legal behavior *must* pay attention to the theory and practice of sanctions. Whether sanctions are the "essence" of law or not, they are real enough in the world, and one cannot explain how law works without explaining the work of its sanctions.[8]

In modern nations—France, the United States, or India—the legal system produces and uses a stupefying volume of rules. National statutes, city ordinances, administrative regulations—all are made up of rules. In the United States, one must reckon with state as well as federal laws. The total number of rules in force can hardly be counted; judicial doctrines add thousands more. There are many ways to classify

---

[7]Michael Barkun, *Law Without Sanctions* (1968), p. 92.

[8]To say that nothing is a rule that lacks a statement of sanctions does not mean that the sanctions are always used. Obviously, some laws are not enforced, and it is also certainly true that there is more to the law than its rules.

these rules and reduce them to some kind of order. One way is to divide them by topic: rules of criminal law, tort law, or maritime law; rules about food and drug inspection; traffic rules of Rome or New York. Another way is by source: federal statutes, ordinances of Miami, rules of the Dayton police force, doctrines of the Maine supreme court. Or by formal type: constitutional rules, statutes, executive orders, interpretative rules of the high courts of Spain.

Each of these methods of classification has its uses. An observer of the legal system also notes that some rules are very precise, very objective; others seem little more than vague generalities. The rule that sets the voting age at eighteen is much more precise than the rule that a negligent driver must pay damages to someone he injures. Extreme examples of the second type include the lapidary statement of the Uniform Commercial Code that the performance of contracts imposes an "obligation of good faith" or the "general clauses" of the continental codes that require "good faith" in contracts or the like.[9] Vague rules require someone to exercise judgment or discretion before making a decision in a particular case. We can call this kind of rule *discretionary.* Some rules are explicitly discretionary. They tell the judge or other official that he may choose either *A* or *B* or *C,* or they give him power to choose from an unlimited number of options. For example, the law of Connecticut allows a judge in divorce cases to "make any proper order as to the custody, care and education of the children," and, "at any time thereafter, annul or vary such order."[10]

In other statutes, the grant of discretion is implicit. A judge, in a case arising under the Uniform Commercial Code, will presumably have to decide what is or is not "good faith," just as judges and juries have made up their minds whether it is negligent to drive a car at 30 m.p.h. during a blizzard, or to fail to put a fence around a buzz saw, or whether an injured leg is worth $300, or $3,000, or $3,000,000 in damages in some particular situation. A discretionary rule is a rule which is, in a sense, not final. It always involves some sort of delegation to another: The power to reduce discretion to certainty flows downward. All rules contain a jurisdictional side; hence, delegation is a pervasive feature of rules. But not all grants of authority are grants of discretion. Rules of the other sort—*objective* rules—are quite final in a way; someone will have to apply the rule, but this can be done "mechanically," that is, the rule itself leaves little official room for further choices

---

[9]For example, in Germany, under Art. 138, BGB, a legal act is "void" if it is offensive to morality; Gunther Teubner, *Standards und Direktiven in Generalklauseln* (1971).
[10]Conn. Rev. Stat. §§ 46–23.

among alternatives. The voting age is eighteen, and that is that. The registrar has no right to say that seventeen and one-half is close enough, nor does a judge.

Many rules have a discretionary form, which does not necessarily mean that there is real choice at the point of application. As we have said, every rule has a jurisdictional side. A statute may lay down the rule that factory owners must keep their premises "safe." This rule is, in the first place, elliptical. Very likely, the law will provide for inspection of factories. Very likely, too, the inspecting agency or board will have power to make rules about safety. A court, too, might decide, in a particular case, what makes a factory "safe." Courts do not enact codes of safety as such. They decide matters case by case. An agency or board *might* draw up a code. If so, it would surely take some guesswork—some discretion—out of the concept of "safe." Regulations might, for example, set out a table of specific rules: A factory is safe when: (a) there is not less than one fire extinguisher for every six workers. . . . A discretionary rule, in short, *delegates* power to make decisions. One must look further, then, to see whether some agency or officer lower down in the legal system can and does make sub-rules that are more objective. Does the real discretion go to the bottom, to the point of application, or does it turn into objective sub-rules somewhere in between?

Later, we will discuss objective and discretionary rules in more detail, particularly how and why one kind of rule changes into another over time.[11] For now, we would like to make one cautious point. It might seem, on the surface, that the two are distinct, exclusive types at opposite poles. In fact, they are two ends of a continuum with many shadings in between. No rule is perfectly discretionary or perfectly objective. This is because no *concept* is completely objective, and no concept is completely bloodless and abstract. "One fire extinguisher" is a fairly objective phrase, but any law student could easily dream up a situation in which the meaning was in doubt. Is a broken fire extinguisher a fire extinguisher? What of an extinguisher that works but is hard to reach on the wall? On the other hand, some situations are so "unsafe" or "unreasonable" that one can not imagine much doubt. "Safe" is a discretionary term, but a factory shed made out of dry, rotten wood, with no fire extinguishers or sprinklers, full of oily rags, its floors too weak to bear the weight of the workers, is unsafe under anybody's definition. Discretion in a rule, then, is a matter of more or less.

---

[11]See Chapter X.

ON LEGAL DISCRETION

Discretion is a term with many meanings. Discretion commonly refers to a case where a person, subject to a rule, has power to choose between alternative courses of action. Since rules have a double aspect —they speak to officials and to some or all members of the public as well —a rule may carry a grant of discretion in one aspect and not in the other. This yields four types of formal rules. Some rules are doubly fixed—neither public nor official has a choice. The rules of the penal code, generally speaking, take this form. They forbid murder, arson, and theft; the rules are, on paper, absolute. Violators must be punished. No one is allowed to violate, nor does any official have the (formal) right to let a criminal go. Another kind of rule, which we can call an *authorization*, is discretionary with the public but not with officials. A man and woman *may* apply for a marriage license; a person may decide to bring a lawsuit; these are personal choices in the eyes of the law. If the couple or the plaintiff meet legal requirements, civil servants have no choice but to react in the prescribed, official way. The clerk must give the license; the clerk of the court must put the case on the docket.

A third type, the *privilege,* is doubly discretionary: An eligible person may apply or not, as he wishes; there is discretion on the public side as well. Technically, the applicant has no right. Privileges are common in the legal system, especially in the allocation of scarce goods. The Federal Communications Commission gives out licenses for radio stations. No one *has* to apply; if someone does, the FCC acts under an umbrella of rules giving vast, almost amorphous discretion.[12] In the fourth type of rule, only the official has leeway. This too is common. Criminal statutes often give, for example, wide discretion to judges in sentencing and disposition. The convict himself has no say in the matter.

These are four types of *formal* rules—rules which not only can be written down on paper but actually have been. Many rules look hard-and-fast on paper but are different in the real world. There are innumerable examples. Police will fail to arrest, or prosecutors will drop a case for one reason or another, even though "the law" makes no mention of such power.[13] Contrariwise, a family court judge may have full

---

[12]See 47 U.S.C.A. § 309(a); the commission grants application when "public interest, convenience, and necessity would be served."

[13]Wayne R. La Fave, *Arrest: The Decision to Take a Suspect Into Custody* (1965); John Kaplan, "The Prosecutional Discretion: A Comment," 60 *Nw. U.L. Rev.* 174 (1965); Robert L. Rabin, "Agency Criminal Referrals in the Federal System: An Empirical Study of Prosecutional Discretion," 24 *Stan. L. Rev.* 1036 (1972); Brian A. Grosman, *The Prosecutor, An Inquiry into the Exercise of Discretion* (1969).

discretion to award custody, limited only by some vague formula about the benefit of the child, but in practice, the mother almost always gets the custody.[14] Commercial arbitration seems open and discretionary— no tight rules, no written opinions; in fact seller-claimants almost always win their claim.[15] Also, concepts such as murder, arson, and theft do not have self-evident meanings. There are always borderline cases. This fact, which we ignore for now, is very general; it builds an unavoidable amount of discretion into the real operation of rules.

A modern legal system contains immense numbers of rules, some objective and some discretionary.[16] The *proportion* of one type to the other is more or less constantly changing. Discretionary rules are more interesting to legal scholars; objective rules seem primitive or formalistic. But the most cursory glance at the statute books of any country reveals thousands upon thousands of objective rules. They are the workhorses of the law. Modern regulatory law demands precise, detailed rules. A discretionary rule does not govern; it only delegates authority. As we pointed out, discretionary rules often have objective sub-rules. If one took a worm's eye view of modern law, many "discretionary" rules would vanish. As vague rules are handed down from level to level, they tend to become more specific.[17] The legal system, formally speaking, has more discretionary rules than rules that really operate that way.

From another standpoint, legal rules can be divided into three general groups. First, some rules are *dormant*—that is, no one makes any real attempt to enforce them. Second, other rules are more or less *part of the living law,* but raise classic problems of uncertainty. Exactly what do they mean, and how far do they reach? What is due process of law? What makes a ship "seaworthy" in admiralty law? When is a person not guilty of crime, because he suffers from mental disease? Many of these rules are couched in discretionary *language,* but not all. In some, uncertainty exists not because but in spite of the text. What unsettles these rules is social controversy—challenge, social demand. Many rules are doubly uncertain. The First Amendment to the American Constitution prohibits restrictions on freedom of speech. No one can give an exact definition of freedom of speech, and the First Amendment did not try. Hence the language itself is not free from difficulty.

---

[14]The *reason* may be that the judge, like members of the public generally, believes that children are better off with their mothers.

[15]Robert L. Bonn, "The Predictability of Nonlegalistic Adjudication," 6 *Law and Society Rev.* 563 (1972).

[16]See, in general, the treatment of the subject in Lawrence M. Friedman, "Legal Rules and the Process of Social Change," 19 *Stan. L. Rev.* 786, 791–792 (1967).

[17]The opposite process can also take place.

However, the limits of meaning would be clearer than they are, if there were *social* consensus about obscenity, or sedition, or "symbolic speech."

A third—and equally vital—part of law consists of *well-settled* rules. That is, the rules are alive and work, and no one challenges them. There is no doubt that an ordinary check is negotiable or that a will needs two witnesses, not more, in West Virginia. "Well-settled" does not necessarily mean that the rule is objective in form. Clever people can always dream up dubious or borderline cases. Does an eighteen-year-old have the right to vote, if his birthday falls on Election Day? Can he cast an absentee ballot before his eighteenth birthday, to be counted *after* his birthday? "Well-settled" does not mean that the meaning of a rule is inherently free of doubt. It means that the rule is *actually* free of doubt as a matter of ordinary behavior and ordinary understanding.

It is in this sense that real rules, working rules, are well-settled. Indeed, they must be. Otherwise, in the modern world the life of society and the market could hardly go on. A legal system would be an intolerable nuisance if all rules were open-ended, if every proposition and concept raised "nice," debatable issues. People need to know what is lawful and unlawful in everyday life—what is valid and what is not. For example, a couple has a license, they have taken a blood test, and they have gone through a ceremony. Are they legally married or not? They are, since no one will challenge the marriage, and, if someone dared, his challenge would fail. People need to know how fast they can drive their cars on the road. A speed limit is better than a sign that reads "drive at a reasonable speed." People need to know that a deed made out in such and such a way will validly transfer a house; a buyer must be reasonably sure that he can move in, stay, sell, or trade the house without difficulty. The economy could not go on in its present form, if every little act had to be funneled through an agency with discretionary power. A market economy—for that matter, a socialist economy—imposes on the legal system a heavy demand for certainty, not in the abstract rules that jurists debate but in those parts of law which regulate everyday affairs. A society which makes the market one of its central institutions has a "peculiar need to create and maintain a framework of reasonably well defined and assured expectations as to the likely official and nonofficial consequences of private venture and decision."[18] The economy is the most obvious case of the need for such certainty. Other parts of the social system, which law touches or regu-

---

[18]J. Willard Hurst, *Law and the Conditions of Freedom in the Nineteenth Century United States* (1956), p. 22.

lates, have their own degree of demand for certainty—whether for efficiency's sake or to fill sociocultural needs.

The case for certainty seems obvious, but legal scholars in the nineteenth century vastly overdid this point, and twentieth-century thought reacted against them. Nineteenth-century thought, for a variety of reasons, stressed the formal, mechanical, deductive aspects of law. The legal realists, roughly from 1920 on, ridiculed the hunger for certainty; Jerome Frank, for one, called it an "illusion or myth" that law "either is or can be approximately stationary and certain."[19] Lawyers and laymen, he thought, were really searching for a father figure ("the child's Father-as-Judge") when they dreamed of this unattainable ideal. Notice that Frank lumped certainty and immutability together, but they are very different things. Perhaps it is "primitive" to conceive of law as eternal and unchanging. To want short-run fixity and certainty, however, is not primitive at all—not that perfect certainty is attainable, especially in cases that go to trial. Many factors are unpredictable, and the longer and more elaborate the trial, the more of them. The point is even stronger for cases on appeal. In everyday affairs, however, and in routine matters, reasonable certainty *is* attainable—indeed, it must be attained.

The legal system, then, must somehow keep discretionary rules in proper bounds. These are rules that do not govern directly; they do not give clear-cut guides to expected behavior. Economy and society can put up with some such rules as luxuries; and there are areas where society chooses to have or must have justice slowly and carefully cut to the individual case—for murder trials, yes; parking violations and garnishments, hardly. To deal with transactions in the mass, one needs snappy, objective rules. The rule that a will must have two witnesses is hard-and-fast, inflexible, "primitive" if you like, but better than a rule requiring a "reasonable" number of witnesses according to the nature of the case. Open, flexible rules are arguably fairer, less harsh, more in tune with the sense of justice, but flexible rules are inefficient. They also give enormous discretion—and therefore power—to those officials or judges who apply them. They invite corruption or caprice.[20] In operation, such rules may offend the moral sense of society rather than fulfill it.

---

[19]Jerome Frank, *Law and the Modern Mind* (1930), pp. 13–21.

[20]Tight rules, of course, do not guarantee against corruption. In fact, one might argue that when rules are *too* tight, corruption is bound to occur: A rationing scheme breeds a black market. Corruption and abuse of discretion also vary from legal culture to legal culture. See Chapter IX, pp. 224–225. All that one can safely say is that, other things being equal, objective rules do serve a somewhat prophylactic purpose. See Kenneth C. Davis, *Discretionary Justice: A Preliminary Inquiry* (1969).

To be sure, fixity also has its costs and its limits. The legal system is not a machine; it is run by human beings. In a sense the larger society gives the orders, and the cogs in the machine mostly do as they are told. Any theory of law, however, must assume a lot of slack, leeway, discretion, and downright disobedience within the system. Every study of the legal system confirms this. Discretion is, of course, not evenly distributed throughout the system. In part, higher levels have more than lower ones. The president of the United States has an awesome range of options; postal clerks have very few as far as postal rules are concerned. Administrators in high or middle posts tend to have a good deal of discretion,[21] while low-level functionaries, most of the time, have no official discretion—no power or very little power to change any rules.[22] An absolute dictator, whose word is law, stands at one extreme; at the other extreme, behind his cage, is the marriage license clerk whose job is narrowly defined and who takes the rules as given.

We say that the clerk has no discretion. What does this mean? Obviously, he has a choice in the physical sense, but "choice" also has an ethical or normative meaning. An institution or person can lack legal or moral discretion. By this we mean that, by some standard, the actor behaves properly *only* if he performs in such and such a way. We recognize, at the same time, that some people do misbehave. We can say that a policeman is "bound" by the rules, that he is not authorized to act on his own to arrest the innocent without cause, to beat prisoners, or to take bribes. Policemen sometimes do these things and with impunity. This behavior, of course, is defined as illegitimate. It is considered a defect in the system, to be rooted out if possible.

Somewhat different is this situation: The actor has a choice in fact; there also exist standards and norms about what is and what is not the actor's duty, yet "wrong" actions are neither illegitimate and illegal. This situation occurs when, for example, an appellate court "wrongly" decides a case. When we say this, we mean it chose the wrong rules, or applied them incorrectly, or made a mistake, according to some external standard. However, even if we "catch" the court, nothing can be done about this "abuse" of discretion, either in theory or in fact.

---

[21]See, for example, the study of the work of the Immigration and Naturalization Service, Abraham D. Sofaer, "The Change of Status Adjudication: A Case Study of the Informal Agency Process," 1 *J. Legal Studies* 349 (1972).

[22]The point can be carried too far. Even the president must bow before the will of Congress and the courts, while, on the other hand, the lowly patrolman on the beat has tremendous discretion in his sphere. Wayne R. La Fave, *Arrest: The Decision to Take a Suspect into Custody* (1965); Johannes Feest and Erhard Blankenburg, *Die Definitionsmacht der Polizei* (1972).

This example suggests an important, perhaps central, meaning of *discretion*. A decision-maker has discretion to choose between two alternatives, *A* and *B*, when no one else has the right, on review, to correct the decision, good or bad. This is what is meant when we say that a judge or jury has discretion over guilt or innocence or over the sentencing of persons convicted of crime. It means that there is no appeal or review of that aspect of their activity. Of course, how far judge and jury have such rights is a complicated question. Much of what they do *can* be reviewed, but it is the unreviewable, untouchable aspect or part that we call their discretion.

This is a useful definition of discretion, because it is empirical rather than normative. With it, one might perhaps measure how much discretion there is in a legal system. We can observe which actors and what actions can be reviewed and which cannot, either according to the rules of the system or according to patterns of behavior valid by some standard. The task would never be easy. Indeed, the very rules of the system are sometimes paradoxical or contradictory. A jury in the United States has real discretion to set free an accused killer; jury decisions are final. Yet there is a theory or doctrine that jurors are "bound" by the law and must decide in accordance with law. This pious sentiment as such does not limit their power. Jury decisions cannot be questioned or reviewed. It is not illegal for a jury to set a guilty man free.

The jury has both real and formal discretion. A policeman or a judge may corruptly use discretion he is not supposed to have, or corruption may remove some discretion which law formally grants. Judges may feel bound, despite the formal law, to favor political bosses, or the party, or the powerful. Norms and values also limit discretion, even when formal law does not. The exercise of *discretion* is merely one kind of legal behavior. It is behavior not controlled by formal sanctions or review. As we will develop at more length in later chapters, there are three general clusters of control over legal behavior. Even when the sanction is missing, two of these clusters are left: the opinion of significant others and the actor's own values and norms. Many loose guidelines *do* predict behavior despite "full discretion," because they embody public opinion or express or invoke the actor's values or norms. There is no one who can review what the Supreme Court does or the House of Lords or the Cour de Cassation. These courts, in other words, have enormous discretion. Yet they do not behave arbitrarily or whimsically; they pay great attention to rules, values, and norms.

Formal discretion in a legal system, then, is quite different from real discretion; one cannot be deduced from the other. Still, formal discretion is a fact of great interest and importance. It also tends to be rather controversial. Discretion means, in its sphere, unbridled power. On any issue, final power must rest somewhere in the legal system. There must be some place of last resort; otherwise, disputes could drag on forever from forum to forum. Where this power should lie and for what issues is constantly under debate. At this time in American history, presidential power is one major focus of discussion, particularly as regards foreign affairs. For a preceding generation, administrative power was hotly debated. Big government generates hordes of agencies, bureaus, boards, and commissions. They need freedom to plan and to govern, but they also seem to threaten the liberty of the citizen, unless they are controlled. There must be some scope and freedom, too, at the bottom as well as at the top—for clerks, patrolmen, trial judges, and others. It would be both wrong and impossible to treat these men as machines or to review their every step.

At least three prerequisites are needed to control or reduce discretion. First, there must be a rule book—literally or figuratively. There must be some source, in other words, which states plainly and flatly what it is that the actor must do. Discretion thrives on vague, open-ended rules.[23] Second, there must be a system of communication, up and down—some way to bring the rule book home to the actor and communicate its terms; and some way to discover how he is doing, whether he is carrying out the letter and the spirit of the rule. Lastly, there must be some way to keep the actor in line, to enforce compliance. This would include rewards and punishments, primarily, although perhaps a superior could find some way to invoke the power of peers or induce some other tool of "voluntary" compliance.[24] These methods and prerequisites, as we shall see, are the same as those for "enforcement" of any rule, discretionary or not. In other words, the techniques

---

[23]See, in general, Davis, *supra* note 20.

[24]The rules, rule book, and enforcement are not necessarily drawn up by the government. Consider the case of a surgeon in government service, whose job it is to operate on army personnel. Most of his "rules" are not prescribed by the army, but by his *profession;* he learns them as he learns to be a surgeon; the values of the medical profession, which he has internalized, do much of the "enforcing" of the norms. The legal system uses professionals in many areas—doctors, accountants, nurses, engineers, biochemists. When they perform their roles, they use their well-known and reliable rule books. Professionals can be given "discretion" to ply their trade, partly because one knows that they will follow definite rules most of the time, and will be guided by known standards. They will be given discretion, of course, only when the system wants those rules and standards of the profession followed. The army wants the surgeon to act like a doctor, in operating on military personnel. Where "professional" rules would not produce desired results, they will be superseded or supplemented by other rules.

for reducing discretion are only a special case of a more general subject: How to make, influence, or change legal behavior. Because administrators armed with broad discretion are so pervasive a feature of modern life, the problem is particularly thorny and acute.[25]

ON AUTHORIZATIONS

Not all rules are orders, commands, or prohibitions. Some give privileges and authorize action: You *may* do this, if you wish. Like all rules, authorizations attach consequences to statements of legal fact. If the bank does not honor your check, you may sue it for damages.

Authorizations are dominant on the civil side of the law; prohibitions are dominant in criminal law. All legal rules, however, are aimed at conduct. Rules, in general, express a collective decision— that society or some ruling part of it wants behavior to bend in some particular direction. The penal code expresses a policy that people should not kill, rape, or steal. It backs up its words with formal sanctions. But punishment is not the only way to bend conduct. Some statutes offer flat out rewards. Other rules, and networks of rules, offer subtle mixes of punishment and reward. The federal tax code, for example, taxes some kinds of income, excuses other types from tax, offers tax benefits to people who drill for oil or give money to charity, and threatens cheaters with fines and imprisonment. A subsystem of rules is a complex arrangement, a kind of legal supermarket; a wide range of products is for sale with various prices, packages, and inducements to buy. The freedom to buy or not buy apples does not mean that the owner is indifferent to their sale or that he could not sell more apples by cutting the price, improving the service, or providing more carts.

The rules of contract law are typical of the civil side of the law. The rules include few do's and don't's and many statements about duties, rights, privileges, and authorizations. *X* agrees to sell a carload of lumber to *Y*. He fails to deliver the lumber which *Y* then buys on the open market. *Y* can now claim damages amounting to whatever he spent for the lumber over and above the contract price. This and similar rules offer *some* inducement to lumber dealers to stick to their bargains and have at least some modest deterrent effect on breach of contract. Yet breach of contract is not *forbidden*. It is not "against the law" to fail to deliver the lumber, nor does the buyer have a duty to

---

[25]See the perceptive essay by Joel Handler, "Controlling Official Behavior in Welfare Administration," in Jacobus ten Broek, ed., *The Law of the Poor* (1966), p. 155.

sue for breach of contract; it is entirely up to him. Unless the price of lumber goes up, he has no money incentive to sue. He may ignore the breach, if he wants to, or settle the matter out of court. Either of these alternatives is a more likely outcome than full trial.

The rules about breach of contract may or may not influence contractual behavior; they certainly have *some* effect on a party's decision to sue. Changes in rules can raise or lower incentives to sue. Rules that offer higher damages would encourage more lawsuits. Outside of court, the rules affect negotiation. They influence the settlement process. Most cases of personal injury never get to court, but the lawyers argue rules of tort law in trying to strike a favorable bargain. How the (imaginary) trial *would* come out affects the balance of negotiating power.[26] Rules about court costs and jurisdiction also affect bargaining power and act as incentives and disincentives. Authorizations are like other rules, except for the strength of the inducements they offer, and the institutional arrangements they imply.

THE HIERARCHY OF RULES

Some rules, like Orwell's pigs, are more equal than others. Rules can be ranked in a kind of pyramid from lower- to higher-order rules. When rules conflict, higher rules control the lower ones. In a constitutional system, the constitutional rules have higher validity than ordinary statutory rules. A statute in turn has more authority than a city ordinance or an administrative regulation. Usually, higher validity does not mean that the rule is morally more perfect, merely that those who made it stand higher in the pyramid of government.

Some scholars, however, draw a line between *principles* and rules. Principles are super-rules. They are rules from which one makes other rules—in other words, patterns or models for rules. Some people use the word "principle" in a slightly different sense. A "principle" serves as a standard, that is, a rule by which one judges the worth or validity of lesser rules. Still another meaning of the word "principle" is that of an inductive abstraction. A principle, in this sense, is a broad, general rule that sums up many smaller, particular rules.

In the well-known case of *Riggs* v. *Palmer*,[27] a sixteen-year-old boy had poisoned his grandfather. The question was whether he could inherit from his grandfather's estate. The court said he could not and

[26]Alfred Conard et al., *Automobile Accident Costs and Payments* (1964); H. Laurence Ross, *Settled Out of Court, the Social Process of Insurance Claims Adjustments* (1970).
[27]*Riggs* v. *Palmer*, 115 N.Y. 506, 22 N.E. 188 (1889).

referred to the "principle" that "no one shall be permitted to profit by his own fraud, or to take advantage of his own wrong, or to found any claim on his own iniquity, or to acquire property by his own crime." What makes this maxim a "principle"? It fits each of the three meanings mentioned. It is, first of all, a broad statement from which one could cut a number of sub-rules; it is also an ethical proposition that could be used to test the validity of sub-rules; and it might well be an induction, summing up, at a higher level of abstraction, many prior decisions and holdings.

The three meanings have a common core: A principle is some sort of higher-order rule. There are ordinary workaday rules, the drudges and drones of the legal system, and there are principles which have higher morality or at least greater abstraction. Because of their abstraction, principles are more *discretionary* than rules which fall under them. ("Fall under them," either because these rules are the raw material from which some mind has abstracted the principle or because the principle was the pattern or model from which they were cut or against which they were tested.) To hold that a man should not profit from his wrong does not automatically decide a particular case. A plain, flat rule that a murderer cannot inherit from his victim comes much closer. Between principle and decision, leeway and judgment intervene; the principle, in other words, is highly discretionary.

A principle, in short, can be seen as nothing more than a certain kind of rule, a rule phrased in abstract general language.[28] All principles have this character. Still, people commonly speak about principles in a normative way, as something higher, nobler, and finer than a rule. Whether an abstract statement has this quality is not due to its abstractness, but because it states norms that command ethical allegiance in the community. Some principles and some rules do, and some do not. Principles which do will, in fact, *control* the use of rules, that is, act as a standard, as an agent for legitimizing rules. They tell us *why* some rules are valid and some are not in a given society, or why some are more valid than others. The "principle" that no man should profit from his wrong both *explains* and *validates* the rule that a murderer cannot inherit from his victim's estate. Principles of this

---

[28]To the contrary, see Ronald Dworkin, "The Model of Rules," 35 *U. Chi. L. Rev.* 14 (1967), arguing that principles are fundamentally different from rules. But Dworkin uses the term "rule" in a more restrictive sense than it is used here. For him, a "rule" becomes more rule-like, the more objective it is. For another view of the distinction between rules and principles, see Joseph Raz, "Legal Principles and the Limits of Law," 81 *Yale L.J.* 823 (1972).

kind, then, are rules of special importance in the study of legal culture and popular attitudes toward law.

ON THE REALITY OF RULES

The *operating* norms of a legal system are not principles or abstract standards, by and large. The law works with rules that are much more down to earth. One can question whether even these humdrum rules really work. After all, one never *sees* a rule; one only sees patterns of behavior. We can describe the behavior and wrap it up neatly into packages of rules. Much of the behavior *seems* to conform to preexisting formal rules. How do we know, however, that the rules "caused" the behavior? The rules are there—on paper, but paper rules may be and often are ignored. Or the behavior and the rules may be unconnected; the rules rationalize the behavior, after the fact. Do rules decide cases? A judge, for example, may shovel a flock of rules into his opinion or cite whole sections of a code. He claims he was "bound" by these rules, that they dictated his decision. How do we know if these rules were really responsible for his decision? Does the judge *himself* really know?

Nineteenth-century legal thought took quite seriously the reality of rules and their powerful impact on legal behavior. Twentieth-century thought has been far more skeptical. In the United States this skepticism is associated with the legal realists, who burst on the scene with great flair in the 1920s and 1930s. Their zeal and electricity have passed into history, but some of their ideas have percolated into the minds of many judges and lawyers. Karl Llewellyn[29] and Jerome Frank[30] were among the most notable spokesmen for realism. Actually, realism was a complex movement. The realists shared a distaste for the older jurisprudence, which they derided as "mechanical" or "conceptual." Otherwise, individual members of the movement had little in common. Llewellyn, in a well-known essay, did point to some common themes: The realists, for example, generally thought of law "as a means to social ends and not as an end in itself"; it therefore needed "constantly to be examined for its purpose, and for its effect." Rule skepticism, too, was of the essence of realist thought. The realists, Llewellyn pointed out, had a "distrust" of "traditional legal rules and concepts insofar as they purport to *describe* what either courts or

---

[29]See, for example, "A Realistic Jurisprudence—the Next Step," 30 *Colum. L. Rev.* 431 (1930); and "Some Realism about Realism," 44 *Harv. L. Rev.* 1222 (1931); the movement is generally treated in Wilfrid E. Rumble, Jr., *American Legal Realism* (1968).

[30]*Law and the Modern Mind* (1930).

people are actually doing"; they also distrusted "the theory that traditional prescriptive rule-formulations are *the* heavily operative factor in producing court decisions."[31]

The rule skeptic started out with an undeniable insight. He saw that some rules were enforced rarely, others not at all. He also saw that judges and lawyers often used rules to rationalize after the fact. Many rules were highly abstract or even tautological. Such rules could not possibly govern the conduct of judges, who were free to "interpret" according to their discretion. The rules, in short, did not rule by themselves. No one could look at rules on the printed page and deduce or guess what the behavior of judges was like.

If one carried this viewpoint to an extreme, one might conclude that rules meant nothing. Judges do as they please, plain and simple. The idea may seem absurd, but it is not *logically* impossible. Even if rules *were* meaningless or totally ignored, it would not follow that chance and caprice would govern the courtroom. It would mean only that something other than the official rules—the judge's attitudes and values, for example—would determine decisions. Imagine a secret, fanatical Marxist, taking office as a judge in a non-Marxist country. Imagine him utterly determined to decide every case according to Marxist principles, as he understood them, but also determined not to tip his hand. This judge would use rules cynically, as excuses, rationalizations. Actually, his ideology would decide his cases for him. The outcomes would not be random or accidental; once one cracked his code, they might be easy to predict. Yet the opinions would not *look* any different from those of his colleagues. The reader who doubts this statement might consider known cases of corrupt judges sitting on the bench.[32] Until exposed, these judges fooled the legal community; a bribed decision looked no worse or less convincing than an honest one.

Social scientists who study law tend to be rule skeptics, too. They assume that there is a "code" and look unceasingly for ways to crack it. They go beyond rules and written opinions, read outcomes as true data, and explore personality, attitudes, and values of the judges in their search for an explanation of decisions.[33]

The results have been sometimes interesting, often disappointing. The flaw in rule skepticism, if there is one, is not a logical flaw. It is

---

[31]Karl Llewellyn, "Some Realism about Realism," 44 *Harv. L. Rev.* 1222, 1236, 1237 (1931); on the instrumental view of law, see also pp. 204–209 of this book.

[32]See Joseph Borkin, *The Corrupt Judge* (1962), for examples.

[33]The literature is considerable. See, for example, Glendon Schubert, *Quantitative Analysis of Judicial Behavior* (1959). Most of the work has focussed on the United States Supreme Court, but not all; Daryl R. Fair, "An Experimental Application of Scalogram Analysis to State Supreme Court Decisions," 1967 *Wis. L. Rev.* 449. See also Chapter VII.

an empirical failing. The fact seems to be that some people follow some rules some of the time; probably all people follow some rules some of the time. We say, "seems to be," because the fact is hard to prove. Most law clerks and most students of the courts feel that judges in many or most cases do honestly or guilelessly search for rules and try to follow them. This is an impression—an untested hypothesis and nothing more. On closer analysis, it might be dead wrong, but the burden of proof is on those who deny *all* efficacy to rules. Certainly, if *lower* functionaries in a hierarchy were not bound to *some* degree by rules, it is hard to see how government would function. Marriage license clerks, white-collar workers in pension bureaus, inspectors of meat, wool, and elevators must and do follow the rule book most of the time —indeed, they follow it all too blindly, if we believe studies of bureaucratic behavior. In short, some rules really govern, but since some do not, one must always explain why these govern and not those; why these people and not those follow rules. It may be force or threat of force—the clerk's fear that he will lose his job. Perhaps it is loyalty or pride. In any event, deciding which rules govern, when, and why is a major research problem in the social study of law.

What of principles? Since principles are merely a kind of rule, it is as easy to deny the reality of principles as it is to deny the reality of rules. Indeed, it is easier, since principles have the vice of abstraction, and hence less real power to govern behavior. A rule skeptic is almost always a principle skeptic, too. This skepticism, too, can be carried to excess. In their role as guardians, judges, and standards of validity, principles are a solid social fact—as solid as the social fact of rules and sometimes more so. The reality of principles, how they govern, when, and why, is also an empirical question on the agenda of research.

Chapter III

On Legal Impact[1]

A crucial function of rules is guiding behavior. It follows that one major aim of any scientific study of law is to discover the impact of law on behavior.[2] Under what conditions do people react to legal rules or make use of them? Under what conditions do they defy, misuse, or ignore the law? This chapter introduces the subject with some distinctions, definitions, and propositions. The following two chapters deal with specific factors that mold or change legal behavior.

Legal acts take many forms. Any decision by a legal authority, any new rule, or affirmation of an old one is a legal act. A legal act has an *impact*, when it is causally related to somebody's conduct. The legal act is said to be "effective" when behavior moves in the desired direction, when the subjects comply or obey. Many legal acts are not "effective" in this way. People ignore them or violate the command. Deliberate disobedience may be part of a system of behavior which does, however, take a legal act into account. For example, armed robbery is prohibited by law. One would not say that armed robbery is part of the "impact" of rules that forbid it, unless the crime were somehow causally related to the norm. The norm, however, makes some difference in the way that robbers behave; they may, for example, wear masks, which they would not ordinarily do, except to avoid being caught and punished for breaking the law. Wearing the mask, then, *is* part of the impact of a concrete

---

[1]An earlier version of this chapter has appeared in *Zur Effectivität des Rechts, Jahrbuch für Rechtssoziologie und Rechtstheorie* (1972), vol. 3.

[2]See, in general, Harry Jones, *The Efficacy of Law* (1969).

legal act. Impact, in other words, is more than the degree of obedience; it is the total effect of a legal act on behavior, positive and negative.[3]

Impact refers to behavior, and behavior can sometimes be quantitatively measured. There are legal acts for which one might even construct an impact scale, measuring impact from 100 (perfect *positive* impact) to zero (for total indifference), with various scores in between. Imagine an army unit made up of 100 men standing in a row. The commander orders the men to take one step forward. If sixty-five of the soldiers each take a full step forward, the command has achieved a score of sixty-five on our imaginary scale. If not a single soldier budged, the command would score zero in impact. There could be *negative* responses as well. Some of the men might step backwards, or run away, or shoot their guns at their commander. In other words, simple noncompliance stands at a sort of neutral zero point—if the men, perhaps, did not hear the command or are mulling it over. We can assign a negative score to more aggravated types of refusal to obey, especially as part of a movement or plot to revolt, and to behavior that frustrates or nullifies the command. The negative, then, is an attack *on the order itself* or on the *authority of the person who gives it.* From the standpoint of a commander, this is worse than simple noncompliance.

The example of the soldiers represents a fairly simple situation. Even here, the type of noncompliance made an enormous difference. If a few soldiers stood still or took less than a full step forward, the small subsystem could probably deal with them adequately, less so, if they ran away, still less, if they shot at the officer or attempted a coup. The officer's order called for a positive response: a single, discrete piece of behavior. For many orders of this kind, there are, as in our example, sharply distinct grades of impact from full, swift compliance through simple noncompliance to defiant and rebellious behavior. A person can file his tax returns on time and honestly; he can file late or not at all, or late and fraudulent. Not every legal order or rule has this characteristic. Some call simply for a single negative response. They tell people *not* to rob, or murder, or rape. For these rules, we do not usually think

---

[3]A growing literature is devoted to legal impact. In the United States, much of it deals with the effectiveness of particular decisions of the United States Supreme Court. For this literature, see Stephen L. Wasby, *The Impact of the United States Supreme Court, Some Perspectives* (1970), especially Ch. 2; Theodore L. Becker, ed., *The Impact of Supreme Court Decisions* (1969); James P. Levine, "Methodological Concerns in Studying Supreme Court Efficacy," 4 *Law and Society Rev.* 583 (1970); see also Harrell R. Rodgers, Jr., "Law as an Instrument of Public Policy," 17 *Am. J. Pol. Sci.* 638 (1973).

The emphasis on "effectiveness" has not gone without criticism. See Donald J. Black, "The Boundaries of Legal Sociology," 81 *Yale L. J.* 1086 (1972).

about grades of compliance and noncompliance. Murder is a violation of the law against murder; there is no obvious equivalent to the difference between simple and aggravated noncompliance.[4] Of course, there are differences between murders and murderers that are relevant to the question of how well the system can absorb or tolerate disobedience. A crime of passion is as much a "murder" as a political assassination, but the consequences for society might be worlds apart.[5]

Compliance and deviance are sometimes easy to distinguish and mutually exclusive. More typically, however, it is hard to tell what is compliance and what is not. For our soldiers, it is clear that a full step forward is compliance. But there are steps and steps—half-steps, side-steps, grudging and imperfect steps. The legal system gives out thousands of orders, many of them very subtle and very intricate. The subjects respond too in subtle and intricate ways. Some responses are obviously compliant, some are obviously deviant, others are very much in the middle. There are endless ways to "fudge" on a tax return.

Roughly, a subject can be said to *comply* when he honestly tries to live up to what the rule-maker expects, as the subject understands it. Compliance is, in other words, knowing conformity with a norm or command,[6] a deliberate instance of legal behavior that bends toward the legal act that evoked it.[7] Compliance and deviance are two poles of a continuum. Of the legal behavior in the middle, one important type might be called *evasion.* Evasive behavior frustrates the goals of a legal act, but falls short of noncompliance or, as the case may be, legal culpability. Every legal system is a storehouse of historical examples. In the United States, the southern states twisted and turned every legal, and illegal, way to avoid obeying the 1954 court decision ordering schools to be open to black and white children alike.[8] Tax practice, too,

---

[4]Also, it is hard to quantify compliance: How do you measure the number of acts of compliance to the rule "thou shalt not kill"? See Erhard Blankenburg, "Die Selektivität Rechtlicher Sanktionen," 21 *Kölner Zeitschrift für Soziologie und Sozialpsychologie* 805, 808 (1969).

[5]See Gusfield's distinction between "enemy" and "repentant" deviants, discussed on pp. 128–133.

[6]Johannes Feest, "Compliance with Legal Regulations: Observation of Stop Sign Behavior," 2 *Law and Society Rev.* 447 (1968).

[7]Sometimes, to be sure, commander and subject are on different wave lengths. In law, there are often problems of communication. The roar of an airplane engine can drown out the officer's command, so that the soldiers cannot hear. Or they may misunderstand. Subjects and commanders can honestly differ in their mental picture of what deviant behavior would be.

[8]*Brown* v. *Board of Education*, 347 U.S. 483 (1954). Federal courts spent years deciding, case by case, whether this or that district had crossed the invisible line.

is a veritable factory of evasion. Courts and tax agencies are continually called on to decide whether a taxpayer has remained inside the law or has "gone too far."[9]

The terms *compliance, deviance,* and *evasion* best fit one sort of legal behavior—behavior in reference to commands or regulations. However, there are many important parts of law where the rules, by and large, are not "commands" at all but authorizations or blueprints for structures and facilities. All rules tend to channel behavior, but many are not phrased in terms of do's and don't's; these lack any concept of "noncompliance." For example, many rules of law deal with the making of contracts and wills. A contract for the sale of land must be in writing. So too must a will. An oral will or land contract will not be enforced, but it is not "deviant" to make an oral will or to die with no will at all. Nor is it "compliance" with the law to put a land contract in writing. Contracts and wills are matters of choice. In much of the civil law, the rules are not commands; and such terms as *use, nonuse,* and *misuse* (parallel to *compliance, deviance,* and *evasion*) fit these rules better. The law of wills and contracts has, to be sure, an impact on behavior. People use, misuse, or ignore these rules too.[10] The civil law is, on the whole, less colorful than the law of crime and punishment, yet the modern state could hardly go on without it.

IMPACT AND CONCEPT OF PURPOSE

The term *impact,* as used here, means behavior causally linked to a rule or command, regardless of what the rule-maker had in mind. Yet, in everyday language at least, there is a competing model of positive impact or effectiveness, which does depend upon the purpose or intent of a rule. When people say that such and such a law failed or succeeded in its purpose, they are measuring impact by how well behavior conforms to some purpose or goal. Behavior in conformance with the purpose is positive; behavior that moves away is negative.

---

[9]Whatever the court or agency decides, the behavior is, in our terms, evasive when it comes close to the limits and has, as its intent, to frustrate the apparent purpose of the norm. It is not simple, of course, to decide when this occurs.

[10]Impact research has been rather anemic in areas of civil law, but see, for example, M. B. Sussman, J. N. Cates, and D. T. Smith, *The Family and Inheritance* (1970); Vincenzo Ferrari, *Successione per Testamento e Trasformazioni Sociali* (1972); Lawrence M. Friedman, *Contract Law in America* (1965); Stewart Macaulay, "Non-Contractual Relations in Business: A Preliminary Study," 28 *Am. Soc. Rev.* 55 (1963); N. William Hines, "Personal Property Joint Tenancies: More Law, Fact and Fancy," 54 *Minn. L. Rev.* 509 (1970).

Other behavior, even though causally connected with the rule, counts only when it bears on the purpose or goal. Hence, a law can "fail," even when the subjects comply literally with its directions or make full use of it, if the purpose is not fulfilled. People also commonly distinguish between the "spirit" and the "letter" of the law. Without this distinction or something like it, it would be hard to speak about "evasion" or "misuse" of law at all, except in the sense of sly but definite violation.

Purpose and goal are difficult concepts to work with. Purpose means, in the first instance, the *intent* of the lawmakers. It is hard enough to know what a single authority wants. A legislature is made up of hundreds of men. Many decisions are made by panels or committees. Lawmakers may have many or different intents. They may say one thing and mean another.

Again, does purpose or intent mean the *original* understanding? Is it what the legislature had in mind when it made law, perhaps centuries ago? Are new social needs and ideas relevant to the "purpose" of a law? The concept of "intent" and its bearing on statutory interpretation are endlessly discussed in the literature of the law.[11] A judge faces this problem when he is called upon to "apply" a statute or regulation. The problem also arises for other legal actors, administrators, policemen—even for the ordinary citizen called on to comply with some norm or command in his everyday life. Purpose is not the same as a *stated* goal. The rhetoric of a rule is often not the "real reason" behind it. There may be layers and hierarchies of purposes. What, for example, are the goals of the system of rules about automobile accidents? One goal, which Guido Calabresi calls "justice," is to adjust costs or consequences fairly among people involved in an accident. Another quite separate goal is to reduce the number and severity of accidents themselves. Still another is to lower the *social* costs of accidents, whatever their number. An important subgoal is to reduce the costs of administering the system of treatment of accidents. Different accident rules and their corollaries serve different purposes. For example, tort law includes a statute of limitations. After a certain deadline, an injured man may not sue the other party for damages. This rule does not prevent accidents or cut down their social costs. It serves an administrative goal and, arguably, accords with some community notion of fairness as well.[12] Even a single legal act may raise

---

[11]See, for example, Karl Engisch, *Einführung in das Juristische Denken*, (3rd ed., 1964), pp. 63ff.; Charles R. Curtis, "A Better Theory of Legal Interpretation," 3 *Vand. L. Rev.* 407 (1950); François Geny, *Méthode d'Interprétation et Sources en Droit Privé Positif*, trans. Jaro Mayda (1963).

[12]Guido Calabresi, *The Costs of Accidents* (1970), pp. 24–33.

questions of conflict of goals. Why do we have stop signs and traffic lights? Is it to avoid accidents? To speed the flow of traffic? To make clear who has the right of way? All of these or some combination?

We should distinguish, too, between *direct* and *indirect* goals. The direct goal is the precise behavior commanded or allowed. The underlying point or aim is the indirect goal. Rules commonly have both direct and indirect goals. In the nineteenth century, rules of tort law made it hard for workers to recover damages for industrial injuries. Why? We can assume a belief, current among the elites, that the rules would save new industries from heavy damage costs and thus promote economic growth—an indirect goal that carried great weight.[13] During the war in Vietnam, Congress made it a crime to burn a draft card. An indirect goal was to hurt the campaign against the draft and the movement against the war in Vietnam.

In short, what the law tells you to do or not do is the *direct* goal; the *indirect* goal is what it hopes to accomplish, if you obey. There is also a difference between primary, immediate conduct, which a rule requires, encourages, or forbids and the unintended consequences or *side effects*. During Prohibition, sales of liquor were illegal in the United States. Gangsters took over the trade in alcohol, and courts became jammed with Prohibition cases. These were *side effects*. Side effects need not be negative. We can call a positive side effect a *function* —an unforeseen, unintended, but beneficial, result.[14] Driver's license laws, for example, have the additional *function* of furnishing people with a handy identity card, useful for credit and cashing checks.

Joseph Gusfield draws a line between symbolic and instrumental purposes of a rule or a law.[15] A law is instrumental if it aims at concrete behavior; such a law has "little effect" unless actually enforced. Symbolic laws "do not depend on enforcement for their effect." They take on meaning by "symbolizing the public affirmation of social ideals and norms as well as [by] direct social control." A liquor law has an instrumental effect, if people stop drinking. It may have a symbolic effect, if

---

[13]Lawrence M. Friedman, *A History of American Law* (1973), p. 262. Whether the rules *actually* had this effect is, of course, another question.

[14]On the general meaning of *function*, see Robert K. Merton, *Social Theory and Social Structure* (1968), pp. 74–79. On indirect consequences of legal acts, see also James P. Levine, "Methodological Concerns in Studying Supreme Court Efficacy," 4 *Law and Society Rev.* 583, 586–588 (1970).

[15]Joseph Gusfield, "Moral Passage: The Symbolic Process in Public Designations of Deviance," 15 *Social Problems* 175 (1967); Gusfield deals with the liquor laws in more detail in *Symbolic Crusade, Status Politics and the American Temperance Movement* (1963).

it persuades people that it is wrong to drink; or that the norms of people who do not drink are better than those of drinkers. In other words, symbolic laws are directed at *attitudes;* instrumental laws, at behavior. Presumably, a temperance law could have symbolic effect, even if nobody drank one drop less; such a law could be *instrumentally* a failure, *symbolically* a success. On the other hand, a law may succeed instrumentally and fail in the symbolic realm.

There are problems with Gusfield's distinction. Does the distinction rest entirely on intent? Were the temperance leaders really struggling to put their norms on top, regardless of the number of drunks? Or were they fanatically opposed to drinking—real, actual drinking? One doubts that they would have considered a purely symbolic victory worthwhile. Social movements, one suspects, are at bottom instrumental. Rarely are they *primarily* concerned with symbolic values. Yet the symbolic realm is important. The dominance of norms is itself instrumentally useful. Symbols are weapons if not goals. A movement that captures control of official norms gains a foothold on a small, but strategic, hill. Moreover, there are subtle interactions between official rules and what the public senses as legitimate law; in the end, official norms may have some kind of magnetic pull on behavior. For now, we simply note that Gusfield's point complicates even further the study of the impact of law, since there is no yardstick to measure *symbolic* effect.

THE MEASUREMENT OF IMPACT

Many problems can be ignored or sidestepped, if we return to a simpler model of impact. Any behavior causally related to a legal act is impact, regardless of the meaning or purpose of the act. The measurement of impact is difficult even so. First, there is the question of cause and effect. How can we know that a rule affected conduct? Can we disentangle *legal* effects from effects of other causes? The problem is most acute for old, long-standing laws and especially laws deeply imbedded in the moral consciousness of a people. Every civilized state has some form of law against murder and some sort of staff to enforce this law, among others. But what roles do the law, legal process, and the staff actually play in keeping the murder rate low? What, in other words, is the *impact* of the legal system? No one, as of now, really knows. *and perhaps never will*

The problem, then, is to untangle the various strands of behavior, assigning the proper share to legal norms and institutions, custom, habit, conscience, and the pressure of other social forces. For new laws, demanding precise, objective pieces of behavior, the causal chain is sometimes easier to follow. It is, for example, possible to count how many people apply for a driver's license and, with some effort, to find out how many people carry them. There was no "norm" or "custom" about driver's licenses before the law was enacted. When states set up these laws, then, they set a process in motion which does have a causal effect on the behavior of drivers of cars. Of course, we do not know what feature of "the law" actually led to changes in behavior. Surely, it was not the mere act of passage or the pure existence of the norm. There might have been a publicity campaign; the sanctions used to enforce the law may have had some effect. We cannot, then, simply say that the law "caused" this behavior change. But we are closer at least to measurable data on *impact*.

Two factors, in other words, make some effects of a rule relatively simple to measure. First, the rule itself must call for behavior that is easily seen or observed. Second, one must be able to separate *this* behavior from what would have happened in the absence of the law. If we lower the speed limit, we must be able to tell not only how many people obey it, but also how many people have *changed* their behavior. For this, we need before-and-after data or some substitute—interviews with drivers, comparisons with similar towns with a different speed limit, etc.

"Old" laws and rules, rooted in the "mores," particularly lack this second feature—data on what would have happened but for the law. The law against murder is a classic old norm. For murder, we are at least roughly aware of the *rate* of deviance, an essential feature in the study of impact. Many other violations, though measurable, are hard to detect, especially the so-called victimless crimes where the "dark figure" (the rate of unknown crime) is unusually high. Many crimes are not reported.[16] Many are undetected as studies of shoplifting show.[17] The most difficult effects to measure are those of rules which use vague, open-ended terms—words like "reasonable" or "safe" or "good faith."[18] Long-range and indirect effects are hard to measure for any rules. What do driver's license laws do to the accident rate? To traffic patterns? To society in general?

---

[16]Crime is consistently underreported in American cities; aside from the failings, and they are many, of police statistics, many crimes, even quite serious ones, are not brought to police attention. *Newsweek,* Apr. 29, 1974, p. 60.

[17]Erhard Blankenburg, "Die Selektivität Rechtlicher Sanktionen," 21 *Kölner Zeitschrift für Soziologie und Sozialpsychologie* 805 (1969). An American study is Donna E. Gelfand, Donald P. Hartmann, Patrice Walker, and Brent Page, "Who Reports Shoplifters? A Field-Experimental Study," 25 *J. Personality and Soc. Psychology* 276 (1973).

[18]On this type of rule, see Lawrence M. Friedman, "Legal Rules and the Process of Social Change," 19 *Stan. L. Rev.* 786 (1967).

The *time* when one measures effects is also important. Compliance may be seasonal or it may take time to penetrate. Often, change in behavior is subtle and slow. Study it one day and one gets one result; on another day, another. "Compliance to many court orders," Martin Shapiro has remarked, "takes a long time and may be mediated by many social learning phenomena. . . . At the very least, new court 'orders' . . . are likely to create periods of confusion and disequilibrium in complex social systems."[19] The impact of the *Brown* decision, desegregating schools, has not spent itself after twenty years. Many rules, in time, ripen into custom. Whatever the first impact of the laws on driver's licenses, carrying a license in a wallet or purse has become a practice, then a habit almost universally accepted, part of one's daily life, as natural as breathing. By now, it is hard to tell how much of the load is carried by knowledge and acceptance of the formal norms, how much by threat of enforcement, how much by habit, and how much by the inner sense of right and wrong.[20] Clearly the impact and the motives for compliance are not the same at various stages in the life cycle of a law.

A person complies with a legal act only when he knowingly alters some bit of behavior in an observable way. Compliance, then, is knowing behavior, not unconscious or inevitable behavior. How can we separate the knowing from the unknowing, the caused from the uncaused? The scientific method would be through controlled experiment. Scholars have studied attitudes about law in controlled experiments,[21] and there have been some studies of legal behavior;[22] but impact studies suffer as a rule for want of control groups.

Ordinary experience sometimes can act as a partial substitute for the missing control group, at least in measuring precise, direct, and short-run impacts. Americans must file an income tax return on or before April 15 of each year. If we know roughly how many people have reportable incomes, we can count the returns and measure the defi-

---

[19]Martin Shapiro, "The Impact of the Supreme Court," 23 *J. Legal Ed.* 77, 80 (1970).

[20]See Harry V. Ball and Lawrence M. Friedman, "The Use of Criminal Sanctions in the Enforcement of Economic Legislation: A Sociological View," 17 *Stan. L. Rev.* 197, 220 (1965).

[21]E.g., Leonard Berkowitz and Nigel Walker, "Laws and Moral Judgments," 30 *Sociometry* 410 (1967).

[22]See, for example, Richard D. Schwartz and Sonya Orleans, "On Legal Sanctions," 34 *U. Chi. L. Rev.* 274 (1967), with reference to income tax compliance and evasion. In an interesting experiment on how and why people make rules, a small group was shut in a penthouse on the Berkeley campus and studied to see what norms they developed. Walter O. Weyrauch, "The 'Basic Law' or 'Constitution' of a Small Group," 27 *J. Soc. Issues*, no. 2, 49 (1971). On the general subject, see Hans Zeisel, "Reflections on Experimental Techniques in the Law," 2 *J. Legal Studies* 107 (1973).

ciency. We know that without an income tax *law* or an equivalent legal act, nobody would file a tax return. Hence, we do not need a control group. We can rely on experience to tell us what the control group would have done, when the behavior in question is precise, detailed behavior, created by or through law. Even here, we must add a word of caution. It does not mean much to say that "the law" made people file their tax returns. It was not the words of the statute acting magically by themselves but those words *plus* publicity, supporting institutions, and threats of sanctions. Which of these and in what proportions "caused" the behavior, we cannot know.

Other techniques can make up more or less for a missing control group. One technique is simulation: mock juries, make-believe trials, and the like.[23] Three scholars, for example, tried to measure differences in outcome between adversary and "inquisitorial" trials through experimental study of simulated trials.[24] Another technique is the quasi-experiment. Donald Campbell and Laurence Ross studied the effect of a crackdown in Connecticut on speeding.[25] They compared the death rate before and after the crackdown; they also compared Connecticut's rates with those of neighboring states. Here the "before" served as a rough control group for the "after," and the neighboring states served as natural controls for the state to be studied.[26]

Governments, too, often run pilot and demonstration projects. These are, in a sense, quasi-experiments. For example, the California Youth Authority conducted a controlled experiment in two California cities. The authority took two groups of delinquent boys: One group was put on probation and given "intensive counseling"; the other group was "assigned to California's regular juvenile penal institutions." Later,

[23]Rita J. Simon, "Murder, Juries, and the Press," 3 *Transaction* 40 (1966); Rita J. Simon, *The Jury and the Defense of Insanity* (1967); William L. Walker and John W. Thibaut, "An Experimental Examination of Pretrial Conference Techniques," 55 *Minn. L. Rev.* 1113 (1971).

[24]John Thibaut, Laurens Walker, and E. Allan Lind, "Adversary Presentation and Bias in Legal Decisionmaking," 86 *Harv. L. Rev.* 386 (1972).

[25]Donald T. Campbell and H. Laurence Ross, "The Connecticut Crackdown on Speeding: Time-Series Data in Quasi-Experimental Analysis," 3 *Law and Society Rev.* 33 (1968); see also Richard Lempert, "Strategies of Research Design in the Legal Impact Study," 1 *Law and Society Rev.* 111 (1966).

[26]H. Laurence Ross applied similar techniques to test the results of the British Road Safety Act of 1967. H. Laurence Ross, "Law, Science, and Accidents: the British Road Safety Act of 1967," 2 *J. Legal Studies* 1 (1973); see also Gene V. Glass, George C. Tiao, and Thomas O. Maguire, "The 1900 Revision of German Divorce Laws: Analysis of Data as a Time-Series Quasi-Experiment," 5 *Law and Society Rev.* 539 (1971); Leon S. Robertson, Robert F. Rich, and H. Laurence Ross, "Jail Sentences for Driving While Intoxicated in Chicago: A Judicial Policy that Failed," 8 *Law and Society Rev.* 55 (1973).

the authority compared the results.[27] Comparison of legal systems or institutions also sheds light on impact. Justice Brandeis referred to the American states as "laboratories" of social reform.[28] An important new law, passed in a single state, sets up a kind of natural experiment. The controls are other states, similar in culture and economy, which do not have the new law. Countries may float trial balloons in one or more regions. France, in the 1960s, instituted a new form of civil procedure in a piecemeal fashion, trying it out in some courts before generalizing it to all.[29] One can also compare the legal experiences of nations.[30] Japan, France, and Australia are all industrial countries with some form of market economy. To compare their legal systems might suggest which laws are economic catalysts and which ones are irrelevant. Here, however, so many other factors may enter in that it is at present impossible to expect scientific rigor.

Social theory is an important substitute for a missing control group. If we know how something *must* behave when factors A, B, C, and D are present, then, when we add factor E (and only E), we can attribute any changes to E. Economists, for example, tend to agree on certain basic propositions about economic behavior. This means that economists can use theory as a base line. An economist knows, or thinks he knows, how the economy will behave under perfect competition. He may therefore be able to "prove" the effects of legal intervention even without a control group of unregulated societies.[31]

But all social sciences, even economics, have wide gaps in their theories and many areas of vigorous dispute. Therefore, they cannot provide, at present, much help in the study of legal behavior at many points of great importance and interest.

---

[27]Described in Martin A. Levin, "Policy Evaluation and Recidivism," 6 *Law and Society Rev.* 17, 32 (1971).

[28]"There is a great advantage in the opportunity we have of working out our social problems in the detached laboratories of the different states," Brandeis to Mary E. McDowell, July 8, 1912, in Melvin I. Urofsky and David W. Levy, eds., *Letters of Louis D. Brandeis* (1972), vol. II, p. 640.

[29]Jean Carbonnier, *Sociologie Juridique* (1972), p. 246. See also Richard G. Salem and William J. Bowers, "Severity of Formal Sanctions as a Deterrent to Deviant Behavior," 5 *Law and Society Rev.* 21 (1970), comparing the effect of sanctions on the behavior of students in different colleges.

[30]See Andreas Heldrich, "Sozialwissenschaftliche Aspekte der Rechtsvergleichung," 34 *Rabels Zeitschrift für ausländisches und internationales Privatrecht* 427 (1970).

[31]See, for example, Henry G. Manne, *Insider Trading and the Stock Market* (1966), pp. 77–110, on the effects of securities regulations; Michael Levine, "Is Regulation Necessary? California Air Transportation and National Regulatory Policy," 74 *Yale L. J.* 1416 (1965).

IMPACT: SOME PREREQUISITES

To build a theory of legal behavior, one must begin with a list of prerequisites to impact and some empirical statements about those prerequisites. Such a theory would also, as we shall see, contain propositions about sanctions, legal culture, legitimacy, social learning, peer group influence, and other factors which affect legal behavior.

At least *three* conditions must be fulfilled before a legal act, i.e., a rule or norm, can have an impact on a particular target person. First, the rule or norm must be *communicated* to the subject. Second, the subject must be *able* to perform or, as the case may be, *not* to perform. Third, the subject must have a *disposition* to perform—from desire, fear, or some other motive. The second condition is a weak one, easily met in the ordinary case. A law that ordered people to fly would be pointless. There are examples of behavior—rape may be one—where, arguably, most violators are people who cannot help themselves. We will return to this point. The third prerequisite, the disposition to perform, is the subject of the next two chapters. The theory of *sanctions,* for example, deals with those legal techniques which dispose people to follow, use, or ignore the law.

Something, however, must be said about *communication* of norms. It is obviously vital to any legal system.[32] "It is axiomatic that no person can guide his conduct by a law unless he knows what that law is."[33] The legal system as a whole or some network of rules within it may, by creating and maintaining symbols, processes, and structures, alter behavior even when the person who changes his behavior is unaware of the rules or norms. But a communication network is absolutely vital for particular rules in the short run.

Communication is built into the legal system. Laws and decrees are published. So are important judicial decisions. In addition to whatever else they are, all judicial decisions, along with laws, ordinances, rules, or decrees, are messages. Decisions, indeed, are a "principal mode of communication" in the legal system.[34] The message of a case

---

[32]See Richard Fagen, *Politics and Communication* (1966); Vilhelm Aubert, *Elements of Sociology* (1967), pp. 35–39.

[33]Daniel J. Gifford, "Communications of Legal Standards, Policy Development, and Effective Conduct Regulation," 56 *Cornell L. Rev.* 409, 410 (1971); for a specific example of the effect of failure of communication on impact, see John A. Robertson and Phyllis Teitelbaum, "Optimizing Legal Impact: A Case Study in Search of a Theory," 1973 *Wis. L. Rev.* 665, 695–699, on new procedures for dealing with drug abuse cases in Massachusetts.

[34]Martin Shapiro, "Toward a Theory of *Stare Decisis,*" 1 *J. Legal Studies* 125, 134 (1972).

may have direct and indirect audiences. For example, *Gideon* v. *Wainwright* (1963),[35] an important case about the right of an accused to counsel, sent a direct message to the courts of Florida where the case arose. This was an order to give Gideon another day in court. The opinion also carried a message, less immediate to be sure, to other judges and officials in Florida, in other states, and to criminal lawyers in general, prescribing what the Supreme Court expected as to future behavior. This was the "rule" of the case: States must provide lawyers, free, as of right, to people accused of serious crimes. This message went as well to everyone who was or might be charged with a crime. The case carried other, dimmer messages (hints one might call them) about the line the Court was likely to take in analogous cases. This message might create new hopes and fears among law enforcement officers, lawyers, perhaps even among thieves or potential thieves. Civil cases, too, carry messages—to the litigants, to other courts, even at times to the general public—about what courts are likely to do about negligence, shoddy goods, slander, or variances in zoning.

A message can be given directly—face-to-face or by telephone. It can also travel by less direct means—by mail, telegram, or a personal ad in the newspaper. The message can specify its audience one by one or it can be sent diffusely, by loudspeaker, television broadcast, or printed in the paper. Other things being equal, the more direct the means of communication, the more likely that the message will reach the right audience in accurate form. If Smith gives an order to Jones, face-to-face, Smith can make sure Jones hears and understands. If necessary, Smith can repeat the message louder or clarify it.

A general broadcast, on the other hand, has tremendous advantages too; it is cheap in cost per thousand of listeners; but it scatters its shots, and the broadcaster has less control over the receiver's behavior—whether the set is on or off. Broadcasting has to make up in frequency or intensity what it lacks in clear focus. It is something like the sex life of fish, where the female lays thousands of eggs in the water, and the male lays down milt, leaving the rest to the current. Direct face-to-face communication is the rule in small societies and subgroups and in primary groups like the family. Face-to-face contact, in fact, defines the *primary group*, a term invented by Charles Horton Cooley.[36] Immediacy, however, is not necessarily small scale or primitive. Trials are face-to-face proceedings in most societies, and even in the most highly formalized systems, many messages carried by legal acts are

---

[35]372 U.S. 335 (1963).
[36]L. Broom and P. Selznick, *Sociology* (4th ed., 1968), p. 120.

given in person and through the spoken word.[37]

Another dimension of a message is *generality*—that is, the size of the audience, real or potential. Many commands, orders, or warrants are issued directly to a single person. The *decision* in a court case binds the immediate parties—two people, sometimes more—and a small circle of officials who may have to help carry it out. The indirect message, of course, runs to a wider group. Orders, warrants, and commands are *usually* less important than more general messages—doctrines, laws, principles, or rules. However, an order in wartime, appointing a general or relieving him, may affect the fate of the world; *decisions* in a class action may bind thousands of people. An antitrust decree breaking a giant corporation into parts may set loose shock waves in the stock market.

An order or command is more likely to hit home than a rule. When one speaks to a person directly, he has to be deaf not to hear. But many messages sent "through channels" get garbled or lost, or noise drowns them out. When a message is *specific*, it is likely that the intended listener will pick it up out of the air, like a radio receiver tuned to the proper station. So too, when a message relates directly to the person who receives it. People listen to messages selectively, the way they read a newspaper. This person looks mainly at the sports pages, this one at fashions or news. Some skim, some read carefully, some are distracted —all have different mental filters. When a person sees his own name in print or if the story seems to affect his life, his work, his group, his home, he reads on with great interest. The death of one neighbor intrigues or horrifies him more than a thousand dead Bulgarians. The homeowner reads about property taxes; the convict on death row, about capital punishment.

These simple truths suggest, in other words, that there are inherent aids to effective communication. Specificity is one. (It may, of course, have other drawbacks.) Importance and exclusivity are others. If a person thinks he is one of a chosen few to get the message, he is more likely to pay attention.[38] Clarity of language is still another. An

---

[37]Common-law countries may, however, put a special value on spoken messages as an element of fairness in trials and other proceedings, preferring the verbal to the written message. "Not only is the spoken word predominant, but there is also an *immediacy* in the relationship between the parties, counsel and witnesses on the one hand, and the entire adjudicating body on the other hand." Mauro Cappelletti, *Procédure Orale et Procédure Écrite* (1971), p. 102.

[38]Howard L. Fromkin and Timothy C. Brock, "Erotic Materials: A Commodity Theory Analysis of the Enhanced Desirability that May Accompany Their Unavailability," 3 *J. Applied Soc. Psychology* 219 (1973). They add that "a communication will increase

officer hands an order to a soldier, telling him by name to report for duty on a certain Monday at a certain place. This is one polar type. A vague, general message, by way of contrast, even if it reaches its audience, may make no impact. The audience can easily misunderstand or think: "It was not intended for me" or simply not know what to do. A court, deciding a case, states the "principle" that no one can profit from his own wrong; or that businessmen must deal with each other in good faith. These messages are not likely to reach *any* audience; if they do, they are so colorless and vague that subjects can define them almost any way they wish. Such messages, in short, are not likely to alter behavior.

Legal scholars tend to lavish their attention on general principles, on concepts and rules with open texture. These subtle phrases and rules may be useful in many ways; they may lend themselves to logical analysis or express high ethical ideals. But as messengers, they fail. For *this* purpose, more humdrum rules are superior—the speed limit, for example, which lacks conceptual beauty, but is expressed in simple, forceful English and sits in huge letters by the side of the road.

The speed limit, again, is quantitative; its meaning is therefore hard to misjudge. Numbers are "objective"; this means that everyone in society shares an understanding of their scope. One person's concept of "sixteen" is the same as the next one's, which is more than can be said about "reasonable," "safe," or "good faith." When a big, bold sign announces that the speed limit is sixty, the driver can hardly mistake the content of the norm. If the sign said "Drive at a reasonable speed," the most conscientious driver could hardly avoid inconsistency, nor could an outsider tell for sure which drivers were deviant except in the most flagrant cases.[39]

The key to clarity is not the words but the social understanding. Actually, people who read a sign that says 60 m.p.h. understand it to mean, in fact, that 65 m.p.h. is what is allowed. Clear words cannot, moreover, convey a message by themselves; there has to be some track or path along which the message can travel. Vilhelm Aubert and associates, in a well-known study, tried to discover the impact of a Norwegian law on the work conditions of housemaids. They found that maids were aware of *some* behavioral norms—those that were rooted in custom. They knew much less about new rules set out in the statute. The

---

in effectiveness to the extent that the recipient perceives that few other communicators exist who might have delivered the same message," that is, the message is rare and exclusive. Ibid., pp. 222–223.

[39]See Chapter X pp. 295–296.

maids were poor, uneducated women; they had no unions; and they worked in a place (the home) which, by tradition, has been largely immune from intrusions of law. The statute sent out a weak and flickering signal; it had no natural channel in which to flow toward its audience. That audience never heard and thus could not obey.[40]

Many fields of law have highly discretionary rules. As we shall see later, such rules serve various purposes. In any event, not all messages *can* be clear. A modern nation could hardly write an income tax law as stark and unambiguous as a speed limit. In general, each segment of the tax law is more or less objective, each term rigorously defined. But the whole is so monstrously large and so intertwined that ordinary mortals cannot cope with it; only specialists can.

In Western societies, these specialists are lawyers, who serve as intermediaries in the communication net. They interpret fuzzy or complex messages. Where there is a problem of finding a channel, lawyers also act as brokers or middlemen of information, receiving, storing, intensifying, and transmitting signals. The tax lawyer knows his way through the tangle of tax laws; he translates its rules into terms and behaviors his client understands. He keeps books and files about tax law and follows changes in regulations, reading new matters as they appear. Rules and regulations, as one might expect, are diffuse messages, broadcast into the air. Usually, the state does not send them directly to users—often because there is no way to know who the users are and because new users constantly enter the circle of relevance, by getting married, creating trusts, incorporating, giving money to charity. The lawyer stores the message until some future client needs it. Then, when he gives advice, he passes the ruling on. In so doing, he makes possible a level of compliance that would be unthinkable without him. Yet he is a kind of double agent: Both government and client depend on him—the one, to ensure compliance; the other, as advocate and counselor, and on occasion, carrier of feedback information. It goes without saying, then, that he has a certain amount of unconscious power; he can, knowingly or not, bend the messages going each way.[41] His advice and consent stand between citizen and state.

---

[40]Vilhelm Aubert, "Some Social Functions of Legislation," 10 *Acta Sociologica* 98 (1967); reprinted also in Vilhelm Aubert, ed., *Sociology of Law* (1969), p. 116.

[41]On the lawyer's role in the communication net, see Victor Thompson, *The Regulatory Process in OPA Rationing* (1950), with rich material on the subject. In Herbert Jacob's study of bankruptcy proceedings in four Wisconsin cities, it was the lawyers who guided debtors into bankruptcy. Herbert Jacob, *Debtors in Court, the Consumption of Government Services* (1969), p. 62. In another study, Abraham Blumberg found that it was the lawyers who first suggested to their clients in criminal cases that they might plead guilty to the charge. Abraham Blumberg, "The Practice of Law as Confidence

Lawyers are not the only ones who play the role of middlemen. Some societies have no lawyers. Elders, wise men, or priests store up or possess knowledge about rules of right conduct.[42] In modern society, the need to know law is pervasive; in a large business firm, hundreds of employees may work with rules of law—receiving, processing, storing, or acting on them as at least one part of their job; most of these employees will be laymen, not lawyers.

As one might imagine, knowledge of law is unevenly distributed in society. In a small, face-to-face community, most people probably know the main operating norms. This cannot be the case in countries like France, Mexico, or the United States. There are large parts of the law which only experts know, or a small group of people who are directly concerned. Taxicab drivers may know about the regulation of taxicabs; the general public will not. A social scientist studied policemen in four Wisconsin cities; most policemen knew, because it concerned their work, that the Supreme Court had laid down rules about legal and illegal confessions. But most of them could not answer correctly when asked about the meaning of these subtle new rules.[43]

Research on knowledge of the law is a growing field of study.[44] The more a person knows, the more he is able to enforce rights, prevent injustice, and take advantage of law. In general, the public, or most of it, will know enough to carry on its work or to conform. People know that breaking into a house and stealing silver is illegal, whatever they know about the technical details of criminal law. They have never heard of negotiable instruments, but they know how and when to endorse a check.[45] In general, however, knowledge of law tends to be greater among those with better income and education.

So far, we have talked mostly about messages traveling downwards

Game: Organizational Cooptation of a Profession," 1 *Law and Society Rev.* no. 2, 15 (1967).

[42]See, for example Max Gluckman, *The Ideas in Barotse Jurisprudence* (1965), pp. 16–17.

[43]Neal Milner, "Comparative Analysis of Patterns of Compliance with Supreme Court Decisions," 5 *Law and Society Rev.* 119, 125–126 (1970).

[44]European research is reported in Adam Podgórecki, et al., *Knowledge and Opinion about Law* (1973).

[45]On the distinction between "official" and "popular" versions of law, see Daniel J. Gifford, "Communication of Legal Standards, Policy Development, and Effective Conduct Regulation," 56 *Cornell L. Rev.* 409, 410–418 (1971); compare the distinction made by Adam Podgórecki between "familiarity with legal principles,"—that is, "the nature of basic rights and obligations," and "broad categories of what is allowed and forbidden" —and familiarity with "the precept of law," the technical rules for realizing these principles. Adam Podgórecki et al., p. 71.

from authority to subject. Government, big business—institutions in general—bombard their employees and subjects with orders and rules. Public opinion, flowing upward, is diffuse; so much so, that Vilhelm Aubert thought he sensed a "higher likelihood of transmission of the sender's intention when the message passes downward than when it passes upward."[46] This may be true of bureaucracies. Whether it is true of the law as a whole is another question. The terms "up" and "down" are metaphors, not physical facts. There are many channels for upward movement, too—for example, *appeals* in the judicial system. If channels are clearly marked and easy to use, there is no reason why messages should not move as swiftly and smoothly in one direction as in the other.

To be sure, governments often feel they must shield themselves against a flood of messages from below. The social order has the shape of a pyramid. The top is more lightly populated than the bottom. If everybody below sent up messages, the circuits could get overloaded. Government tries to limit communication from the public and also wraps its actions and decisions in secrecy. Government is also large and has many structures and rules; hence, the public finds it hard to talk to government—and vice versa. Here too the lawyer is a valuable middleman. He knows his way through the thickets of rules, and often, too, through the corridors of power. In many societies, specialists (not necessarily lawyers) work to untangle red tape and cope with bureaucracy. In Brazil, there is the *despachante*, an intermediary who, "in return for a commission or fee," will "lubricate" Brazil's "sticky administrative process," filling out forms, seeing the right people, getting a needed permission or document. As of 1970, in Rio de Janeiro, the yellow pages of the phone book listed more than 300 *despachantes*.[47] Other societies, too, develop "underground lawyers." Unlicensed and untrained, these people make a living because they have, or pretend to have, a particular skill; they carry messages from ordinary people to the officials above in Kafka's castle.

THEORIES OF BEHAVIOR

Communication is vital to impact. But it is only a prerequisite; it does not explain how people who receive a message act and why. There

---

[46]Vilhelm Aubert, *Elements of Sociology*, p. 38; see, in general, Herbert Kaufman, *Administrative Feedback* (1973).

[47]Keith S. Rosenn, "The Jeito, Brazil's Institutional Bypass of the Formal Legal System and Its Developmental Implications," 19 *Am. J. Comp. L.* 514, 536 (1971).

are several competing models of legal behavior. One we can call the *cost-benefit* model. It assumes more or less rational behavior. Before a person acts, he calculates what he stands to gain and the risks he runs. He acts only if, in his opinion, he is likely to profit from behavior. For this actor, *sanctions* have tremendous importance. He molds his conduct in the light of rewards and punishments.

No scholar, of course, would try to reduce *all* legal behavior to this calculus. It seems obvious that *social* factors, "social relationships"[48] —surrounding culture and the peer group—influence legal behavior, by threats of ostracism, for example, or through praise and blame. Still a third model explains behavior on the basis of norms that the actor has internalized. We may call this third cluster of factors *conscience* for short. In stateless societies, the peer group—public opinion—and conscience may be the only real hammers of enforcement. It was the peer group that served as the court among Hoebel's Eskimos.[49] In any society, the peer group is powerful. "The law" about sexual misconduct, if enforced at all, is enforced more by culture, peer group, and conscience than by the police.

There is, in a sense, a fourth source of conduct—laziness, habit, or inertia. People take some paths of conduct out of cognitive poverty and because the paths are *there*—easy and available. It is the line of least resistance. Society, to be sure, carved out the original channel, but strong moral tone is absent by now. The law creates forms—a road, the language of a check, the income tax form—and people follow them. Much legal behavior is of this dry and convenient sort.

These models of legal behavior do not, on the whole, contradict each other. They can all be true, in part. Some legal acts rely for impact more on one type than another. Rewards and punishments are everywhere in the law. Lawmakers clearly assume that people will think twice before they run the risk of jail or a fine and that they will rise to the bait for money and other rewards. Government propaganda certainly assumes the force of conscience and public opinion. The whole legal system relies on voluntary action. The money spent, and not spent, on inspectors, detectives, police, and courts assumes that society expects compliance without force from most of us most of the time. That law relies on habits and cuts paths of least resistance is also easy to demonstrate. Rules of law point to or create standard ways to behave. Legal forms reduce to a favored few the disorder of infinite possibility. What people buy is influenced by what the market offers

---

[48]Michael Banton, *The Policeman in the Community* (1964), p. 2.
[49]See Chapter I, pp. 6–7.

them; few people make their own soap or weave their own clothes. Legal forms also strongly affect their customers and markets.

There is a sense, however, in which structured, habitual behavior does build on the other three types of motivation. It is the residue of one or more of them. Before forms for wills were habits, or routines, some act or acts or some patterns of legal behavior cut the channel that later became routine, in response to one or more of the livelier factors. As for the factors generally, one might reduce or combine all of them, in one sense, into a single theory of legal behavior. On a highly abstract level, all behavior can be analyzed in cost-benefit terms. The peer group, for example, is a kind of rival government giving out its own punishments and rewards. The rational actor would therefore include "public opinion" in his calculus. Conscience, the sense of right conduct, is the inner voice of a general standard. It is intensely personal, but men grow up in society, and conscience represents, on the whole, a social code of right and wrong. At any rate, a bad conscience is painful, while virtue brings a glow of satisfaction. Structured behavior, too, follows lines of rational calculation. A person crosses a river on a bridge, preferring not to swim; he uses ordinary forms for wills or contracts rather than inventing something new. These ways are the easiest, the least costly, and the most beneficial. Ostracism, bad words from peers, a troubled conscience, the labor of breaking new paths— all are real costs, even though "the law" does not inflict them and even though it is hard to reckon them in dollars and cents and compare them with subsidies and fines. Moreover, social behavior means behavior that is learned. Words and phrases, such as habit, conscience, and obedience to peers, describe what social learning has deposited inside the self. Reward and punishment, stimulus and response are the mechanisms, ultimately, that implant these habits and feelings in the mind.

Despite this last point, it is worthwhile, practically speaking, to keep the theories separate. Whether or not on a high plane of abstraction, they all merge into one, down below, on earth, they are very distinct. What is distinct about them is what they imply about likely or typical reactions to legal acts; when will a legal act produce impact and how much, on whom, and what sort. *Some* behavior is best explained by one theory rather than another, but no one theory holds the exclusive key. At least that is what the available evidence suggests.

To show how sanctions work is probably simpler than to show the results of moral pressures and pressures of peers. William Chambliss has described one study of sanctions. A college campus enforced parking rules very weakly, charging low fines. Later the school increased the fines and tightened enforcement. Compliance dramatically improved.[50] In any city, more police, or higher fines, or both will reduce illegal parking. A towaway program, which puts owners to the bother and expense of reclaiming their cars, wrings still more compliance from the public.

The parking study showed what is almost self-evident: Rewards and punishments have at least some effect on legal behavior, but sanctions do not *totally* account for driver behavior. Even when the fines are low and there is no enforcement at all, some people obey, or seem to. Some people put out their cigarettes when they see a "No Smoking" sign, even with no one around to enforce the rule and even though "enforcement" would consist of a single harsh word.

The parking study is instructive. It shows that sometimes one can pick apart strands of behavior and measure the components one at a time. Parking behavior is *not* pure reward and punishment; but it is partly that, and that part can be measured. Hopefully, social science will be able to frame and test propositions about other factors too, their relative strength, and how they act in combination or conflict. A theory of sanctions will not solve *all* the mysteries of legal behavior. It will illuminate *marginal* behavior. That is, more units of reward or punishment will induce *more* or *less* of particular kinds of behavior. But sanctions do not explain the *base* on which changes are rung. In the parking study, the theory suggested (and research confirmed) that higher fines and better enforcement would cut down violations. But the study gives no tools to predict how many people will violate parking rules in New York, or London, or Athens, or Green Bay, in summer or winter, or at 10:00 A.M., when the fine is $1 or $10, and with high or low or medium efforts at enforcement. Nor do we know why one person, town, or society is more likely to obey the law than another at the *same* level of delivered sanction. Sanctions are like prices. A higher price for roast duck lowers the demand for this product, but we cannot tell how much demand will decline until we know what the substitutes are and who likes roast duck, and why, and the place of roast duck in the culture.

A full theory of legal behavior must therefore include more than the theory of sanctions. It must also include, among other things, a theory of normative behavior.[51] In the legal context, this means con-

---

[50]William Chambliss, "Types of Deviance and the Effectiveness of Legal Sanctions," 1967 *Wis. L. Rev.* 703.

[51]Another way of putting this point is to say that a full theory of sanctions would take account of normative factors, and a full theory of normative behavior would take account of sanctions.

science and the concept of legitimacy. We will discuss these in more detail in Chapter V. In the broadest sense, a theory of legitimacy means a theory of those elements—cultural or psychological—that move persons toward compliance with law, or when absent, toward noncompliance, apart from motives of personal loss or gain. Here research lags, understandably. It is hard to test propositions in the field. Compared to the effect of a sanction, the effect of peers' attitudes toward authority, ideas about legitimacy, and the force of conscience are more slippery. These depend more on history, context, and tradition and (short of some unforeseen breakthrough) seem less likely for now to yield up their mysteries to quantitative test. This, of course, is no reason to neglect these factors as aspects of legal behavior.

Chapter IV
When Is Law Effective?
Part I

This chapter will deal with legal behavior, that is, with conduct that follows on and is causally related to a legal act. Strictly speaking, only behavior which is not absolutely, physically coerced can be legal behavior. If a policeman drags a man kicking and screaming into a police van, the latter's behavior is not legal behavior. The policeman's is. If the man enters the van on his own two feet at the command of the police, even though he does it because he *knows* the police will drag him aboard if they must, his behavior is for our purposes voluntary, and therefore legal behavior.

Hence, although the terms "force" and "coercion" crop up in discussions of legal behavior, particularly sanctions, we generally mean the threat of force and coercion, not force and coercion themselves. The legal system to be sure makes use of force. It puts burglars and rapists in prison. Many systems put people to death. But the system mainly moves people, or tries to, through the *threat* of force. We define legal behavior as voluntary, even when powerful threats work on the will of the subject. And what we discuss here are those elements of legal acts which induce behavior, that is, which work on the motives and will of the subject. In general, rules of conduct in the abstract do not produce behavior. People do not react automatically or by instinct. They react to threats, promises, and other mechanisms. A rule, then, is a message, carrying a promise or a threat; it is delivered to one or more persons, and they react to the promise or threat or to normative elements of the rule, or neither, or both.

Legal behavior does not spring from a single motivation. Different situations trigger different motives and responses. Since people in general do not want to die, except for rare and magnificent causes, it is no trick to explain why most people obey a policeman with a gun. Nevertheless, opinions can and do differ on where the *dominant* power of a legal system lies. Is it the arsenal of promises and threats or some aspect of group life, the appeal to conscience or indwelling norms? The historical school of the nineteenth century, of which the German jurist Friedrich Carl von Savigny (1779–1861) was a prominent member, stressed the normative, customary elements in law.[1] Adherents of the historical school in the United States argued that legislation could not change strong, bedrock customs—the mores.[2] These alone, not formal norms and their sanctions, guaranteed behavior.

Carried to an extreme, this idea would eliminate the formal law. If rooted in mores, law would enforce itself; if not so rooted, no one could enforce it at all. In other words, formal law was either futile or unnecessary. Probably no one took so extreme a view. Mores alone, obviously, cannot guarantee an orderly society. If legal restraints are lifted, if enforcement breaks down, violence and disorder increase despite mores. Similarly, when tyrants rule a state, mores do not prevent wholesale terror and torture. It is enough to cite Germany under Hitler.

In fact, few social norms are so deeply implanted that they enforce themselves completely with no help from the law. The taboo against cannibalism may be one of these. In most societies, the very thought is disgusting. Violations are rare—almost unknown. When they occur, people assume, almost automatically, that the violator must be insane.[3] Yet there have been societies of cannibals; the taboo is a matter of culture, not of instinctive disgust. Murder, rape, and arson are repellent to the average man; but they do occur and must be guarded against. No doubt, if the penal code through some technical error were suddenly suspended, people would not rush out to butcher their enemies. Strong moral chains would keep people in control, at least for a

---

[1]On the origins of this school of thought and the relationship of its ideas to the earlier school of natural law, see Franz Wieacker, *Privatrechtsgeschichte der Neuzeit* (1952), pp. 217–252; Roscoe Pound, *Interpretations of Legal History* (1923), pp. 9–20.

[2]The idea that legislation cannot change mores is attributed to William Graham Sumner. His views have often been exaggerated; see Harry V. Ball et al., "Law and Social Change: Sumner Reconsidered," 67 *Am. J. Sociology* 532 (1962). In the United States, James C. Carter used the notions of the historical school to argue against codification of the common law. See his *Law, Its Origin, Growth and Function* (1907).

[3]Except, as in the case of the athletes who crashed in the Andes, when human flesh is the only food that stands between people and starvation.

while, but not everyone and not in every respect. Occasionally, laws *do* take a holiday—when police go on strike, for example—and what happens sheds indirect light on the matter. Johannes Andenaes has recounted one such episode. In occupied Denmark in 1944, the Germans arrested the entire police force. During the rest of the occupation, an unarmed watch corps served as makeshift police, but they were not very effective. Robbery increased tremendously, rising from ten cases a month to a hundred. Other crimes, such as embezzlement and fraud, did not increase, but these were crimes "where the criminal is usually known if the crime itself is discovered."[4]

The case is clearer for minor, detailed rules of modern law which lack strong moral supports—the precise time limit on a parking meter, for example. Unenforcement leads to wholesale violation. Hence, those theories of law which stress the role of custom and history in enforcement illustrate their point with "old" and nearly universal rules (such as the rules about murder) or rules heavily charged with custom, religion, or culture (such as rules about incest). A more instrumental theory of legal behavior, which stresses rational calculation, looks for proofs and illustrations in laws about parking rather than murder.

Scholars generally agree, however, that a theory of legal behavior must be multiple; legal acts work on the minds of subjects in various ways. These ways, we repeat, can be grouped into three main categories. First, there are *sanctions*—threats and promises. Second, there is the influence, positive or negative, of the social world: the *peer group*. Third, there are internal values: *conscience* and related attitudes, the sense of what is and is not legitimate and what is or is not worthy to be obeyed. Each of these factors is itself complex. We will discuss them in turn.

SANCTIONS

We begin with the model of legal behavior that stresses reactions of subjects to sanctions. In one form or another, this idea is basic to law. People comply with rules or use the law for their own benefit or to avoid punishments, penalties, and pains. These do not always come from the government. One of the most powerful motives for obeying speed limits is that people are afraid of an accident. This is self-interest, pure and simple, but it is as potent as any sanction offered by the state.

---

[4]Johannes Andenaes, "The General Preventive Effects of Punishment," 114 *U. Pa. L. Rev.* 949, 962 (1966).

Of course, self-interest will not guarantee compliance with law. This is certainly true of the speed limit. Even the rational driver is often willing to run a slight risk of accident to avoid losing a business deal, missing a plane, or coming home late for dinner. Also, many laws extend general benefits; a noncomplier might hitch a "free ride," unless sanctions were imposed to change his cost-benefit structure.[5]

Sanctions are ways to implement a norm or a rule. Legal sanctions are sanctions prescribed or authorized by law. Every legal rule contains or implies a statement of legal consequences. These consequences are sanctions—promises or threats. Much of the social energy of law and much of society's investment in law goes to support the system of imposing or threatening sanctions: detectives, police, bailiffs, prosecutors, and jails (on the criminal side); courts of law and a vast administrative apparatus (on the civil side). Yet the study of legal sanctions and their effect on behavior is barely beginning. Only in recent years has there grown up a substantial body of research. Most of it has focussed on one particular point, the question, crudely put, whether punishment deters. Almost all of the studies deal with deterrence of crime or other blameworthy acts, such as cheating on exams.[6] One overpowering subquestion has been whether capital punishment is of much use as a deterrent. People feel strongly about capital punishment. They would

[5]See Malcolm Feeley, "Coercion and Compliance, a New Look at an Old Problem," 4 *Law and Society Rev.* 505 (1970).

[6]A recent and excellent overview of the whole question of deterrence is Franklin E. Zimring and Gordon J. Hawkins, *Deterrence, The Legal Threat in Crime Control* (1973); earlier and briefer was Franklin E. Zimring, *Perspectives on Deterrence* (1971); another fundamental essay is Johannes Andenaes, "The General Preventive Effects of Punishment," 114 *U. Pa. L. Rev.* 949 (1966); more recently, his "Deterrence and Specific Offenses," 38 *U. Chi. L. Rev.* 537 (1971). Many recent studies have tried to prove, disprove, or measure the deterrent effect. Maynard L. Erickson and Jack P. Gibbs, "The Deterrence Question: Some Alternative Methods of Analysis," 54 *Soc. Sci. Q.* 534 (1973); Frank D. Bean and Robert G. Cushing, "Criminal Homicide, Punishment, and Deterrence: Methodological and Substantive Reconsiderations," 52 *Soc. Sci. Q.* 277 (1971); Theodore G. Chiricos and Gordon P. Waldo, "Punishment and Crime: An Examination of Some Empirical Evidence," 18 *Social Problems* 200 (1970); Charles R. Tittle, "Crime Rates and Legal Sanctions," 16 *Social Problems* 409 (1969); Jack P. Gibbs, "Crime, Punishment and Deterrence," 48 *Southwestern Soc. Sci. Q.* 515 (1968); Frank Brooker, "The Deterrent Effect of Punishment," 9 *Criminology* 469 (1972); James J. Teeven, Jr., "Deterrent Effects of Punishment: the Canadian Case," 14 *Canadian J. Criminology and Corrections,* no. 1, 68 (1972); Richard G. Salem and William J. Bowers, "Severity of Formal Sanctions as a Deterrent to Deviant Behavior," 5 *Law and Society Rev.* 21 (1970); Roger C. Cramton, "Driver Behavior and Legal Sanctions: A Study of Deterrence," 67 *Mich. L. Rev.* 421 (1969); see also, on the possible application of behavior modification techniques to law, James P. Levine, "Implementing Legal Policies through Operant Conditioning: The Case of Police Practices," 6 *Law and Society Rev.* 195 (1971).

like to prove that it does not work. Some go on to doubt whether punishment deters at all.[7]

Any theory of sanctions, however, must start out by accepting the fact that the threat of punishment tends to deter, just as rewards tend to encourage rewarded behavior.[8] As a general rule, people want what is pleasant and rewarding, and they avoid costs, punishments, and pains. These propositions are basic to learning theory and to the study of human behavior. Skepticism about legal punishments arises out of the fact that under *some* circumstances, *some* kinds of sanction do not seem to produce much effect, but the basic proposition must be taken as unassailable.

Another proposition must also be taken as true. Suppose a rule of law threatens behavior X with a sanction. If we increase the sanction, behavior X will decrease, all other things being equal; and all other things being equal, if the law promises a reward for behavior X, an increase in reward will bring an increase in X.[9] This follows from the first proposition. No one doubts that a merchant can sell more soup or more soap by lowering his price and less soup or soap at a higher price —all other factors held constant. The *rate* of change may not be predictable, of course. Some kinds of behavior are elastic, some inelastic. There is no way to say crudely and flatly that 10 percent more punishment buys 10 percent more deterrence, ounce for ounce. What one can say is that more units of genuine punishment will discourage, not encourage, whatever behavior is the target of the sanction. To take the simple example of parking behavior, if the fine for illegal parking goes up, illegal parking goes down, not vice versa. The basic propositions

---

[7]The thesis that punishment is inefficient, once bolstered by studies largely confined to rats, has now been abandoned by psychologists. Barry F. Singer, "Psychological Studies of Punishment," 58 *Calif. L. Rev.* 405, 413–4 (1970).

[8]Isaac Ehrlich, "The Deterrent Effect of Criminal Law Enforcement," 1 *J. Legal Studies* 259, 261 (1972); see also C. Ray Jeffery, "Social Change and Criminal Law," 13 *Am. Behav. Scientist* 523 (1970); C.J.M. Schuyt, *Rechtssociologie, een Terreinverkenning* (1971), pp. 142–151.

[9]One must not, of course, confuse "attitude" with "behavior." These propositions in themselves say nothing about the effects of sanctions on attitude. In a famous experiment, Leon Festinger and James C. Carlsmith hired students to empty and refill trays of spools. The job was dull and frustrating. Then the students were paid to tell the other subjects that the job was really quite enjoyable. Some students were paid $1 for this little fable; others, $20. It turned out that the $1 students tended to *believe* their story more than the $20 people. The extra money did not, in short, produce more attitude change; it produced less. But note that the very power of extra money to alter behavior might help explain this effect; there was less need to justify the white lie internally. "Cognitive Consequences of Forced Compliance," 58 *J. Abnormal & Soc. Psychology* 203 (1959); see also Alan C. Elms, ed., *Role Playing, Reward, and Attitude Change* (1969).

have empirical backing; they are in accord with common experience and with theory in other branches of social science.

Are there exceptions to the basic propositions? Are there cases where, if one threatens to punish behavior, the behavior will actually be encouraged? In rare situations, the sanction may give conduct some symbolic meaning that increases its importance. The United States Congress passed a law, during the war in Vietnam, which made it a crime to burn one's draft card.[10] There was only one reason to burn a draft card: as a symbol of defiance toward the war. It is possible that Congress heightened the meaning of the act by passing the law, making it more attractive to people looking for some way to express their disgust for the war. Possibly these people more than offset those *deterred* by the law. Supposedly, some products (cosmetics, for example) will sell more at a higher price, because the consumer thinks a cheap product cannot be any good. There is some research support, too, for the "forbidden fruit" idea: Because pornography is illegal, scarce, and slightly risky, it becomes more erotic and desirable. At least such cases are *theoretically* possible.[11]

The basic propositions assume a certain degree of rational, or cost-benefit, behavior. They do not assume that people are nothing but unfeeling machines. People do act unselfishly at times, and at times irrationally, in every sense of the word. But social science deals with group or mass behavior—with general, typical, modal tendencies. It does not matter if a few people murder, pillage, and rape, regardless of punishment, and are incapable of responding to threats. Some of these people will be considered insane—not legally responsible for their acts. Most *potential* murderers and rapists are not outside the reach of sanctions. And one cannot leap from murder to less "expressive" crimes—crimes without passion (except the passion for money), economic crimes, regulatory crimes, or violations of small rules of order —overtime parking, walking on the grass, or littering the streets.

The deterrent (or incentive) effect of sanctions means, first of all, *general deterrence*, that is, the likelihood that the population or part

---

[10]See *U.S.* v. *O'Brien* 391 U.S. 367 (1968); 50 U.S.C.A. 462 (b) (3).

[11]See Howard L. Fromkin and Timothy C. Brock, "Erotic Materials: A Commodity Theory Analysis of the Enhanced Desirability that May Accompany Their Unavailability," 3 *J. Applied Soc. Psychology* 219 (1973). The authors argue that, for example, requiring "the potential recipient of erotic materials . . . to sign a statement that he is over 21 years of age," while only "a minimal effort," might "make materials more desirable than equivalent materials for which no such statement is requested" (ibid., p. 229). What they do not take into account is the possibility that any such effect would be more than offset by the deterrent effect—the embarrassment, the bother—of the signing.

of it, hearing about a sanction or perhaps seeing it in operation, will modify its behavior accordingly. *General deterrence* is distinguished from *special deterrence* which, on the punishment side, means the "asserted propensity [of punishment] to reduce or eliminate the commission of future crimes by the person being punished."[12] The idea of general deterrence is, for example, that the law against armed robbery will frighten people into thinking twice about committing armed robbery for fear of arrest, conviction, and jail; special deterrence means that a robber, once sent to jail, may think twice about robbing again.

In either case, the deterrence lies mainly in the threat. An armed robber *in* jail cannot rob; that much is obvious. He, of course, is deterred in the physical sense, that is, by walls, bars, guards, and guns.[13] The interesting and important questions have to do with verbal legal acts. The assumption is that people react to these acts. If we threaten a punishment and enforce it, there may well be *some* deviance left, but other potential deviants have been deterred.

The propositions assume, in short, a theory of behavior similar to that assumed in economics. Consumers of legal acts have choices and preferences. Each possible piece of legal behavior promises costs and rewards. A change in cost or price makes for a change in aggregate behavior, but we cannot predict how any particular person will react. If an opera house suddenly lowers the price of its tickets from $10 to $5, the company will obviously be able to sell more seats. Still, some people will not go, even if you paid them; others are too busy to go, too poor, live too far away, or prefer some other entertainment, at the same or lower price. There will be more violators of rules if fines are low than if they are high. The propositions, in other words, are propositions about marginal behavior. They do not pretend to tell how a certain Mr. Jones or Mrs. Smith will act; or even how *many* people, at the margins, will change their behavior as the fine goes up and down.

DETERRENCE AND CAPITAL PUNISHMENT

If we assume a deterrent effect for punishment, what shall we make of the literature on capital punishment, denying any deterrent effect? We have no quarrel with the argument that capital punishment is immoral, and it is certainly possible that it produces harmful side

---

[12]Herbert L. Packer, *The Limits of the Criminal Sanctions* (1968), p. 45.

[13]Even here, what really deters is the threat. Walls themselves are purely passive. A prisoner stays put because he is afraid that he will get caught, get a long sentence, or be shot by a guard if he tries to escape.

effects. Indeed, the case against capital punishment is strengthened if it rests on moral grounds rather than if one insists, against all reason, that the threat of the ultimate punishment has no effect on behavior. In fact, capital punishment is atrociously efficient in the hands of a tyrant like Hitler. The killing of dissidents is an instrument of "horrible and tragic effectiveness"; it forces "the great majority of subjects . . . into conformance."[14] Its very strength is an argument for denying it to governments or to judges who are merely flesh and blood.

Many studies of capital punishment, however, claim to be based on empirical data. In the last generation, capital punishment declined dramatically in the United States. Yet the murder rate remained stable. The murder rate was 4.8 per 100,000 population in 1951; in the same year, 105 persons were put to death. In 1960, the rate was 5.1 per 100,000, and fifty-six persons were executed. In 1964, the murder rate was exactly the same as in 1955 (4.8 per 100,000), but only fifteen persons were put to death, as opposed to 76. In 1966, the murder rate was 5.6 per 100,000; only one man was executed.[15]

These figures, however, do not prove the case, one way or the other. It is clear from the data that capital punishment had gone largely out of fashion in the country. It had become a rare form of punishment—so rare that perhaps it added little or nothing to the risk a rapist or murderer ran. In 1951, about 7,500 people were murdered; yet only 105 killers were executed—about 1.4 percent.[16] A number of states had abolished the death penalty; some had never had it; those who kept it fussed over it so, with so many appeals and delays that convicts spent ten years or more on death row. This further diluted the risk and made the condemned into objects of sympathy—victims themselves—rather than objects of hatred. Differences in risk, like differences in price, may be so small that they do not matter. If a dealer in sports cars raised the price of one model from $7,000 to $7,000.20, one would not expect sales to decline. Airplane passengers do not cancel a trip if the chance of a crash rises from one chance in ten billion to two. Capital punishment may have become such a rare, remote risk, and so far removed in time, that it added no *significant* deterrent. Any potential murderer ran the risk of arrest, prosecution, and a long term in jail. A truly *tiny* added risk of death might not mean very much. By the late 1960s, then, it was

---

[14]Leopold Pospisil, *Anthropology of Law, A Comparative Theory* (1971), p. 91.

[15]William J. Chambliss, "Types of Deviance and the Effectiveness of Legal Sanctions," 1967 *Wis. L. Rev.* 703, 705; see also, in general, Thorsten Sellin, *The Death Penalty* (1959).

[16]These murders took place, of course, before 1951; for the sake of simplicity, we will assume the execution rate was about the same in the year the murders did take place.

safe to abolish the death penalty under any view of its value as deterrent. Abolition would make only a slight difference, because the effect of the penalty was already virtually gone.[17]

Deterrence, it must be repeated, does not imply that people obey a law only because they fear some immediate punishment. All it implies is that a rise in *actual* costs, sanctions, punishments will produce *more* deterrent and *less* forbidden behavior. Capital punishment need not deter everybody, so long as it deters some people; and if an increase in punishment has a marginal effect, that is enough. It therefore will not do to show that many people, caught and punished, commit crimes once more. A high rate of backsliding does *not* prove that deterrents do not work or that lawbreakers become so addicted to crime that they cannot be broken of the habit. In the first place, as Herbert Packer notes, "we do not know how much higher the recidivism rate would be if there had been no criminal punishment in the first place."[18] Secondly, society treats criminals harshly, restricting their chances to rejoin society. It may be "rational" for an ex-con to steal, rather than starve. Other citizens stand to lose more than they gain through crime, but not the ex-convict.[19] Rates of recidivism tell us, at best, something about *special*, not general deterrence. The death penalty is perfect as a special deterrent: The dead can commit no more crimes.

THE DETERRENCE CURVE

In any case, there is no simple, linear relationship between sanctions and sanctioned behavior. Suppose we plotted on a graph the rate

---

[17]Public support for the death penalty had also oozed away; polls showed that, by 1966, a majority opposed the death penalty, even for convicted murderers. There was a sharp upturn later, when "law and order" became a burning issue. Hazel Erskine, "The Polls: Capital Punishment," 34 *Public Opinion Q.* 290 (1970); *New York Times*, Nov. 23, 1972, p. 18, col. 4; *Furman* v. *Georgia*, 408 U.S. 238 (1972). Many states have since reinstituted capital punishment in a limited form and in such a way as to avoid, they hope, the constitutional problems of *Furman*.

[18]Herbert L. Packer, *The Limits of the Criminal Sanction* (1968), p. 46.

[19]Isaac Ehrlich, "The Deterrent Effect of Criminal Law Enforcement," 1 *J. Legal Studies* 259, 264–265 (1972). Compare Daniel Glaser's conclusion, in *The Effectiveness of a Prison and Parole System*, abridged ed. (1969), p. 337, that correctional treatments work best at "reforming" a person when they "enhance a prisoner's opportunities in legitimate economic pursuits" and also "improve his conception of himself when he identifies with anticriminal persons." For firsthand confirmation, see Harry King, as told to William J. Chambliss, *Box Man, a Professional Thief's Journey* (1972), pp. 144–145; See also Robert A. Stebbins, *Commitment to Deviance, The Nonprofessional Criminal in the Community* (1971), pp. 93–109.

of overtime parking at given levels of fine. As fines rose, we would expect the violation rate to fall, but we do *not* expect a perfect straight line on the graph. Doubling a $5 fine, in other words, will (enforcement staying constant) increase compliance, but compliance will not necessarily double. A threat of twenty years in jail will probably *not* be twice as effective as a threat of ten years. We expect some sort of curvilinear relationship, a gradual flattening out. At some point, new inputs of fine will produce less and less new compliance, and one may or may not reach a zero effect. This is because, as compliance rises, there are fewer people to affect, and those few are the most difficult cases. One approaches a saturation point, a point of diminishing returns. This is another reason why capital punishment seems to have so little effect in the United States; murder is so heavily sanctioned by peers, conscience, and the state that the pool of potential murderers is small. Also, a person or group may become so saturated with punishing stimuli that nothing worse or more punishing is possible. A man about to be shot will risk anything; he has nothing to lose. His tormentors have lost the power to deter him with additional actions or threats. Totalitarian societies can reach this point. Gestapo tactics, concentration camps, and indiscriminate shooting may produce an atmosphere where many people feel life is intolerable, and nothing could be worse. Hence, more terror will have no effect; it merely drives people to join the resistance. If even the innocent face random, senseless terror, then revolution seems little more fearful than the risks of everyday life.

There are, alas, ample historical examples of such societies of terror. Gresham Sykes has made a similar point about prison life. He studied prisoners in the New Jersey State Prison and found that they misbehaved at what he thought a very high rate. The custodians, "far from being omnipotent rulers," were "engaged in a continuous struggle to maintain order"; in the struggle, they frequently failed. One reason was that officials were "dangerously close to the point where the stock of legitimate punishments has been exhausted and . . . the few punishments which are left have lost their potency." In this prison, Sykes felt, the curve had flattened out.[20]

Each legal act will have its own deterrence curve. Perhaps no two curves are exactly the same. That is, any intervention of the legal system—any rule or order communicated to one or more subjects and

---

[20]Gresham Sykes, *The Society of Captives: A Study of a Maximum Security Prison* (1958), pp. 42, 51. Sykes also felt that "the reward side of the picture has been largely stripped away." The prison gave away all its privileges at the outset—time off for good behavior, for example, was subtracted from the prisoner's sentence the day he entered prison. The prisoner therefore found himself "unable to win any significant gains by means of compliance."

buttressed by a sanction, positive or negative—will affect behavior more or less, depending on the level of sanction threatened or promised. Many factors affect the slope and the shape of this deterrence curve. The following are some of the basic factors; we will discuss some of them later in more detail.

I. *Characteristics of the threat or promise*
   A. The nature of the sanction. Is it a reward or a punishment? Is it light or severe?
   B. The perceived risk of suffering a negative sanction or enjoying a positive one.
   C. The speed at which the sanction is delivered. Is it immediate or far in the future?

II. *Characteristics of the persons subject to the sanction*
   A. How many people are subject to the sanction? It is easier, for example, to achieve high enforcement of rules that apply only to a few prominent people or entities.
   B. The personality type of the subjects, or the culture in which the subjects live.

III. *Characteristics of the behavior to be controlled*
   A. How easy or difficult is it to detect and visit punishment on the behavior? For example, it is very hard to stamp out dangerous thoughts, much easier to burn dangerous books.
   B. What is the nature of the demand for the behavior to be controlled? Some behavior is hard to control, because people find it so desirable that they will not readily give it up, or so unpleasant that the law cannot easily stimulate it. For some behavior, there is strong and relatively inelastic demand; sanctions have comparatively little effect; other behavior is quite elastic and responds very quickly to sanctions.

CHARACTERISTICS OF THE THREAT OR PROMISE

THE NATURE OF THE SANCTIONS

Conventionally, sanctions are divided into two large divisions, rewards and punishments, that is, positive and negative sanctions. The idea is that people subject to law will choose one and avoid the other. Lawmakers assume that the sanctions labelled as "punishments" are actually painful and the "rewards" actually pleasant, so that the desired behavioral consequences will follow more or less automatically.

The common forms of punishment in criminal law are fines and imprisonment. Corporal or other physical punishment was, in the past, often used in the law. Whipping was a normal means of social control in colonial America, especially for servants and slaves and especially for sexual transgressions. Servants and slaves had no money to pay fines, and to put them in jail would rob their masters of their labor.[21] The death penalty is rare today but has been frequently used in the past. Other punishments include reprimands, demotions in rank, and losses of privilege—forfeiture of the right to vote or to drive a car.

Each punishment has its own social meaning. Since the power of a sanction depends on how people perceive it, it may make a difference whether "death" comes through hanging or shooting or the electric chair; and "three years in prison" may mean different things to different classes of people. It may also depend in part on the kind of jail. History records many extinct and obsolete deterrents: exile, the whipping post, castration. Ideas about the morality of punishments change; these ideas increase or reduce the options open to the legal system. There seems to be a general trend in the modern world toward leniency. The Eighth Amendment of the United States Constitution prohibits cruel and unusual punishment. The clause forbids torture and probably all but a narrow band of conventional deterrents,[22] such as fines and imprisonment. Corporal punishment has declined, officially, at least,[23] and jail sentences have become shorter over the years. Punishments, however, are hard to compare—is a whipping worse or better than a month in jail? And their effect may vary with culture and time.

The civil side has a rich armory of penalties too. The most familiar is money damages; another is forfeiture of privileges. A corporation can lose its charter; the party "at fault" in a divorce case loses the marriage, not to mention his car, children, and house. Civil courts can impose *injunctions* which bind a party to act as the court directs. If the party steps over the bounds of the order, he may go to jail. Every court order, injunction or not, is a restriction of freedom, laying the subject open to further penalty (usually money) if he fails to obey.

The most obvious form of *reward* is cash for performance. Many states offer bounties for killing predators—Arizona, for example, will pay up to $100 for killing a mountain lion, $3.50 a head for coyotes.[24] Tax laws are riddled with direct money incentives. Governments have paid out billions in subsidies—to farmers, for example, for price supports and soil bank payments. Positive sanctions also include titles, honors, medals, and positions of power, and smiles, handshakes, and

---

[21]See Edwin Powers, *Crime and Punishment in Early Massachusetts, 1620–1692, a Documentary History* (1966), pp. 164–177.

[22]As is well known, the United States Supreme Court has held that capital punishment in its present form violates the Eighth Amendment. *Furman* v. *Georgia*, 408 U.S. 238 (1972).

[23]This statement is, however, not necessarily true of totalitarian states.

[24]Ariz. Rev. Stat. § 24–821 (1956).

praise. Anything of value may act as an incentive; a prisoner, who satisfies the parole board, can win early release.

Legal scholarship pays little attention, on the whole, to rewards. On the surface, the legal system seems to use punishment more than reward. Punishment seems, in a sense, more efficient. The mere *threat* of it has a deterrent effect, while the hope of reward is a flimsy incentive. A subsidy might provoke more discontent than action, if only one out of three actually collected it. (Sometimes, of course, people expect to take a chance on a reward, most obviously in state-run lotteries.)

It is, however, difficult to count and compare formal punishments and formal rewards in order to measure empirically the use of one or the other by the law. A count, on the books, hardly tells us which technique the law "uses" more. Moreover, the terms *reward* and *punishment* do not describe very well the way rules channel conduct outside the criminal law. Let us take, once again, the law of wills as an example. Each American state has an intestacy statute. This sets out the procedure for disposing of a person's goods at death, if the deceased left no will. In Pennsylvania, for example, the widow, if there is one, will receive at least one-third of her late husband's estate, more if no children survive. Other members of the family will take specified shares of the estate.[25] The law also sets out rules for drawing up a will. The will must be in writing, it must be signed by the testator, it must have at least two witnesses.[26] A will that meets these standards is valid. One that does not is a worthless piece of paper.

It is possible, of course, to describe this set of rules in terms of rewards and punishments. One might say that a person who does not follow the rules—who uses only one witness, for example—will be *punished.* His will fails, his wishes are ignored, and the intestacy statute takes over. We might just as well say that a person who does follow the rules is *rewarded;* he gains freedom to ignore the intestacy law and leave his estate as he pleases. Since we can describe the same matters just as plausibly as reward or as punishment, it is fair to conclude that the terms do not fit. This in-between situation, very common in the law, uses channeling techniques, not straight punishments and rewards. It sets up structures and makes them easy to use. It fosters habits and routines. The man who makes out a will uses the structure which was created or shaped by the law. We called this kind of legal behavior *use;* its negative is *nonuse.*

---

[25]Pa. Stat. Ann. Title 20 § 1.2, 1.3.

[26]In a few states, three witnesses are needed. In a number of states in the West and South, a testator may do without the witnesses, but only if he writes the will entirely by hand and dates it. This is called a holographic will, Cal. Prob. Code § 53.

Formally at least, *use* is a matter for actors to decide for themselves. The law does not "care" whether one makes out a will or not. We may ask, of course, *why* the law does not "care." In a sense, the law *does* care; it does not treat intestacy and testacy with total indifference. Under the present system, a certain number of valid wills are produced each year. It may be that, from some social viewpoint, this is the "right" amount. If so, and if more coercion will cost more than more right conduct is "worth," then it is preferable to leave matters where they are. We can make small changes by changing law or procedure. If we want *more* testacy, we can try to make wills more desirable, or "punish" intestacy (with a tax perhaps), or both. The state does not, for example, collect rent for landlords. The landlord does it himself. He *can* invoke legal process, if his tenants do not pay. Often he will. His right to collect rent through the legal process is the right to gain a reward and inflict a punishment. If the amount of *use* by landlords is acceptable or optimal, we can let the matter lie. We can adjust the level up or down by tinkering with rules or procedures. We can make it harder or easier to evict. If we go to the extreme, we can make nonpayment of rent a crime. This tilts the scale even farther. Rules of law, then, by their structure and content channel conduct with varying degrees of success. Rewards and punishments are alternative methods of channeling.

A further point: The terms *reward* and *punishment* refer to intended results of legal acts. It is assumed that the message is the same for sender and receiver—that both see punishments as punishments, rewards as rewards. This is usually the case but not always. Some people, subconsciously perhaps, may want to be punished and treat punishment as a reward. Some psychoanalysts feel that punishment is "an unconscious and most dangerous incentive to crime. The forbidden deed relieves . . . an overly great feeling of guilt. The prospect of punishment does not deter the criminal, but unconsciously drives him to the forbidden deed."[27] A dedicated revolutionary might want to be arrested to publicize his cause and become a martyr. More prosaically, a homeless drunk on a cold, lonely night in December may want to be thrown into jail.

No form of sanction, then, has *universal* effect, although physical punishment comes close, and money is a powerful and general

---

[27]Theodor Reik, *The Compulsion to Confess, On the Psychoanalysis of Crime and Punishment* (1959), p. 295. The American Psychiatric Association filed an *amicus curiae* brief before the United States Supreme Court in a capital punishment case, claiming there were men "for whom capital punishment served as an incitement to kill rather than a deterrent," quoted in Michael Meltsner, "Litigating against the Death Penalty: The Strategy behind *Furman*," 82 *Yale L.J.* 1111, 1137 (1973).

reward. The effect of a sanction is an empirical question. People assess sanctions differently. They have different tolerances for pain and different responses to money incentives. Economic status may matter; a thousand-dollar fine is a trifle to a large corporation, a hardship to a workingman. The threat of prison, it is said, is more devastating for a middle-class, white-collar criminal than for other violators.[28] Conceivably, there are subcultures where arrest and imprisonment are badges of manhood, not of shame. Conversely, not everyone wants an official reward; a teacher's high praise might embarrass a boy in the class.

In some modern political trials, defendants have acted "irrationally," goading the court into punitive acts. This occurred at the trial of the "Chicago seven" in 1970 before Judge Julius Hoffman.[29] Here the punisher and the punished had different goals and constituencies. The defendants were eager to make their case against the American system of justice. They wanted to show that the judge was harsh and prejudiced.[30] The judge punished, however, for social control, for deterrence, for his own satisfaction, and to please an unseen audience of solid citizens outside.

REWARD VS. PUNISHMENT

Is reward more effective than punishment? Suppose the government is anxious to promote racial integration in a housing project. Would it produce better results to pay whites $10 a month to live in an integrated project or to fine them $10 a month for living elsewhere? Questions like this cannot be answered with confidence. Studies of animals and children, along with a certain amount of wishful thinking, have led some psychologists to conclude that punishment (a painful stimulus) is not as good as reward (or "positive reinforcement") in inducing learning or change of behavior. Shakespeare's Hermione said, in *The Winter's Tale*, "you may ride 's/ With one soft kiss a thousand furlongs ere/ With spur we heat an acre."[31]

---

[28]In the famous electrical equipment cases of 1961, prominent businessmen were charged with gross antitrust violations. To judge by the outcry, the prospect of jail horrified the executives accused of these crimes. See Gilbert Geis, "The Heavy Electrical Equipment Antitrust Cases of 1961," in Gilbert Geis, ed., *White Collar Criminal* (1968), p. 103; Alan M. Dershowitz, "Increasing Community Control over Corporate Crime: A Problem in the Law of Sanctions," 71 *Yale L.J.* 280 (1961).

[29]See the discussion in Harry Kalven, Jr., " 'Please Morris, Don't Make Trouble': Two Lessons in Courtroom Confrontation," 27 *J. Soc. Issues*, no. 2, 219 (1971).

[30]They might also have felt they were bound to lose and wanted to build up a case for appeal.

[31]*The Winter's Tale*, Act I, scene 2.

Even so, it is not clear that these statements apply to legal behavior.[32] Most of the studies have not dealt with adult human behavior. In the studies, rewards and punishments usually followed immediately after behavior—an electric shock, a bit of food. Legal punishment is rarely certain and almost never immediate. A person who cheats on his income taxes will surely not be caught right away, and trial, fine, and sentence may take years. Many rewards and subsidies are certain and almost immediate; hence, it is hard to compare the effect of the two. It would be a more realistic comparison, if every tenth white family won a claim to $10, payable some time in the future. Punishment is more like a lottery than like a bond coupon due on a definite date.

Also, there is no reason to believe that *all* forms of reward are superior to *all* forms of punishment for *all* acts.[33] Fear of jail may be a more powerful sanction than promises of money for many people and for many acts. Any sweeping generalization will no doubt turn out to be wrong.

Moreover, what is the unit of reward or punishment for purposes of comparison? Is a $10 fine the same *unit* of sanction as a $10 reward? How do you compare units of imprisonment or beatings with units of money? How many strokes with a whip equal a medal for bravery?

THE PERCEPTION OF RISK

It goes without saying that it does not deter to make punishment more severe—on paper. Many people who argue that punishment is futile mean that words in a book are futile in themselves. This is correct. Evidence for the deterrent effect of purely *formal* sanctions is, as expected, slight.[34] The deterrent effect comes from the force of a threat. An unenforced sanction is a poor deterrent, because it is so weak and so flabby a threat. It may work, but only if people do not know that the threat is an empty one.

It has been often said that what is important about a sanction is its

---

[32]See Barry F. Singer, "Psychological Studies of Punishment," 58 *Calif. L. Rev.* 405, 411ff. (1970).

[33]There has been some laboratory work on the comparative effect of different punishments. See Joseph C. LaVoie, "Type of Punishment as a Determinant of Resistance to Deviation," 10 *Developmental Psychology* 181 (1974); Jeffrey I. Rubin and Roy J. Lewicki, "A Three-Factor Experimental Analysis of Promises and Threats," 3 *J. Applied Social Psychology* 240 (1973). The applicability to legal phenomena is questionable.

[34]Richard G. Salem and William J. Bowers, "Severity of Formal Sanctions as a Deterrent to Deviant Behavior," 5 *Law and Society Rev.* 21 (1970).

certainty.[35] This is what makes surveillance so strong. No one parks in a "No Parking" zone under the policeman's nose. It seems likely that fewer people would drive when drunk, if they were sure that they would be caught and given a year in jail. A five-year penalty would be even more effective. How effective, we cannot tell, but suppose that as the penalty increased to five years, the chance of arrest and conviction retreated to one out of five. We are now unsure whether we have increased the punishment at all. Perhaps we have only changed its form. Deterrence depends on the perceived *risk* that a sanction will actually fall on a person's head. By raising the level of enforcement, one gets more deterrence out of the same formal punishment. If every thief was caught and jailed and this fact became known, a small fine and a week in jail might provide as much general and specific deterrence as harsher but less certain punishments. In the nineteenth century, penal laws became more humane, prison terms shorter, and the death penalty shriveled to a shadow of itself. But perhaps techniques of enforcement improved. Society could then afford to inflict mild penalties on the many who were caught instead of great cruelty on the few.[36]

What deters, however, is not the real or objective risk. It is *perceived* risk—the risk as a potential violator sees it. This fact, of course, adds another complication. Certainly, punishment can discourage shoplifters; but not all shoplifters are caught, not all are prosecuted, not all those prosecuted are convicted. What do shoplifters know about their chances? Different types of shoplifters probably have different perceptions. Professionals have one idea of the risk, amateurs (housewives and teenagers) another. (On the other hand, the housewife may dread getting caught more than the professional.)

In short, then, for deterrence to work, a sanction must be real or *seem* real. Paper tigers do not bite or deter, unless their weakness is kept secret. In one study, students in a Florida college were asked what they thought the penalties were for possession of marijuana, whether they thought offenders were likely to be caught, whether they knew people who had been arrested, and whether they themselves were violators. Nonviolators tended to assess the risks as greater than violators. This is what deterrence theory would expect. Other results of the study were less clear-cut.[37] In general, we know little about perceptions

---

[35]See the studies cited in note 6, and, especially, George Antunes and A. Lee Hunt, "The Impact of Certainty and Severity of Punishment on Levels of Crime in American States: An Extended Analysis," 64 *J. Crim. L. and Criminology* 486 (1973).

[36]J. Tobias, *Crime and Industrial Society in the Nineteenth Century* (1972), p. 289.

[37]Gordon P. Waldo and Theodore G. Chiricos, "Perceived Penal Sanction and Self-

of risk. It is a promising area for study. Jonathan Casper, who interviewed convicted burglars in Connecticut, quoted one as saying that "you can . . . get a lot of breaking and entering, and it's very hard to catch you on one." Most burglars, Casper felt, "assume that for any given job they will not be caught, though in the long run they will."[38]

We are also not sure how to affect perceptions of risk. Some communities boldly mark their police cars. The idea is to make the police as visible as possible, increasing the perceived risk to bad drivers. One could also make an argument for unmarked cars; drivers might then imagine police lurking everywhere and over-assess the risk of getting caught. A study of the effect on crime of increasing subway police in New York found a "phantom effect"—"deterrence caused by a police activity that is not actually present." Crime on the subway decreased even during times when the police were not there, probably because of "an incorrect perception of the threat of apprehension."[39]

THE SPEED OF ENFORCEMENT

The *speed* with which a punishment or reward is delivered is as important as its certainty and severity. An immediate punishment or reward has more impact than a delayed one. A dollar in the hand is worth a dollar; the right to a dollar tomorrow, or next week, or next year must be "discounted." It is the same with other goods and services —and punishment and reward. Experiments show that "the effect of a delay is to lessen severity, and manipulations of severity have little effect at long delays." Laboratory experiments call it "delay," if the punishment comes thirty seconds later than the act to be punished. The lag in the legal system may be years. Still, it seems logical that "a five-year sentence beginning a year after the commission of a crime may not be as effective as a six-month sentence administered without delay."[40]

Reported Criminality: A Neglected Approach to Deterrence Research," 19 *Social Problems* 522 (1972). The study also included questions about petty larceny. The results here are harder to explain—perhaps because "stealing" is a much vaguer idea in people's minds than "using marijuana." See also Daniel S. Claster, "Comparison of Risk Perception between Delinquents and Nondelinquents," 58 *J. Crim. L. C. & P. S.* 80 (1967).

[38]Jonathan D. Casper, *American Criminal Justice, the Defendant's Perspective* (1972), p. 159. This is the philosophy of the cigarette smoker, too, in the face of a risk of cancer.

[39]Jan M. Chaiken, Michael W. Lawless, Keith A. Stevenson, *The Impact of Police Activity on Crime: Robberies on the New York City Subway System* (1974), p. 23.

[40]Barry F. Singer, "Psychological Studies of Punishment," 58 *Calif. L. Rev.* 405, 421 (1970).

This sensible proposition should apply to civil damages too. The possible "costs" of breach of contract (the liability for damages) will be incurred in the remote future, while there may be immediate gains in getting out of a losing deal.[41] Consequently, even generous damages for breach of contract, and interest from the date of breach, will not be very effective in forcing people to live up to their bargains. Yet the law of contract does not allow "extra" damages—for pain, suffering, or inconvenience—as does the law of tort. Society may not be that eager to "deter" breach of contract; that is, contract law does not aim to "stamp out" breach of contract, while tort law does aim to reduce accidents; and criminal law aims to control behavior and suppress the tendency toward crime. Areas of the law that are seriously concerned with ideas of deterrence tend to "over-punish," that is, they make the wrongdoer pay and pay and pay. A man can go to jail for years for stealing a battered old car; he pays a price far out of line with the market value of the car.

CHARACTERISTICS OF THE PERSONS SUBJECT TO THE SANCTION

THE NUMBER OF SUBJECTS

Another factor in determining effectiveness of a sanction is the *number* of persons whose compliance is required. Obviously, other things being equal, a legal act is more likely to achieve an impact if only a few people need comply rather than many.[42] Enforcement will be cheaper. It is easier to guard five people than five hundred. The practical advice that flows from this fact is that lawmakers should look for rules and strategies that attack a problem at its bottleneck points. The goal, let us say, is to make cars safer to drive and reduce accidents. Assume we have two choices, the inflatable air bag and the seat belt; they cost the same to manufacture and produce the same safety results. Under these conditions, the air bag is much to be preferred. It is built into the car; hence compliance is needed from four to five auto manufacturers, not, as is the case with seat belts, from a diffuse group of millions of drivers and passengers. To ensure the quality of meat, it is

---

[41]Of course, there may also be immediate losses, too—goodwill, future business, etc.

[42]For a similar point about "moral suasion," (i.e., governmental threats, "guidelines" with controls lurking in the background, and similar techniques), see J. T. Romans, "Moral Suasion as an Instrument of Economic Policy," 56 *Am. Econ. Rev.* 1220 (1966).

easier to inspect packing plants than butcher shops. Of course, when regulations fasten on the few, those few are usually a *powerful* few whose capacity to resist surpasses the ordinary citizen's. But when those few—for example, large companies—are indifferent as to modes of enforcement, the better choice is the device that calls for fewer compliers.

THE PERSONALITY OF THE SUBJECTS

It seems reasonable to suppose that personality of subjects affects the impact of sanctions. To begin with, people differ in their taste for risks. Few people will violate a law when detection and punishment are *certain*—when the policeman is standing on the corner. At a lesser level of enforcement, some people violate laws even though the chances of getting caught seem very great. They are risk-lovers who knowingly take a chance; they gamble on the cards, even though they know that the house does not lose in the long run.

Actual evidence on the differential effect of sanctions on risk-avoiders and risk-takers is, however, quite limited. Indeed, there is little on the whole subject of the effect on enforcement of what Zimring and Hawkins call "differences among men."[43] Berkowitz and Walker found differences in attitude toward moral and legal propositions among British college students, which they thought they could relate to scores on personality tests.[44] It is some distance, however, from attitude to behavior.

Clearly too, culture is a crucial determinant of legal behavior. Moral and cultural factors affect the deterrence curve. These are often the factors hardest to manipulate or synthesize. To this extent, William Graham Sumner was right. Behavior imbedded in the mores and supported by the mores changes slowly and at great pains. Since there is no single world culture, there is no reason to expect the same deterrence curve for armed robbery or drunkenness in Hungary and Honduras.

CHARACTERISTICS OF THE BEHAVIOR TO BE CONTROLLED

EASE OF DETECTION AND ENFORCEMENT

Some breaches of norms are harder to detect than others. Hence they are harder or more expensive to deter. A dollar spent to spot and

---

[43]Zimring and Hawkins, *supra* note 6, pp. 96–129.
[44]Leonard Berkowitz and Nigel Walker, "Laws and Moral Judgments," 30 *Sociometry* 440 (1967).

catch speeders on the open road in broad daylight is a more productive dollar than one spent to catch parole violators or persons guilty of monopoly, sedition, and illegal sex acts. Some kinds of "victimless" illegalities[45] are hard to police, because these "crimes" are committed behind drawn curtains. Homosexual acts between consenting adults, for example, are both victimless and private.[46] These crimes are hard to detect, because the police must do the work all by themselves. Normally, they cannot rely on victims to report these crimes.[47]

Again, it has been hard to enforce laws against dumping oily bilge into the sea. The ocean is huge and too expensive to patrol; ship captains have endless privacy for dumping filth overboard. Some laws are hard to enforce satisfactorily, because violations, though rare, are terribly serious, and deterrence is no use unless it approaches 100 percent. Skyjacking and political assassination are examples. For some acts, on the contrary, there are many potential violators, and they can violate in many places. To catch jaywalkers, one must watch a whole network of streets. Every pedestrian—young or old, man, woman, or child—is a possible jaywalker. On the other hand, only coal mining companies can violate mine safety laws and only in the mines. Coal mines are easy to count, and the number of inspectors needed can be easily calculated.

THE DEMAND FOR THE BEHAVIOR TO BE CONTROLLED

Norms that seek to limit or control behavior are always aimed at behavior that at least someone does or might find desirable. There is, in other words, a *demand* for the behavior. We can assume that there is a demand for murder, arson, breach of contract, illegal parking, adulteration of milk—every act which sanctions try to reach, but the demand curve is different for different behaviors.

Some scholars have tried to classify types of legal behavior in terms of their demand curves. Some such notion lies behind the classification of crimes by William Chambliss, who distinguishes between two polar types, which he calls "expressive" and "instrumental."[48] A criminal act is "expressive," if it is pleasurable in itself—committed, in other words, for its own sake. He cites rape and drug addiction as examples.

---

[45]See Edwin M. Schur, *Crimes without Victims* (1965).

[46]Troy Duster, *The Legislation of Morality: Laws, Drugs, and Moral Judgment* (1970), p. 26, distinguishes between "public" and "private" victimless crime. The former are committed "in a public arena," e.g., prostitution or sale of alcohol during Prohibition. These "public" types are hard to control, too, without disguises, entrapment, and other devices, but the "private" acts are still more difficult.

[47]Except, of course, for informers and undercover agents, whose services cost money.

[48]William J. Chambliss, "Types of Deviance and the Effectiveness of Legal Sanctions," 1967 *Wis. L. Rev.* 703.

An instrumental crime—embezzlement, income tax evasion—is only a means to an end. Punishment, Chambliss feels, deters instrumental crimes more readily than expressive ones, but this cannot be taken as an absolute rule. Some expressive acts seem quite easy to deter. People hunt for the pleasure of it, but there is no reason to believe that rigorous enforcement would be less effective against illegal deer hunting, than against overtime parking, which is plainly instrumental. Andenaes points out that "the fear of even mild social sanctions often leads to the suppression of expressive acts (for example, yawning, picking one's nose, or crying out angrily)."[49] The better distinction might be between controllable and uncontrollable acts. The drug addict *must* get his drugs; sex crimes may stem from overpowering urges. If so, then the distinction means little more than that punishment deters only the deterrable—hardly an earthshaking discovery.[50]

Chambliss, however, is right in trying to sort out types of legal behavior and in insisting, although not in so many words, that different courses of conduct have different deterrence curves. Most persons would concede that punishment does deter a great many instrumental acts. "Expressive" acts are supposed to be exceptions to the rule, yet few if any crimes are purely expressive. Murder is usually expressive, in Chambliss' terms. But a hired killer is an instrumental killer; and so is an amateur, who kills his uncle to get his insurance, even perhaps a man who poisons his wife to clear the way for his mistress. If punishment deters insurance murders, then additional real punishment ought to bring more deterrence, until, as the curve flattens out, only a small "expressive" residue is left. At least, we may presume as much, unless there is proof to the contrary.

Whatever the problems with Chambliss' typology, it does seem clear that the demand for deviant behavior (the desire or predisposition to violate) can be inelastic or elastic, that is, responsive or unresponsive to sanctions. Where it is elastic, improvement in enforcement, or enforcement technology, can show good, and perhaps permanent, results. If demand is inelastic, investment in enforcement shows a poor return. The "demand" for illegal parking seems fairly elastic. Busy drivers are

---

[49]Johannes Andenaes, "Deterrence and Specific Offenses," 38 *U. Chi. L. Rev.* 537, 538 (1971).

[50]Chambliss also distinguishes between *actors* with a "high commitment" to crime and those with a low commitment—i.e., professionals and amateurs. The amateur is presumably more easily deterred. This seems clear enough for some kinds of crime—for example, shoplifting. For other crimes, however, it is much less clear—for example, "amateur" murder. In addition, the line between amateurs and professionals is not always distinct.

greatly tempted to park illegally. Moreover, the behavior is sensitive to ups and downs in enforcement and severity. The demand for rape, on the other hand, seems to be fairly inelastic, at least as things now stand.[51] So, it seems, is the demand for hard drugs. Heavy penalties do not "work"; they lead mainly to frustration. It is like pouring water into a sieve. If the police try to crack down on prostitutes, prostitutes raise their prices or, more likely, go in for bribery and corruption. A crackdown on drugs drives the price of drugs higher. The supply shrinks and the risk to the dealers rises. When we make a commodity illegal, we make it harder and more distasteful to go into the business. This gives a special profit "to the entrepreneur who is willing to break the law." This profit is what Herbert L. Packer, in a suggestive phrase, called the "crime tariff."[52] Similarly, cities occasionally get tough with owners of slum tenements, who violate the housing codes. These episodes are usually ineffective. In many cities, the network of rules is so thick that government has imposed a sort of crime tariff here too. Demand is relatively inelastic; poor people must live somewhere. The tariff discourages all landlords except those willing to break the law. If higher costs result, the poor will bear them.[53]

One should not overemphasize, however, the chasm between controllable and uncontrollable behavior. It is certainly easier to give up overtime parking than drug addiction. Nonetheless, some people experiment with drugs, yet retain control over the habit. If punishments for use or possession of drugs became *very* certain and very severe (the death penalty or torture), some addicts might force themselves to try to quit. The penalties might also have a strong effect on *potential* users of drugs. Each increment of punishment drops off a few more potential actors, like bidders at an auction who quit as the bidding rises. Some people are so rich and so desperate that they will pay any price. The addict cheats and steals to raise money for drugs. He is desperate; he is willing to go to great lengths, but this does not call into question the law of supply and demand. Hard drugs might become so costly that addicts would be literally unable to steal enough money. The punishment "price" could also reach (in theory) so high a point that all but a few would drop out.

It remains true that some kinds of deviance are hard to deter,

---

[51]We have to allow for the possibility that the "demand" was great but easily deterred by threat of punishment; the curve then flattened out.

[52]Herbert L. Packer, *The Limits of the Criminal Sanction* (1968), pp. 277–282.

[53]Lawrence M. Friedman, *Government and Slum Housing: A Century of Frustration* (1968), pp. 39–44.

because they are deeply rooted in habit, tradition, or desire. It would be hard to stamp out illegal sexual intercourse. The "noble experiment," Prohibition, showed that the urge to drink, at least in the United States, was almost as intractable. "Deeply rooted," however, is only a way of saying that one can deter only through generating huge voltages of sanction and that the price of deterrence runs high. Every act (perhaps) has its price; but the prices are variable. Chambliss' "expressive" crimes,[54] drug addiction or murder for passion, are hard to deter because the actors have such strong incentives to commit them. Punishment, then, must outbid a mighty opponent. Full deterrence would be astronomically expensive; even modest enforcement runs up an enormous bill.

This situation is not limited to "expressive" acts. Bank officers embezzle because money is tempting. The risks must be high to deter this crime. As we noted, for some kinds of deviant behavior the demand is strong and inelastic. Any culture, looked at in cross section, that is, frozen in a snapshot at some point in time, stands in some rough sort of equilibrium. It will seem hard indeed to raise the level of enforcement against particular crimes. In the short run, if we try to increase this level, leakages in enforcement will frustrate our attempts. The system is like a garden hose, punctured with holes. If we turn the pressure up at one end, more water may or may not flow out the other; it depends on the number of holes and how much pressure is applied. Prohibition was a very leaky hose. State and federal governments did reach a certain level of enforcement. People were arrested, tried, and put in jail; by 1932, there were 70,242 Prohibition cases in the federal courts. This was, of course, a drop in the bucket compared to the rate of violation. Yet the "machinery of justice" was, in the words of one authority, "inadequate to cope with this volume of business," suggesting a failure of will to enforce. Periodic crackdowns produced poor results. Juries refused to convict people arrested for drinking; prosecutors sometimes looked the other way; judges gave light sentences or dismissed cases; federal agents were bribed and corrupted.[55]

People violated prohibition laws, because they wanted to drink and enjoyed the culture of drinking; millions thought the law was foolish or pernicious. Today, the marijuana laws—which John Kaplan calls

---

[54]See pp. 87–88.

[55]The administration of President Hoover seriously considered trying, finally, to enforce Prohibition sternly. The attempt would surely have failed; indeed, it has been suggested that the very idea was what finally sealed the doom of the "noble experiment." Andrew Sinclair, *Prohibition: The Era of Excess* (1962). See also Paul E. Isaac, *Prohibition and Politics: Turbulent Decades in Tennessee 1885–1920* (1965), especially chs. 12 and 14 on enforcement of Tennessee's prohibition laws.

the "new prohibition"[56]—are also unpopular. The number of people who smoke marijuana is increasing rapidly; so is the number of arrests. Still, trivial percentages of violators are caught, and sentences are getting lighter. This, too, is a leaky hose.[57] As the Vietnam war became less and less popular, in the late 1960s, draft evasion lost its stigma among college men. Draft evasion increased, and, although more men were arrested, sentences declined.[58] In both these cases, the larger culture was in conflict. Failure of consensus meant that society would not even try to spend enough to control marijuana. Nor was there agreement about the methods to use; draconian measures could not command enough support. The moral code is, hopefully, a strong curb on "efficient" law enforcement. When behavior is strongly rooted in the culture, or difficult to detect, or for other reasons responds only sluggishly to increases in ordinary forms of enforcement, laws to control that behavior may be unenforceable—by legitimate means. The laws *might* be enforced, but society is not willing to pay the price or to use the stringent methods necessary. The rule of law means a society too bashful to use murder and torture—or wiretapping, sabotage, and blackmail—to enforce "unenforceable" laws.

The leaky hose is a sign, then, of equilibrium. A delicate balance is natural, if legal acts have a social genesis—that is, if we can "explain" the laws at any particular time in terms of social and economic forces in society. Social forces determine "the law," meaning not the rules as such but the system in actual operation. An outside observer of American society would find marijuana laws utterly baffling as they appear on the books. In actual operation, they are conflict-ridden, inconsistent, and confused, but they mirror in that regard the conflict, confusion, and inconsistency in society's views on the subject.

The idea of an equilibrium cannot, of course, be pushed too far. Legal systems are in constant movement and change. Each working part serves some function, has some cultural support, but there is also slack in the system, leeways, room for practical reform. We will return to the subject of legal change in Chapter X.

---

[56]John Kaplan, *Marijuana, the New Prohibition* (1970).

[57]Thirty-one percent of those convicted in California in 1960 for violation of marijuana laws, who had no prior drug record, were put on probation. In 1967, the percentage had risen to 53 percent; and even 20 percent of those with "serious" prior records got probation, compared to 6 percent in 1960. Stanley E. Grupp and Warren C. Lucas, "The 'Marihuana Muddle' as Reflected in California Arrest Statistics and Disposition," 5 *Law and Society Rev.* 251, 262 (1970).

[58]See the data for northern California, in Jeffrey A. Schafer, "Prosecution for Selective Service Offenses: A Field Study," 22 *Stan. L. Rev.* 356 (1970).

TECHNIQUES OF DELIVERING THE SANCTION

A legal sanction operates by actual application or, more characteristically, through threat or promise. The means of delivering the sanction and the rate of delivery make up a process called *enforcement.* Behavior can be modified by actual enforcement, by threat or promise (deterrence), or by more indirect means, for example, by modifying the social surroundings. There is a big difference between a threat to throw leaders of a juvenile gang into jail and opening a settlement house in the neighborhood. Oaks and Lehman speak of various ways of controlling "an objectionable pattern of individual behavior." One is "by eliminating the circumstances (other than the individual's system of values) that give rise to the behavior."[59] Thus, one could try to fight crime by getting rid of slums or by building a society in which crime would wither away.

But this technique or hope is in a sense not a method of "controlling" behavior at all. Opening a settlement house is like prescribing the form of a will. Certain rules of law and other legal acts have the indirect goal of reducing crime. If we want to destroy the slums, we might enact a law giving tax incentives to people who build low-income housing. Crime control *might* be one ultimate purpose, but the law would do nothing more than channel the behavior of housing developers and investors, in the first instance. Thus, this technique of Oaks and Lehman can be reduced to other techniques—deterrence, incentive, and various kinds of non-state persuasion.

Most discussions of sanctions blur the distinction between the sanction itself, the way it is communicated, and the way it is carried out. "Reward," "punishment," "fine," "subsidy," and similar terms refer to end-states. What goes on between a decision to punish or reward and the delivery of the sanction is vitally important. The process —from the rule against murder to the arrival of a murderer in jail— involves a whole social system, significantly different from the system and process that follow other legal acts. It is somewhat artificial to ignore the separate parts of the process.

Many techniques for controlling behavior and carrying out policy are half-communication, half-enforcement. Eugene Litwak and Henry J. Meyer in an interesting essay catalogued some of these techniques, although without special reference to law.[60] One technique is the use

---

[59]Dallin Oaks and Warren Lehman, *A Criminal Justice System and the Indigent* (1968), p. 188.

[60]Eugene Litwak and Henry J. Meyer, "A Balance Theory of Coordination between Bureaucratic Organizations and Community Primary Groups," 11 *Admin. Sci. Q.* 31 (1966).

of the "detached expert," the professional—a social worker or street gang worker—who moves directly among subjects, trying to induce or force them to change their behavior. An organization can try to reach its public through enlisting opinion leaders, using mass media, or setting up enclaves, such as settlement houses. The organization may also use "common messengers," that is, it may send "messages intended to influence," through "an individual who is regularly a member" of both camps, the rulers and the ruled.

None of these techniques is a sanction in itself. Each is a delivery system—a way to communicate and at the same time to threaten and persuade. They have the advantages and disadvantages of modes of communication. The detached expert, for example, gives out a strong signal. He works on a one-to-one basis. He is effective but expensive. The general broadcast reaches a lot more people, but in a weaker, less persuasive way. The presence of a policeman in a trouble-making bar is more effective than a policeman who strolls by every hour or a message that floats into the bar from police headquarters on a loudspeaker. To control behavior at a busy intersection, a city can put in stop lights or post a patrolman. The two techniques have different costs; they produce different results. In general, rules backed by *surveillance* produce more compliance than rules communicated but left unpatrolled or controlled by spot checks.[61] Enforcement is so much more probable, but the norm is also *communicated* more effectively.

Litwak and Meyer speak about particular techniques; one can also group large clusters of similar techniques together into basic *mechanisms*. These are fundamental choices about how society will control and channel behavior and carry its policy into effect.

The market is one of these mechanisms. The market is private, but state action creates, invokes, or encourages it. The criminal justice system with its heavy use of coercion is another mechanism. Licensing and administrative regulation make up another common mechanism. Another mechanism is the allowance or promotion of bargaining and negotiation among affected parties; still another is choice through free elections; still another is random selection. These mechanisms are not exclusive. Every major modern society makes use of all of them. Each aspect of government or law—cartel policy, fish and game control, Sunday blue laws—is a system of its own with its own unique, subtle

---

[61]On rules and surveillance, see William A. Rushing, "Organizational Rules and Surveillance: Propositions in Comparative Organizational Analysis," 10 *Admin. Sci. Q.* 423 (1966). It strikes us as incorrect to contrast "surveillance" with "rules," as if these were two separate techniques. An overseer must be enforcing rules—and not necessarily informal ones. Rules never enforce themselves; there must be some check or surveillance.

mixture of methods of persuasion and control.[62]

Societies, however, can be classified according to whether they choose more or less of one mechanism or another: liberal, nineteenth-century England obviously encouraged the free market, while Maoist China does not. Mechanisms analytically break down into clusters of rules; each rule, in itself, contains a threat or a promise and creates its effect through sanctions, the peer group, or internalized norms. So, for example, the classical rules of contract law in Europe and the United States were rules no different in *form* from other rules, even though their overall effect may have been to sustain and promote a free market. Rules of criminal law (about theft, for example) supported these rules. Formally, such rules differ little from rules about contract and theft, promoting state socialism in the Soviet Union today.

ON NONENFORCEMENT OF LAWS: THE DECISION TO INVEST IN LEGAL EFFECTIVENESS

Nonenforcement is common in the law, perhaps as common as enforcement. Indeed, total enforcement of a rule is almost unknown. Low levels of enforcement balance high paper punishments. There are endless examples. In eighteenth-century England, death was the official punishment for most crimes including theft, but few thieves ended on the gallows. Juries refused to convict, or they brought in verdicts that allowed the convicted to live.

The opposite case is also possible—people can respond to sanctions that are illegitimate, unenforceable, or simply an invention. A hospital threatens to hold a patient until he pays his bill. In fact, a hospital is not a prison and has no right to keep people locked up, but patients may not know this. Enforced non-law—that is, false sanctions, inflicted illegitimately but under color of law[63]—thrives on victims who are powerless, ignorant, or insecure like the patients in the hospital. Among the poor, rights often lie fallow; lazy or overburdened civil servants prefer it that way.

Probably it is less true that non-law is enforced than that real law is unenforced or half-enforced. Nonenforcement is everywhere in the legal system. Hundreds of laws on the books are rarely or never en-

---

[62]See Robert A. Dahl and Charles E. Lindblom, *Politics, Economics and Welfare* (1953), for a perceptive discussion of these mechanisms.

[63]As distinguished from private or illegal sanctions, also often imposed on the helpless, but which everyone *knows* to be illegitimate—for example, keeping blacks out of a community by force and intimidation.

forced—many sex laws, for example. Prohibition was a famous case of partial nonenforcement.[64] In 1919, by constitutional amendment, the sale of alcohol became unlawful in the United States. Despite the law, millions of people drank. Everyone knew that liquor was available. Per capita consumption of alcohol actually rose during Prohibition. Many people were arrested, but compared to the number of drinkers, the arrests were minimal. One had to be blatant or unlucky to get caught. This fact diluted the deterrent effect of arrests. As more people drank, enforcement became even weaker, since the money and effort spent on enforcement did not keep pace with the public's drinking habits. The marijuana laws seem to be entering the same cycle of violation and unenforcement.

An unenforced law, known to be unenforced, may not be completely powerless. So long as it *exists*, there is some slight risk of revival. The law may have symbolic strength, or it may act as a draft on the bank of conscience. The very fact of nonenforcement, however, tends to cut the ground out from under a rule; it loses legitimacy. Imagine a room with a large "No Smoking" sign hanging on the wall. A man enters the room and sees dozens of people smoking. Then, he too smokes. He has caught a cue that the rule about smoking is not really enforced. The very *fact* that the rule is not enforced suggests a further point: that people in authority—whom he might otherwise respect—do not take the rule very seriously. When a rule is not enforced, the threat *and* the legitimacy of the rule both grow weaker.

A bare change in a sanction on paper does not add to or detract from the normative force of a rule. That much is obvious; but a huge leap one way or the other might give people a message: Society takes this conduct seriously (or has changed its mind in the opposite direction). If the law threatened to hang all jaywalkers or if the penalty for sodomy went down to a $1 fine, and if likely offenders knew about these changes, behavior might be altered for two reasons: the change in the sanction and what people thought of the change. Suppose an unenforced abortion law is abolished; the number of abortions increases. Was it the paper change that brought about this result—a signal that society had changed its collective mind, leading individuals to rethink the question on their own? Or is it that people never knew the odds against enforcement? What makes research, and even speculation, so difficult is that many factors may have influence. A city raises the fines

---

[64]See, in general, Andrew Sinclair, *Prohibition: The Era of Excess* (1962); Herbert Asbury, *The Great Illusion* (1950).

for jaywalking. There is a certain amount of propaganda, stories in the newspaper, etc., but enforcement remains feeble. Still, *something* is afoot, or the city would not have wanted to change the formal rules. Someone or some group must have agitated; some new factor must have intruded. If jaywalking now declines, we cannot be sure whether the new rule in some way led to attitude change and then behavior change, or whether the social cause of the change in the rule (whatever it was) led also to change in behavior.

Recent studies of criminal justice have shown a healthy realism on the subject of enforcement. The actors in the system do not behave as official rules decree. The police cannot and do not arrest everyone who commits a crime; they do not try.[65] They make choices constantly. The enforcement process is a gigantic filter.[66] At every stage, more people wriggle out of the net, even some who are clearly "guilty" of crime. For one reason or another, they are not caught, or not arrested, or not prosecuted. This nonenforcement is accepted as natural by almost everybody. Why not treat first offenders leniently? Why not let the policeman on his beat show some mercy?

Other nonenforcement and sporadic or unfair enforcement is more controversial. A notable recent literature sharply criticizes these as evils. Full enforcement is an ideal toward which the system should strive; what it cannot fully enforce, it should abandon, stripping away the criminal label. "Making and retaining criminal laws that can be only sporadically enforced," writes Herbert L. Packer, "can result in actual harm." "Respect for law" is likely to suffer; enforcement officers will be tempted "to use unsavory methods"; discretion is "unlikely to be exercised in any but an arbitrary kind of way"; this arbitrariness "is bound to contribute to the unfortunate sense of alienation on the part of those who see themselves as its victims."[67]

This critique is the more forceful, in that it is the laws regarding so-called "victimless" crimes—adultery, and homosexual behavior between consenting adults—which are sporadically enforced rather than, say, the laws regarding murder. These crimes, it is argued, hurt no one, and the laws that make them crimes should be abolished. Partial enforcement also has the look of oppression. The middle class gets away with its crimes; the lower class, especially blacks, falls victim to arrest. White-collar crime is punished more leniently than working-class

---

[65]See, in general, Wayne R. LaFave, *Arrest: The Decision to Take a Suspect into Custody* (1965); Johannes Feest and Erhard Blankenburg, *Die Definitionsmacht der Polizei* (1972).

[66]See, in general, Dallin H. Oaks and Warren Lehman, *A Criminal Justice System and the Indigent* (1968).

[67]Herbert L. Packer, *The Limits of Criminal Sanction* (1968), p. 287.

crime.[68] This is the argument. Morally, it is highly persuasive, but some of its conclusions—loss of faith in the law—remain to be proved.

Enforcement, of course, depends on the *resources* put into it. Ten policemen on busy streets can catch more speeders than five. Enforcement reflects, then, a two-stage decision: First, how much is the community willing generally to invest in law enforcement; and second, once that decision is made, how will the funds be doled out? Of ten policemen, how many are assigned to the traffic squad? How many will walk the beat at night? How many will help bring sick people to the hospital? How many will attack gambling and vice? Those who make these decisions will not only weigh traffic against burglary against vice, they will also weigh traffic control on Main Street against traffic control on Oak Street; vice in the white neighborhood against vice in the black neighborhood, and so on.[69] Two-stage decisions occur also on the civil side: how many courts, and what kind, how much subsidy to poor plaintiffs, how much investment in divorce courts, how much decentralization of justice, etc.

The quality and nature of justice depends on these decisions. Some societies spend more on enforcement than others, some spend more on investigation (perhaps to make sure the innocent do not suffer) or on police to exercise more social control. Amounts invested in the legal system are a rough key to what society expects the system to do and what functions it values most highly. Investment is not easy to measure. Bordua and Haurek, in an interesting essay, show that the increase in money spent on police between 1902 and 1960—on the surface a spectacular rise—shrinks to insignificance once one takes into account such factors as the explosive rise in the number of automobiles.[70]

Investment in enforcement can take many forms. To attack the problem of illegal parking, a city might raise fines to or keep the same fines and hire more policemen. The second plan is more expensive to institute, but might bring more compliance, or pay for itself in fines, or both. The city might also try new techniques—speed up court processes, slow them down, force people to appear in court rather than pay by mail.[71] The city might search for some technical improvement in

[68]Edwin Sutherland, *White Collar Crime* (1949); Steven Box and Julienne Ford, "The Facts Don't Fit: On the Relationship between Social Class and Criminal Behaviour," 19 *Soc. Rev.* 31 (1971).

[69]On the actual modes of deployment, see James Q. Wilson, *Varieties of Police Behavior* (1968).

[70]David J. Bordua and Edward W. Haurek, "The Police Budget's Lot," 13 *Am. Behav. Scientist* 667 (1970).

[71]The city might, of course, also create more parking spaces, improve public transportation, or close streets to all parking.

detecting violators. It might try to use methods of education or propaganda. To fight theft, a city can hire more police, buy more equipment, light the streets better, or set up youth clubs.

Each technique has its own cost and rate of return. It is difficult to generalize about investment decisions. One can only say that the decisions are value choices. The police have their zone of discretion and their values; so does the larger society. The police chief may deploy men as he sees fit, limited, of course, by the danger of some public outcry. A police chief can also try to get stiff ordinances passed or raise money for more policemen. (A stiff ordinance, on its face, is much cheaper than authorization for more men.) His decisions and those of other agencies about investment are legal acts to be explained on the same basis as other legal acts, such as "the laws" themselves.

Often, if a law is imperfectly enforced, the reasons lie in the history of the law and, beyond that, in the social forces at work outside in society. Quite commonly, a law is born crippled, designed or doomed to nonenforcement. When this happens, we suspect some sort of rough trade-off, ending the struggle behind passage. Those who wanted the law get it for symbolic effect, but in a toothless or unfunded version. Early fair housing ordinances in American cities can serve as examples. Often they set up mechanisms to "conciliate" or "mediate," but lacked machinery for enforcement. What had happened? The forces on both sides of the issue were strong. Blacks and their allies were perhaps strong enough to get an ordinance passed, but not to get both passage *and* enforcement—even the threat of enforcement on paper. This, we suspect, is one reason why so many laws on the statute books are merely symbolic. Not that interest groups are so hungry for symbols, but because symbols are what they must settle for.[72]

The Sherman Antitrust Act (1890) was another sort of compromise.[73] This famous law was worded very vaguely. It made monopolies and contracts "in restraint of trade" illegal. The statute did not define these terms or set up any mechanism to enforce the law. These deficiencies were not accidental. In the background was a major political struggle. Small businessmen and the ordinary, middle-class citizen demanded action against the trusts; big business was powerful and resisted. The Sherman Act was a compromise. Congress had indeed done something about the trusts: It had outlawed them, on paper. But

---

[72]See pp. 50–51; on housing statutes, see Davis McEntire, *Residence and Race* (1960), pp. 278–280; an excellent account of the passage of a compromise civil rights law (Massachusetts) is in Leon Mayhew, *Law and Equal Opportunity* (1968), ch. 4.

[73]On its background, see William Letwin, *Law and Economic Policy in America, the Evolution of the Sherman Antitrust Act* (1965).

the law was vague and tentative. Real decisions on enforcement were yet to be made; they would be delayed until some later time and delegated to the Department of Justice and the courts.

The history of the death penalty in the United States is also instructive. In recent years, public opinion has fluctuated radically. Probably, by the 1960s, a bare majority of articulate, vocal people were against capital punishment, but the defenders were also strong.[74] The death penalty was on the books, but it was rarely carried out. There were so many appeals, petitions, stays, and delays that persons could and did sit on death row for ten or fifteen years. This was the form this "compromise" took. Of course, the delays merely strengthened the conviction of those who thought the penalty was cruel and unfair. It made the convicts into victims and weakened public support. It helped bring about the intervention of the Supreme Court, which tipped the scales against the laws.

Many compromises of the type we are discussing are apparent on the surface of the laws. Others are not; they are matters of enforcement. Nothing is more typical of law than the constant internal haggling over deployment of money and troops.

THE TECHNOLOGY OF ENFORCEMENT

One way to change the level of enforcement is through technology. Someone might invent, at last, a leak-proof hose. Society as a whole may not feel like investing more money in law enforcement, but a breakthrough might possibly produce a better yield, just as better seeds and machines can grow more corn from an unchanging acreage of farmland.

Fingerprints, ballistic science, the "breathalyser," radar to catch speeders—all these have benefited law enforcement along with such illicit means as wiretapping. Technology also lends a hand in civil suits —through photography, forensic medicine, blood-typing for paternity suits, etc. Many technical advances are neutral, that is, they make processes quicker or more accurate but do not tilt the scales toward one side or another. The impact of science on criminal justice, however, is subtle and far-reaching. New ways to detect crime and catch the guilty mean that fewer cases of real doubt need to be brought before judge and jury. The judge and the jury weigh evidence and make judgments only on matters far more individual and discretionary.

Police science, then, revolutionizes criminal justice. The trial is less common in the life cycle of criminal justice than it was a century

---

[74]The minority seems to have become a majority again.

ago. Most of those accused of crime plead guilty; most who go to trial are convicted. In 1850, for example, the guilty plea was less common, and the judge and jury tended more to acquit than today.[75] Only a few big cities had police; fingerprinting and ballistics were unknown. The modern crime-fighter catches more criminals; also, in the past, the innocent were not so efficiently filtered out *before* trial. Technology has shifted the balance away from judges and juries toward professionals and the police.[76]

Social investment in enforcement, of course, is not static or unchanging; indeed, the great concern about crime in the cities has touched off a wave of big spending on police and police technology. This is important, because technical improvement is no accident; it comes from investment in research. Some crimes, no doubt, will yield to technology just as some diseases yield to modern medicine. We noted, for example, how hard it is to detect and control the crime of polluting the sea. But satellites might patrol the sea lanes. General Electric has developed a technique to "tag" oil tanker cargoes with magnetic dust; ships that pollute the ocean would leave a telltale chemical track.[77] Technology might also reduce or eliminate the side effects of some sanctions, producing, as it were, a pollution-free engine. Prisons, for example, leave prisoners bitter and scarred. Some have suggested letting prisoners roam free, watched by electronic eyes; the men would live in prison without stigma or walls. The idea raises moral and technical issues, but it is worthwhile to explore.[78]

Generally, we assume that it is good to make crime-fighting more efficient, that the more control, the better. This may be true for murder and rape. But technological change has nontechnological consequences. It can alter a delicate balance between subjects and authorities. People do not always *want* more efficiency. They resent the use of radar in enforcing speed limits. They like speed limits, in general, and support, in other words, a particular level of enforcement. At this level, only blatant violators are arrested. Radar threatens to upset this balance. Similarly, many people feel uneasy at the thought that a com-

---

[75]On this point, see Lawrence M. Friedman, *A History of American Law* (1973), p. 252. The evidence is fragmentary.

[76]Interestingly enough, these changes can take place without changing formal rules in the short run.

[77]*New York Times*, Nov. 13, 1972, p. 73, col. 4.

[78]See Ralph K. Schwitzgebel, "Issues in the Use of an Electronic Rehabilitation System with Chronic Recidivists," 3 *Law and Society Rev.* 597 (1969).

puter may check their tax returns. They do not object to enforcement, but enough is enough.

A NOTE ON STIGMA AND SHAME

Most of the rewards and punishments discussed so far have been open, official, and direct. There are other, unofficial ways to punish and reward; some are intended, some may be latent or unconscious. Shame and degradation are forms of punishment. Arrest and trial inflict great suffering, even on those who are ultimately set free. It is punishing to wait for trial in a dirty cell, anxious, ashamed, alone, exposed to cruelty and indifference, eating bad food, breathing foul air, cut off from family and friends, and fearful of the future. Many employers fire a worker who is arrested. Shame, loss of status, hostility of neighbors and friends, and personal discomfort are common penalties on top of the official ones. The state may deliberately work up these side effects. Harold Garfinkel, in a striking phrase, has called the criminal trial a "status degradation ceremony."[79] It prepares a man for descent into the hell of a lower, less honorable existence. It strips him progressively of honor. In the military, after a soldier was found guilty, insignia of rank were publicly ripped from his uniform. The trial as drama and ritual leads the accused ceremonially to his lower status.

Stigma is a pejorative label attached to a person or group.[80] *Shame* is the inner state of the person stigmatized.[81] Legal and quasi-legal systems frequently try to induce shame as a sanction. The reprimand is a common punishment. It works, when it does, because it stigmatizes (influencing onlookers) or produces repentance through shame. The Uniform Code of Military Justice names "admonition or reprimand" as a form of sanction[82]; judges make use of it all over the world instead

---

[79]Harold Garfinkel, "Conditions of Successful Degradation Ceremonies," 61 *Am. J. Sociology* 420 (1956).

[80]For a perceptive treatment, see Erving Goffman, *Stigma, Notes on the Management of Spoiled Identity* (1963).

[81]Supposedly, shame affects the lower orders less than the middle class, just as the white-collar criminal is supposed to have a greater horror of jail. Whether this is so or not remains to be investigated. A study of men on skid row in Seattle found, somewhat surprisingly, that these men were extremely sensitive to "degradation." Half of them, asked to name "the worst thing about appearing in court on a drunk charge," answered: "public humiliation." To stay several days in the "drunk tank" made a man look unkempt, "sick and dirty." "To have to appear in front of a lot of people in that condition is very humiliating." "You look like a bum." James P. Spradley, *You Owe Yourself a Drunk* (1970), pp. 190–191.

[82]See 50 U.S.C.A. § 571 (a).

of or on top of other forms of punishment. Maureen Mileski, observing a lower criminal court, noted that judges used "situational sanctioning"—scolding, warning, and lecturing—in a definite minority of cases.[83]

Stigma and similar side sanctions are dangerous weapons—the more so because they are tempting to the state. Ordinary sanctions cost money. Degradation, however, enlists public opinion, creating a powerful sanction with few *direct* costs. There is a similar temptation to make prisons unpleasant. Of course, the crueler aspects of prisons, present and past, have many explanations.[84] Legislatures were never willing to spend money on prisons; people are disinclined to "coddle" criminals, and an unpleasant place seemed all the more likely to deter.

Before 1800, prison was not as dominating a punishment as it is today. The prison rose, in part, in response to the decline in other means of delivering stigma. The tight-knit colonial communities used whipping, branding, and the stocks to punish deviants. These were painful, of course, but they also held deviants up to the scorn of their neighbors. The colonials thought or hoped that public scandal would bring black sheep into line. They also hoped to induce a healing measure of *shame.* For incorrigibles, there was banishment or death.[85]

Stigma is built into civil law as well. Here too it has social and economical overtones. Welfare law is a notable example. Political leaders, among others, have felt that it is important to keep welfare shameful and painful, so that only the most destitute and desperate would be willing to go on welfare.[86] Big signs identify and label public housing

---

[83]Maureen Mileski, "Courtroom Encounters: An Observation Study of a Lower Criminal Court," 5 *Law and Society Rev.* 473, 521–531 (1971).

[84]The penitentiary, an American invention of the early nineteenth century, imposed utter solitude and silence on its prisoners, but this was ruthlessness with a point. The theory was that this kind of regimen would cure criminals of their propensity for crime. See David Rothman, *The Discovery of the Asylum, Social Order and Disorder in the New Republic* (1971); Lawrence M. Friedman, *A History of American Law* (1973), pp. 259–261, 519–524; W. David Lewis, *From Newgate to Dannemora, the Rise of the Penitentiary in New York, 1796–1848* (1965).

[85]In Massachusetts Bay Colony, under laws of 1648, first offense burglars were to be "branded on the forehead with the letter (B)." The second offense brought a whipping and another branding; third offenders were to be "put to death, as being incorrigible." *Laws and Liberties of Massachusetts, 1648* (ed. Max Farrand, 1929), p. 4. The avoidance of shame is another reason why people do not park overtime, when a policeman is around. Of course, the punishment—a ticket—is absolutely certain; but in addition, the policeman can and will give violators a dressing-down.

[86]The amount of stigma and its effect on behavior are disputed. See Joel F. Handler and Ellen J. Hollingsworth, *The "Deserving Poor," A Study of Welfare Administration* (1971), pp. 164–178.

projects in the United States. Council housing in Britain is anonymous. New York has begun to insist that people on welfare must come in personally to pick up their checks. This may be enough to discourage thousands from collecting their money.

In some societies, it is shameful to go to law at all. For example, Koreans feel strongly on this point:

> The vast majority of the population . . . has never been to a courthouse. Furthermore, they were proud of that fact. [Going to a courthouse] . . . they regarded . . . as tantamount to being asked whether they had ever been convicted of a crime. . . . [T]o the average Korean the courthouse . . . symbolizes a dehumanized mode of sanctioning the public order.[87]

Even in the United States, where litigation is common, divorce and bankruptcy carry a certain flavor of failure if not of stigma and shame. Actions for libel, contested divorces, and paternity suits may ruin lives and careers. They may also bring about open, public vindication. In any event, civil trials are tedious and disruptive, which may be their most serious side effect. For these reasons, people tend to avoid lawsuits, if they possibly can, except where the money incentives are overwhelming, as in certain personal injury cases. Stigma and shame, in short, often add to the power of a sanction and discourage use of law. In either case, the public saves some money.

Stigma and shame are side effects of the processes of justice. The impact of stigma depends on the audience. The point of it, like the point of the sanction itself, is to act as a deterrent. Great crowds used to watch public hangings. Presumably they learned a lesson from the hanging and from the derision and public display. At school, when a child is put in a corner with a dunce cap, shame is supposed to teach him a lesson, and the stigma teaches the same lesson to his classmates.

One problem with stigma is that it may overpunish; as a sanction, it is difficult to control. Nor does it have a clear beginning, middle, and end like a prison term. Schwartz and Skolnick, in an interesting study of stigma, found that ex-convicts had a hard time finding jobs. Employers did not want to hire them. Malpractice suits, on the other hand, did not hurt doctors' careers; doctors who lost these cases did not suffer in their practice. This was because the "institutional environment" was "protective." Other doctors rallied to their defense; local medical societies supported their cases; in one instance, a doctor even thought that

---

[87]Pyong-Choon Hahm, "The Decision Process in Korea," in G. Schubert and D. Danelski, eds., *Comparative Judicial Behavior* (1969), pp. 19, 22.

other doctors sent him referrals out of sympathy.[88] Since stigma is a *community* reaction, it varies with the community. Jail stigmatizes, but northern liberals, convicted for civil rights work in the South, did not lose status with their peers. Convictions for draft evasion during the Vietnam war probably carried far less stigma than similar convictions during World War II.

Stigma has definite limits, and it can suffer from overkill.[89] If a person labelled "thief" is cut off from normal society, he may be driven to the point where he must steal or starve. Stigma needs a public. The victim or his group must agree that the behavior is shameful, that the punishment degrades. Stigma, then, is blunted for people who go to jail out of principle or whose peer group does not buy the official label. For those to whom jail is a mark of manhood, a prison record is not a source of stigma or shame. Also, if everybody goes to jail, jail loses stigma and therefore shame as well. Hence, stigma and shame are, in a way, self-limiting. Finally, stigma and shame are not "pure" sanctions at work. Stigma is a mixture of official sanctions and the social factor; shame is a mixture of official sanctions and the inner voice.

---

[88]Richard D. Schwartz and Jerome H. Skolnick, "Two Studies of Legal Stigma," 10 *Social Problems*, 133 (1962).

For a recent attempt, by German criminologists, to explore the concept of status degradation empirically in traffic court—alas, not too favorable a locale—see Karl F. Schumann and Gerd Winter, "Zur Analyse des Strafverfahrens," 3 *Kriminologisches Journal* 136 (1971).

[89]The so-called "labeling theorists" argue, in essence, that deviance "is *not* a quality of the act the person commits but rather a consequence of the application by others of rules and sanctions to an 'offender'." Howard S. Becker, *Outsiders, Studies in the Sociology of Deviance* (1963), p. 9; see Edwin M. Schur, *Labeling Deviant Behavior, Its Sociological Implications* (1971); Bernard A. Thorsell and Lloyd W. Klemke, "The Labeling Process: Reinforcement and Deterrent?" 6 *Law and Society Rev.* 393 (1972). They stress the importance of stigma. Labeling transforms people into "outsiders"; this makes it more likely that they will break the law; or, what is equally important, more likely that others will treat them *as if* they were breaking the law. The labeling process—the use of stigma—will often be counterproductive; stigma generates behavior that earns the stigma rather than reducing it. Convicts may not get "cured" by prison and post-prison life but become "hardened criminals" instead. One reason is that society labels them as criminals and gives them no way out.

Chapter V
When Is Law Effective?
Part II

THE IMPACT OF LAW: PEER GROUPS AND SUBCULTURES

Throughout the discussion of sanctions we assumed, on the whole, a fairly simple situation: A legal actor, with authority, gives orders to a subject or lays down rules for him to follow. No doubt it is good to begin with this simple model in mind. The subject makes his private calculus of benefits and costs and decides how to respond. If we raise his costs or change his benefits, he moves his behavior from one square to another on the checkerboard.

But we know life is rarely that simple. First, "the law" is not the only source of punishments and rewards. The subject lives and works in society. He has a family, friends, co-workers; he is a member of a church, club, clan, or gang. All of these groups are sources of rewards and punishments too. Second, he is not a machine but a moral being with ideas and values of his own. Commands filter through his moral screen; they do not come out unscathed. Third, we cannot assume that our subject is entirely inert. A person stopped by a policeman does not always take the ticket sheepishly. He can argue with the policeman, he can make excuses, or he can offer a bribe. These activities are neither compliance nor noncompliance. They are, rather, attempts to bend the sanction in one direction or another. We can call this behavior *bargaining* or *interaction*. Also, a driver can pass up the opportunity to bargain, take the ticket, pay the fine, but at the same time complain to the mayor and police chief about the way things are done. If he feels strongly enough, he could try to change the law; in extreme cases, he might lead a revolution. We call these reactions *feedback.* Or he might alter his conduct in some other way, in the light of the rule—for example, forbidden to steal, he may set fires. We call these *side effects.*

We begin with some discussion of the complications that come from the fact that the people to whom rules are addressed are not isolated beings but creatures in society. They are subject to social influences. For convenience, we can call these influences those of the peer group, with a certain loss of accuracy, since the family is hardly a peer group. In all societies, there are dialects of culture. In a large country, there will be many cultures, that is, many different folkways and norms. Each subculture rewards and punishes behavior, and subcultures are by no means always consistent with other subcultures or the official culture. Quite frequently an official or dominant culture tries to punish behavior, which, at the same time, a subculture rewards or supports; or it may reward behavior that the subculture punishes. There are endless examples. The Mormons practiced polygamy; the general government ruthlessly stamped this out.[1] Every guerrilla is someone's hero and someone's deadly enemy. Cultural pluralism is extremely common and a classic source of unenforceability of laws. An increase in real punishment or reward should bring about behavior change. If, however, a competing culture increases its *own* sanctions to offset the official ones, the effect will be lost. A government fighting guerrillas offers money to informers, sends troops, and punishes those who give food to the rebels. But the rebels themselves may escalate their acts—extorting grain, killing informers, and so on. Again, the government cracks down on drug sellers, arrests smugglers, and cuts off part of the supply. Demand is inelastic, and the drug culture offers more money for drugs. The increased reward can offset the higher risk of punishment from the state. In plural societies, it may be nearly impossible to enforce laws strongly opposed by a compact subculture. The Soviet government learned this, to its grief, when it tried to change the status of Moslem women in the traditional societies of central Asia.[2]

We do not need a subculture to find such results. Peers are a mighty power even in homogeneous countries. There are always groups and cliques: the dental society, the family, the children in school, the union. Each can be, at times, as powerful a source of rewards and punishments as the state. Particularly interesting and important are

---

[1] Gustive O. Larson, *The "Americanization" of Utah for Statehood* (1971).

[2] Gregory J. Massell, "Law as an Instrument of Revolutionary Change in a Traditional Milieu, the Case of Soviet Central Asia," 2 *Law and Society Rev.* 179 (1968).

those pressures on young people to do acts that earn them the label of "delinquent,"[3] or the pressures of the prison community, the "society of captives," which in many ways pulls harder on prisoners than wardens, guards, or the outside world.[4] A face-to-face group, in particular, has important sources of strength. It may not have a monopoly of power, but it can deliver its rewards and punishments quickly, effectively, and without red tape.

These rewards and punishments, abstractly considered, are no different in their effect on behavior than rewards and punishments that the state administers. The rules of the game are the same. More peer group punishment, other things being equal, will reduce the conduct which is punished. Uncertainty and delay in delivering the sanction have the same effect as they do for state sanctions. The surrounding society can be compared to a little government, and the effects of its "legal" acts plotted on a graph. Here too, different behaviors and groups would produce different curves on the graph. Linear relationships would be uncommon; most curves would flatten out. The comments made in the prior chapter could be repeated with a bit of translation. Again, what counts is not so much peer group reaction as a person's perception of it—what he fears and expects. And the actual sanction is less important than the promise or threat.[5]

The power of the group is a commonplace of social science; and every student of law in action mentions it in some way, but it is hard to find much systematic treatment of the subject. This may be because group behavior varies so from culture to culture. It is not an easy task to generalize. Some subcultures almost amount to shadow governments, dealing out real rewards and punishments very much like the state. Small gangs and cliques, on the other hand, lack many tools that official justice has in its armory. Usually, for example, groups will not give money awards or extract any fines. The power of the peer group sometimes consists of nothing more than the fear: "What will the neighbors think?" This, however, may be a powerful sanction and inflict a terrible wound; ostracism is one of the harshest punishments known.

As we noted earlier, shame depends for effect on whether the person accepts a shameful label. Moreover, in plural societies, the ties

---

[3]See, for example, Richard Cloward and Lloyd Ohlin, *Delinquency and Opportunity* (1960).

[4]See Gresham Sykes, *The Society of Captives* (1958); Stanton Wheeler, "Socialization in Correctional Communities," 26 *Am. Soc. Rev.* 697 (1961).

[5]See, especially, Richard D. Schwartz and Jerome H. Skolnick, "Two Studies of Legal Stigma," 10 *Social Problems* 133 (1962).

of some groups, religions, for example, are weaker than in traditional society; and the disaffected can leave. A Roman Catholic, Mormon, or Jew can walk away from his church in the United States. The state is not so easy to elude. In traditional societies within nations, one can perhaps escape the state more easily than the clan, tribe, or group. The question is, Who exerts close, daily pressure on a person? The strength of the group, like the strength of the state, depends, in part, on its ability to ferret out deviant behavior. The group is not necessarily better than police at detecting violations of incest taboos and enforcing them.

Peers are a source of modeling or inspiration as well as of sanctions. If a person wants to conform, the behavior of his models will powerfully influence his conduct, even when the models themselves do not punish or reward. Also, as we noted before, people pick up cues from those around them on whether to take official norms seriously. The man who walks into a room full of men and women smoking, in total disregard of "No Smoking" signs, may be affected, even though the smokers are strangers and take no notice of him.

There is a certain tendency in legal literature to treat culture as a negative factor. It is recognized that people have habits, customs, and traditions and that the state finds it hard to chip away at strong group habits. Hence, culture is conservative and a barrier to modernization. It is true that a law which goes against the grain, culturally speaking, will be hard to enforce and probably ineffective. Prohibition is the hackneyed example. But the converse is equally true. Laws that make use of the culture and draw on its strength can be tremendously effective. When a legal system contrives to cut with the grain, it multiplies its strength. Actual force—even the threat of force—is costly; if people obeyed speed limits out of deep respect or blind tradition, society could save a fortune in police cars and salaries alone. A law that can tap some underground spring of goodwill or strength in the culture will get vastly more for each dollar of enforcement or persuasion.

To tap the culture does not mean telling people to do what they want to do anyway, such as taking a holiday on Christmas, or forbidding acts they would find abhorrent, such as cannibalism. It means asking them to do *new* things but in a palatable, comfortable, or convenient way. The legal system does this regularly and quite unconsciously. It uses, for example, money rewards in a money economy. The legal day of rest is Sunday in accordance with religious tradition. As this tradition breaks down, so do Sunday laws. Those who think a negative income tax should replace present welfare laws are hoping thereby for a free ride on tax laws and tax institutions which are comfortable and familiar by now.[6] Every law in some way invokes familiar habits, institutions, or symbols. In so doing, the legal system tries to hook on to proven instruments, to husband scarce resources in this way.

What is the strength of the peer group influence on legal behavior? In one study, experimenters put before English college students certain propositions, for example: "A man who is drunk in a public place is acting in an immoral manner even if he is not disorderly." The students were asked whether they agreed or disagreed. Later, the same questions were repeated, but this time some students got new "information." An opinion poll, they were told, showed "strong" reactions of other college students to certain propositions. Another group was told that some of the behavior described in the propositions was against the law. Students tended now to shift their own opinions to conform with the law and with their peers. The shift toward the peers was more marked.[7]

This was, of course, a study of attitude change; behavior was not at issue. The students were all much the same age, all English, and all sharing more or less a common social background. Would middle-aged housewives, Eskimos, or steelworkers have reacted in this way? One wonders, too, why the shift toward the peers took place. Did the students rethink their premises in the light of fresh information? Did they simply want to conform? Again, how typical were the propositions and of what? The "information" in the retest had to be meaningful—it had to be fresh information and credible or else the test would not work. The experimenters, therefore, had to choose propositions which college students on the whole would not *know* as legal or illegal, as popular or unpopular with their peers. One could not ask whether "A man who kills his mother with an axe in a public place is acting in an immoral manner." First of all, no student would change his mind on the retest, regardless of what he was told; secondly, students know that murder is illegal. They could not be told that it was not, nor that a poll of college students showed that 80 percent approved of the act. Hence, the experimenters had to draft rather marginal—one might almost say trivial—

---

[6]See Christopher Green, *Negative Taxes and the Poverty Problem* (1967).

[7]The study is Leonard Berkowitz and Nigel Walker, "Laws and Moral Judgments," 30 *Sociometry* 410 (1967). The study investigated whether shifts in views correlated with how students scored on personality tests. There were some suggestive results. For example, "highly authoritarian" students were "quite susceptible to peer influence" but "not significantly affected by knowledge of the law." Ibid. at 422.

See also D. G. Myers, F. B. Schreiber, and D. J. Viel, "Effects of Discussion on Opinions Concerning Illegal Behavior," 92 *J. Soc. Psychology* 77 (1974).

propositions. These were propositions no one had thought of much, about which no one had firm, fixed opinions. These propositions, then, were not a fair, random, or representative sample of the universe of moral propositions. They represented a special subset. The study opens a door to the study of how peer groups cause shifts in opinion, but many questions remain to be answered.

There are also a few studies of behavior. In one experiment, pedestrians were observed in New York City. Many walked across the street in defiance of a "Don't Walk" sign. If a model, hired by the experimenters, stood on the corner and abided by the rule, the violation rate dropped significantly. If the model broke the rule, there was some tendency for the rate of violation to rise, too. Since, in all cases, the chance of a formal sanction was close to zero, the model seems responsible for these changes. What the mental mechanism is remains unclear. The model was a stranger and hence not *literally* one of the peers.[8]

One final point about the peer group. We have discussed its role as a rival to the state, sending its own sanction messages to persons who are subject to official rules as well. But the group can send messages to the government, too. It can, for example, play a role in *instigating* official enforcement. Many laws depend upon and presuppose informers. There are many crimes where the police arrest only when someone complains. Criminal cases, as Donald Black has pointed out, often "pass through a moral filter in the citizen population before the state assumes its enforcement role." The police are "invoked . . . through a reactive process." Criminal law, then, is not so very different from contract and tort law whose rules lie sleeping until a private citizen brings them to life. The deterrent function often depends upon "citizen willingness to mobilize the criminal law." Without this, there is no enforcement, and no real sanction can be imposed.[9] This, then, is another case where the legal system relies on the culture to breathe life into its rules.

---

[8]Lionel I. Dannick, "Influence of an Anonymous Stranger on a Routine Decision to Act or Not to Act: An Experiment in Conformity," 14 *Sociological Q.* 127 (1973); A. M. Barch, D. Trumbo, and J. Nangle, "Social Setting and Conformity to a Legal Requirement," 55 *J. Abnormal and Soc. Psychology* 396 (1957); M. Lefkowitz, R. R. Blake, and J. S. Mouton, "Status Factors in Pedestrian Violation of Traffic Signals," 51 *J. Abnormal and Soc. Psychology* 704 (1955). See also Stanley Milgram, "Liberating Effects of Group Pressure," 1 *J. Personality and Soc. Psychology* 127 (1965); Johannes Feest, "Compliance with Legal Regulations," 2 *Law and Society Rev.* 447, 453 (1968), noting that drivers who are *accompanied* observe stop sign regulations better than those who are alone.

[9]Donald J. Black, "The Social Organization of Arrest," 23 *Stan. L. Rev.* 1087, 1104–05 (1971).

THE THIRD FORCE: THE IMPACT OF THE INNER VOICE

The third major force in compliance is the inner voice—the conscience, moral feelings, the desire to obey, the sense of right. No one will deny the importance of these factors. People do not always do what their inner voices say, but people respond to this force at least sometimes. Here too the literature is long on speculation and short on measurement and deeds.[10]

We speak about conscience, the sense of right, and related concepts quite loosely. "Doing what is right" can refer to a number of distinct though related motives. One of these we can call *civic-mindedness*. This is the sense that we ought to obey a rule, even though not in our *personal* interest, because it is good for other people or for people as a whole. We can call *morality* the wish to follow norms, because they are God's will, or good ethics, or a religious duty rather than useful to others or to us. Still another motive is the sense of *fairness*, the idea that a rule or behavior deserves adherence, support, or obedience because of some formal quality—for example, that the rule or behavior applies to everybody equally. Regardless of what I think about the rule "Don't Walk on the Grass," if I think it applies to me and to other people too, who are in the same category, and *they* obey, or have obeyed, or seem about to obey, I might decide to obey myself whether or not the rule is otherwise to my liking, because if I exempted myself it would be "unfair."[11] Strictly speaking, then, if I pass up the chance to walk on the grass, I am moved by a sense of fairness only if I think it would be wrong for me to walk, because others had not, regardless of whether I thought the rule made sense in any way. Fairness might also influence my perception of an institution—whether I think courts behave "fairly" in general has an effect on my opinion of the courts[12] and perhaps on how willing I am to comply with what they say.

So far we have mentioned motives that do not depend on any sort

---

[10]But see the study by Leonard Berkowitz and Nigel Walker, "Laws and Moral Judgments," 30 *Sociometry* 410 (1967) already discussed, and Richard D. Schwartz and Sonya Orleans, "On Legal Sanctions," 34 *U. Chi. L. Rev.* 274 (1967).

[11]"Fairness," of course, is a complex concept. June L. Tapp and Felice J. Levine asked children "What is a fair rule?" The children, in the main, gave three answers: A rule is fair when it applies to everyone equally, when the rule is rational or reasonable, and when there is consensus or participation in making it. Tapp and Levine, "Persuasion to Virtue, A Preliminary Statement," 4 *Law and Society Rev.* 565 (1970). In our terms, the first of these is "fairness"; the second probably means merely that the rule is substantively sound; the third is "legitimacy."

[12]See Richard L. Engstrom and Micheal W. Giles, "Expectations and Images: A Note on Diffuse Support for Legal Institutions," 6 *Law and Society Rev.* 631 (1972).

of general faith in law or in authorities. That faith may be a motive in its own right. *Trust* is the idea that people in authority must know what they are doing, must be experts, must be wise, and must have information and good policies. The president mobilizes troops; he must know something about the situation that we do not understand. The Food and Drug Administration orders a chemical to be removed from our food. The administration must have tested it and found it harmful. The city turns a two-way street into a one-way street. It must have consulted a traffic engineer.

Quite different from this is faith or trust in structures or procedures. This is what we call *legitimacy*. The concept, in legal and political thought, owes much of its currency to Max Weber. According to Weber, a rule, custom, order, or system is "legitimate," when it is "endowed with the prestige of exemplariness and obligatoriness."[13] Put more simply, but negatively, when people obey a rule, not because of self-interest, trust, or a belief in the *substantive* value of the law, the rule has legitimacy. Legitimacy refers to a general attitude toward law, or the rules, or the system. It is not an attitude about the content of rules, nor about their rightness or wrongness in an ethical sense. Judgments about legitimacy are judgments about form, procedure, or source—about the way the rule came about or about the rule-maker and *his* authority. Legitimacy is different from *trust*, because trust rests on beliefs about facts. Even a very trusting person admits that he might be wrong. We can persuade him, for instance, that the FDA made a mistake or that the president did. But legitimacy does not rest on facts and in the individual case cannot be rebutted. For example, a law is legitimate, because it was passed in some proper, legal way. A verdict in a trial is legitimate, because the judge and jury followed the rules and gave the defendant his proper day in court, as prescribed by law.[14] A devout Roman Catholic accepts as legitimate the church's rule against birth control pills. The rule comes from the pope, and the pope, he believes, is the vicar of Christ. This rule, then, is *moral* as well as legitimate to him; here two categories overlap.

---

[13]Max Rheinstein, ed., *Max Weber on Law in Economy and Society* (1954), p. 4; see also Michael J. Petrick, "The Supreme Court and Authority Acceptance," 21 *Western Pol. Q.* 5 (1968); Ted Robert Gurr, *Why Men Rebel* (1970), pp. 183–192.

[14]Niklas Luhmann, in his interesting book, *Legitimation durch Verfahren* (1969) defines legitimacy as a "generalized willingness to accept decisions whose content is as yet undetermined, within certain limits of tolerance" (p. 28). This definition is quite congruent with the remarks in the text; legitimacy is an attitude toward norms that result from certain *procedures*.

See also David Adamany, "Legitimacy, Realigning Elections, and the Supreme Court," 1973 *Wis. L. Rev.* 790, 801–807.

Each component that makes up the third factor is an assumed attitude or feeling that serves as a *motive* inducing compliance. Each one, therefore, has its negative side—an attitude or feeling that serves as a motive for not complying or, in aggravated cases, for flouting or disobeying a norm. For example, we assumed that some people might feel they ought to keep off the grass, because it would not be "fair" to disobey. This attitude depends on the fairness of the *norm;* if the norm is felt to be unfair, there may perhaps be some tendency to disobey or to discontinue using the norm. Similarly, one might feel inclined to disobey because the civic-minded or moral thing to do is *not* to obey (or to disobey) perhaps because the norm in question is itself uncivic-minded or immoral. The opposite of trust is distrust; and the opposite of legitimate is illegitimate. Norms that are not legitimate, or are downright illegitimate, will generate quite different motivations than those that are legitimate.

LEGITIMACY AND CULTURE

The elements of the third factor are inner attitudes, and they vary from culture to culture. For example, the degree of respect for law is different in different countries. In a poll, 66 percent of a sample of Germans agreed with the statement "You should obey the laws, even if you do not think that they are just." In Holland, only 47 percent and in Poland, only 45 percent agreed with a similar statement.[15] Questions on specific institutions, such as the courts, would probably also uncover cultural variations. Adam Podgórecki, in a related study of Polish attitudes toward law, found that women, older people, better educated people, and white-collar workers agreed that legal norms deserved "respect" as "valid . . . law" rather than for instrumental reasons, compared with men, younger people, the less educated, and unskilled workers.[16]

Some research has been done in the United States on attitudes toward the United States Supreme Court, and, interestingly, how particular decisions of the Court *affect* these attitudes. The results so far seem inconclusive.[17] And some research suggests that "general compli-

---

[15]Wolfgang Kaupen, "Public Opinion of the Law in a Democratic Society," in Adam Podgórecki et al., *Knowledge and Opinion about Law* (1973), pp. 43, 46.

[16]Adam Podgórecki, "Public Opinion on Law," ibid., pp. 65, 83.

[17]Much of the research is on the impact of the so-called school prayer cases in the 1960s, when the Court outlawed the practice of reading the Bible and saying prayers in public schools. *Engel* v. *Vitale,* 370 U.S. 421 (1962); *Abington School District* v. *Schempp,* 374 U.S. 203 (1963); see Kenneth M. Dolbeare and Phillip E. Hammond, *The School Prayer Decisions, from Court Policy to Local Practice* (1971); Donald R. Reich, "School-

ance attitudes correlate poorly with specific compliance attitudes," that is, people who eagerly tell an interviewer that people should always obey the law or that the law is always just will violate their own principle when asked about specific legal or ethical dilemmas.[18]

Max Weber distinguished between three "ultimate principles" of legitimation, that is, three types of valid authority; these principles reflect differences in culture. *Traditional* authority is, for example, the authority of a patriarch. A second type of authority is *charismatic;* it is a "surrender to the extraordinary"—authority that flows from "belief in *charisma,* i.e., actual revelation or grace resting in . . . a person as a savior, a prophet, or a hero."[19] Charisma is the authority of a Moses, a Christ. There are charismatic elements in the presidency, if not in the president, and in heads of state generally, especially in non-parliamentary countries. But as Weber used the word, charisma represented a dramatic, personal magic that validated legal acts without recourse to tradition or utility. This magic has always been rare.

Weber's third category of authority is the *rational.* One obeys norms because they are "law." Society makes rules about rules. The rules made by the rules have rational authority. The process is "rational" in the ordinary meaning of making sense; it is certainly conscious and deliberate. When *rational* legitimacy prevails, obedience "is . . . given to the norms rather than to the person." There is nothing mystic about this obedience. It stems from respect for the underlying process. People obey the law, "because it is the law." This means they have general respect for procedures and for the system. They feel, for some reason, that they should obey, if Congress passes a law, if a judge makes a decision, if the city council passes an ordinance. If they were forced to explain why, they might refer to some concept of democracy, or the rule of law, or some other popular theory sustaining the political system.[20]

---

house Religion and the Supreme Court: A Report on Attitudes of Teachers and Principals and on School Practices in Wisconsin and Ohio," 23 *J. Legal Ed.* 123 (1971); William K. Muir, Jr., *Prayer in the Public Schools: Law and Attitude Change* (1967); Richard M. Johnson, *The Dynamics of Compliance* (1967); H. Frank Way, Jr., "Survey Research on Judicial Decisions: The Prayer and Bible Reading Cases," 21 *Western Pol. Q.* 189 (1968); William M. Beaney and Edward N. Beiser, "Prayer and Politics: The Impact of *Engel* and *Schempp* on the Political Process," 13 *J. Pub. L.* 475 (1964).

[18]Harrell R. Rodgers, Jr., and Edward B. Lewis, "Political Support and Compliance Attitudes: A Study of Adolescents," 2 *Am. Pol. Q.* 61 (1974).

[19]Max Rheinstein, ed., *Max Weber,* p. 336. The word, "charisma" has become quite voguish; in newspaper columns it means little more than whether, for example, a candidate for office looks good on television.

[20]The basis for judicial legitimacy would probably give the average person more

Most people, of course, do not think deeply about the subject. They accept these trite judgments and the outer signs of procedural legitimacy on faith. In modern society, too, fairness and *legitimacy* tend to blur about the edges in regard to courts and court-like institutions. "Due process" is both fair and legitimate. Bland acceptance of law has its limits, especially if, as we suspect, the feeling-tone is rather shallow. Cultural changes affect theories of legitimacy: The shift from traditional to rational is one of the hallmarks of modern law. Within a culture, too, attitudes toward law are affected by events and socioeconomic change. By 1975, the political events in the United States, summed up under the heading of "Watergate" and following years of an unpopular war, seem to have impaired both legitimacy and trust.

LEGITIMACY AND COMPLIANCE

What is the relationship between legal behavior and the *attitude* that certain norms or processes are legitimate or not? Or fair or not? Or moral or not? One would expect that when people *approve* of rules, as validly made, they will be more likely to obey than if they thought otherwise. In other words, legitimacy tends to lead, through approval, to compliance. The study by Berkowitz and Walker, mentioned earlier, points in this direction. Students tended to change their mind about moral propositions when they found out what "the law" had to say.[21] Another study of American doctors found substantial changes in attitudes toward medicare *after* the plan became law; doctors who had opposed it now felt more favorable toward it.[22] Still another study found that students judged a line of conduct more harshly, if they were told it was against the law as well as in violation of social norms. For example, they were more disapproving of a bystander who refused to rescue a drowning man, when they were told that the law imposed a duty to help.[23] These studies did not measure legitimacy in so many

---

trouble probably, than the basis for the legitimacy of laws passed by the legislature. Many people see "law" as an objective, impersonal body of norms which are reasonable and just. Judges are trained to pull these norms out of the mass of law, following fair, time-honored procedures.

[21]Leonard Berkowitz and Nigel Walker, "Laws and Moral Judgments," 30 *Sociometry* 410 (1967); see p. 111.

[22]John Colombotos, "Physicians and Medicare: A Before-After Study of the Effects of Legislation on Attitudes," 34 *Am. Soc. Rev.* 318 (1969).

[23]Harry Kaufman, "Legality and Harmfulness of a Bystander's Failure to Intervene as Determinants of Moral Judgment," in J. Macaulay and L. Berkowitz, eds., *Altruism and Helping Behavior* (1970), p. 77.

words, but "against the law" means forbidden by rules validly adopted, that is, legitimate rules.

These studies at least suggest that *procedural* legitimacy leads in the end to *substantive* approval of rules or to what we call *trust*. Of course, such a statement must be carefully qualified and explained. Clearly, the public relies on its experts—displays trust—in some areas of life but not in others. Many people are willing to accept the surgeon-general's word that cigarettes are harmful to their health. (They may or may not act on their belief.) These same people, however, may reject the opinion of "experts" that pornography is harmless. The difference between these two reactions must depend on the prior state of mind. Americans did not *want* to believe what experts told them about pornography. They also distinguish among doctors, economists, psychiatrists, and sociologists.

For all we know, legitimacy may be as variable as trust. Legitimacy is said to be a powerful social force. People accept "the law." They go along with rules and orders, insofar as they understand them, when authority has been properly designated or elected and when authority itself follows proper form. Many people will grumble about outcomes but in the same breath concede that society must have faith in its institutions, for stability's sake. Yet some institutions earn more respect than others. People are quite capable of believing that Congress is honorable; the city council, a den of thieves.

We have defined legitimacy as basically procedural—that is, as a faith in processes and institutions, independent of how the process turns out or what the institution does. But what if outcomes *consistently* go against a person's interests, or his moral sense? What does it do to a loyal, law-abiding Puritan, when case after case allows nude shows, topless bars, and dirty books? What does it do to a white supremacist, when the Supreme Court consistently decides in favor of the black man's rights?[24]

One wonders, in other words, how deep legitimacy goes. How much different is legitimacy from trust? Do people believe in law, because they generally feel the government does the right thing? No one, after all, has the time, energy, or inclination to investigate every subject. A person must mostly rely on others. A plumber does his own plumbing but hires doctors, lawyers, and carpenters as he needs them. Similarly, in political affairs: People are attracted to the general program of a

---

[24]More liberals than moderates and conservatives, in a California poll, thought that the Supreme Court was doing an "excellent" or a "good" job—40 percent, compared to 28 percent. *San Francisco Chronicle,* Dec. 14, 1971, p. 16, col. 1.

party; once they climb aboard, they may follow the whole party line, perhaps out of expediency, but also perhaps out of trust. They like some aspects of the program, and they assume the rest must be equally good.

Again, there are many reasons why law-abiding people feel they ought to obey the law. Procedural legitimacy may be nothing more than a way to recognize laws that are generally right. The real reasons may not be procedural at all but substantive. That is, we ought to obey because law is *generally* sound, or because if we do not, violence and anarchy will follow. Or people might feel that *on the whole* the laws will serve their interests or the interests of their group; since this is so, people should support the law, even if once in a while the law turns out unfavorably for them.

This, if true, is a rather subversive suggestion. It means that a subtle, long-run selfishness undergirds "unselfish" judgments. The liberal believes in freedom of speech—"even for those whose ideas he abhors"—but, in fact, he expects *liberal* views to prevail under freedom of speech. A restrictive regime, he suspects, would begin by restricting him. If he was really sure that the state would repress *only* fascists and racists, might he not subconsciously rethink his premises? Many liberals find censorship acceptable, so long as it affects only "smut." Indeed, many people have a selective view of civil rights. They believe in it in the abstract, but they make all sorts of exceptions for harmful or dangerous acts.[25] It may be, then, that what bolsters legitimacy (whatever people say) is the smug conviction that legitimate institutions, although we back them "right or wrong," are actually right; they feather *our* nest. If they become consistently wrong, then legitimacy totters.

Of course, sophisticated people give sophisticated reasons for obeying the law; they do not rely on crass personal interest. Research on the socialization of children suggests that sophistication grows by stages. As they get older, children give more complex reasons for obeying the law.[26] But these overt reasons may tell only part of the story. What happens to people who have actual contact with law? A suggestive little study of lawsuits between landlord and tenant was carried out in three German cities. Winners and losers were interviewed; their attitudes

---

[25]See Samuel A. Stouffer, *Communism, Conformity, and Civil Liberties* (1955). Similarly, a study of adolescents found that although very strong majorities stated that people should always obey the law, and that all laws are just, attitudes toward specific situations were quite different. Harrell R. Rodgers, Jr. and Edward B. Lewis, "Political Support and Compliance Attitudes: A Study of Adolescents," 2 *Am. Pol. Q.* 61 (1974).

[26]See June L. Tapp and Lawrence Kohlberg, "Developing Senses of Law and Legal Justice," 27 *J. Soc. Issues*, no. 2, 65 (1971).

were measured. As one might expect, a huge majority of the winners (78 percent) were completely satisfied with the way their cases came out; 82 percent of the losers were not satisfied at all. Interviewers asked the litigants whether their personal experiences had "strengthened or weakened their confidence" in the system of justice; none of the losers felt their confidence was strengthened; 67 percent found it weakened; the rest were indifferent.[27]

All this seems obvious enough, even trivial; but how does it square with the conventional wisdom about the strength of the idea of legitimacy—win or lose? Attitudes about legitimate authority may be quite frail. People who feel injured by the system do not remain confident in institutions that did them wrong—whatever they felt before. Oddly enough, the German study found that the opposite was by no means so striking a case: Winners were *not* strengthened in their feelings to the degree that losers were weakened.[28] Perhaps one *expects* vindication; the real shock is to lose.

How far can we generalize these studies? What does it do to *behavior*, when a person feels a law is unfair or certain legal acts are not legitimate? Or that certain legal actors are not deserving of his trust? We might expect some diminution in compliance at any given level of enforcement. In other words, the authorities, following a loss of faith, or trust, or legitimacy, will have to intensify delivery of sanctions, if they want to achieve the same amount of compliance as before.

There is a serious question, however, about what we might call the "spill-over" effect. If a person sees unfairness or illegitimacy or unworthiness of trust in *one* instance, how far does his disillusionment extend? How much of his attitude spills over into other areas and into his actual behavior? The hypocrisy and unfairness of Prohibition, it is said, brought the whole legal system into disrepute. Legal scholars claim that marijuana laws "hasten the erosion of respect for the law."[29] But how much "erosion of respect"? And where? And what are the conse-

---

[27]Hartmut Koch and Gisela Zenz, "Erfahrungen und Einstellungen von Klägern in Mietprozessen," in Manfred Rehbinder and Helmut Schelsky, eds., *Zur Effectivität des Rechts*, vol. 3, *Jahrbuch für Rechtssoziologie und Rechtstheorie* (1972), pp. 509, 527–528.

[28]Herbert Jacob, in a study of the way blacks and whites in Milwaukee felt about police, reported a similar finding: "Satisfactory experiences do not elevate evaluations of the police. On the other hand, bad experiences seem to deflate evaluations considerably." Herbert Jacob, "Black and White Perceptions of Justice in the City," 6 *Law and Society Rev.* 69, 78 (1971).

[29]Herbert Packer, *The Limits of the Criminal Sanction* (1968), p. 340; John Kaplan, *Marijuana, The New Prohibition* (1970), p. 30.

quences? Compliance itself is selective; as Harry Jones has remarked, "there are bank robbers who obey traffic laws and burglars who pay their debts."[30] A person disgusted by police brutality, or by selective enforcement of drug laws, does not necessarily turn against the Supreme Court or the Civil Aeronautics Board. Is he any more likely to embezzle, or rape, or cheat on his income tax?

Perceptions of justice are a significant item for research. Harry Ball, in a study of rent control in Hawaii, found that landlords who overcharged their tenants also expressed the opinion that rent control laws were unfair.[31] Arguably, the rent laws *were* unfair, and this made a difference; perceptions of the police as brutal and unfair may reflect the fact that they *can* be brutal and unfair. Exactly how these attitudes translate into behavior, of course, is an open question, and the direction of the causal flow is uncertain. For example, in Ball's study, was it landlords who thought the law was unfair who broke the law; or did landlords who broke the law rationalize by deciding the law was unfair?

Trust and legitimacy perhaps had power in traditional society that is lacking in modern society. In traditional society, presumptions of legitimacy are etched in the soul during socialization; it may take a huge amount of preaching or evidence to overcome these. In modern society, many people are more skeptical, more "rational"; trust and legitimacy then may be more fragile, more dependent on actual outcomes.

The feeling of legitimacy in our own society probably attaches most firmly to areas of law which are of personal interest or benefit or are at least not harmful. Legitimacy leads people to approve of what the system does. This, in the language of systems theorists, is "support," especially diffuse support, the "more generalized favorable attitudes or goodwill exhibited by the members of a system that is not associated with specific outputs."[32] Note that "support" refers, not to

---

[30]Harry Jones, *The Efficacy of Law* (1969), p. 81.

[31]Harry Ball, "Social Structure and Rent-Control Violations," 65 *Am. J. Sociology* 598 (1960); see also N. Friedland, J. Thibaut and L. Walker, "Some Determinants of the Violation of Rules," 3 *J. Applied Soc. Psychology* 103 (1973).

[32]Sheldon Goldman and Thomas P. Jahnige, "Eastonian Systems Analysis and Legal Research," 2 *Rutgers-Camden L.J.* 285, 291 (1970); David Easton, *A Systems Analysis of Political Life* (1965), p. 273; for an attempt to measure support, see John E. Conklin, "Criminal Environment and Support for the Law," 6 *Law and Society Rev.* 247 (1971); see also Richard L. Engstrom and Micheal W. Giles, "Expectations and Images: A Note on Diffuse Support for Legal Institutions," 6 *Law and Society Rev.* 631 (1972); Harrell R. Rodgers Jr., *Community Conflict, Public Opinion and the Law: The Amish Dispute in Iowa* (1969), pp. 111–118.

obedience to rules but to a kind of warm glow about rules in general or rules addressed to somebody else. This "support," we suggest, is a fragile thing. The right-thinking and the righteous stagger under the blows of permissive cases. They can tolerate a few "mistakes," but if the results keep on coming in "wrong," they will have to decide whether continued "support" of such a doubtful system is worthwhile —they may even question obedience. For the disappointed, much depends on whether, *in the main*, they feel that the law does or will turn out right. "Let justice be done, though the heavens shake." But do we really agree? If the sky began to fall, if the plaster cracked, the dishes broke, the walls trembled, we might wonder whether justice was worth such a terrible price.

FACTORS IN HARMONY, FACTORS IN CONFLICT

It is easy to see that when official norms *and* the subculture reward or promise to reward or punish or threaten to punish the same behavior, the two will powerfully reinforce each other. The case is even stronger when some moral factor pulls the same way. It is not hard to think of examples. The state, the gang, the family, the boys at work, every ethnic group and culture, and almost every individual conscience feel the same way about murdering one's mother. A rule so universally supported will have a tiny rate of deviance. If every factor is neutral except one, that one is likely to have its way. So, if society around us and our consciences have nothing to say about breaking the speed limit, behavior will be unusually sensitive to the rise and fall of sanctions.

The interesting question is, which factors are the strongest? And which prevail in case of conflict? Nothing in existing literature furnishes a satisfying answer. It is doubtful that a *general* answer exists. Much depends on the particular subjects and the particular behavior. Moreover, it is hard, in most cases, to compare state with nonstate sanctions. Dodge City offers $1,000 reward for information leading to arrest of a rustler. But the townspeople ostracize informers. We cannot predict, in advance, which of the two will prove more powerful with any one person or with people in general. If we know that a $1,000 reward will produce a certain amount of information, we assume that $2,000 may produce somewhat more. But we certainly cannot know whether the extra money can offset a heightened threat from the citizens.

Richard Schwartz and Sonya Orleans, in a notable study, tried to discover whether threats to punish or appeals to conscience brought about more compliance with the income tax laws.[33] They concluded that, on the whole, appeals to conscience seemed to bring more results. These conclusions, however, hang by a rather slender statistical thread.[34] It is also not clear how far one should generalize their results. Their subjects were middle-class Americans. Tax laws may or may not have some special sort of deterrence and conscience curve. Almost certainly, further research would *not* show that conscience is always stronger than threats of sanction regardless of time, place, and subject.

Schwartz and Orleans did not pit their two factors *against* each other. On the problem of conflict of factors even less is known. Will a norm be obeyed if conscience *and* the state support it, though not the peer group? The state should find it hard to enforce a norm opposed by conscience *and* the peer group. Beyond this, it is hard to guess.

Moreover, it is an oversimplification to speak of *three* factors. Each factor is in fact made up of subfactors; and subfactors too may conflict. A person living in Birmingham, Alabama, might find himself impelled in one direction by city ordinances, in quite another by state or federal laws. His family may support one norm; his fellow workers, another. Members of his church, his friends, his neighbors all support sets of norms, and by no means the same ones. Some groups may agree with each other or with one or more official norms; not all will administer sanctions. Within the third factor, we distinguished civic-mindedness, morality, legitimacy, and trust. These also may be in conflict. Morality, legitimacy, and trust need not and often do not express the same demands.

Another question is, in any real life situation that law deals with, what behavior is explained by each factor and subfactor? Take a simple command: An army officer orders his company of troops to march a mile down a dusty road. Sometimes the men quickly and dutifully obey. Down the road is the mess hall, and the men are hungry. Those who disobey, they know, face court-martial. Once some men begin marching, others feel foolish or conspicuous if they hang back. Moreover, the order seems reasonable; and the men have been trained to do as officers command.

In this case, all the motives reinforce each other: The men march down the road and that is that. When each factor is present and working in harmony with others, the engine of social control works

---

[33]Richard D. Schwartz and Sonya Orleans, "On Legal Sanctions," 34 *U. Chi. L. Rev.* 274 (1967).

[34]See the remarks by Stewart Macaulay in Lawrence M. Friedman and Stewart Macaulay, *Law and the Behavioral Sciences* (1969), pp. 262–267.

smoothly and efficiently. As each factor drops off or is impaired, it becomes harder to make the men move. If the men are indifferent (the march is not especially irksome or dangerous, but they see no benefit) and if they do not like to obey orders, if it is late, and they are tired, and if they do not know the officer, and they feel the order is on the whole unjustified—then the officer will probably still get results, but only if he threatens the men. He may have to send a lieutenant along to prove the reality of enforcement; or he may have to punish an offender or two. All this inevitably means that the march costs more in real resources. Finally, the men may be absolutely mutinous. The road, they know, is booby-trapped; the command they think is wholly illegitimate for some reason; they hate army life; they have absorbed subversive ideas from a radical coffee-house near the base, and the first to obey will be branded a traitor by his comrades. Here only a staggering input of resources can force the men to move—in the most extreme case, violence, or dragging the men one-by-one down the road. This would not only be terribly costly, but the coerced "compliance" would be useless.

The example is extreme, but the basic point is clear. Free will obedience, that is, compliance that the culture supports and that the third force supports, or both, is fundamental to law as we know it. This kind of compliance is indispensably efficient from the point of view of those in command. Force is wasteful, by and large. If everyone cheated on his income tax or most people did not file a return, the government might simply have to give up collecting the tax. This is apparently the case in some countries. Prohibition was, as we have noted, a classic example of mass disobedience. Other instances could easily be named.

These general observations are, however, hard to turn into testable propositions. For one thing, behavior does not break down into separate little sticks, which we can label force, peer group, conscience, and the like. Rarely is there hard information on the *share* each factor contributes. A Polish sociologist asked people whether they crossed the street against a red light, when no cars were around. Forty percent said they never did; 32 percent said they did it only occasionally. Observation of actual behavior at the crossings confirmed what people reported: These proportions were just about right. The sociologist then asked *why* people obeyed: 16.3 percent said they were afraid of a fine; 36.5 percent said they liked "order"; 19.6 percent thought it was habit—they were "used" to observing the lights.[35] If these statements can be believed,

---

[35]Jerzy Kwasniewski, "Motivation of Declared Conformity to a Legal Norm," *Polish Soc. Bull.* no. 1, 74, 76 (1969); 21.6 percent gave other reasons, but most of these were

then we have for this one case some clues about the mix of sanction, legitimacy, and habit (whatever this means) in causing one type of legal behavior.

At any rate, the mix will vary from law to law. The typical "old" law (against murder, for example) is sustained by the culture, by its legitimate origins, by its morality, and by its place in the individual conscience. The threat of force is a sheep dog that no doubt keeps some marginals in line. "New" laws, regulatory laws, laws devoid of history and affect have other behavioral dynamics. For them, total relaxation of enforcement *could* lead to massive disobedience. This would surely happen if a city stopped enforcing parking laws. Automobile drivers as a group would probably concede that parking rules are legitimate; moreover, they would probably agree that the rules make sense, since without the rules, the traffic and parking situation would deteriorate. But the moral element is missing or weak. The convenience of parking overtime or at a crosswalk easily outweighs claims of legitimacy and conscience in the private calculus of many people. Here, only the threat of real sanctions can tip the scales.

Deep moral conviction, in other words, delivers compliance more effectively than simple legitimacy without the aid of other factors. Morality is a much better watchdog against murder than the *law* against murder; if morality and legitimacy conflict, the legitimate law will have to give way. Most laws, of course, do not rest on the bedrock of morality. They are legitimate, but no cultural pillars support each facet of the norm. Morality and custom do not dictate that the speed limit on Elm Street should be 35 m.p.h. or that the amount of butterfat in ice cream should be not less than such and such percent. There are hundreds and thousands of these workaday rules in the modern state. Legitimacy and trust give them important supports, but not as to every jot and tittle, and only when the norm does not press against some vital personal need. Ordinarily, people will not park in a no parking zone for fear of a ticket. If it is a matter of urgency, these people will even double park. Yet legitimacy, civic-mindedness, and trust support these rules, and the peers seem on the whole indifferent. For these rules, violation is elastic, and small increases in real enforcement make a sizeable difference.

Force, opinion, and conscience do not live in separate worlds of behavior. They are in constant interaction. We have used the example of the man who sees people smoking in a room with a "No Smoking" sign. What he sees tells him that no one is enforcing the rule and that

---

people who sometimes violated, and the reasons they gave were reasons for crossing against the light.

whoever might enforce it does not take the rule seriously. At this point, the legitimacy of the rule begins to erode. Clearly, then, the smokers may influence the attitudes, and ultimately the behavior, of new people entering the room. If nobody enforces the law, then perhaps "they" don't really "mean it"; it is not "true law," "nobody follows it anymore." Especially in a society with ideas about majority rule, the unenforced rule can end up losing its legitimacy, and with it, its life.

LAW AS A LEARNING PROCESS

Legitimacy is a word for an attitude; the idea is that this attitude, other things being equal, affects people's behavior. People obey legitimate laws. One model of how law works, then, is that it produces an attitude—legitimacy—and the attitude in turn brings about new behavior.[36] But obviously, legitimacy is not inborn, and feelings about government and law do not come out of thin air. A regime gains legitimacy after people have "a considerable period of experience" with the regime, are trained by it and gain "symbolic rewards from it."[37] Legitimacy must, in short, be earned and learned; it is something which legal systems try to teach. The *process* of teaching and learning legitimacy—how it is suggested, communicated, reinforced, extinguished, and impaired—badly needs research.

One way legitimacy is learned is through behavior. Laws backed by threats of force induce conduct; when conduct is repeated often enough, becomes familiar enough, it turns into habit, and a kind of coral reef of attitude builds up. One can speak, then, of an "intergenerational 'drift' toward increased moral justification of required conduct."[38] Much modern law, as natural to us as the air we breathe, was once novel and controversial. The income tax law of 1894 set off a storm of protest from business interests and the well-to-do; a test case was brought, and the Supreme Court voided the law.[39] The highest tax rate under this law was 2 percent. Today rich men and big business—indeed, the public at large—accept tax rates unthinkable in the 1890s. Tax rates have gradually risen. The laws and their enforcers set a

---

[36]See William K. Muir, Jr., *Prayer in the Public Schools, Law and Attitude Change* (1967), ch. 8.

[37]Richard M. Merelman, "Learning and Legitimacy," 60 *Am. Pol. Sci. Rev.* 548, 552 (1966).

[38]Harry V. Ball and Lawrence M. Friedman, "The Use of Criminal Sanctions in the Enforcement of Economic Legislation: A Sociological View," 17 *Stan. L. Rev.* 197, 221 (1965).

[39]See Arnold M. Paul, *Conservative Crisis and the Rule of Law* (1969), pp. 185ff.

process in motion, and induced behavior which became more or less a habit, and (at last) produced a different frame of mind.[40] People still grumble about taxes and about details of the tax laws, but they accept the tax itself without a murmur. If the government passed a law to make Americans carry an identity card, there would be some fuss about privacy and Big Brother. But driver's licenses, draft cards, and social security cards have paved the way for identity cards (perhaps even made them unnecessary). Legal institutions act as learning theorists, almost without knowing it. They induce reactions more or less like conditioned reflexes. Added to this is the influence of observing *other* people's behavior, which produces "vicarious learning."[41]

Equally, an unlearning process may take place when law is not enforced. A person "gets out of the habit" of obeying a law, but what started him on the road to noncompliance? As a concrete example, take the common case of driving faster than the speed limit. Most people are not speeders as a rule, but in many towns there are places where, by common consent, the speed limit is unreasonably slow, and everyone goes 40 m.p.h. rather than 25 m.p.h. It is easy to see the behavior, but how did it begin? How does it spread? Is it sheer imitation? How do people justify their behavior? Do their attitudes and behaviors affect their idea of the legitimacy of this speed limit, or speed limits in general, or laws in general?

THE THIRD FACTOR AND THE STATE

Internalized values are usually ascribed to that amorphous entity, society, but the *state* may be their source. Officials can and do try to raise or lower levels of conscience, ideas of legitimacy, feelings of trust, and so on. The modern state spends a good deal of money on education or, to be more accurate, on propaganda. It tries to generate feelings of duty to conform, to enlist public opinion in aid of obedience to law. In this way, the state buys more conformity than it would get from sanctions alone. In legal behavior, then, the line between the influence of the state and that of nonstate sources does not coincide exactly with the line between "social" forces and sanctions.

There are many reasons besides cost why the authorities wish to

---

[40]This statement, of course, conceals much complexity. "Law" in the sense of words does not change attitudes or behavior. It must be communicated. Communication already implies institutions and behaviors, and these are the aspects of "law" which actually influence behavior.

[41]Richard Schwartz, "A Learning Theory of Law," 41 *So. Cal. L. Rev.* 548, 578 (1968).

manipulate public opinion rather than invest more heavily in enforcement. Law puts limits on government action, limits that do not apply to private citizens. When, at the height of the Cold War, Senator Joseph McCarthy of Wisconsin and his followers in and out of government leveled wild charges of subversion against political enemies, the idea was, in part, to induce the public to vote against these enemies, to condemn and avoid them—in a word, punish them—when they stood in McCarthy's way. It was easier and safer to use these back door methods than to try to pass repressive laws which the courts might overthrow.[42] The United States may be particularly prone to the use of this sort of subterfuge. The written Constitution, flamboyantly interpreted by federal courts, imposes many constraints on government. In 1970, after terrorists from Quebec kidnapped a government official and another prominent man, the Canadian government suspended civil rights and took vigorous, perhaps too vigorous, action. Emergency measures of this sort are not legally feasible in the United States. The government does not and cannot invoke a state of siege. This is all to the good, but an unscrupulous government can search for other ways to subdue insubordination and suppress deviance. These are secret ways; they can be vicious, and they are not easily exposed to the withering glare of public opinion.

DEVIANCE AND INTERACTION

As we noted, people to whom rules are addressed are not always passive. They may obey or disobey for a number of reasons, and they may also actively interact or communicate with authority. A person may, for example, try to change the rule; we have called this *feedback.* Or he may bargain in some way with rule-makers or rule appliers. Bribery and corruption are forms of bargaining; so is begging for mercy. Private citizens to a lawsuit bargain with each other, when they settle a case out of court. Enforcement or threat may induce third persons to take some action or induce behavior of some sort (other than compliance, evasion, noncompliance, bargaining, and interaction) on the part of the persons to whom the rules are addressed. We call these *side effects.* If people deprived of liquor during Prohibition turned to chewing gum, soft drinks, or organized crime, these were side effects.

Each of these phenomena is an important subject in its own right. The question of side effects, for example, is inseparable from the ques-

---

[42]Congressional committees continue to use such methods. See Ted Finman and Stewart Macaulay, "Freedom to Dissent: The Vietnam Protests and the Words of Public Officials," 1966 *Wis. L. Rev.* 632.

tion of the impact of law except in the narrowest sense of impact. Rewards and punishments have many indirect consequences. When a thief is put in jail, he cannot rob houses; jailing him will be a lesson to other potential thieves. On the other hand, a man in jail has to be fed at public expense; society has lost a worker; his family may have lost their breadwinner; his children, now fatherless, may drift into delinquency.

Rewards can have serious side effects too: price supports for peanuts and cotton distort the market, keep the price of food high, disturb the balance of trade—even when the system is "effective" in buying the behavior of farmers. When the legal order tries to forbid or discourage behavior which people find pleasant or profitable, we can expect some countermotion. The state, to avoid a glut of grain, pays farmers to retire some of their land from production. But the farmers let their worst land lie fallow and raise bumper crops on the rest.

This is an example of an important type of side effect: the purpose of a rule is frustrated because the person who "obeys" finds a substitute avenue of conduct. A crackdown on one dangerous drug, raising the risk and the price, sends addicts scurrying into the market for another drug. Often, out of experience, as here, we can predict some side effects. Where demand for some bit of deviant behavior is high or the behavior brings a great reward and a substitute is feasible, people will turn to the substitute just as they turn from beef to pork or lamb, if the price of beef goes too high.

Side effects need not be bad, of course. The literature puts heavy emphasis on negative side effects in criminal justice. Prison ruins the prisoner's life and disrupts his family, but it may also bring satisfaction to the victim and family and a sense of security (perhaps false) to possible victims. In fairness and in scientific honesty, these must be reckoned into the calculus. The main issue, indeed, in the struggle over capital punishment relates to the side effects. For many legal acts— outlawing race discrimination, redistributing income, cleaning up air and water, establishing new parks—the hope of positive side effects is at the very heart of the policy.

Bargaining and *interaction* also have their positive and negative sides and can take legitimate and illegitimate forms. Interaction can be deviant or nondeviant, that is, illegal or not. A person arrested for assault can beg for mercy—or offer a bribe. Under what conditions can we expect deviant interaction? And under what conditions can we expect successful bargaining? It takes two sides to strike a successful bargain; the official side must want to acquiesce. Sometimes this is due to corruption. Some legal cultures are more corrupt than others; but where corruption occurs, we often find the "leaky hose" syndrome—pressure on the system to enforce rules against lucrative, or pleasant, or unavoidable behavior. Interaction also often reflects the fact that the rulers and the ruled are for some reason dependent on each other, perhaps because of a shortage of enforcement resources. Plea bargaining in criminal trials is a kind of interaction that comes, in part, from the fact that the criminal justice system cannot afford full-scale trials in every case. Criminal justice then becomes a "set of interorganizational exchange relationships"[43] in which police, prosecutors, and judge all take part, as well as the accused. Gresham Sykes, in his study of a New Jersey prison, pointed out how guards bargain and interact with prisoners, excusing some offenses, going light on others, extending favors. The prisoners outnumber the guards, who badly need their cooperation; otherwise, discipline would be utterly impossible.[44]

Much has been written about the so-called "capture" of regulatory agencies by industries they are supposed to regulate.[45] This is an important example of interaction. The ICC works hand in glove with railroads, the FCC with the networks, the CAB with the airlines, and so on. In some ways, what happens is strikingly similar to the situation in prisons as described by Sykes. The agency has to live and work with its industry day-by-day. If the industry does not cooperate, the agency can hardly do its job. High agency officials serve limited terms; they hope for well-paying jobs from their former subjects. If regulation becomes too harsh, the companies may appeal to Congress or the press. This form of feedback could make life miserable for the agency which thrives on anonymity. Bargaining, then, is a way to prevent harmful feedback.[46]

Joseph Gusfield has classified labels placed on deviant behavior in a way that helps in understanding deviant interaction.[47] Gusfield observed that society's attitude toward deviants depends on the deviant's own assumed attitude toward the broken norm. A *repentant* deviant is

---

[43]George F. Cole, "The Decision to Prosecute," 4 *Law and Society Rev.* 331, 332 (1970).

[44]*The Society of Captives* (1958), pp. 55–58. The guards are also aware of a contingent dependence. If a riot ever broke out, guards might fall into the hands of rebel prisoners. There would be a grim day of reckoning for guards who had incurred too much ill will.

[45]Marver H. Bernstein, *Regulating Business by Independent Commission* (1955); Samuel P. Huntington, "The Marasmus of the ICC: The Commission, The Railroads and the Public Interest," 61 *Yale L.J.* 467 (1952).

[46]The situation is, of course, complicated by the active intervention of public interest lawyers and reformers such as Ralph Nader.

[47]Joseph R. Gusfield, "Moral Passage: The Symbolic Process in Public Designation of Deviance," 15 *Social Problems* 175 (1967).

one who accepts the norm. The "reckless motorist," for example, "admits the legitimacy of traffic laws"; he may even be sorry he broke the rule. His deviation is a moral lapse, a fall from grace. "Consensus" exists "between the designator and the deviant." A second label is that of the *sick* deviant. Alcoholics and members of sexual minorities, who accept this label, resemble the repentant in one important way: They do not threaten or oppose the norms they violate. "Acts which we can perceive as those of sick . . . people are irrelevant to the norm; they neither attack nor defend it." A professional thief is an example of the third type, the *cynical* deviant. He does not attack the norm but violates it without regret or feeling. Finally, the *enemy* deviant does not accept the deviant label at all. He "is neither repentant nor sick." Instead, he upholds "an opposite norm. He accepts his behavior as proper and derogates the public norm as illegitimate."

The labels are not static; they change during periods of "moral passage." Homosexuality was once branded as an infamous crime; later it was generally accepted that homosexuals were "ill." In the last few years, however, many homosexuals have rejected these labels, formed a movement and are lobbying to change the laws. They are now enemy deviants, from the standpoint of the norm.

The type of label affects the techniques of bargaining and interaction. Begging for mercy or pleading guilty are forms of *repentant* interactions. They can be highly effective. Judges welcome those who affirm the norms even, or especially, repentant deviants. Individually, the repentant deviant is antisocial, but he does not threaten the normative order. Repentance is conservative and individual, not social and reformist. From the standpoint of the people on top, cynical and enemy deviants are more serious threats to society. But the cynical deviant merely breaks the rules, and he is not part of a social movement. His behavior is normally a threat only if there are too many of him. A single burglar, or even a thousand burglars, does not bring down the state. The enemy deviant, however, is a rebel and a danger at least to the norms.

In some ways, Gusfield's terms are not ideal. The word "cynical" conjures up the picture of a hardened professional; the enemy deviant suggests a revolutionary. It might be more realistic to think in somewhat different categories. Some people deny the *general* validity of a norm; some only deny that it applies to *them*. Some keep the idea to themselves; others spread the word, or form or join movements to destroy or change the norms. People who used contraceptives in Massachusetts, when contraceptives were illegal, were "deviants." Most of these people broke the law quietly and did nothing more about it, although they probably greatly disapproved of the law. The true "enemies" were those who actively worked to destroy the rule. In other words, some deviants do not interact with each other or with authorities or interact only personally and individually; or, if they form a group, form it as quietly and secretly as possible.[48] The sit-ins in the South, however, were a *movement*. When members of the movement resisted the police, they were engaging in a form of interaction. At the same time, they went beyond the local authorities; they fought to change the law in court; they lobbied; they carried on campaigns—all of which was feedback.

Enemy deviance, then, is deviance of the type called *feedback* or *interaction* supported by some movement or subculture. In history, we see many examples of "moral passage" (Gusfield's phrase) among labellers; what they once considered sin, they come to consider sickness. At the same time, moral passage among the labelled is equally important. These people change their own self-concept and behavior. The repentant or sick lose faith in the norm, first inwardly, then actively, as part of a group. They become enemy deviants.

What sets off this chain of events? Some enemy deviants belong to well-defined groups with their own norms in opposition to the state— the devout Mormon in the late nineteenth century, for example, was caught in the cross fire over polygamy. Enemy deviance, then, is often a case of conflict between official and nonofficial norms. The person in the middle will have to be a deviant from the standpoint of one or the other. Which one will depend on whose sanctions are more powerful and which norms are more firmly imbedded in his heart.

The Mormon church was strong and well-structured. It is fascinating to watch a movement rise up out of much less promising material, for example, the unorganized, the oppressed, the sexual minorities. Information plays an essential role. Isolated deviants cannot turn into a *society* of deviants—a subculture—if they are unaware of the norms of their group. Hence, merely spreading information may have an important long-run effect. When the Kinsey report revealed the sexual behavior of Americans, people found out, perhaps to their surprise, that their secret vices were not so special or so rare. They gained a sense that they were not alone; some may have begun to wonder whether the rules that labelled them as criminals or as sick were all that just.[49]

---

[48]See Howard S. Becker, *Outsiders, Studies in the Sociology of Deviance* (1963), pp. 67–69.

[49]Naturally, there is far more to the sexual revolution than the splash made by the Kinsey report and similar communications, although we suspect these did play a part. On this point, it is interesting to note the study described in D. G. Myers, F. B. Schreiber, and J. Viel, "Effects of Discussion on Opinions Concerning Illegal Behav-

To be sure, this primitive realization is only part of the way to enemy deviance. Something must trigger a new frame of mind, something must build an organization. But information comes first. Nineteenth-century intellectuals, who helped revive language and culture among such submerged peoples as the Czechs or the Basques, acted as carriers of revolution whether they meant to or not. The sense of heritage made subject people into real subcultures. These people lived in compact areas in towns and villages. It takes a rather different flow of information and opinion to make homosexuals join a liberation movement, to encourage nuns and priests to defy their bishops, or to turn the sullen resentment of convicts into riots and revolts.

In the modern world, the weakening of faith in authority seems to provide a fertile field for such revolts. Information flow—messages from or about others—is also smoother and quicker. But a subgroup must nonetheless provide rewards and punishments for members; or depend on the force of group opinion; or on the sense of legitimacy among its crowd of adherents. Without these elements, any movement will perish.

Society responds in many ways to attacks on its norms. All attacks are not equally threatening. Modern systems accept without question the idea that rules are in flux. They expect change and make provision for it. They tolerate, in other words, attacks on some norms. Anyone who opposes a norm is an enemy of the norm, in a sense; but he is not an enemy *deviant* unless he violates it as well. Everyone has the right to press for reform of the law though not to violate it meanwhile. Yet deviance is extremely common precisely in the case of a dying norm. Since the norm has lost its normativeness, many people see no reason to adhere to it. In World War II, draft dodgers were ashamed to be so labelled; during the Vietnam war, particularly toward the end, people openly flaunted this deviance and were proud of it.

Every existing norm is, in a sense, part of the status quo. But some norms mean much more than others to the people who hold power. Some parts of the status quo are flabbier than other parts. There is a good deal of leeway, slack, and give in the system. When the Supreme Court abolished racial segregation in the schools, the deep South resisted bitterly; but the border states, where segregation was less deeply entrenched, gave up more quietly on the whole. When students began

---

ior", 92 *J. Soc. Psychology* 77 (1974). Subjects were asked their attitudes toward "ethical-legal dilemmas," for example, whether a poor man with a hungry family should keep some money he found on the street. After group discussion, attitudes shifted *toward* favoring the illegal behavior. One explanation offered is that the discussion revealed that the illegal behavior was *not* as strongly disapproved of by peers as the subjects might have thought.

to rise up in revolt against universities, they demanded mixed dormitories, more freedom in their personal lives, and a voice in running the faculties. The universities easily and quickly gave up on the personal issues which meant little to them, but they bitterly resisted giving up faculty control. It is not always easy to tell in advance where the slack is. Often it takes a genuine battle to discover which are the lightly held outposts, and which is the citadel itself.

In general, elites can put up with less enemy deviance than with deviance of other kinds. Society can tolerate a good deal of speeding; most speeders are what Gusfield would call repentant deviants.[50] Illegal speeding is common; in absolute terms, there are millions of violations every day. Speeding is dangerous and expensive, but on the whole we live with it. On the other hand, enemy deviance must be resisted and repressed, or the norms will change. Social reaction to enemy deviance will tend to be stronger than the reaction to other forms of deviance, even when the behaviors in themselves seem equally serious. Society does not tolerate much murder; murder threatens the social order, regardless of what murderers think of the validity of criminal law or do about it. But society has an even lower threshold of toleration for assassination and revolution.

Most people assume that crime and deviance are absolute evils that must be overcome, like poverty or disease. Yet arguably, deviance is inevitable. Any society or social group has rules or norms. Most people conform in an average way. Behavior distributes itself along a bell-shaped curve. Hence, whatever the rules, some people, compared to others, will not meet the standards, and some will be extremely saintly, again compared to the mass. This in no way depends on whether the society is wicked or not. A nunnery filled with holy women will call certain acts, trivial by worldly standards, deviant. Some nuns will violate these rules, and the bell-shaped curve may look much the same as the curve for legal behavior outside the convent walls. It follows from this line of argument, with roots in the sociological thought of Émile Durkheim, that no society can abolish deviance. Deviance remains a constant—perhaps at a constant rate,[51] And it has a function of sorts: It defines the boundaries of a group. In Kai Erikson's words, "[M]orality and immorality meet at the public scaffold, and it is during this meeting that the line between them is drawn."[52]

---

[50]A few may be sick and some may be cynically or passively opposed to the norms.

[51]See Kai Erikson, *Wayward Puritans* (1966), p. 13; Edwin H. Schur, *Labeling Deviant Behavior, Its Sociological Implications* (1971), p. 147.

[52]Erikson, p. 12.

Do deviance rates in any society tend toward a constant? This intriguing idea might lend itself to empirical test. Yet, the thesis cannot apply to *all* deviance. Enemy deviance will not follow normal distribution. It is the intrusive, the unpredictable element, the engine of social change. There is no reason to believe that rates of enemy deviance are the same, more or less, in all societies. The nunnery may be, and probably is, completely free of it. Russia in 1917 was seething with rebellion; Denmark in 1974 is not. The theory predicts deviant behavior aboard every ship (and ship of state). But mutiny takes place only on the *Bounty*, and only when Captain Bligh is in command.

A NOTE ON THE CIVIL SIDE

The discussion in the last two chapters has drawn most of its examples from criminal justice. But any theory of legal behavior should apply to legal behavior in civil affairs as well. When we ask who will make *use* of a particular rule and when, the general answers should look much like answers to questions about who and when punishment deters, and the like. Basically, an increase in perceived benefit produces more use at the margin. Higher farm subsidies produce more crops but do not turn everyone into a farmer. Cheap, easy divorce does not ruin a happy marriage. Under the British health system, visits to the doctor are "free," but there is no stampede to the doctor's office. It still costs time and trouble to go, and people still hesitate to waste the doctor's time. Changes in benefits and costs, however, do bring changes at the margin in the rate of legal use.

Use rules are, of course, different in many ways from rules of the penal code. For one thing, the state has assumed many of the costs of enforcement. Public taxes pay for police, detectives, juries, and prisons. Civil costs fall more heavily on the individual. This is most striking in private lawsuits. Court costs and salaries of attorneys hardly enter into the district attorney's decision to bring one more armed robber to trial. (He must, of course, worry about budget and staff.) For the ordinary plaintiff—individual or business—the investment in time and money, win or lose, may be significant for the single case. The public pays for the judge's salary and courtroom overhead; the rest must be privately borne. In the United States, winner and loser each pays his own lawyers. In Great Britain and in other countries, loser pays all.[53] In both countries, in a commercial case, tort case, or land case, potential ben-

---

[53]See Albert A. Ehrenzweig, "Reimbursement of Counsel Fees and the Great Society," in Jacobus tenBroek, ed., *The Law of the Poor* (1966), p. 468.

efits must be large to outweigh the costs and risks of losing the case.[54]

Cost is a heavy barrier to access to court. Litigation, quite apart from dollars laid out, can be very burdensome. Macaulay has shown that businessmen shy away from litigation and with good reason. Lawsuits are highly disruptive. Managers and engineers may have to take out from their normal work to appear in court. When two firms have ongoing relations, they prefer not to litigate but to compromise and continue to do business.[55] Ordinary citizens have good reasons to avoid court too. It is troublesome and time-consuming, as well as expensive.

American courts, then, are not open door, popular institutions where people go with troubles and disputes. The courts in other modern Western countries have similar limitations. It is as if society had decided that litigation was unhealthy, that it must be discouraged, and that, therefore, the price must be high.[56]

Yet, in many simple societies, courts *are* popular, busy, and open to all. Tribal courts tend to be free in a double sense. First, many of them charge no fees of any kind. (The judges are not professionals, and there is no salaried staff.) Second, there is nothing shameful about going to court. Lloyd Fallers, discussing the Soga of Uganda, calls their law "popular" and "accessible." It is popular in that "knowledge of the legal subculture . . . is widely shared. . . . The language of the law is mostly everyday language." It is "accessible" because the court is "cheap—fees amount to a few shillings" as well as "permissive with respect to grounds for action."[57] Village courts the world over are popular and accessible. They must be, in order to do their job, to settle disputes and to restore that social harmony which rancor threatens to disrupt.

These courts are concerned with "making the balance." The phrase is Laura Nader's. She has used it to describe the legal methods of the Zapotecs of Oaxaca, Mexico.[58] "Making the balance" is hardly a phrase anyone would use about American litigation. American courts perform many functions, but restoring social harmony among squabbling neighbors and kin is hardly one of them. A policeman on the beat

---

[54]The British system would tend to discourage very risky lawsuits but to encourage plaintiffs who are bound to win—routine debt collection cases, for example.

[55]Stewart Macaulay, "Non-Contractual Relations in Business: A Preliminary Study," 28 *American Soc. Rev.* 55 (1963).

[56]See Lawrence M. Friedman, "Legal Rules and the Process of Social Change," 19 *Stan. L. Rev.* 786, 798, 798–810 (1967). Some societies feel an even stronger distaste for litigation—Korea, for example—although for quite different reasons.

[57]Lloyd A. Fallers, *Law Without Precedent* (1969), p. 313.

[58]Laura Nader, "An Analysis of Zapotec Law Cases," 3 *Ethnology* 404 (1964).

in the big city may have more in common with a Zapotec law court than the local trial court, state or federal—or even the downtown court of small claims.

Western societies, in short, through decisions about structures and institutions, encourage the use of some legal rules and discourage others.[59] The high cost barrier is selectively discouraging. Notably, it is the *courts* that are expensive. The justice of the peace marries people for a paltry sum; registering deeds is relatively cheap; applying for a veteran's pension costs nothing. Use of a rule or institution will, of course, go up as the costs of use go down. Court costs and lawyer costs are quite fixed and discouragingly high in the short run. But cost is also a function of the chances of winning the case. If victory becomes more likely or if the potential gains go up (for example, when the law allows punitive or extra damages), the use of the court is encouraged. This happens, too, when a court develops doctrine that promises new gain for some class of litigants.

Because litigation is so expensive, American law has evolved many devices to mitigate these costs, where litigation is socially approved or publicly encouraged. Legal aid plans in many countries provide some help for very poor litigants. The contingent fee, used in accident cases in the United States, shifts risks from the litigant to his lawyer who spreads them out among many clients. A contingent fee is one which "becomes payable only if the lawyer is able to accomplish a specified benefit for his client."[60] Many accident victims could not afford to sue if they had to pay their own costs, win or lose.[61]

Change in a rule of law could change the balance of costs and benefits for those subject to the rule, if it has any impact. Legal rules prohibit some activities, limit others, attach bad consequences to others. Rarely does the law restrain an act in the physical sense.[62] Generally the law prescribes sanctions after the fact. The law "forbidding" murder does not make murder impossible; it merely tries to put a terrible price on murder. One may pay the price and commit the murder, despite the law.

This analysis blurs the distinction between criminal and civil pen-

---

[59]Court costs and lawyers' fees are probably more of a barrier in the United States and England than in parts of continental Europe, but even there, the courts are far from "popular" in the same way that the courts of the Soga are.

[60]F. B. MacKinnon, *Contingent Fees for Legal Services* (1964), p. 18.

[61]In tort cases, the two parties are usually strangers, who meet only when their cars collide. Hence there are none of the disruption costs so common in business cases.

[62]An injunction is no exception; it restrains only in the sense that it increases the risks: Those who disobey may go to jail.

alties. Breach of contract is no crime, not even a sin, but it does lay one open to an action for damages. Theoretically, the risk of a lawsuit raises the price of breach of contract and makes it a bit less worthwhile. Rules of civil law, then, presuppose the cost-benefit model of behavior just as much as the criminal law if not more. The same is true of rules that channel behavior without telling people what they *must* do. We used the law of wills as an example.[63] Any changes in the rules may change the cost-benefit balance and hence the rate or the manner of use.

Civil law, of course, does not rely on sanctions only, that is, on the cost-benefit balance. It too relies on inner feelings and on public sentiment for its efficacy. A rule of civil law "succeeds" if it provides incentive enough to encourage its use. Incentives and disincentives need not come from the state. To use a familiar example: Many an unhappy wife will shy away from divorce because of religious scruples or because she is ashamed. Legal culture is operative here too.

Civil law does in the main lack the feeling-tone of some parts of the criminal law. Even tort law, which, unlike contract law, sometimes allows punitive damages and recovery for pain and suffering and emotional injuries, is a relatively cold-blooded affair. Most cases are about money, not morality or feelings. But, as we noted, neither does every crime offend some deep moral feelings. Criminal law does not have a monopoly on moral indignation, nor is all "crime" conduct that makes the blood boil. Criminal law is, among other things, law open to state or public enforcement; civil law is law relegated largely to private initiative. Many "crimes" are breaches of regulatory law which the private sector cannot or will not efficiently enforce. If a grocer sells ten baskets of rotten strawberries, no one buyer or even ten buyers would find it worthwhile to sue. Food laws may be far more effective when publicly enforced, regardless of what one feels about the morality of selling substandard fruit.[64]

Some parts of the civil law—divorce and bankruptcy—do carry some stigma and shame. But on the whole, stigma and shame are not salient in civil litigation. This fact may have consequences. A fine of $1,000, and $1,000 in civil damages, are *not* exactly the same. Other things being equal, the criminal penalty is more powerful for many groups and individuals, because of the unofficial penalties it drags along in its wake. But the line is by no means hard and fast.

---

[63]See p. 48.
[64]See Lawrence M. Friedman, *A History of American Law* (1973), p. 258.

Chapter VI

On the Origin of Law and Laws

Earlier chapters dealt with conditions under which laws became
more or less effective. This chapter asks what is, in a sense, a prior
question. Where do laws come from? What social forces produce law,
the laws, the legal system, and legal change?

It is possible to answer this question only in a broad and general
way. Legislatures, courts, and administrative bodies grind out new
rules every day. Each legal act, each fragment of legal behavior, has
its own special history. Each is unique, like a set of fingerprints.
Nonetheless, legal acts fall into types, patterns recur, and some gener-
alizations are possible.

Two questions can be distinguished. The first is the question of the
origin of law in general in any society or system. But all modern
societies and many subsystems already have legal systems. For them,
the second question is the more important one: What forces produce or
thwart change in the law? What brings about new legal acts or keeps
old rules and institutions alive?

There are many general theories about the origins of law, but they
reduce to a few basic types. Some have few adherents today. Not many
people in the West believe that God, through revelation and inspiration, is the immediate source of their law. Such theories of law were
once very important and are still significant, for example, in traditional Moslem nations. In European history, there were many theories
of natural law. They had in common the idea of a body of law that stood
outside of any historical or social process. They identified law with pure
reason or with innate ideas implanted by God or some supreme being.
Many traces of these beliefs remain in modern legal thought. In gen-

eral, however, modern theories of law begin and end with human beings; philosophers may use meta-human concepts to judge the laws but
not to account for the laws themselves. Dominant opinion has it that
law is, and always has been, man-made.

Indeed, it takes no special talent to see society at work influencing
law. Any issue of the daily newspapers is full of examples, especially
for statutory law. The question is, How *much* of the story do social
forces explain; and what, if anything, is left over. There is a strong
tendency among legal scholars to downgrade the importance of outside
forces and to explain legal development internally, referring to legal
concepts and legal habits of thought. These are treated as *in some sense*
resistant to social pressure, in some sense independent of external,
social force. Those who feel this way assume that law, like language,
has some life of its own; that legal phenomena, like the phenomena
studied in chemistry or geology, have external reality and can be made
the subject of a "science."[1] If law is a science, one can study its propositions apart from any social context, and new generations will make
new "discoveries" all the time.[2]

We have earlier expressed our skepticism about this idea of legal
science.[3] Some versions of it, however, were very strong in nineteenth-
century thought, especially in Europe. The theories are still vigorous
today. In a less rigorous—and perhaps more important way—these
"theories" are implicit in everyday thinking, writing, and talking
about law. It is part of the folklore, even in modern cultures, that law
is in some sense beyond culture and certainly is or should be beyond
the ebb and flow of momentary public opinion. Lawyers and judges tend
to think, or say, that "the law" transcends time and space. After all,
this idea inflates their importance and the importance of the law. They
would rather be craftsmen and professionals than tradesmen, politicians, or puppets of history. Perhaps this kind of theory is essential for
public respect for the law. An institution, which is fair, idealistic, and
long-term and which stands apart from the selfishness of politics and
the market, should command great respect. Respect means, presumably, legitimacy; and although we voiced some skepticism in the last

---

[1]Still another possibility is what N. S. Timasheff has called "legal monism"—the
theory that law is not determined by "other elements of culture," but, on the contrary,
law determines them. Natural and divine law theories have something of this flavor. See
N. S. Timasheff, *An Introduction to the Sociology of Law* (1939), pp. 327–328.

[2]Law is obviously not an experimental science; hence, geometry might be a better
model than any natural science. Geometry is rigorous and deductive and is not culture-
bound, at least not to the naked eye.

[3]See p. 11.

chapter about how long legitimacy can sustain itself without delivering the goods, it may be, while it lasts, a powerful prop for the social order.

In any event, legal writing generally presupposes the second broad theory: the independence of law from politics and culture. We see the palm prints of this view whenever a writer argues, in some connection, that legal craft (or craftiness), as such, has been responsible for some great and permanent difference, has made an impact on society through its own inherent force. As an example, we might cite the so-called "conspiracy theory" of the Fourteenth Amendment (1868) to the United States Constitution. The amendment, enacted after the end of the Civil War, forbade the states from depriving "any person" of "life, liberty, or property," without "due process of law." The amendment was part of a package which had as one goal guaranteeing the rights of the former slaves. One generation later, however, the Supreme Court and some state courts built a whole castle of doctrine out of the words "due process of law." The phrase was used, for example, to protect businesses against unfriendly regulation. In the Minnesota Rate Case (1890), the Supreme Court held that a Minnesota law, which delegated to a commission power to fix freight rates without judicial review, took away the "property" of the railroads without "due process" of law.[4] In 1905, the Supreme Court held unconstitutional a statute fixing the maximum hours bakers could work.[5]

How had this strange transformation come about? The "conspiracy theory" suggested that the Fourteenth Amendment intended the protection of business. The word "person," rather than "citizen," was secreted into the text, presumably because the word was broad enough to cover big business. There it waited like a dormant spore for the right time to germinate.

Whether the conspiracy theory explains the events of 1868 is much disputed.[6] It is another question entirely whether the thoughts and hopes of 1868 could determine the results of cases argued in 1890 or 1905. The dispute *assumes* that the "intention" of the draftsmen in 1868 made a real difference in 1890 or 1905, that the due process clause acted as a kind of "carrier" of the later decisions, and that somehow the results of these later cases were latent or inherent in the text. To assume so, downplays or ignores the concrete social and economic forces, which pressed in on the courts, not in 1868 but in 1890 and 1905. A social theory of legal change would pay less attention to text, more

---

[4]*Chicago, Milwaukee & St. Paul Ry. Co.* v. *Minnesota,* 134 U.S. 418 (1890).

[5]*Lochner* v. *New York,* 198 U.S. 45 (1905).

[6]See Howard Jay Graham, *Everyman's Constitution* (1968), especially chs. 1 and 2.

attention to social forces. It would begin by presuming that forces at work at the time, in 1890, bear the major responsibility for the legal acts of 1890 and that it was these forces that put protection of corporate enterprise into the Fourteenth Amendment, whether that protection was "really" there in the words or not.[7]

The "conspiracy theory," as a theory, is a curious hybrid. In essence, it suggests that one social force (big business) succeeded in molding the law, by drafting the Fourteenth Amendment in a crafty way. Once the *words* were on paper, however, they took on a life of their own. Most popular "theories" of law are hybrids of this sort, that is, rather inconsistent. An orthodox Marxist should, in principle, adopt a strict social theory of law, but the less rigorous left has a less rigorous view. One hears that "the law" is torpid, unjust, glacial, reactionary, and unresponsive; by implication, it is unresponsive even to society's masters and useful only to the lawyers that pull on its strings. Those who agree reject to that extent the social theory of law.

General theories of law have political consequences. Theories in themselves are not "progressive" or "reactionary," but their consequences may be depending on the time and place. Some Soviet lawyers now argue that law *should* be impersonal, self-contained, and independent of the government. They see law as a way to balance the overpowerful state.[8] American liberals in the 1930s on the other hand, argued for a social theory of law; they wanted to liberate law from conservative judges whose neutrality masked a bias against progressive social reform.

The legal and social theories are in reality large conceptual umbrellas. An odd collection of thinkers is gathered under each of them. Modern social science in dealing with law more or less takes some form of social theory for granted. This is clearly true of work on the impact of pressure groups on legislation. It is also true of behavioral study of courts. Starting in earnest in the 1960s,[9] a school of political scientists

---

[7]For examples of this kind of analysis, see Arnold M. Paul, *Conservative Crisis and the Rule of Law: Attitudes of Bar and Bench, 1887–1895* (1960) and Lawrence M. Friedman, "Freedom of Contract and Occupational Licensing, 1890–1910: A Legal and Social Study," 53 *Calif. L. Rev.* 487 (1965).

[8]Some German jurists, too, reject the theory that law is merely social and utilitarian. The idea that law merely expresses social forces, they feel, paved the way for the amorality of Nazi justice. See, for example, Ilse Staff, ed., *Justiz im Dritten Reich* (1964), pp. 11–16.

[9]The opening salvo was C. Herman Pritchett's book, *The Roosevelt Court: A Study in Judicial Politics and Values, 1937–1947*, published in 1948, which was, in Glendon Schubert's judgment, the "first really major break with the past." Glendon Schubert, *Judicial Decision-Making* (1963), p. 2.

has tried to unravel the mystery of how and why judges decide as they do.[10] They have mostly examined the work of the United States Supreme Court. Their techniques are quite sophisticated, for legal studies, at any rate, ranging from survey research to scalogram analysis and game theory.

These studies, however diverse, generally reject the idea that judges primarily decide according to "the law"—the dictates of prior doctrines and cases. Rather, they look for the key to judicial behavior in the judge's background, attitudes, or his conception of role. Few modern scholars really think that social forces determine every legal act. They feel that legal training, thought, and concepts make some difference. The law itself, banished from center stage in their theories, creeps back in, rather surreptitiously, under the code name of "judicial role." That is, they feel that judges are "role players" and that the "role" they play often calls for following "the law." Yet, on the whole, social theory dominates their work.

Social explanations govern, too, in Marxist theories of law. In Marxist thought, law is the "aggregate of the rules of conduct . . . expressing the will of the dominant class"; it is guaranteed by the "coercive force of the state" and put into operation "to the end of safeguarding, making secure, and developing social relationships and arrangements agreeable and advantageous to the dominant class."[11] The social point of view is common too in more bourgeois circles. It is a factor in the historical school of jurisprudence, founded by the German jurist Savigny, in the early nineteenth century. Savigny insisted that true law was rooted in the history and genius of a people.[12] The American counterparts of this school, William Graham Sumner and James C. Carter, were the very epitome of late Victorian conservatism.[13] As we

---

[10]The literature is large. See Glendon Schubert, *Quantitative Analysis of Judicial Behavior* (1959) and *The Judicial Mind* (1965); Joel Grossman, "Role Playing and the Analysis of Judicial Behavior: The Case of Mr. Justice Frankfurter," 11 *J. Pub. L.* 285, 293 (1962); Theodore L. Becker, *Political Behavioralism and Modern Jurisprudence* (1964) and *Comparative Judicial Politics, the Political Functionings of Courts* (1970).

[11]S. A. Golunskii and M. S. Strogovich, " The Theory of the State and Law," in *Soviet Legal Philosophy*, trans. Hugh W. Babb (1951); see "Marx et le Droit Moderne," essays collected in vol. 12, *Archives de Philosophie du Droit* (1967); for a succinct overview, see Harold J. Berman, *Justice in the U.S.S.R.* (1963), ch. 1; K. Zweigert and H. Kötz, *Einführung in die Rechtsvergleichung* (1971) vol. I, pp. 349–358.

[12]See Julius Stone, *Social Dimensions of Law and Justice* (1966), pp. 86–111. Yet curiously enough, Savigny's own research focused not on German customary law, but on Roman law and led to the conceptual excesses of the Pandektist school. K. Zweigert and H. Kötz, pp. 170–172.

[13]See p. 68.

shall see, the popularity of social theories after 1800 was a reasonable and predictable development.[14]

Theorists who stress social forces differ too on *which* social forces influence law and in what proportions. The Marxists emphasize the economy. Owners of the means of production mold the law to protect their interests. The economic system is the base of society; law is part of the "superstructure." Even non-Marxists find it hard to deny the powerful pull of economics on law.

That culture, in the broader sense, is a molder of law also seems undeniable. The anthropological study of law shows legal diversity of a quite astounding sort, yet each distinct culture seems to generate a legal system in its image, one that suits its own style and own needs like a costume cut to specifications. Psychological laws and impulses, common to mankind in general, are another source of explanation.[15]

Probably there is some truth in both major theories of law. But do they share truth equally? If we had to choose one general theory of law, it would have to be a *social* theory. Clearly, law, in the long run, is a product of culture and society; in the short run, law constantly shows the impress of current social forces, current struggle. The values and concepts of the law come from society, too; in particular, they are the values and concepts of the powerful and influential. If this were not so, if the legal system reflected values other than the values of those in control of the political, social, and economic systems, then it would produce consistently "wrong" results—wrong, that is, from the standpoint of the powerful. (If they were consistently "right," it would be plausible to assume some connection between social forces and the outcomes of the legal system.) "Wrong" results may be tolerable for a while and in occasional cases or in minor matters, so long as the legal institutions which turn out "wrong" results have a stock of good feeling or legitimacy to fall back on. But in the long run, this kind of goodwill could hardly succeed in keeping the system going.

This is the point made, or suggested, in the last chapter, about the

---

[14]See pp. 205–207.

[15]Jerome Frank, writing in 1930, in *Law and Modern Mind* (Anchor ed., 1963), observed that judges decided cases not by reference to the law, but by following emotion and intuition. "That law is, or can be made unwavering, fixed, and settled" was a "myth," the product of a "childish need for an authoritative father." He felt that law schools and judges should "come to grips . . . with human nature," pp. 21, 22, 156, 158. On the psychological makeup of jurists, see Walter O. Weyrauch, *The Personality of Lawyers* (1964) and Wolfgang Kaupen, *Die Hüter von Recht und Ordnung* (1969), both dealing with West Germany.

relationship between legitimacy and outcomes. This relationship, we suspect, is particularly strong in modern law. Modern law is fundamentally utilitarian or instrumental. Law is right because it is useful. In any event, why would rulers, power holders, influentials put up with law, if it was consistently "wrong"? A dictator could change the law to suit his desires. So, too, could an elected body of men. Less obviously, so could the judges. Conceivably, the holders of power might stay their hand for some reason—to avoid trouble, to appear virtuous, to emphasize that their own position was peaceful and just. But the burden of proof is on those who feel that the powerful will not normally advance their own interests, as they see them. If they claim that legal concepts override self-interest, as people see them, they bear a heavy burden indeed.

Some form of social theory, then, must occupy a central place in the theory of law. This much is generally conceded. The dispute is over details. For example, how shall we account for the growth of tort law in the nineteenth century? Roscoe Pound strongly attacked the "economic interpretation." The "taught tradition of law," he felt, rather than class interests, explained the *particular* decision. Yet Pound admitted that in the long run, the economy prevailed: "With an economic interpretation of the general course of . . . legal history one can have no quarrel."[16] Indeed, one must accept the ultimate dependence of law on society. No other point of view makes sense. Roman law fit Roman society; medieval law was medieval; Islamic law was Islamic; the law of the South was a slaveholder's law; the law of the Soviets is cut to their model of society. We can concede with Pound that "legal tradition" may best explain some *particular* decision, but rarely a trend or a drift.

We noticed in Chapter I that various theories about law had or implied their own view of what law consists of, how broad is its domain. Social theories of law are most comfortable with *whole* legal systems and with long-term spans of time. This is the point that Pound was making. Social theories also suit statutes, regulations, and administrative law rather well. The case is trickier for lawyer's law and judicial doctrine. Events and ideas wholly *inside* the legal system do quite nicely, on the other hand, in explaining certain minor and short-run legal acts. What is plausible, however, may or may not be true. We suspect that many bits of legal change *seem* more "legal" on the surface than they would if we knew what went on underneath.

---

[16]Roscoe Pound, "The Economic Interpretation and the Law of Torts," 53 *Harv. L. Rev.* 365, 366 (1940).

ORIGINS: OF LAW IN GENERAL

Every society, indeed every group, needs some way to settle disputes and enforce essential norms; probably every society needs some mechanism for changing norms and applying them to novel situations. In these senses, at least, every group or society has law. On the other hand, many simple societies do not have courts, judges, and lawyers, neither do most schools, businesses, families, or clubs. They lack a "legal system," meaning formal *institutions* that specialize in rules, settling disputes, and social control. At what stage in the life of a group do these appear? So long as *informal* controls work smoothly, societies can do without *formal* controls. When social life becomes very complicated, the general public can no longer enforce norms exclusively through informal pressure and internalized norms. At that point, the group may feel the need for formal structure.

For most communities, the origins of "law" in this sense are lost in the dimness of the past. In a striking study, however, Richard Schwartz gives us a glimpse of the process.[17] Schwartz compared two Israeli settlements, a *moshav* (cooperative) and a *kvutza* (a collective community). The *moshav* had a formal legal structure; the *kvutza* did not. In the *kvutza*, children were communally raised, and meals were eaten in a common dining hall. The *moshav*, on the other hand, was less ideological. Members lived and ate with their own families in small bungalows screened by hedges and fruit trees.

The *moshav* had a judicial committee which handled disputes among members. The *kvutza* had no such body. The hammer of enforcement in the *kvutza* was public opinion—informal controls. In the *moshav*, informal controls had proven "ineffective"; the members felt a need for "legal controls." These controls then, according to Schwartz, develop "where disturbing behavior" cannot be "adequately controlled informally" without the "aid" of law.

The implications of this study are plain. Small face-to-face communities can often survive without formal law. In these communities, people generally agree about the norms. They hold common allegiance to rules of conduct, to what H.L.A. Hart called "primary rules of obligation."[18] No matter how small the community, informal social control does not work without consensus over norms. If consensus fails, then

---

[17]Richard D. Schwartz, "Social Factors in the Development of Legal Control: A Case Study of Two Israeli Settlements," 63 *Yale L.J.* 471 (1954). An interesting theoretical treatment of the process of formalization of law, and why it occurs, is in Austin T. Turk, *Legal Sanctioning and Social Control* (1972). Turk calls the process "legalization."

[18]H.L.A. Hart, *The Concept of Law* (1961), p. 89.

public opinion (the peer group) cannot enforce the rules and punish any lambs that stray from the flock. A society without formal law, with no rules but primary rules of obligation needs consensus, because such rules, Hart argues, are *static* (they evolve but cannot rapidly adapt), are *uncertain* (there are no mechanisms for resolving doubts about the scope or application of rules), and are *inefficient* (they have no method for ending a dispute once and for all).[19] If consensus about rules is lacking, consensus about rule-makers and authorities—legitimacy, in short—can substitute. A family does not need formal law if the members agree about the rules or if there is absolute agreement about authority—for example, if the children accept their father's and mother's word as law.[20]

Informal systems do not work, then, in any society badly split down the middle. (There is a question of how well *formal* systems work.) They do not work in the presence of "class struggle" or sharply contentious ethnic groups. They do not work in communities with a shifting population, where public opinion has no force, and the people warned, threatened, or "educated" today are far off tomorrow, replaced by new, raw, and unwarned populations. The police chief in a small Massachusetts community with 6,000 people does not feel the need, we are told, to write out traffic tickets; it is enough to give violators a good lecture and threaten to take their licenses away, if they repeat.[21] But in a large city, full of strangers, these tactics do not work.

Conflict and competition, as such, are not fatal to informal social control. Society can contain and control its conflict and competition, so long as people generally agree about *aims* and *means*—what things one may compete and conflict about and how. The economists' free market, for example, assumes vigorous competition. This can go on without too much formal regulation, as long as business people agree on the rules of the game and how to deal with those who violate the rules. Competition is, in Vilhelm Aubert's terms, a "conflict of interest."[22] Two businessmen, for example, both want to win a contract to

---

[19]Hart, pp. 89–91; see Stuart A. Schlegel, *Tiruray Justice* (1970), pp. 54–57.

[20]Hence, the existence of many simple societies that lack formal institutions for enforcement, but who invest mediators or other third parties with "sanctity" and accept their decisions on faith. See John H. Hamer, "Dispute Settlement and Sanctity: an Ethiopian Example," 45 *Anthropological Q.* 232 (1972).

[21]John A. Gardiner, *Traffic and Police, Variations in Law Enforcement Policy* (1969), pp. 147–148.

[22]See Vilhelm Aubert, "Competition and Dissensus: Two Types of Conflict and Conflict Resolution," 7 *J. Conflict Resolution* 26 (1963). A "conflict of interest" is to be distinguished from a conflict of values, facts, or beliefs. See pp. 225–227.

supply steel to a bridgebuilder. They compete, but they agree on the rules of competition. Underbidding is acceptable; advertising is acceptable; extortion and blackmail are (usually) not; bombing a rival's factory is not, presumably for moral reasons as well as out of fear of criminal sanctions. They also agree or assume that bidding is an acceptable way to award contracts. They accept the value of the game as a whole and its subgames along with its supporting institutions.

Whether informal systems "work," of course, is a matter of more or less. Informal sanctions do have some effect even in complex societies riddled with dissension. Indeed, as we have suggested, a legal system could hardly work without some support from social groups. The question is, Will group support work so well that no sanctions will be needed? That is, will informal pressure bring enforcement to a level that the *community* will define as good enough for the community's needs?

Schwartz's observations fit in nicely with others made by Joseph Gusfield. Gusfield studied American temperance and drug laws. These laws were the product of "moral crusades"; they bred "strong countermovements." The "deviants" fought back; they threatened the very legitimacy of the norms. The battle acted as a "spur" to those who felt the "need for symbolic restatement" of the embattled norm "in legal terms." As the struggle became more bitter, more temperance laws were passed in reaction to the threats. This legal activity was not a sign of "consensus within the community." Rather, legal norms revealed cracks in the social armor; "it is when consensus is least attainable that the pressure to establish the legal norms appears to be greatest."[23]

Gusfield's point sheds light on an important process. We can see it, for example, in the history of school law. American schools operated, on the whole, with few formal rules. They did not need many rules, so long as students and teachers agreed on basic values—or agreed who was boss. Few schools had formal dress codes. Students dressed the way they were expected to dress. But then students began to grow their hair long and to wear "hippie" clothing. Some teachers were offended. Students also began to show less deference. At this point, schools and school boards felt they had to lay down definite rules. At this point too, litigation began, and long hair in school became a judicial issue.[24]

---

[23]Joseph R. Gusfield, "Moral Passage: The Symbolic Process in Public Designations of Deviance," 15 *Social Problems* 175 (1967).

[24]See Stephen R. Goldstein, "The Scope and Sources of School Board Authority to Regulate Student Conduct and Status: A Nonconstitutional Analysis," 117 *U. Pa. L. Rev.* 373 (1969).

Schools had never worried about procedure before—hearings, rules, judges. Discipline was discipline, and teachers and principals did their job. When deference slipped, however, the schools, in part under pressure, had to look to their forms and formalities.[25] Here again, we see formal law and legal institutions thriving at a point of balance, halfway between two "states of nature"—the primary group, controlled by informal means and the society of revolutionary anarchy where everyone does as he pleases. For societies as a whole, neither pole is common. But there are small groups and subsystems that conform to these ideal types.

Rules of a modern legal system are not, in the main, "shared norms." This is so in two distinct ways. First of all, there are culture clashes in every modern society. Every country has ethnic minorities or at least classes, interest groups, and strata. Some laws—on adultery, murder, polygamy, and rape—do rest on "shared norms," but even these are hardly universal. Polygamy was once a burning issue in the United States; it is still an issue in African countries with Moslem minorities. Opinion about adultery is far from unanimous, too. Some groups do not define revenge-killing as murder.

In addition, literally thousands of rules in a modern state have a purely technical content. Under federal regulations in the United States, no product could be called "ice cream" unless it had 10 percent or more, by weight, of butterfat.[26] This percentage was hardly a "shared norm." There was not even a "shared norm" that ice cream should be rich, tasty, and full of cholesterol. The rule about fat, of course, was not pulled out of thin air. Those who promulgated it based their decision on known criteria. These criteria probably commanded a good deal of agreement. No doubt people generally feel that food should be wholesome and safe, that food makers should not cheat the public, that the government has a duty or right to keep the industry honest, and that it should use scientific methods in regulating food. At the same time, these norms are not precise, detailed, or concrete enough to solve any particular problem. No one could deduce from these principles the proper percentage of butterfat. It cannot even be deduced from *scientific* norms.

The expression, "shared norm," seems to refer to some sort of

---

[25]Compare, also, the case of the California Industrial Accident Commission, as described in Philippe Nonet's *Administrative Justice* (1969), pp. 174–175, where informal procedures, under the pressure of interest groups, had to be replaced by more "legalistic" procedures.

[26]21 C.F.R. 20.1 (a).

moral principle which has substantive legitimacy. Realistically speaking, most rules do not have this quality—or not enough or not precise enough to give them the support that a "shared norm" is supposed to have. People believe that food should be wholesome, and they will agree that cyclamates should be banned from diet soda, but only if these chemicals are actually a danger to health. People will support or approve the rules, if they have faith in those who made the rules and the way they made them, insofar as people know. What the rules say is not "shared" or universal at all. Quite the contrary: These rules are often in dispute—or are rules *created* by dispute, rules that arise, as did the liquor laws, out of a climate of conflict.

Formal law presupposes that climate of conflict; modern societies easily meet this criterion. In modern societies, there is no doubt that "law" in the formal sense exists; indeed, it is an overwhelming social fact. For these societies, then, we can move from the general question to the specific—to the sources of legal acts.

ORIGINS: OF LAW IN PARTICULAR

Any form of social theory of law implies one fundamental principle: The living law, observed in cross section at any point in time, reveals the imprint of those social forces which have actually pressed against the legal system. Each fresh legal act results from and reflects the social forces that exerted themselves to produce, block, or change the act. Where the balance of force pushes toward change, change occurs. Where it does not, the state of the system remains as it was before. In general, a look at the law as a whole or any important part is like a slice through the earth; rocks and fossils reveal which forces molded the landscape.

If we analyze some particular bit of behavior, such as a major statute, we can grasp the point more clearly. An elaborate statute can be broken up into smaller acts, each of which lends itself to yes–no decision. Tiny indivisible acts seem to be either–or decisions. There is a vote; one side wins, the other loses. In life, however, bits do not exist in isolation; the pieces are interrelated. Individual acts are part of a chain of acts; trade-offs and compromises are always possible. A major statute, pages and pages long, can be broken down by the legislature into smaller units, each unit subject to majority vote. When it comes time for a final vote, the bill stands or falls as a whole, yet any strong minority will have left its mark on the bill in the form of amendments, modifications, and compromise provisions. The final statute, then, will not *merely* reflect which social group had the upper hand; it will reflect he losers' influence, too, insofar as they had any power to exert and actually exerted it. The final result will show who played in the game, how strong the players were, and how they were distributed in teams. For example, when a health insurance plan for the elderly was enacted in the United States in 1965, the organized doctors seemed the losers.[27] Yet they left their mark on the law in many ways—the plan was restricted to the elderly, for example, and doctors were left free to charge as much as they pleased.

One point about social explanations of law should be stressed, however. Social forces in the abstract do not make law. They must actually press against the system by making demands. A person who understood the social structure of a society could not deduce the legal system from this structure. Among social structure, social forces, and the law, a complex cultural variable intervenes. We call it, in brief, *demand.*

In other words, mere forces and interests do not make law; what makes law are forces and interest that express *demands.* A group can have strength but choose not to use it; it can forego the pursuit of its "true" interest as others might see it. Power and (objective) interest, as far as the law is concerned, are irrelevant, unless and until they turn into demands.

Here is where ideology makes a crucial impact on law. The working class had the right to vote in the nineteenth-century United States. They could have voted themselves into power and redistributed income to themselves. Arguably, this looked like their best interests. Of course, there were many reasons why no such revolution took place, but it is possible that *one* of the reasons was how deeply many members of the working class shared the dominant feelings of their time. Many people were convinced that only a business economy could bring lasting prosperity. This was the goose that laid the golden eggs. There were strong ideas abroad about the practical and moral limits on demands. These ideas, whatever their ultimate causes, had a powerful short-run effect on the pattern of demands.

Ideas and ideals move people. They mold the very way people see their interests. They ultimately change the structure of government and law and cut the grooves along which conceptions of interest run. People feel they must follow their ideals; they also believe they should disguise their interests in idealistic clothing. They talk about states'

---

[27]The law is the "Health Insurance for the Aged Act," 79 Stats. 290, Act of July 30, 1965; on the background, see Richard Harris, *A Sacred Trust* (1966); Max J. Skidmore, *Medicare and the American Rhetoric of Reconciliation* (1970).

rights, decentralization, community control of schools, abolition of the jury, expansion of the jury, etc. as outright rationalizations. What they want are specific outcomes, but they cannot always openly admit this. Politicians talked states' rights when they meant keeping blacks in their place. The audience understood. Still, casting the debate in such terms *might* influence some people, especially people hanging in the balance. Finally, ideas and ideals have power, because they intervene between objective interests and actual demands. A person can have power to press forward but hold back because of ideas and ideals. If a businessman can be persuaded that lobbying is immoral or corrupt, or that, in the long run, what he thinks he wants will hurt him or the country, he might decide not to fight for a particular beneficial legal act.

Social explanations of law, then, assume the existence of *interests*, which are converted into *demands* and then produce responses in the legal system. It is the legal culture that presides over the conversion of interests into demands. The response of the system depends on the structure of the legal system itself (we will call this the "structural variable") and on the structure of the outside society, that is, the distribution of power and influence. The legal culture will be discussed in Chapter VIII. We will now discuss, briefly, *interests* and the *structural variable*. In Chapter VII, we will discuss power, influence, and the relationship of law and class structure.

A CATALOGUE OF INTERESTS

We have spoken loosely about "interests" without making clear what we mean. Interests come in various types and shapes.[28] First of all, there are *direct* interests, mostly economic. A person has a direct interest in any proposed legal act that will put money in his purse or take it out. If Congress proposes a 1 percent tax increase to provide pensions for war veterans, a veteran would have a direct interest (negative) because of his tax load and a direct interest (positive) in the pension. His positive interest will probably be many times larger than his negative interest. The larger the direct interest, the more likely a person will exert social force with regard to a proposed legal act, for or against.

There are direct interests that are less crudely economic. Individuals and groups will favor measures that add to their power, prestige,

---

[28]See Lawrence M. Friedman, *Government and Slum Housing: A Century of Frustration* (1968), pp. 184–186.

or sense of well-being; these are institutional, bureaucratic, or status-group interests. Jews, businessmen, blacks, actors—any group—tend to support measures good for other Jews, businessmen, blacks, or actors, even when they themselves do not stand to gain.

Other interests are much more *indirect.* No sharp line divides a direct from an indirect interest. A city has an urban renewal scheme; a building contractor has a direct interest in winning a contract to build an apartment house. He has an indirect interest in the renewal scheme in general, because it will help contractors, generate business, and vitalize his city. He may have no guarantee that the business will actually come to *him.* Even a cold-blooded calculator has trouble with indirect interests. They are difficult to reckon. The contractor knows he will have to pay taxes to finance renewal. This is a direct interest, and it cuts against the plan. The benefits are latent and distant. How can he know how to balance one against each other?

All other interests we will call *reform* interests. A reformer is a person who spends his energy on an issue where he has nothing *personally* at stake—no interest, direct or indirect. In modern society, the reform interest is common and important. Nonetheless, as a rough general rule for the mass of humanity and for most issues, we expect *direct* interests to pull more powerfully than indirect interests; reform interests less than direct interests and less than many indirect interests as well. Even reformers can only spend themselves on one or two areas of reform; in others, direct interests continue to rule. For the day-by-day run of humanity, reform is a luxury few can afford: "Experience tells us that a bill to abolish liquor stores will be opposed by people who own liquor stores. If a proposal is made to build an eight-lane highway through Manhattan, storekeepers who would lose their shops will oppose the plan, even though the highway in the long run is 'good for business'. In a copper mine, a worker who is ideologically opposed to war will probably support the stockpiling of copper 'for defense reasons,' if it means that his job is saved."[29] These observations hold as a general rule.

Interests are not always obvious. People can be, and often are, grossly ignorant about their own self-interest. People guess about their interests; they often guess wrong. On many issues, only a tiny minority is directly interested. Shall the state of California license electricians? Shall a national park be created in northern Minnesota? Shall the United States move to the metric system? In each case a few people have strong direct interests on each side of the issue—the electricians

---

[29]Lawrence M. Friedman, *Government and Slum Housing* (1968), p. 186.

in California, the landowners in northern Minnesota, the publishers of textbooks in arithmetic. The interests of others are real but very slight. The park would cost a bit in taxes; many people might visit it and enjoy themselves. If California licensed electricians, the cost of wiring might go up. The metric system would change the habits of a lifetime, but it would be simpler in the long run, and it would be good for international trade.

In real life, people with small interest or no interest in these proposals would pay no attention. A congressman from Florida will have the right—even the duty—to vote on the park in Minnesota. He may follow the party line, or trade with the Minnesota delegation for some Florida bill, or vote one way or the other, storing up credit for the future. The people who want the park badly are a minority; to win, they must bargain and trade for a majority coalition. The same is true of the people against.

Where an issue *directly* affects a small minority, partisans and reformers have a particular opportunity and role. They try to persuade the neutrals—those with unused power and influence—to cast their lot on one side or another. Some neutrals are people who think the act will affect them, but they are not sure whether the effect will be good or bad. Others see nothing for them in the act one way or the other. Partisans and reformers will try to get the first group off the fence and the second group aroused. They may use a mixture of moral and economic arguments. They will try to show people what the law might mean for them. Spokesmen for the electricians will argue that the public might get better electrical work, if the licensing law is passed. Conservationists will talk about the need for wilderness, for open space, for national parks. On the other side, we may hear about lumberjacks thrown out of work. Trade unions may take a stand for the sake of solidarity or to win future support from lumber workers. The arguments, in general, will try to rouse the sleeping giant—dormant perceptions of latent interest.

These efforts go on unceasingly. They are part of the life cycle of most legislation. But enactment is only a beginning. Legal dynamics continue long after the ink dries on a bill. Reformers and partisans arouse expectations and interests, but many of these are diffuse and unstable. The arguments were exaggerated guesses. Law in action often turns out very different from the glittering promises and the colorful packages. Reality sets up fresh fields of force. People demand wage-price controls to beat inflation. A law is passed, but shortages and black markets develop. Now people want amendment or repeal. Many people thought Prohibition would be an excellent idea; it was a monster in practice. Sometimes law disappoints expectations because of the way it is enforced. The Interstate Commerce Commission, set up in 1877, was supposed to tame the big, bad railroads. At least, farmers and shippers hoped so. But they came to think of the agency as a puppet of the railroads, consistently doing their bidding.[30]

People also commonly change their minds about where their interests lie. In the United States, urban renewal drew political strength from the hopes of good middle-class people that such plans would bring new life to their communities.[31] The streets would be safe to walk on, the dead downtown areas would come to life, the slums would disappear. But when it turned out that their own neighborhoods might be destroyed, many people, who had favored the plan, turned to the opposition. The proof of the pudding, after all, is in the eating.[32] On the other hand, many programs, bitterly disputed before enactment, disarm the opposition once in force simply because the sky does not fall in. Regulation turns out not to be onerous; novelties grow into habits. In a 1955 referendum in Sweden, 82.9 percent of the voters voted against changing from left-hand to right-hand driving. After years of debate, the country made the change. Once done, it became a fait accompli; the grumbling diminished. Clearly, as time passes, less and less will be heard about the old way of driving.[33]

Moreover, the "social force" that makes law is itself quite volatile. Within any society, an enormous amount of social energy lies inert; but this energy can be mobilized within limits by firebrand reformers or

---

[30]Samuel P. Huntington, "The Marasmus of the ICC: The Commission, the Railroads and the Public Interest," 61 *Yale L.J.* 467 (1952). There are other views of the history of railroad regulation. Gabriel Kolko, for example, has argued that this outcome was preordained; the railroads had made their mark on the original legislation, molding it in such a way as to ensure that the commission would be tame and unthreatening, *Railroads and Regulation, 1877–1916* (1965). In any case, farmers and shippers, weakly organized, were unable to exert much strength, once the law was passed. (They had some power and access in the legislature.) The ICC, however, had to live with its railroads every day; they were the day-to-day source of pressure and strength.

[31]There is a large literature on urban renewal. See, in particular, Scott Greer, *Urban Renewal and American Cities* (1965); Herbert Gans, *The Urban Villagers* (1962).

[32]Two scholars studied attitudes in Holland toward a value-added tax. A slight majority of their sample favored the law, before it was enacted. But later many people soured on the subject. The government campaign to whip up support for the tax had been successful, but information "loses its meaning and force, when the actual effects of the law become palpable." Cees J. M. Schuyt and Joop C. M. Ruys, "Die Einstellung gegenüber neuen sozialökonomischen Gesetzen," in *Zur Effektivität des Rechts*, vol. 3, *Jahrbuch für Rechtssoziologie und Rechtstheorie* (1972), pp. 565, 582.

[33]See the discussion in Britt-Mari P. Blegvad and Jette Moller Nielsen, "Recht als Mittel des sozialen Wandels," in *Zur Effektivität des Rechts*, p. 430.

galvanized into life by some scandal or incident. Upton Sinclair's novel *The Jungle* (1906) nauseated the public with its description of filth in the meatpacking plants; it paved the way for passage of new food and drug laws.[34] Violent, horrible crimes touch off demands for sterner laws.[35] When the noise dies down, quite different dynamics take over.

For many reasons, then, the course of legal development does not run smooth. There are few straight lines, even few gentle curves. Uneven development does not mean that legal institutions are "unresponsive" to social forces. Rather, they are extremely responsive, extremely sensitive. It is this responsiveness that makes development follow a zigzag path, reflecting the complexity and constant change of social, political, and economic life.

THE STRUCTURAL VARIABLE

When we say that social forces "make" the law, we do not mean that this precise law, word for word, was the *only* possible product or result of social forces. Chance and choice continue to operate within constraints imposed by social forces.

Social theories are most likely to lead to satisfying answers about long-run trends and those legal acts that have the most social impact. Minor and short-run events may call for minor, short-run explanations. Some of these can be structural; and even chance can be pressed into service. If the question is, why Congress did not enact a national health law *yesterday*, it is a fair answer to point out that yesterday was Sunday, and Congress did not sit. There is no need to drag in big business, doctors' groups, or even legal doctrine.[36] In the short run, the shape and structure of the legal system, the *structural variable*, puts its stamp on events. Only in the long run does it melt away as a *causal* factor. Hence *time* is an important variable in the theory of law and society.

William F. Ogburn, writing in the 1920s, argued that, often, when "one part of culture changes" (because of new technology, for example), other parts of the culture do not catch up right away; there is a period of "delay" or "readjustment." Ogburn found, for example, a fifty-year "lag" between the time the problem of industrial accidents emerged

---

[34]See Lawrence M. Friedman and Stewart Macaulay, *Law and the Behavioral Sciences* (1969), pp. 561–565.

[35]Edwin H. Sutherland, "The Diffusion of Sexual Psychopath Laws," 56 *Am. J. Sociology* 142 (1950).

[36]Although why Congress observes Sunday ultimately calls for a social explanation.

and the time when workmen's compensation plans were adopted in the United States. During this period, "the old . . . culture . . . hung over after the material conditions had changed."[37] Many people, in and out of law, agree that law or parts of it are or can be "behind the times," archaic, out of touch. The common notion, then, is that legal structure does make an important difference, particularly in retarding change.

If, however, the fundamental framework of the social theory is correct, we must be skeptical about any hypothesis of "culture lag" in the law. Not that culture lag is an entirely useless idea. It expresses a moral point of view. It describes delays and barriers which prevent those solutions that, in the speaker's view, would be fairer or more just. What is wrong about the concept is not the moral tone, but the assumption that something *in the legal system*, something structural, some loose bolts in the concepts or machinery of law makes the system "unresponsive" or by nature slow to move, keeping the system from adapting to social demands. To say this is to conjure up a picture of the legal system as some sort of obstacle, an enormous fat man collapsed in the middle of the road blocking traffic, and too heavy to move. There is a grain of truth in the notion but only a grain. What keeps old-fashioned laws alive (abortion laws, drug laws), what hinders enactment of strict controls over noise and smoke, what preserves the class structure, and what maintains a brutal prison system is not the legal system in itself, not structure, not the network of legal concepts, but real forces, real people—the concrete opposition of interest groups expressed *through* or *in* the legal system.

Any social theory of law implies a great deal of caution before one attaches the word "unresponsive" to the legal system or some parts of it. It is easy to show that the system is very fast and very responsive, when no one stands in the way. Congress is often described as hidebound and immobile in its structures. But in December, 1941, when the Japanese attacked Pearl Harbor, both houses of Congress roused themselves to declare war with incredible speed—not in years, months, or days, but in hours.

This speed shows that structure can be short cut under ideal circumstances, and the "drag" of the legal system, its resistance to social change, can melt away like butter. What are these conditions? Basically, where there is no opposition. When *all* force is directed toward

---

[37] William F. Ogburn, *Social Change with Respect to Culture and Original Nature* (1950), pp. 199–280; see also Yehezkel Dror, "Law and Social Change," 33 *Tulane L. Rev.* 787 (1959); Lawrence M. Friedman and Jack Ladinsky, "Social Change and the Law of Industrial Accidents," 67 *Colum. L. Rev.* 50, 72–77 (1967).

one goal, structures crumble; or rather, they too work toward that goal. A consensus among the powerful cannot be stopped. The structures do not and cannot interfere.

What role, then, does the structure of the legal system play? As a rough approximation, we can compare it to a rope in a tug of war. Imagine two teams pulling on the rope, one at either end. The stronger team drags the other forward against its will. The rope does not "cause" this movement. The rope is only an instrument, a means. Of course, the game could not take place *without* the rope; it is the medium along which force moves. The legal system is such a medium.

Social theories pushed to their limit treat the legal system as a conduit, a medium, a kind of permeable membrane. Social demands flow in at one end; legal acts come out the other, producing legal behavior. The medium does not influence the outcome or the message.

Classical legal thought tended to overrate law as an independent variable in at least two ways: first, as a system which imposed its own values and forms on the outside world; second, as a structure which bent and distorted the energies flowing through it. No one would deny *any* power of its own to the structure; in the short and middle run, the *structural variable* must make some difference. Even the rope in our metaphor of the tug of war had some function, and its physical properties—roughness, thickness, type of material—affected the chances of the players. Almond and Powell speak about "interest aggregation"— the "function of converting demands into general policy alternatives." As they explain it, a "political party convention, as it receives the complaints and demands of labor unions and business organizations, and juggles, bargains, and compromises these conflicting interests into some sort of policy statement, is engaging in interest aggregation."[38] This is roughly the role of the rope, the role of the legal system. It provides a structure for aggregating interests, for expressing demands, for converting demands into rules and decisions. It is, in a way, a kind of prism in reverse. It takes in various bands of light, the colors of the rainbow, and converts them into a single white beam.

These, however, are metaphors. Granted, legal structure does make some difference; exactly how much, we do not know. If we found two societies, whose social demands on the legal system were identical but whose structures were different, and if we found different outputs and impacts, we could ascribe the variance to structure. Such societies, however, do not exist. The structures themselves come out of history,

---

[38]Gabriel Almond and G. Bingham Powell, Jr., *Comparative Politics, a Developmental Approach* (1966), p. 98.

culture, and tradition, that is, from past and present social forces. Where social demands are the same, structure should gradually melt into similar forms. Structures change, in short, along with society, interacting constantly with other forces, other institutions.[39]

People have values as well as interests. The structure may allow free rein to the values of people in strategic places in the short and middle run. A congressman votes for a bill because of civic-mindedness, even though his mail runs heavily against him. This congressman is no mere conduit. If we looked closely enough at his background, we might find that his values were the residue of old interests and pressures, concealed or congealed. In any event, it is a question how often congressmen behave "in the public interest" or according to conscience, rather than as straight political beings with their eyes on the next election. In the long run, the good conduits get reelected. Those who are *too* courageous lose their seats, but the structure allows many leeways in the short run.

The study of the structural variable, then, is an important part of the study of legal behavior. In one guise or another, the question runs through the literature: What difference does federalism make? What is the impact of an activist court? Of a legislature with one chamber instead of two? A civil service dominated by lawyers?[40] Judges sitting in panels rather than alone? It is hard to do much better than mere speculation. Experiment is rare and difficult. There are so many intrusive factors, which doggedly insist on clouding the crystal ball. Still, some work goes on. Maurice Rosenberg, investigating the value of pretrial conferences in personal injury cases, studied a matched set of

---

[39]We might get some ideas of the strength of the structural variable by looking at the matter the other way around. If political systems which seem structurally very different produce the same results, perhaps the structure has had little effect. See Thomas R. Dye, *Politics, Economics, and the Public: Policy Outcomes in the American States* (1966). Dye found that "economic variables" were "more influential than political system characteristics in shaping public policy in the states" (p. 296). Such factors as the way the state was apportioned or the vigor (or lack of vigor) of its party system did not explain differences in, for example, the amounts states spent on schools and highways. Of course, these "system characteristics" are not quite what we mean by structure, but the study is still rather suggestive.

[40]Gerhard Brinkmann, discussing the case of West Germany in "Die Diskriminierung der Nicht-Juristen in allgemeinen höheren Verwaltungsdiensten der Bundesrepublik Deutschland," 129 *Zeitschrift für die Gesamte Staatswissenschaft*, no. 1, 150 (1973), suggests that this makes a big difference, but he brings no evidence to bear on this particular point. On the impact or nonimpact of lawyers in legislatures, see Heinz Eulau and John D. Sprague, *Lawyers in Politics, A Study in Professional Convergence* (1964) and Justin J. Green, John R. Schmidhauser, Larry L. Berg, and David Brady, "Lawyers in Congress: A New Look at Some Old Assumptions," 26 *Western Pol. Q.* 440 (1973).

New Jersey cases, some with and some without such conferences.[41] Harry Kalven and Hans Zeisel published a massive study of the criminal jury. The main question they asked was structural: Do jury cases come out differently from cases decided by a judge alone?[42] A team at the University of North Carolina tested the adversary system against the "inquisitorial" system, using mock trials.[43]

Most of these are studies of one piece or element of the legal structure. The legal system in a country is made up of countless elements of structure. Federalism, for example, is a cluster of structures; so, for example, is the French legal system compared or opposed to that of England or Japan. Whole books have been written about such structural variables as federalism. One modest point can be made: A structure like federalism is both a cause and an effect. It is surely an effect of the culture, especially in so far as federalism is a *living* organism.[44] Federalism, however, may also be a fact; its ideas and shapes become part of the common stock of beliefs and expectations. People accept the federal system and act accordingly, because they do not find anything else really conceivable. Structure becomes, in short, custom or habit. This means that the threshold of skepticism, or rebellion, is that much higher. We expect federalism to survive and to influence life in the United States: But how? And how much?

Within any legal system, living institutions and structures have histories and mean something to people. These meanings change only slowly, with some traumatic exceptions. The United States Supreme Court is a structural fact, an institution with body and shape; it has social and psychological boundaries, and, in the short run, it is certainly not infinitely plastic. This is because social meanings clump about each structure. The Court means the majesty of the law, John Marshall, marble columns, robes, prestige, *Brown* v. *Board of Education*, a concept, an image. Structures have social-psychological and cultural boundaries. For this reason, there may be consequences, in the short run, when a job is transferred from one institution to another— when cases about freight rates are taken away from the courts and given to the Interstate Commerce Commission. Nothing inherent in a "court" makes it unsuitable for this work. The commissioners know more about railroads than judges, but judges could learn about rail-

[41]Maurice Rosenberg, *The Pretrial Conference and Effective Justice* (1964)
[42]Harry Kalven and Hans Zeisel, *The American Jury* (1966).
[43]John Thibaut, Laurens Walker, and E. Allan Lind, "Adversary Presentation and Bias in Legal Decisionmaking," 86 *Harv. L. Rev.* 386 (1972).
[44]There are any number of federal states that are federal on paper only. The sovereignty and "independence" of the Soviet republics, for example, is a myth.

roads, too, if they tried or were trained. The difference lies in the social meanings that attach to institutions. "Courts" have a social definition, which, in the short run, they cannot and will not shake off. This is more than the matter of a label; it is a matter of culture, which judges and lawyers share and which affects their behavior. When society transfers job *X* to institution *Z*, it usually *intends* to make a difference; one way in which social forces act on the law is by shuffling functions from court to agency to police to president and back again.

THE SOCIAL THEORY OF LAW: SOME QUESTIONS AND ANSWERS

If the metaphor of the rope aptly describes the role of the legal system and if the concept of "culture lag" does not fit, why are contrary opinions so widely held? One reason is the old problem of the meaning of the word "law" or the phrase "legal system." People talk about "law" or "the legal system" when they mean not the whole but some part. Social forces may have a different effect on different legal acts—statutes, case-law, administrative behavior. The legal system *as a whole* will reflect with fair accuracy how social power is distributed, but each part of the legal system need not be a little mirror of society in itself. The parts are like pieces on a chessboard; they can make different moves and play different roles in the game. Because of this, they may serve different masters. The police have their constituency; so do the Supreme Court, Congress, and the president. It is not the structure that attracts a constituency; output is what counts. In the United States, blacks find the Supreme Court more congenial than, for example, white city councils in the South. The preferences of white supremacists are the other way around. Both institutions create legal acts. A complete picture —an accurate picture—of the legal system would include them both. Jurists, however, are interested mostly in "lawyers' law"—in common-law countries, courts, above all; the codes and their glosses on the Continent. The habit is a natural result of their training, but it infects other scholars, too, who get their outlook on law secondhand through the books that the jurists write. A narrow view of "the law" distorts one's view of the relationship of law and society.

A second caution is that "legal system" must refer to the real legal system, not the system on paper. There can certainly be "lag" in the paper legal system. In many legal systems, it is easy to find useless survivals from the past. But what do they mean? A leading American treatise on property law flatly states that a form of the ancient fee tail still exists in Maine, Massachusetts, and Delaware.[45] The question is, "exists" in what way? Doctors or farmers in and around Wilmington, Portland, or Plymouth do not leave or give land to the heirs of their body in fee tail. This "survival" survives by not surviving at all. Behaviorally, it is absolutely dead, but for one reason or another, no one has bothered to remove the corpse from the books. The common law is notoriously sloppy in these matters; unlike the codified systems, it is slow to bury its dead.[46]

These survivals make good stories, and they do tell something about legal culture. Perhaps training in common-law law schools exaggerates the survivals. The survivals tend to cluster in areas of law— property, for example—which have the most archaic *language* and are least disturbed by statute. The continental codes, on the other hand, are deceptively rational. They are basically the work of jurists for jurists. They emphasize clarity, elegance, and system. But one cannot deduce from the codes how the law really works—not even from the gloss that courts have put on them. In every mature, Western system, living law is different from the law on the books; both are social facts, but it is above all living law that the social theory tries to explain.

Another point, too, is worth making. Any general theory of law, stressing interest groups and social forces, must have room for lawyers and judges as an interest group in its own right. The profession has values, traditions, and habits and strong economic interests and political strength. Lawyers are, on the whole, well-to-do, articulate, and influential. In the United States, they sit in great numbers in the legislatures.[47] Some "archaism" or "lag" in law is nothing more than the result of orthodox interest group behavior by bench and bar. This noisy, numerous group, nimble in defense of its economic interests, battles against no-fault insurance and has fought similar battles to protect its fees in the past. Government in modern society with its millions of employees is also a powerful interest group; the bureaucracy fights for its interests as greedily as any trade group.

---

[45]1 *Am. Law of Property* § 2.13. Land held in fee tail—common in the Middle Ages —descends to the "heirs of the body" of the holder. In medieval law, such land could not be sold, given, or willed away.

[46]A classic instance in English law was trial by battle, that staple of medieval romance. It was not actually abolished until 1819 after a litigant, through a mistake in pleading, accidentally invoked the right to battle. An embarrassed Parliament then did away with it. Theodore T. F. Plucknett, *A Concise History of the Common Law* (5th ed., 1956), p. 118; see also p. 272.

[47]See Heinz Eulau and John D. Sprague, *Lawyers in Politics, A Study in Professional Convergence* (1964); J. Willard Hurst, *The Growth of American Law: The Lawmakers* (1950), p. 47.

ARE SOCIAL THEORIES TAUTOLOGIES?

From one point of view, grand social theories of law cannot be proven, because their argument is circular. One can hardly *prove* that the Social Security Act in all its details, as enacted in the 1930s, reflected exactly those social forces that pushed and pulled in Congress, for and against, at exactly that time. If we assume this, however, we can use the shape and scope of the law to point out what those forces must have been. The law, passed in 1935,[48] did not allow pensioners to earn more than a small amount in wages after retirement age. It was all right to have income from stocks, bonds, or rents or gifts from children, but not income from a job. This was a period of tremendous unemployment. Labor wanted to get older workers out of the job market, hence provisions reflecting the power and interests of organized labor.

This reasoning *is* circular, of course. But the point of the theory is not to prove but to suggest hypotheses and lead the way to strategies for research. Suppose the question is raised, *Why* a particular rule of law took on a particular form? How does one research this question? Where does one look first? What is the starting hypothesis? If social pressures bring on legal change, then this is where one begins—not with legal concepts, not with formal legal thought, not with logical analysis of the prior state of the law, not with structure, not with history, in the doctrinal sense. The idea is that it will yield the best, most reasonable results to begin the search for explanation in society. Social "theories," then, are useful conceptual frameworks for studying legal phenomena. The "social theory of law" does not explain legal behavior by itself. It may not even deserve the name of a "theory" at all.[49] Alternative ways of looking at law, however, suffer from worse defects and have not produced satisfactory results. The social theory is an attitude, an approach, a conceptual framework, a start toward building explanations of legal acts and legal behavior. It is not necessary to banish other doctrines, frameworks, or theories entirely. The facts may serve them up so forcefully that we cannot resist them. But that will come later, if at all.

A complete theory of law would be largely a social theory, but it would take into account social structure and the values held by legal actors. Ultimately, the culture manufactures these values, which people select or which their parents and teachers drill into them. Values

---

[48] 42 U.S.C. § 403.

[49] See Theodore J. Lowi, "American Business, Public Policy, Case-Studies, and Political Theory," 16 *World Politics* 677 (1964), questioning whether the related interest group theory of politics is truly a theory.

and ideals are like clothes on a rack in the store. People choose what they like in their size; the store and the manufacturers set the short-run limits of choice; customer tastes have a long-run effect. Structure, too, is ultimately a product of culture. Structures are patterns of behavior that persist over time—vessels or containers that the culture slowly welds into shapes. In the long run, structure and values and social forces blend into one. But the phrase "the long run" is not very precise. As a practical, everyday matter, the three concepts—structure, value and immediate social force—can be and probably should be kept distinct.

LAW AND PUBLIC OPINION

One commonly hears that law does (or does not) "reflect public opinion." The phrase "public opinion" can be rather misleading. Majority opinion does not make law the way majority votes make a president. It would be naive to imagine that the opinions of a majority of ordinary people become automatically law. Authoritarian countries do not even pretend this is so. There are vast inequalities in parliamentary systems too despite their elections. The legal system faithfully reflects these inequalities of wealth, power, and prestige. Moreover, people have different skills and intensities of feeling. They may choose to exert influence on some subjects but not on others. The public opinion measured by a Gallup poll would not describe the *actual social force* on law, even in a perfect democracy with complete equality of income.

Studies of law and public opinion are not common. One well-known study was conducted by Julius Cohen, Reginald A. Robson, and Alan P. Bates.[50] They were interested in the "moral sense of the community." They interviewed a cross section of the population of Nebraska. They asked questions about the rights and duties of parents and children and put forward for discussion some imaginary situations. For instance, they asked whether people thought parents should control their children's religion, and whether parents should be able to disinherit their children. They counted and sorted the answers and matched these with the actual state of the law. They claimed to find a large gap between "public opinion," as they measured it, and the law, as they understood it. For example, Nebraska law, like American law in general, allows parents almost total freedom to disinherit grown children. But almost two-thirds of the people of Nebraska felt this was wrong, and 93.4 percent thought the law should not let a parent disin-

---

[50] *Parental Authority: The Community and the Law* (1958).

herit a minor child, although in fact this can be done.

Cohen and his associates certainly measured some kind of public opinion, but not the "public opinion" which is or could be the fountainhead of law. They chose their subjects at random; they asked abstract questions, ignoring whether the respondents had children, had any experience with family law, or had any opinions on the matters up to the moment of the poll. How real were these problems to the subjects? Had they or some relative ever considered disinheriting a child? Did they have enough money to make this an issue at all? What did they know about religious conflict between parent and child? No doubt many had no opinion at all until the man with the notebook arrived. Dormant opinion, latent opinion, is not a social force; and social force makes law.

As we pointed out, it is misleading to assume that all persons are equal, legally and politically. Equality is an ethical idea, but it is not reality. If we asked people what products they would most like to buy, we would get a list of preferences. This would tell us something about consumer wants, but to predict behavior we would have to know what people could afford, how much they would give up for a new car or a color television, and what choices they would make if two wants collided. The market reflects individual preferences. In addition, some people have more money to spend than others; therefore, frankly, their opinions count more. Similarly, if we wanted to explain or predict the repertoire of an opera house, it would be absurd to take a Gallup poll. "Public opinion" *does* affect the repertoire. However, people who hate music and who live 1,000 miles away have no say; if we coax an opinion from them, it will be worthless. Rich patrons are another story. Their influence is naturally greater, too, than that of the poor student who loves music, but who can scrape together only enough money for standing room once a year.

The "public opinion" that affects the law is like the economic power which makes the market. This is so in two essential regards: Some people, but only some, take enough interest in any particular commodity to make their weight felt; second, there are some people who have more power and wealth than others. At one end of the spectrum stand such figures as the presidents of the United States and General Motors; at the other, migrant laborers, babies, and prisoners at San Quentin.

Still, if everyone had the same income, people would not spend money on the same goods and services. One man would buy more clothes; another, fancier food. Similarly, even in a "perfect democracy," where everyone had the same potential stock of influence, people would spend their influence (within limits) on different issues, as they saw fit. People in general may and do accumulate, hoard, or spend their power just as they accumulate, hoard, or spend their dollars. Two people with the same political energy or force may use it quite differently. One may do nothing; the other may write, cajole, speak, and campaign.

Legislators, of course, are quite aware that some people are more equal than others because of money, talent, or choice. They know that 100 wealthy, powerful constituents, passionately opposed to socialized medicine, outweigh thousands of poor, weak constituents, mildly in favor. Most people do not shout, threaten, or write letters. They remain quiet and obscure, unless a head count reveals they are there. This is the "silent majority"; paradoxically, this group matters only when it breaks its silence—when it mobilizes or is mobilized by others.

The sin of Cohen, Robson, and Bates is that they ignore inequality and intensity. Their public opinion is a concept with all intensities drained out.[51] Their data would be a measure of public opinion and its influence, but only if every public issue were decided by referendum, if all issues were independent of each other, no vote-trading was allowed, everyone had to vote, a simple majority ruled, and, therefore, the process necessarily did ignore "the varying intensities of preference among the separate voters."[52] In a society that decided everything by this sort of referendum, if law and "public opinion" *were* very different, one might suspect some sort of "culture lag." No such society exists in the real world, of course. Legal acts are interrelated, and intensities register and make an impact on the law.[53]

The Nebraska study also ignored the problem of structure. The questions had to be asked in a way that left out institutional problems. People were not told, for example, what the implications of rules were for the structures that carry them out. Since people know very little about what makes the legal system tick, it is hard to say exactly what their answers meant. If one asks whether there ought to be a law against obscene books, most people will probably answer "yes." The same people would not *necessarily* still say yes, if one asked whether a committee of three—two retired policemen and a nun—should pre-

---

    [51]See Walter J. Blum and Harry Kalven, Jr., "The Art of Opinion Research: A Lawyer's Appraisal of an Emerging Science," 24 *U. Chi. L. Rev.* 1, 15–19 (1956).

    [52]James Buchanan and Gordon Tullock, *The Calculus of Consent* (1962), p. 132.

    [53]Whatever one feels about inequality of income or power, ethically the case can be made that those who care deeply should be able to accumulate their votes. Equality means equal voting power, but does not mean that the state can coerce a person to distribute his votes a particular way.

view all movies and books and have the right to prohibit offensive ones. Would they want people who read dirty books put to death? Would they like the courts to censor magazines? What would they say to any one of dozens of structural alternatives? Structural implications of a change in "the law" are not irrelevant. They are the very heart of the legal system. Unless one takes them into account, what one is measuring is not attitude toward the *legal system* but attitude about something vague, disembodied, artificial—call it a norm—that cannot live on its own, a mere test-tube creation. Of course, to build in all the structural alternatives might make a questionnaire a hundred pages long. The people of Nebraska or any other place could not cope with it. This fact, sad but true, is a severe constraint on the science of public opinion. It is also a constraint on the effectiveness of "public opinion" itself.[54]

Moreover, issues come in packages. Attitudes relate to other attitudes, behaviors to other behaviors. A. V. Dicey defined public opinion as "the reigning or predominant current of opinion," a "body of beliefs, convictions, sentiments, accepted principles, or firmly-voted prejudices ... *taken* together."[55] Attitudes about children may hang together with attitudes about women's rights; it may be misleading to measure one set of opinions without showing how it depends on the other.

---

[54]On the structural point, see Luke Cooperrider's review of Cohen, Robson, and Bates, 57 *Mich. L. Rev.* 1119 (1959). Alan Milner, reviewing the study in 21 *U. Pitt. L. Rev.* 147 (1957), doubted the value of studying attitudes rather than actual *behavior*. What people say and how they conduct themselves may be quite different. Milner also suspected that the authors took too static a view of the law. The people polled varied their answers when "the authors introduced 'significant factual variations' to gauge the moral sense more accurately. . . . But nowhere is there the slightest suggestion that if a judge were faced with a similar variation, he might find a legal way to label it significant and so come up with a decision to suit his own moral sense." Ibid. at 148.

[55]*Law and Public Opinion in England during the Nineteenth Century* (1920), pp. 19–20. (Emphasis added.)

Chapter VII

Law, Power, and Social Structure

What makes law, then, is not "public opinion," in the sense that Cohen, Robson, and Bates use the phrase, but social force actually exerted. But what is social force? What is "pressure" made of? There is no convenient word for a unit of legal or political force. The unit of economic force is simple: It is money—the dollar. The legal or political unit is more slippery, more abstract. Power, influence, and force are real phenomena. Social forces, power, and influence come in sizes and forms; we can compare them with each other. We can speak of them as big and small, as more or less. We can picture power, influence, and social force as divided into not wholly imaginary units. These units, like dollars in many ways, would have some special characteristics. Some could be used only once, like a dollar bill or the sting of a bee. Others could be reused or recharged, like batteries. One letter to a congressman does not stop a man from writing another—with equal impact up to a point. In some cases, the units of force are like votes— single, one-time rights; in other cases, they are like physical force—a punch or a slap—which can be repeated, although not indefinitely. Like money, the units can be spent, hoarded, or invested.

We call persistent possession of money, wealth. Wealth is influential; it generates credit. A rich man can get goods without cash, because his credit is good. A man of power or intensity has a somewhat similar credit. A legislator will hesitate to propose, fight, or vote for a bill, if he thinks the bill would harm or annoy powerful constituents, even though the group had as yet spent no force against the bill and was not even aware it existed.

This fact, among others, makes power and influence elusive subjects for study. Max Weber defined power as "the probability that one actor within a social relationship will be in a position to carry out his own will despite resistance."[1] Edward Banfield defined "influence" as "ability to get others to act, think, or feel as one intends."[2] Despite the definitions—there are others, of course—and a number of interesting studies of power and influence,[3] many questions remain. In at least one sense, power is too elusive to measure. An observer can see and feel what goes on in a city, he can read the papers, and he can jot down the names of people who seem to have power to settle a garbage strike, block a new airport, or whatever. He may, however, miss the invisible power, the power that determines the very structure of the community, that shapes the very "agenda of alternatives" sitting on the table for discussion.[4] Power makes some plans and ideas inevitable and others unthinkable. No one in the United States seriously proposes seizing department stores, deporting all police chiefs, or handing school boards over to workers and farmers. No one in the Soviet Union proposes selling steel mills to Japanese investors or distributing free a Russian language version of *Playboy*. These plans never reach center stage. No one with power need lift a finger to prevent them. The structure of power, along with the prevailing system of beliefs, prescribes what interests and hopes will become real demands.

Within the legal system are processes and rules which create and maintain the social structure. These rules come *from* society; society, so to speak, is their draftsman. At the same time, these rules help keep society on its track. The track can be revolutionary or conservative. In Western countries, the processes and rules make sure that wealth has the climate to thrive. The rules of law permit people to inherit wealth and leave it to their children; the rules permit a stock market to exist and in general give a snug harbor to private property. Of course, modern societies are not simple or static, nor are they monolithic engines for sustaining the rich and exploiting the poor. These countries provide

---

[1]Max Weber, *The Theory of Social and Economic Organization*, ed. Talcott Parsons (1964), p. 152; on the many definitions of power, see James T. Tedeschi et al., "Power, Influence and Behavioral Compliance," 4 *Law and Society Rev.* 521 (1970).

[2]Edward C. Banfield, *Political Influence*, (1961), p. 3. Note the difference between the two definitions: Influence does not mention resistance.

[3]Ibid.; see also Floyd Hunter, *Community Power Structure* (1953); Robert Dahl, *Who Governs? Democracy and Power in an American City* (1961).

[4]Robert Alford, *Bureaucracy and Participation: Political Cultures in Four Wisconsin Cities* (1969), p. 194.

social services, for example, and in most of them the middle class has considerable power and wealth.

Rules of law and processes of law, to repeat, are products of power. They also define power, and they instruct how power can be used. At the heart of the system, then, are processes and rules that give out units of power, ratify their distribution, and describe their use. They allow or forbid people to accumulate, sell, trade, or give away units, and determine under what circumstances such acts can be done. Under usual voting rules, people vote for representatives; these people then make the rules. There are referenda on some issues, but the referendum is not the norm. In a referendum, each man has a vote; no one has more than one. There is no bargaining, log-rolling, or vote-trading, especially if the balloting is secret and honest.[5] But usually, bargaining and trading are in some sense possible. In legislatures, log-rolling is an everyday affair. It is open and notorious in so-called "pork barrel" bills, where a congressman from Florida promises to back a dam in Wyoming, if his colleague from Wyoming returns the favor for a barge canal back home.

Even more common is what Buchanan and Tullock call "implicit log-rolling." The "political 'entrepreneurs' who offer candidates or programs to the voters make up a complex mixture of policies designed to attract support. In so doing, they keep firmly in mind the fact that the single voter may be so interested in the outcome of a particular issue that he will vote for the one party that supports this issue, although he may be opposed to the party stand on all other issues."[6] A candidate, of course, is also a human being with values and attitudes. A legislator, like any other legal actor, will sometimes follow his own conscience and sometimes respond to pressure from the voters, party leaders, or the White House.

To oversimplify and summarize: There are long-term and short-term pressures at work in the law. Some social forces work slowly, producing structures and institutions, creating model and modal personalities. Short-term pressures act swiftly, like lightning, striking directly in the form of sharp, concrete demands. Short-term pressure is like weather; long-term pressure is like climate. Ultimately, air, water, and wind are elements of both.

---

[5]James M. Buchanan and Gordon Tullock, *The Calculus of Consent* (1962), p. 132. Sometimes politicians are glad to throw touchy issues, such as fluoridation or some school bonds, to the electorate, and avoid the responsibility of choice.

[6]Ibid., pp. 134–135.

JUDICIAL BEHAVIOR

It is no trick to see social force at work in elected assemblies. Lobbyists buzz around the halls. Legislators make campaign promises. Voters approach congressmen directly. They openly threaten to take political revenge on a congressman who votes what they consider to be the wrong way. Unions, farmers, manufacturers, and consumers frankly announce the price of their support. In court, however, parties do not talk about their interests. They do not openly threaten the judge, even an elected judge. Litigants follow strict rules of the game. They appeal to "the law" and hide their motivations behind legal phrases.

This style conceals social issues and social demands. On the surface, other factors seem to account for judicial behavior—the *structural variable,* for one—that is, rules of procedure and jurisdiction, the etiquette and habits of the court. Another explanation is "the law" itself. The judge searches for the principle that is legally correct or listens to the better legal argument.

No doubt, these factors are important in individual cases and in the short run. Perhaps they are overrated even there, compared to the impact of the judge's values and attitudes and the pressures of interests and events. In the long run, these factors melt away: the judge's values, the rules of procedure, the skill of the attorneys, and logic of the law. What is left is society: concrete social and economic forces. Basically, the argument is the same as for the legislature. Why would society tolerate a court system, which consistently produced "wrong" results?

Legal scholars, especially in common-law countries, spend much of their time discussing the work of the courts. Their special skill is analysis of legal rules as announced by and changed by appellate courts. They tend to inflate the importance of cases and judges. A good example, already mentioned, was Benjamin Cardozo's opinion in *MacPherson v. Buick Motor Co.*[7] In this famous case, a wheel fell off MacPherson's car; he was injured and sued the manufacturer. Cardozo's opinion, in the New York Court of Appeals, expanded the liability of manufacturers. The case found "immediate acceptance," and within forty years, was "universal law" in the United States.[8]

This is the bare record. Undeniably, products liability has had a meteoric growth in the twentieth century. Law gives more and more protection to the consumer as against the producer. If the Buick Motor Company Case had gone the other way, would this have smothered products liability in its cradle? Why did Cardozo's opinion influence

---

[7]217 N.Y. 382, 111 N.E. 1050 (1916).
[8]William Prosser, *Handbook of the Law of Torts* (3rd ed., 1964), p. 661.

other courts, if it did? Was it the skill of the opinion? Or simply the result?

We do not know the answers, but we can make a guess or two. Cardozo was a skillful, famous judge, but dull, inept opinions have become "leading cases" in many areas of law. Arthur Goodhart has written: "Paradoxical as it may sound, the law has frequently owed more to its weak judges than it has to its strong ones. A bad reason may often make good law."[9] As an example, he gives Priestley v. Fowler,[10] which launched the notorious fellow-servant rule. "The two reasons on which Lord Abinger based his judgment," Goodhart states, were "palpably incorrect"; and the rule of the case proved to be "absurd" and "unjust."[11] Perhaps products liability was an idea whose time had come. Goods are produced and nationally advertised, and there are new ideas among citizens about where responsibility should lie for harm caused by products. If so, then Cardozo's opinion was only an incident. Perhaps it pushed the movement slightly in one direction institutionally speaking, but that was all. Cardozo's opinion, in other words, may well have helped to shape the *rhetoric* of case law—what arguments would be used. It may have had some influence on how far *courts* would go, as opposed to legislatures or other agencies, in putting together the law of products liability. This is not trivial, but it is far from "social engineering." Lord Abinger probably had the same long-run impact on industrial accident law as Cardozo had on products liability. His "absurd" and "unjust" rule succeeded, not because it persuaded, but because society was moving toward a pattern of industrial relations in which his rule had a definite function and place.

THEORIES OF JUDICIAL DECISION-MAKING

What elements go into the decision of a Cardozo or for that matter any judge? As we mentioned, modern political science has tried to attack the question with scientific rigor. Scholars have concentrated on the United States Supreme Court, using a variety of methods and materials. Some have made use of the papers of the justices and other archives.[12] On the whole, this is a limited resource. The Court works in secret, nor do judges like to grant interviews or answer question-

---

[9] Arthur L. Goodhart, "Determining the Ratio Decidendi of a Case," 40 *Yale L.J.* 161, 163 (1930); on the fellow-servant rule, see pp. 275, 305.

[10] 3 M. & W. 1 (1837).

[11] Goodhart, *supra* note 9, pp. 162–163.

[12] See, for example, Walter Murphy, *Elements of Judicial Strategy* (1964); David Danelski, *A Supreme Court Justice is Appointed* (1964); Alexander M. Bickel, "Mr. Taft Rehabilitates the Court," 79 *Yale L.J.* 1 (1969).

naires. Hence, students of the courts have relied heavily on reported cases.

Almost to a man, political scientists who use behavioral techniques reject traditional legal thought. They do not feel that rules of law determine how a case will turn out, automatically or otherwise. Rather, they see the *judge* himself as the key—his attitudes and values. They try to classify or label judges according to these attitudes; they then verify the labels by checking to see how the judges vote in cases which ought to evoke the particular attitude. Suppose we label Judge X as a friend of civil rights and Judge Y as an enemy. (We get these labels by reading older cases or from what we know about the judges off the bench.) In a series of cases, we find that Judge X consistently does vote for the side we consider favorable to civil rights; Judge Y votes against. This verifies the labels; at the same time, it strengthens us in our opinion that the judge's attitude determines the outcome of his cases.[13]

Scaling was a technique which lent itself to this enterprise. Political scientists invented scales to measure sensitivity to civil liberties, economic liberalism, sympathy for disadvantaged parties, etc.[14] They then arranged justices in line from liberal to conservative, according to the way they voted in nonunanimous cases in a particular period. The scale worked, if it met certain mathematical tests. When this occurred, the researcher could be confident he was tapping an attitude that actually influenced outcomes. Some successes have been reported, although other scholars have questioned both the methods and the results.[15]

There are other sources of data. David Danelski analyzed off-the-bench speeches, looking for judges' "values."[16] Other scholars have sent out questionnaires or otherwise studied the backgrounds and party affiliations of judges.[17] These studies have produced *some* results.

---

[13]See Kenneth N. Vines, "Federal District Judges and Race Relations Cases in the South," 26 *J. Politics* 337 (1964). See, in general, Glendon Schubert, *The Judicial Mind* (1965); John D. Sprague, *Voting Patterns of the United States Supreme Court* (1968).

[14]These scales are described in Daryl R. Fair, "An Experimental Application of Scalogram Analysis to State Supreme Court Decisions," 1967 *Wis. L. Rev.* 449.

[15]See, for example, Joseph Tanenhaus, "The Cumulative Scaling of Judicial Decisions," 79 *Harv. L. Rev.* 1583 (1966).

[16]David Danelski, "Values as Variables in Judicial Decision-Making: Notes Toward a Theory," 19 *Vand. L. Rev.* 721 (1966).

[17]See Joel B. Grossman, "Social Backgrounds and Judicial Decision-Making," 79 *Harv. L. Rev.* 1551 (1966); S. Sidney Ulmer, "Social Background as an Indicator to the Votes of Supreme Court Justices in Criminal Cases: 1947–1956 Terms," 17 *Am. J. Pol. Sci.* 622 (1973).

One study showed that Democrats on the supreme court of Michigan were "more sensitive" than Republicans to the "claims of the unemployed and the injured."[18] The differences, however, were not very startling, and a later study of federal district court judges failed to find a relationship between party affiliation and outcomes in civil liberties cases.[19] Judges' backgrounds do not, in general, carry us terribly far. "That judges are (or were) Republican or Catholics or corporate lawyers or law professors," Joel Grossman concludes, tells "only part of the story." Moreover, scholars have measured attitudes rather crudely and have ignored unanimous cases which are the overwhelming majority in state courts at least.[20]

The shortcomings of attitude research spur on those who are on the lookout for other factors in decisions. Some, for example, think it is time to reexamine *law* itself as an influence. Law is often, as we noted, furtively returned as a factor under the code word "role." Judges have values, attitudes, and intuitions, but they have also accepted the "role" of the judge; and this "role" requires them to play the game of law. Judges, in this view, are as much products of their "institutional setting" as of their backgrounds.[21] Or judges' concepts of "role" might lead them to take up an attitude of restraint, deferring to other branches of government. Judges who play the role of restraint move slowly and abide by past decisions.[22]

Stuart Nagel tried to measure the effect of the background, skill, and experience of lawyers on decisions. He found that older, richer lawyers tend to win cases slightly more often than younger, less established ones; but many other factors (membership in the ABA, type of

---

[18]S. Sidney Ulmer, "The Political Party Variable in the Michigan Supreme Court," 11 *J. Public L.* 352 (1962); see also Stuart Nagel, "Political Party Affiliation and Judges' Decisions," 55 *Am. Pol. Sci. Rev.* 843 (1961).

[19]Thomas G. Walker, "A Note Concerning Partisan Influences in Trial-Judge Decision Making," 6 *Law and Society Rev.* 645 (1972); see also David W. Adamany, "The Party Variable in Judges' Voting: Conceptual Notes and a Case Study," 63 *Am. Pol. Sci. Rev.* 57 (1969). Kenneth Dolbeare, studying suburban trial courts in New York state concluded that "over-all . . . there is no general correlation between party identification and decision-making" and that "individual values and attitudes" were determinative, *Trial Courts in Urban Politics* (1967), pp. 77, 79.

[20]Grossman, *supra* note 17, pp. 1563–1564.

[21]Dorothy B. James, "Role Theory and the Supreme Court," 30 *J. Politics* 160 (1968).

[22]See Joel B. Grossman, "Role-Playing and the Analysis of Judicial Behavior: the Case of Mr. Justice Frankfurter," 11 *J. Public L.* 285 (1962); David J. Danelski, "Conflict and Its Resolution in the Supreme Court," 11 *J. Conflict Resolution* 71, 76–79 (1967); Dean Jaros and Robert I. Mendelsohn, "The Judicial Role and Sentencing Behavior," 11 *Midwest J. Pol. Sci.* 471 (1967); George Otte, "Role Theory and the Judicial Process: a Critical Analysis," 16 *St. Louis U.L.J.* 420 (1972).

legal education) turned out either inconclusive or unmeasurable.[23]

No doubt, some judges play a "legal" role; no doubt, too, lawyers sometimes convince the judges through strictly "legal" argument. At the same time, not *all* judges play the "legal" role, and even extreme role-players do not play the role in every case. If this is so, then what predisposes a judge to play the role in one case and not the other? Perhaps his indifference or indecision. Judges do not react to cases in a uniform way. Passion or conscience or some nonlegal reason may control the important case—the case that makes headlines or poses some challenging problem. Next comes a minor case or a tangled commercial case, where only the facts are in dispute. Now the judge is puzzled and bored. He decides to decide by "the law"—victory will go to the side with better skill at persuading him where "the law" really lies.

Judges will not agree on what is boring, important, trivial, decisive, or whatever. One judge will find criminal cases not to his taste but will savor each detail of the tax code. Another is exactly the reverse. There will be typical and atypical patterns, and, of course, what goes on in society will influence the judge. Every judge would see the drama and significance of a case that attacks the abortion laws or attempts to subpoena the president. If the model described is in any way correct, then we can easily reconcile the social theory *and* the insistence of judges that they often if not always try to follow "the law." What occurs analytically, although not psychologically, is a two-stage process. The primary choice is whether to follow "the law" or not. Attitudes, values, and the concrete social context determine this choice. The second choice is the actual decision. To the judge, however, it will seem as if he usually is "bound" by the law.

Scholars have also looked at *structural* factors in decisions. Appellate cases, typically, are decided not by a single judge but by a panel. The Supreme Court, for example, "is a collegial body of nine men." A decision must gain at least five votes; moreover, it is a problem to get five or more "intelligent, strong-willed and individualistic Justices to agree in whole with an opinion written by one of their number."[24] Judges fall into coalitions and form blocs; this process of gentle battle and accommodation may be uncovered through careful study of voting

---

[23]Stuart Nagel and Felix V. Gagliano, "Attorney Characteristics and Courtroom Results," 44 *Neb. L. Rev.* 599 (1965).

[24]Walter F. Murphy, *Elements of Judicial Strategy* (1964), p. 23. Eleanor C. Main and Thomas G. Walker, in "Choice Shifts and Extreme Behavior: Judicial Review in the Federal Courts," 91 *J. Soc. Psychology* 215 (1973), compared the behavior of single federal judges and judges making collegial decisions; the collegial judges were significantly more likely to declare a challenged statute unconstitutional.

patterns. Courts are also part of a judicial *system.* There are lower courts and upper courts. The upper court reviews and controls the work of lower courts, but it needs their cooperation, too. Judges also belong to organizations and associate with each other. These facts presumably make *some* difference in the way the judging game is played.

There has been surprisingly little study of what might be the most powerful factor: the pressure of the outside world. Research has fixed on intervening variables: the judge's personality, his values and attitudes, role-playing of one sort or another, the give and take in courts on which many judges sit. These variables represent social forces, too, but moving slowly and taking less transient forms. After all, the values of a modern Polish judge are not the values of a judge in medieval Islam, but a particular judge does not change his values overnight. Social theories suggest that judges are not immune to current social forces, to upheavals going on outside their door. Society, one must recall, prepares the docket for the judges. The cases are not imaginary; they come up out of life situations, and decisions have an impact on living litigants, even if they go no further. In some courts, social pressure is easy to see on the surface in the form of test cases, cases brought by interest groups, or cases with *amicus curiae* briefs.[25] But there is little research, almost none outside the federal system.

Even there, it is a disquieting symptom that behaviorists spend so much time on nonunanimous appellate cases. They have been interested most of all in differences among judges. This misses the possibility that social forces might be pushing *all* judges in a certain direction. The judges have had to respond to war, depression, and unrest. They have moved down a road, some eagerly, others reluctantly—but they have moved; events have forced their hand. If one takes a long time span and looks at great sweeping trends, it becomes crystal clear that history helps to write the judges' opinions. It is not easy to measure the impact of social forces, and this has kept researchers shy. But a general theory of judicial decision-making cannot ignore social forces. Decisions are legal acts, as much as statutes are; the same general rule should hold for all legal acts, that is, that legal acts are responses to social force actually pressing in upon the actors—in this case, the courts.

A decision "brought about" by immediate social forces means a

---

[25]Clement E. Vose, "Litigation as a Form of Pressure Group Activity," 319 *Annals* 20 (1958); Nathan Hakman, "The Supreme Court's Political Environment: the Processing of Noncommercial Litigation," in Joel B. Grossman and Joseph Tanenhaus, eds., *Frontiers of Judicial Research* (1969), p. 199; Samuel Krislov, "The Amicus Curiae Brief: from Friendship to Advocacy," 72 *Yale L.J.* 694 (1963).

decision in which the values of the judges and the structure of the court have little impact on the decision. That is to say, all judges—except the most stubborn, or idiosyncratic—living *in* such a society would respond in much the same way to the facts of the case. Cases of this type, unlike the ones studied by political scientists, might well be unanimous. And many cases would be so clear, so self-evident to the judges, that they would all agree. But what is clear to one epoch is unclear or absurd to another.

A study of the law that social forces build would stress cases in the mass, rather than cases picked apart one by one, or in small groups, or dissected and pinned to a "scale." Social force works on law in the form of great irresistible movements. In the nineteenth century, American courts decided that no one could sue a hospital or other charity in tort. In the twentieth century, this doctrine dissolved in state after state, conservative or liberal, Republican or Democrat. Products liability marches on; a cranky judge or court can stop it for a day or a year; eventually it engulfs the courts like a tidal wave. What is even more suggestive is the way courts in different countries, starting with different texts and codes, end up the same. Faced with similar contexts, the tort laws of France and the United States develop suspicious similarities.

It is, of course, not necessary to make so sharp a contrast between decisions "brought about" by social forces and those "determined by" the judge's values. Social forces rarely act like a pistol held to a judge's head. American federal judges have life tenure; European judges are secure civil servants. The judge absorbs social contexts rather differently than a legislator, who is exposed to day-by-day crisis. Then, too, one needs some conceptual spade work. What is a "social force"? What exactly is a "value"? We know that trends outside in society gradually work their will on the courts, somehow forcing the judge to bend this way or that; or because litigants mob the court with one sort of case, demanding change, and refuse to take no for an answer; or because the judge's frame of mind shifts with the times.

Most likely, these processes intertwine. For example, American courts have moved dramatically forward in improving the rights of blacks. But the judges did not initiate this litigation. Blacks and their lawyers brought the cases. They sat in on buses, they pounded on the schoolhouse door, they screamed for the right to vote; and they litigated firmly and persistently.[26] There was, in other words, constant pressure

---

[26]See, in general, Loren Miller, *The Petitioners. The Story of the Supreme Court of the United States and the Negro* (1966).

against the legal system, and it arose out of a genuine social movement, changing the climate of the outside world along with the weather of the courtroom. New judges who came on the bench were not the same as the old men they replaced. They were more likely to favor the cause of the blacks than their predecessors for a number of reasons, ultimately social ones. Finally, some judges, still sitting, may have rethought their own values under the hammer blow of events, the constant pressure of civil rights cases on their docket.

Of course, judges and courts vary greatly. Some differences follow economic, social, or political boundary lines, such as the great North-South isogloss in the United States. Some odd differences are hard to explain. In 1966, at least one judge dissented in almost half of the cases in Michigan's highest court; there were dissents in only 1.2 percent of the cases in Massachusetts.[27] Some courts tend to innovate, others to follow. Judges' ideas about their roles—their theories of legitimacy, their attitudes toward precedent—are also variable from place to place. Socioeconomic differences and differences in tradition explain some of the variance but by no means all.

It is not easy to get inside the judges' heads. One study, by Henry R. Glick, made a hopeful start. Glick interviewed judges, sitting on four supreme courts in New Jersey, Massachusetts, Louisiana, and Pennsylvania.[28] The judges differed greatly in attitude. Glick asked, for example, "How about the influence of nonlegal factors in deciding cases? Of what importance are they?" Every single member of the New Jersey court said "very important." Louisiana judges, with one exception, said that these factors had no importance at all.[29] Out of Glick's interviews, a picture of the four courts emerged. New Jersey was a hotbed of legal realism; judges in the other three states, on the whole, had a more conservative cast of mind.

In another study, Richard Daynard looked at three hundred cases in three intermediate courts to see what style these courts used in deciding cases. He distinguished six styles. Three were narrow—bound to precedent, or the facts of the case, or the governing statutes; three were broader. One style, "the grand style," appealed to the "spirit" of prior cases, rather than to what they literally held; two other styles appealed explicitly to "social policy." None of the courts made much use of "social policy" styles. Only eleven cases out of 300 fell into these

---

[27]Henry R. Glick and Kenneth M. Vines, *State Court Systems* (1973), p. 79.

[28]Henry R. Glick, *Supreme Courts in State Politics, an Investigation of the Judicial Role* (1971).

[29]Ibid., p. 83.

categories; no case rested on "social policy" alone. The portrait of these courts that emerged is conservative. On the whole, styles would not have seemed out of place in the nineteenth century.[30] Of course, between attitude and behavior, between style and result, stretches a great and so far unfathomed gap.

LAW AND CLASS STRUCTURE

Social theories of law start from one basic assumption; economy and society make the law. Law is not impartial, timeless, classless; it is not value-free. It reflects the distribution of power; social forces drive it down the road.

Does this mean that in a country like the United States the law serves only some small but dominant elite? Who has a share in the national storehouse of power? One view, that of Robert A. Dahl, for example, looks on the United States as a "pluralist democracy."[31] No single group is dominant. On most issues, there is no clear majority. Every group is a minority and must bargain with the others. What results is some kind of compromise. No one would call the outcomes ideal, but the system works in a rough and ready way. No one gets exactly what he wants, and no one is entirely left out.

This picture of pluralism was popular in the 1950s. Lately, political scientists themselves have looked at the world with a more jaundiced eye.[32] In the pluralist scheme, critics said, there was too much acceptance of the status quo. Pluralists felt that more people get more of what they want than they would get under alternative systems. Clearly, the theories contained a good deal of truth. In American society, some pigs are more equal than others, but no one group of pigs is *completely* on top for all issues; no group is *completely* without power. But whether the arrangement is ideal or even tolerable cannot be decided theoretically. The question is whether the arrangement satisfies. If the level of satisfaction is falling, then the pluralist solution may *not* be the best.

---

[30]Richard A. Daynard, "The Use of Social Policy in Judicial Decision-Making," 56 *Cornell L. Rev.* 919 (1971). Lawyers in the United States seem to share this traditional view of the role of the courts. See Edward N. Beiser, "Lawyers Judge the Warren Court," 7 *Law and Society Rev.* 139 (1972).

[31]Robert A. Dahl, *Pluralist Democracy in the United States: Conflict and Consent* (1967).

[32]The criticism goes back at least as far as C. Wright Mills, *The Power Elite* (1956), which still stands as a classic attack from the left. The attacks come from all directions now: Theodore J. Lowi, *The End of Liberalism: Ideology, Policy, and the Crisis of Public Authority* (1969).

Critics, too, point out vast inequalities of wealth and power; these load the dice in the bargaining of interest groups. The case for pluralism is like the case for the free market. The market, theoretically, will maximize satisfaction in society, but it cannot guarantee that income will be distributed justly. Pluralism is a market system, with bargaining, vote-trading, compromise, adjustments of prices and wants. It too makes sense, and might be ideal, but only if the distribution of power and wealth is somehow "just."

Social theories of law assume that the legal system emerges from market-like activities. People trade for their interests as they trade for goods in the market; the living code of laws in the society is more or less a catalogue of bargains and preferences, sensitive to dealings and demands like the daily stock market quotations. Some people start with more chips than others and play the game by different rules. The market theory does *not* mean that law never expresses deep values and high aspirations. It does *not* mean that everyone is a rational calculator, that no one makes sacrifices, defers gratification, or acts in the public interest, that is, unselfishly. A person or a group can decide to struggle for social justice just as another group can decide to spend its precious power in the battle for a higher tariff. Indeed, reform lobbying takes place all the time. People do decide collectively that more of the national product should go to the poor—even out of their own pockets.[33] There is no reason to believe that all societies are equally selfish or unselfish. Everywhere, ideals struggle for power along with base grubby interests. In such a struggle, indeed, people turn ideals into interests. The political process in one sense is blind. It cannot tell whether a struggle is selfish or not. A man who fights to feather his nest with a certain amount of force makes the same impact on the law as one who spends the same force fighting for relief of the hungry masses, struggling to save the forests from the lumber barons, or battling to improve the teaching of science in the schools.

INTEREST AND EQUALITY

Power is unequally distributed and unequally exercised. The law cannot help but reflect and sustain this distribution. Between potential

---

[33]The reasons are sometimes coarsely utilitarian. Social reform is one way to prevent a revolution. Presumably, this was why Germany, under Bismarck, pioneered in social insurance in the 1880s. Social insurance was a bribe to the masses to prevent a turn to the left, but there is no need to deny the genuineness of reform impulses in many other cases.

power and its actual exercise, ideology and culture intervene. The ordinary man could, in theory, vote to expropriate the rich; yet he does not. In the first place, as we noted, he may be afraid to kill the goose that lays golden eggs. In Western countries, the ordinary citizen eats better and buys more than was true in earlier generations, and he tends to look forward to a still better life. This expectation helps sustain the current system.

Many of these gains, to be sure, reflect past exercises of power. The middle class was not bashful in the nineteenth century; it bent the law to accommodate its interests. The welfare state is the creation of middle-class pressure. Laissez-faire ideology never gained absolute dominance, even in the mid-nineteenth century. It cast a long shadow on proposals for mild redistribution of income and advancement of social welfare. In hindsight, it is crystal clear how useful the ideology was to business interests and other power holders. The ideology was a way to persuade the middle class and the working class not to use all their formal political power, since social legislation and redistribution would do more harm than good. This interlude of faith was brief, however, and never perfect. The crush of "socialist" legislation passed in the late nineteenth century appalled the true believers.[34]

Not everyone prospered, however, especially minority groups, which the dominant population for one reason or another stigmatized and discriminated against economically and socially. The problem remains in most countries. These groups include racial minorities—blacks, Mexican-Americans, and Indians in the United States; the "colored" people in Great Britain; ethnic minorities, the rock-bottom poor, and extremists of the left in many countries; foreign workers *(Gastarbeiter)* in Germany and Switzerland; criminals; the sexual minorities; the feeble, the old, the insane; hippies; the unpopular, rebellious young. The Western theory of law insists that justice is pure and impartial, but class structure, power, and influence are at the very heart of the law. No wonder, then, that many scholars and laymen doubt that the law lives up to its professed role of protecting the weak and the powerless.

Law discriminates—or, more neutrally put, reflects the existing social structure—in two distinct ways. First, the rules themselves, the official face of the law, are by no means totally impartial even when impartially applied. They come out of the struggle for power, and dominant opinion molds them. Segregation is the law of the land in the Union of South Africa; it was the law of the land in the American South

---

[34]See A. V. Dicey, *Lectures on the Relation between the Law and Public Opinion in England, during the Nineteenth Century* (2nd ed., 1914), introduction to the Second Edition.

until very recently.[35] Penal codes declare "unnatural" sex a crime. The laws punish draft dodgers, seditionists, and drug addicts. American immigration laws excluded the Chinese; public land law ruthlessly exploited the native Indians; welfare law was harsh to the poor. All these are obvious examples and can be matched in many societies. Even more important is the basic structure of the law. The regulatory code, the tax laws—economic legislation in general—are geared to the needs and interests of people who own property. Rules of contract and commercial law are innocent on the surface and seem to the average person to be mere justice and common sense, but it is the justice and common sense of Western society, its economy, its dominant populations. Imperial Rome, the Cheyenne, and the China of Chairman Mao used different rules. Indeed, every area of law—land law, family law, tort law—supports the society which framed the rules and put them to work. To suppose anything else would contradict what we know about the social origins of law.

Many rules, however, do appear timeless and neutral—expressions of abiding faith and high ideals. How they are enforced is another question. The administration of justice is shot through with subtle and blatant forms of social control that official law does not recognize. For one thing, the poor simply cannot afford the counsel they need to enforce their rights against landlords, sellers, and the government in civil[36] or in criminal cases. Disadvantages show up in many ways. A study of criminal justice in Pittsburgh showed that some judges were far more lenient than others; private attorneys with well-heeled clients managed to manipulate the docket, to garner these judges for their clients.[37] Juries are free to translate their prejudices into law; if they do so, it goes unnoticed.[38] Judges have prejudices, too. A study of traffic court cases in Detroit found that a judge was more likely to send a man to jail if he wore "soiled and rumpled" work clothes than if he came to court in a business suit.[39] The police, it is said, are quicker to stop,

---

[35]On the history of segregation laws in the United States, see C. Vann Woodward, *The Strange Career of Jim Crow* (2nd rev. ed., 1966); Ronald Segal, *The Race War* (1967).

[36]See, in general, Jerome E. Carlin, Jan Howard, and Sheldon L. Messinger, *Civil Justice and the Poor, Issues for Sociological Research* (1967).

[37]R. Stanton Wettick, Jr., "A Study of the Assignment of Judges to Criminal Cases in Allegheny County—the Poor Fare Worse," 9 *Duquesne L. Rev.* 51 (1970).

[38]On jury bias, see, in general Harry Kalven and H. Zeisel, *The American Jury* (1966). Simulated jury studies have tended to demonstrate some specific forms of bias. See, e.g., Charlan Nemeth and Ruth H. Sosis, "A Simulated Jury Study: Characteristics of the Defendant and the Jurors," 90 *J. Soc. Psychology* 221 (1973).

[39]Dean Jaros and Robert I. Mendelsohn, "The Judicial Role and Sentencing Behavior," 11 *Midwest J. Pol. Sci.* 471 (1967). Dress had no effect on fines, however, and the results of the study are not easy to interpret.

harass, or arrest blacks, hippies, and other minorities.[40] "In the old days," reports a police officer from Albany, "any Negro who talked back was hammered on the head, right, wrong, or indifferent, and nobody thought twice about it."[41] Blacks were, notoriously, the chief victims of lynch mobs. In the United States, the death penalty fell quite disproportionately on blacks,[42] yet studies often find that race plays only a small part in judicial behavior.[43]

On the whole, it is reasonable to suppose that justice is not as blind and classless as it pretends; it squints in one direction.[44] "White-collar criminals," writes Edwin H. Sutherland, "are relatively immune because of the class bias of the courts and the power of their class to influence the implementation and administration of the law."[45] Henry Mayhew, writing in England, in the middle of the nineteenth century, reported that boys "not even in their teens" were sent to prison "for the heinous offence of throwing stones, or obstructing highways, or unlawfully knocking at doors—crimes which the very magistrates themselves, who committed the youths, must have assuredly perpetrated in their boyhood."[46] Ironically, blacks complain that police do not enforce the laws well in black neighborhoods. The police treat blacks harshly and unfairly; at the same time, law-abiding blacks do not get the protection they want.

Power, it is said, will pervert or color any "reforms" so as to maintain social structure and further the interests of those whose opinions matter. These abuses can be illustrated through considering the histories of many so-called reforms. Juvenile court, for example, seems on the surface a plan to spare young offenders the stigma of criminality and the horror of prison.[47] However, from the

[40]Paul Chevigny, *Police Power; Police Abuses in New York City* (1969).

[41]James Q. Wilson, *Varieties of Police Behavior* (1968), p. 170.

[42]This was one basis on which the death penalty was successfully challenged in *Furman* v. *Georgia*, 408 U.S. 238 (1972).

[43]See, for example, David N. Atkinson and Dale A. Neuman, "Judicial Attitudes and Defendant Attributes: Some Consequences for Municipal Court Decision-Making," 19 *J. Public L.* 69 (1970); see William R. Arnold, "Race and Ethnicity Relative to Other Factors in Juvenile Court Dispositions," 77 *Am. J. Sociology* 211 (1971).

[44]See, Karl F. Schumann and Gerd Winter, "Zur Analyse des Strafverfahrens," 3 *Kriminologisches Journal* 136 (1971) for data from a German study of traffic courts; Edward Green, "Inter- and Intra-Racial Crime Relative to Sentencing," 55 *J. Crim. L., C. & P. S.* 348 (1964), reflects a different point of view.

[45]Edwin H. Sutherland, "White-Collar Criminality," in Gilbert Geis, ed., *White Collar Criminal* (1968), pp. 40, 46.

[46]Quoted in J. J. Tobias, *Crime and Industrial Society in the Nineteenth Century* (1972), p. 65.

[47]See Anthony M. Platt's *The Child Savers: The Invention of Delinquency* (1969), a revisionist history of the movement. Platt argues that the "child-savers" were not

very start around the turn of the century, the juvenile court was a court for the lower class. The well-to-do could buy private care for troubled children and, if worse came to worst, knew who to see, what professionals to hire, and how to behave before judges. The children who came before the court and their parents were "power-less people . . . little equipped to make articulate demands on the court."[48] Judges and social workers had a different class back-ground. The court routinely assumed that the juvenile was guilty whatever he was charged with or had done. Juveniles were sent off to institutions often as bad as regular prisons—or worse. Their "offenses" were often trivial—like the "crimes" Mayhew observed in Victorian London—or not criminal at all but behavior falling under such vague categories as "incorrigible" or "keeping bad company."

In its landmark case of *In re Gault*,[49] the Supreme Court held that proceedings in juvenile court had to meet constitutional standards. Young offenders were entitled to a lawyer, for example. The case seemed revolutionary, but empirical studies suggest that real changes in the short run will be small.[50] The problems of juvenile court are not primarily structural and procedural. The children in trouble and their families lack money and influence. Those who are supposed to act on their behalf themselves have little money or power and at times lack the requisite zeal. Until the situation changes, the problems will be tough and unyielding. The *Gault* case itself came out of a period in which society began to invest more money in reform and reformist lawyers. More investment would yield more improvement; until then, regardless of what is promised on paper, the court will deliver a product that conforms more to what the outside society or the engaged profes-sionals want than to the needs and desires of the class whose children come to court. The presence of a lawyer makes a difference, not so much because of his legal arguments as because he is there to show that what is done to the client will not be meekly and automatically ac-cepted.

A study of civil commitment, by Thomas Scheff, underscores the

---

humanitarians; they actually "invented" new categories of "youthful misbehavior," in an effort to maintain "control of youthful deviance." It was an upper-class intrusion on the life and habits of lower-class city boys. Another review of the history is Sanford J. Fox, "Juvenile Justice Reform: An Historical Perspective," 22 *Stan. L. Rev.* 1187 (1970).

[48]Edwin M. Lemert, *Social Action and Legal Change: Revolution Within the Juvenile Court* (1970), p. 26.

[49]387 U.S. 1 (1967).

[50]See Norman Lefstein, Vaughan Stapleton and Lee Teitelbaum, "In Search of Juvenile Justice: *Gault* and Its Implementation," 3 *Law and Society Rev.* 491 (1969).

point.[51] Who were the people who were locked up in mental hospitals against their will? Scheff's research showed that many people committed to hospitals could not be called insane by any stretch of the imagination; they were no danger to themselves or to others. Many were simply old people, slightly peculiar in their habits, whose families had no patience or room for them any more. A murderer is less likely to be locked away for life than somebody's senile, silly aunt. How did this gross failure of "due process" come about? Scheff drew his data from a liberal state in the Middle West. The law carefully prescribed an elaborate procedure. Three citizens had to apply to court for investigation of the question whether the person was competent. A hospital psychiatrist examined the patient. Then two psychiatrists, appointed by the court, examined the patient once more. The court then appointed a guardian *ad litem* who interviewed the patient. Finally, the judge had to hold a hearing at which he made all necessary orders and decisions.

But this elaborate process did not provide real safeguards. Court hearings were perfunctory; men and women were processed in minutes, even seconds. The courts Scheff studied took, on the average, 1.6 minutes per subject. Psychiatrists, on the average, spent less than ten minutes before deciding whether a patient should be condemned to the asylum or not. Unlike juvenile justice before the *Gault* case, nothing was wrong with the process on paper, but there was a great yawning gap between the power of the patient and the other participants. On one side, were judges, psychiatrists, families of the "mentally ill"; on the other side, a person trapped in the web of the process, typically poor or old, often somewhat befuddled, usually inarticulate. Under such circumstances, "due process" only leads to a meaningless charade. Again, what was wrong was not structure or a plan for proceeding but the proper balance of power.[52]

At law—so runs the legal maxim—every person is presumed to be sane. Scheff found exactly the opposite in practice. Everyone drawn into the net was treated as if insane. Similarly, in theory, every person is presumed innocent until proven guilty. In fact, judges, lawyers, psychiatrists, police, and the general public presume the opposite. The

---

[51]Thomas Scheff, *Being Mentally Ill: A Sociological Theory* (1966); Another study is "Civil Commitment of the Mentally Ill," 14 *U.C.L.A. L. Rev.* 823 (1967).

[52]Dennis E. Wenger and C. Richard Fletcher, in "The Effect of Legal Counsel on Admissions to a State Mental Hospital: A Confrontation of Professions," 10 *J. Health and Soc. Behavior* 66 (1969), show that a patient with a lawyer has a much better chance of escaping commitment; but they do not, unfortunately, tell us *which* patients are more likely to hire lawyers.

criminal justice system preaches the presumption of innocence, but it does not act that way.

Society is not willing to spend much money on legal process. Most persons arrested and accused of crime are found guilty or plead guilty in the end. Indeed, most of them *are* guilty, at least in one sense: They *did* rob the bank, set fire to the house, break into the store, or stab their brother-in-law. The most efficient way to handle these people would be to send them all to jail or shoot them without further ado. Obviously, this would punish some innocent people along with the guilty, and injustice on a grand scale might generate cynicism, fear, outrage, even rebellion. These side effects are kept under control, when the system mistreats only people already disaffected or people with little ability to make trouble and noise. In brief, when resources are short and justice turns to routine, the results work against the poor and weak rather than against the public as a whole. And why are resources so scarce in the first place? Society does not care to spend money on a system that makes too nice distinctions. To give every man due process, to dispense even-handed justice for all would cost a great deal of money. Since "the law" is not severe with elites, they have small incentive to improve it.

This alone would explain the pathologies that Scheff described and many other instances of class-bound justice. But other factors are worth mentioning, too. First, the law is a means of social control, which, in many societies, means that the bulk of the population must be kept in their place. A touch of terror does the job better than pure justice. Hence the elites support a certain callousness in the legal system. In middle-class, liberal societies, these abuses are less widespread, and terror is less useful. Yet even in these societies, a certain ruthlessness in criminal justice may give the bulk of the people a sense of security despite an innocent victim now and then. Legal theory may say it prefers to let ten of the guilty go free rather than convict one innocent man. But the legal system does not *behave* this way, and here, as often, behavior tells more about what people think and where the pressures lie than all the noble words.

One of the most striking facts about modern legal systems is the vast chasm between what they say, what they profess as ideals, and the way they actually work. There are many reasons why this is so. One is that it is functional for the elite if the system *appears* to be classless and just. A certain amount of hypocrisy is twice useful: The double standard works for the benefit of those on top; at the same time, it hides reality from the rest of society. "The law," writes Edgar Z. Friedenberg, is "essentially designed" to impose "miscarriage[s] of justice" on ordinary people—but without admitting that fact. "Weaker members of society are not forbidden access to [law]—which would destroy the integrative power of the myth of 'equal justice under law'—but they find it far more unwieldy in their defense than in the hands of their attackers."[53] Abraham Blumberg, writing in 1967, describes criminal law as a "confidence game." The defendant is the victim. Courts are "bureaucratic," concerned mainly with getting the work done; they process people like sides of beef in a packing plant. The liberal decisions of the Warren court made no dent in actual practices. They only augmented "the existing organizational arrangements, enriching court organizations with more personnel and elaborate structure." "Efficiency" means an "even more sophisticated apparatus for processing" defendants "toward a guilty plea."[54]

Justice, then, is tied to class; the contrary view is a myth. But the general relationship between economy or polity, and justice is not as simple as some left-wing critics would have it. What makes law, we have said, are not interests but demands. Professed ideals, then, can influence the demands made on the legal system. The most obvious examples are ideals that do not work but fool the poor, keeping them in their place; but the process also works the other way. Lofty ideals may exert some pressure on the nonpoor. Through constant hammering in schools, the newspapers, television, people come to believe their myths and perhaps even to act on them. There may be some slight strain toward conformity with the official code.

In Western countries committed to the "rule of law," the system discriminates nonetheless at least *somewhat* against the poor and weak. Totalitarian countries show even less regard for legal ideals. But the precise relationship between political and legal systems is complex. In an interesting essay, Elliott Currie suggests that "repressive" countries tend to define as deviant an "unusually large number of relatively wealthy and/or powerful people, and of solid citizens generally." This is partly because these people provide better plunder. Currie draws examples from Renaissance witchcraft trials, but the purges and expropriations of twentieth-century dictatorships are examples closer at hand.[55]

Obviously, a repressive society cannot take on the whole upper class, but the rulers, in Currie's view, are free to pick off dangerous or

---

[53]Edgar Z. Friedenberg, "The Side Effects of the Legal Process," in Robert Paul Wolff, ed., *The Rule of Law* (1971), pp. 37, 40–41.

[54]Abraham Blumberg, "The Practice of Law as Confidence Game: Organizational Cooptation of the Profession," 1 *Law and Society Rev.* no. 2, 15 (1967).

[55]Elliott P. Currie, "Crimes Without Criminals: Witchcraft and Its Control in Renaissance Europe," 3 *Law and Society Rev.* 7 (1968).

simply vulnerable segments of that class. Perhaps the point is that, in societies governed by the "rule of law," important people more or less harness state power for their benefit; wealth and power pull together, and government is controlled by *them*. In the "repressive" states, the government is a juggernaut, subject to no outside restraints; and even the rich, if they fall afoul of the state, find they cannot buy their way out.

REFORM AND REFORM INTERESTS IN THE MODERN WORLD

In Western countries, official ideals, if they have any effect at all, can work both on the top and the bottom strata—on the top, as a goad to conscience, on the bottom, both as a promise and as a weapon. The *status quo* is by no means ossified. The poor and the weak in recent times have shown more and more signs of banding together to apply collective pressure against the system. The first step is psycho-social. A group that feels oppressed must reject the idea that it deserves its position or that the rules that put its members where they are are just, or sound, or legitimate. Slaves must feel that slavery is wrong or that it is wrong for them to be slaves. At that point, action becomes possible, all the way from orthodox politics to rebellion.

Of course, an oppressed group will almost always lack status and money, and it will often try to make up through intensity what it lacks in resources. Members may, for example, take to the streets; a riot is in one sense an intense form of demand on the system by those who feel they have no alternative. Those who riot are escalating their own demands—in other words, raising the price of order and submission to the rest of society.

Beyond a doubt, these "direct action" tactics or threats of such tactics often bring results. When the Urban League, NAACP, and CORE demanded fair housing legislation, they encountered stony silence. But when the Student Non-violent Coordinating Committee threatened sit-ins, they achieved a more positive response.[56] Dramatic gestures also buy political goods that would otherwise cost hard cash. The press, radio, and television cameras will provide free publicity to someone who brings a dead rat into a.courtroom, chains himself to a tree, or immolates himself. The problem, of course, is that some publicity is bad publicity, and a riot is as likely to unleash repression as to

---

[56]Thomas W. Casstevens, in Lynn W. Eley and Thomas W. Casstevens, *The Politics of Fair-Housing Legislation* (1968), p. 385; see also Michael Lipsky, *Protest in City Politics: Rent Strikes, Housing and the Power of the Poor* (1970).

win results. Nevertheless, when the underprivileged in American society stepped up demands for justice in a variety of ways in the 1960s, they made some considerable gains. Shrill complaints about the failures of justice are themselves signs of movement.

In modern times, the *reform* interest gains constantly in importance. In wealthy societies, more and more people have surplus money and time. People use their surplus in many ways from lying in the sun through stamp collecting to revolution. Sometimes it seems as if radicals come mainly from upper-class backgrounds. This paradox may come about because it is people with leisure who can afford ideologies and hobbies. Most will be content to spend their leisure in the pursuit of happiness. A few will become more actively engaged. The more people with leisure, the more reformers in absolute numbers even if the same large percentage stick to holidays and golf.

Some reformers are professionals; and of these, a few, such as Ralph Nader, are extraordinarily effective, but amateurs also play a vital role. Housewives in Beverly Hills led the fight for smog control in California. Upper-class women, freed from household drudgery, are an important leisure class. Women were prominent in the settlement house movement. The social work profession grew out of the efforts of women like Octavia Hill and Jane Addams. Wilensky and Lebeaux point out that jobs in social work "can be seen as extensions of sex roles derived from norms governing the behavior of wife and mother." Woman is "traditionally expected to provide care to children, the aged, the sick; to be nurturant, gentle, kind, receptive."[57] This, however, goes mainly to explain the *direction* in which some women chose to expend their efforts.

The prominence of women in social reform is a mark of the connection between leisure and reform. Another is the prominence of the nobility in developing the English welfare state. Coal miners had neither the skill nor the time to work for social change, not to mention access to power. As wealth flows downward and spreads out in society, "reform" may claim more and more time and effort in Western countries. The direction of reform is another question. We have defined as reform any movement for legal action that self-interest cannot explain. This definition is politically neutral. The right can agitate for reform as well as the left. The leaders of the DAR are "reformers" too. Probably most reform follows what people would consider a liberal line. One can only guess why this is so: the way the leisure class is educated or

---

[57]Harold L. Wilensky and Charles N. Lebeaux, *Industrial Society and Social Welfare* (1958), p. 322.

the influence of ideals taught in schools, churches, and through the media. Reform means change and hence dissatisfaction.

Public reform has become as important perhaps as private reform. By public reform, we mean reform activities of government—actions that are not merely responses to the pressure of interest groups and that the internal dynamics of bureaucracy cannot adequately explain. In modern times, apparently at an increasing tempo, the machinery of government begins to manufacture, even mass produce, programs, changes, and reforms. Pressure from outside accounts for many of them, but for some reforms, pressure groups are quite invisible. Every year, in the United States, dozens of departments and agencies pour out an endless stream of new ideas, programs, drafts, and proposals. Are *all* of these the children of group conflict? It begins to look as if the machine has gone out of control; like a computer in some science fiction story, the machine had, in Daniel Moynihan's phrase, "begun to think for itself."[58]

If one thinks of law and government basically as conduits, as structures, then law and government should respond, not initiate, react, not produce and anticipate. In general, this remains quite true. "Government is normally passive; it waits for issues to come to its attention."[59] But nowadays one finds more and more proactive "cells" in government, particularly at the upper reaches. First of all, big government is so vast in modern society that it is itself a major interest group. The federal government employs millions of workers all over the country. These workers constitute a genuine pressure group. They lobby for less work and more money like all occupational groups. They also have an interest in a large, expanding government. Each agency, too, will naturally fight to preserve its own authority and to extend it, if it can. A new program, a change, a reform makes an excellent excuse. This certainly does not mean that the reform urge is not genuine, but it is reinforced by institutional necessities.

Is there also pressure on government demanding "reform"—not some particular reform but reform in general? Above the babel of specific demands for subsidies on cotton, lower taxes on cigarettes, an interstate riot bill, hot lunch programs in school, there does seem to be a general call for government to get moving, to earn its keep, to work for the common good. Public opinion in modern legal culture appar-

---

[58]Daniel Patrick Moynihan, *Maximum Feasible Misunderstanding: Community Action in the War on Poverty* (1969), p. 23.

[59]Herbert J. Gans, *The Levittowners, Ways of Life and Politics in a New Suburban Community* (1967), p. 333.

ently expects an active government. Government is supposed to have *programs*. Agencies are supposed to do something, to advance toward some goal. A government with no program is a bad government. An agency without a program is a bad or stagnant agency. Government then takes great pains to show what it is doing. A flock of new programs are announced each year, guaranteed to help the nation or the world. When a new government takes office or when a new man takes the helm at an agency, program-mongering becomes more acute. It may just possibly be true of a new chief justice, too, although judges are among the few civil servants *not* expected to have a new program at all.

What sorts of programs do agencies generate? Mostly, of course, there is no lack of possibilities. Interest groups are happy to make suggestions, but sometimes there are no real demands; sometimes interest groups are in hopeless conflict. Since there must be a program, the program can therefore be more or less spun out of the cloth of pure reform. Some interest groups are weak and inarticulate. Ordinarily, their demands are ignored. If the agency *must* have a program and if the opposition is also weak, the agency assumes the role of surrogate or proxy to the weak. A program will emerge that has some element at least of "pure" reform.

Government is also large and wealthy in the industrial nations. Like rich individuals, it has a feeling of "surplus"; it can afford a luxury or two. The surplus can be invested, as bureaucrats see fit, in reform, that is, in reconstruction of institutions. This process need *not* stem from specific pressure from outside. The surplus could go into building monuments, for example, or trips to the moon, or simply in waste. No doubt waste is amply represented, but there is also some genuine reform. In the modern nations, more and more civil servants are professionals—lawyers, engineers, economists, social workers. Professionals have economic and status group interests. They have also been programmed to work for rational goals, as their profession defines these goals. In their minds, they distinguish sharply between the "scientific" or "professional" and the merely "political." A highway engineer feels that there ought to be a highway through downtown New Orleans, on technical grounds, whatever the politicians think.

Government also attracts real reformers—men and women with more than the common share of zeal. Of course, most civil servants are just people doing their job. But at certain times, government is particularly attractive to idealists. The dawn of the Roosevelt New Deal was one such period. Perhaps the Kennedy administration was another. Some programs—the Office of Economic Opportunity, the Civil Rights

Division of the Justice Department—are especially likely to attract idealists. Their ideals translate themselves into proposals and reorganizations.

Not all actions of government can be explained, then, through resort to the most naked form of interest-group theory. One study of the emergence of poverty as a political issue in the United States in the 1960s argues that the program was incited by reformers such as Michael Harrington, the author of *The Other America*, a study of poverty in the United States, whose work caught the eye and attention of the Kennedy circle.[60]

We should be careful not to exaggerate the impact of such efforts. Many will fail or turn into toothless compromise.[61] Many will be timid and underfunded. The bureaucracy can never stray too far from the firing line of social pressure. What is acceptable to elites and relevant publics sets the boundaries within which reform will have to work. Within these limits, however, the machine does think and act for itself.

For obvious reasons, the judicial system shares these traits only weakly and covertly. Courts in our tradition are passive; they sit waiting for cases. They do not call them up on their own, but they have the option of picking or refusing calls for fresh doctrine. High courts control their dockets. Occasionally, they insinuate doctrine into decisions which no lawyers argued or even suggested, and an activist court can adopt the views of reformist litigants and encourage innovation in this way.

---

[60]Byron G. Lander, "Group Theory and Individuals: The Origin of Poverty as a Political Issue in 1964," 24 *Western Pol. Q.* 514 (1971).

[61]See John A. Robertson and Phyllis Teitelbaum, "Optimizing Legal Impact: A Case Study in Search of a Theory," 1973 *Wis. L. Rev.* 665. The authors studied the impact of a new Massachusetts law (1971) authorizing pretrial or posttrial diversion of persons charged with drug offenses into treatment and counselling services. The law was drafted and pushed through by a "handful of public officials" with "few outside inputs." There was little pressure, "little interest or discussion of the merits" (p. 672). The law was notably ineffective; and the authors argue that one cause was "absence of an organized constituency to monitor implementation and engender commitment among affected actors" (pp. 710–711).

Chapter VIII

On Legal Culture

The basic argument of this book has dealt with legal acts, legal impact, and their relationship. In brief, three clusters of factors determine impact—sanctions, social or peer group influences, and internal values (conscience, concepts of legitimacy). Social forces manufacture law (legal acts) in the first place, but pure "social forces" are too raw to operate directly on the legal system. Individuals and groups have *interests;* interests, however, must be processed into *demands* before they are relevant to the legal system. This means that, while the laws (legal acts) are the product of social forces and result from pressures, bargaining, conflict, etc. as these press in on legal institutions, essential intervening variables are the attitudes and feelings that predispose groups and individuals to turn to or against the law. Similarly, with regard to legal behavior. Pure legal behavior obviously depends on feelings and attitudes; these are also important in determining whether subjects of the law will form groups, exert pressure on the law for change, act as enemy deviants, and the like. Hence, what we call the legal culture must always be taken into account. Indeed, we can rephrase the basic proposition about the making of law as follows: social force, i.e., power, influence, presses upon the legal system and evokes legal acts, when legal culture converts interests into demands or permits this conversion.

The term *legal culture* has been loosely used to describe a number of related phenomena. First, it refers to public knowledge of and attitudes and behavior patterns toward the legal system. Do people feel and act as if courts are fair? When are they willing to use courts? What parts of the law do they consider legitimate? What do they know about the law in general?[1] These attitudes differ from person to person, but one can also speak of the legal culture of a country or a group, if there are patterns that distinguish it from the culture of other countries or groups. A specially important kind of group legal culture is that of legal professionals—the values, ideologies, and principles of lawyers, judges, and others who work within the magic circle of the legal system.[2] The behavior and attitudes of professionals have a great effect on the patterns of demands on the system. To this extent, the legal system *does* seem more than merely a conduit, the rope in our metaphor; but the actions of professionals, too, have their explanation. A judge will decide in such a way as to satisfy demands made upon him when it is in his interest to do so or when his peers or his values so demand. The values, however, as we have suggested, are the long-term residue of social structure, representing old power and influence; and peer pressure depends on who the peers are—on patterns of recruitment into the profession, for example, a factor which is far from politically neutral. Hence the complex behavior of professionals, the legal culture of the insiders, is by no means an autonomous growth and by no means an exception to the general proposition about the primacy of society over law.

ON CULTURAL SPECIFICITY

How culturally specific is law? To what extent is the legal culture of France peculiar to France and French culture? Legal processes certainly look different in different societies. The courtroom world of the English judge in his white wig presents quite a different cultural surface from the people's courts in the Soviet Union and the courts of the Lozi and Zapotec. The substantive law of every country is unique enough to require special study. This suggests that legal cultures are bodies of *custom* organically related to the culture as a whole, not

---

[1]On knowledge and attitude, see Adam Podgórecki et al., *Knowledge and Opinion about Law* (1973); and the essays by Berl Kutschinsky, Klaus Makela, Jan Gorecki, and Adam Podgórecki, in Britt-Mari P. Blegvad, ed., *Contributions to the Sociology of Law* (1966).

[2]This has been a fruitful field for social research on law. There are a number of studies of lawyers and judges—their background, behavior patterns, social characteristics, and attitudes. For example, on American lawyers, see Jerome Carlin, *Lawyers on Their Own, A Study of Individual Practitioners in Chicago* (1962); Joel F. Handler, *The Lawyer and His Community, The Practicing Bar in a Middle-Sized City* (1967); and Erwin O. Smigel, *The Wall Street Lawyer* (1964). Material on Italy is discussed in Renato Treves, *Giustizia e Giudici nella Società Italiana* (1972); on Germany, Wolfgang Kaupen, *Die Hüter von Recht und Ordnung* (1969).

neutral artifacts that a society can pick or buy and which do not bear the genetic mark of any particular society. There are family resemblances, too, among countries with a common legal inheritance.

Differences can be misleading, of course; the white wig of the English judge may be only a trapping. The modern world makes a strong case against cultural specificity. There are tremendous similarities among states that stand at roughly the same level of development. Many countries—Japan, Turkey, Ethiopia—have borrowed whole codes of law from other countries. Borrowing, in fact, is a key theme of modern law. The colonial empires imposed their codes on their colonies; these colonies kept much of this body of law after achieving independence. Borrowing or keeping a foreign code suggests that what is borrowed or kept is *not* culturally specific in the sense of a custom but is rather a tool, a piece of technology—like jet engines, computer hardware, or hybrid corn—that can be packaged in one country and shipped to another.

On the other hand, borrowing is a question of official law; we do not know if borrowed codes and rules set down real roots in national behavior. Some scholars voice extreme skepticism: Robert Seidman even speaks of the "Law of the Nontransferability of Law." The "activity induced by . . . rules," he feels, is "specific to any given situation"; a rule transferred from one culture to another simply "cannot be expected to induce the same sort of role-performance as it did in the place of . . . origin."[3] Moreover, cultural convergence accounts for some of the borrowing. Capitalist economies need capitalist law; socialist economies need socialist law; modernizing societies need modernizing law— rules and institutions to deal with jet engines, computers, hybrid corn. The easiest way to get the appropriate body of law is to borrow it from some convenient source. If similar societies produce similar law, then diverse social structures and economies will produce diversity in law, but this diversity will not be a matter of "culture" in the sense of customs and costumes. We expect great legal variation between a tribal society and Italy, much less between Japan, France, and Finland, although in some ways, language, for example, these three countries have absolutely nothing in common.

---

[3]Robert B. Seidman, "Administrative Law and Legitimacy in Anglophonic Africa: A Problem in the Reception of Foreign Law," 5 *Law and Society Rev.* 161, 200–201 (1970); compare Bernard S. Cohn, "Some Notes on Law and Change in North India," in Paul Bohannon, ed., *Law and Warfare, Studies in the Anthropology of Conflict* (1967), pp. 139, 155. The introduction of British procedural law into Indian courts provoked a "clash of . . . values. . . . [T]he Indians in response thought only of manipulating the new situation and did not use the courts to settle disputes but only to further them."

LEGAL SUBCULTURES AND LEGAL PLURALISM

Legal pluralism is the existence of distinct legal systems or cultures within a single political community. Pluralism comes in many forms. It can be *horizontal,* that is, the subcultures or subsystems have equal status or legitimacy, or *vertical,* that is, they are hierarchically arranged with a "higher" and a "lower" legal system or culture. And pluralism can be cultural, political, and socioeconomic; see Table I. Two forms of *horizontal pluralism* are:

1. CULTURAL FEDERALISM

Some nations or empires contained and allowed distinctive legal subcultures. The Ottoman Empire was a classic case. Within the empire, Moslems, Jews, and Christians each ran a distinct system of courts with jurisdiction over family law and other matters. Modern Israel retains some aspects of cultural federalism. In Israel, family law, and the court which applies it, still depends on the religion of the subject; arrangements are different for Moslems, Christians, and Jews.[4] Islamic courts survive along with state civil courts in Indonesia.[5]

2. STRUCTURAL FEDERALISM

The United States is perhaps the best example of this type. Each of the fifty states preserves considerable legal autonomy. The states are more or less sovereign over commercial and family law, criminal law,

Table I. Types of Legal Pluralism, With Examples

	Horizontal	Vertical
Cultural Pluralism	Eastern empires	Colonial legal systems
Political Pluralism	Federalism	Hierarchical legal systems
Socioeconomic Pluralism	Some forms of status-group pluralism	"Two-nations" pluralism

---

[4]See Amnon Rubinstein, "Law and Religion in Israel," in Haim H. Cohn, ed., *Jewish Law in Ancient and Modern Israel* (1971), p. 190.

[5]Daniel S. Lev, *Islamic Courts in Indonesia* (1972).

torts, contracts, and land law. Switzerland, Canada, and Australia are also organized federally. Many federal states are culturally as well as structurally diverse. Cultural diversity, in fact, is often the excuse for structural autonomy: the "autonomous regions" in the Soviet Union, the South Tyrol in Italy. But the difference between North Dakota and South Dakota is hardly a difference in culture. In Canada, the boundary between Quebec and Ontario is cultural as well as political; the line between Saskatchewan and Alberta, political only.

Vertical pluralism can also be divided into two types:

1. COLONIAL LEGAL SYSTEMS

In the nineteenth-century colonies, there was often an official, usually Western, legal system applicable to the "European" population in the capital and major cities. Indigenous law was in force in the hinterland.[6] It was always clear, however, that the Western system was dominant. In case of conflict, native law had to give way. Independent nations can be "colonial," too. K. Ishwaran reports that villagers in an Indian village make use of customary law, or, when it suits them, the "modern law established by the State." In case of conflict, however, "modern" law prevails.[7] A similar situation can be found among the Mayan Indians of Mexico[8] and indeed quite generally in culturally plural countries with a colonial history.

2. HIERARCHICAL LEGAL SYSTEMS

Colonial legal systems are, in a way, like cultural federalism, only vertically arranged with a bottom and a top. Hierarchical legal systems are the vertical side of structural federalism. For example, in the United States, there is state law and federal law, but when the law of Michigan and the law of the federal government conflict, federal law is supreme.

---

[6]For another definition and view of colonial law, see Paul Bohannon's "The Differing Realms of the Law," in Laura Nader, ed., *The Ethnography of Law*, 67 *Am. Anthropologist*, special publication, no. 6, part 2 (1965), p. 33.

[7]K. Ishwaran, "Customary Law in Village India," 5 *Int'l J. Comp. Sociology* 228 (1964).

[8]Jane F. Collier, *Law and Social Change in Zinacantan* (1973).

STATUS-GROUP PLURALISM

In many legal systems, particularly pre-modern ones, the law that applied to an individual depended on his status or his social class. In England, manorial law ruled the farmers and workmen who lived on the great estates. Knights and nobles used the royal courts and the common law. The merchants had their own rules and courts. To a large extent, status-group pluralism was vertical, but there were horizontal aspects, too, within given strata.

Traces of status-group pluralism still survive, for example, in special rules for "merchants" and special commercial codes in continental Europe. In general, however, modern law tends to eliminate status-group pluralism. "Special law" is abundant but, as Max Weber pointed out, the statuses are "formally and generally accessible to any person."[9] That is, anyone can, formally at least, decide to become a merchant. The laws of modern countries contain dozens of rules about the rights and duties of druggists, but "pharmacist" is not a fixed or inherited status. It is simply an occupation and a role.[10] Modern law, then, does not pay great formal attention to birth or other indices of status; it rather regulates specific roles.

"TWO-NATIONS" PLURALISM

This type probably lurks to some extent in every modern legal system. Official law more or less responds to and governs the well-to-do; the poor stand outside this law for better or for worse. Formal law does not concede any distinction between rich and poor. The law of the poor is informal, unofficial and adverse. In some fields of law, the formal rights of the rich and the poor may be different. Jacobus tenBroek described the family law of California as a "dual system," one set of rules for the rich and a harsh pauper's code for the poor.[11] But some form of pluralism seems inevitable in any complex system. A legal system is plural whenever official, formal law is significantly different from the living law. This is a universal condition of national legal systems.

Structural and cultural pluralism, though distinct, will usually interact. Martin Levin sifted through data on the sentencing behavior

---

[9]Max Rheinstein, ed., *Max Weber on Law in Economy and Society* (1954), p. 144.

[10]See Manfred Rehbinder, "Status, Contract and the Welfare State," 23 *Stan. L. Rev.* 941 (1971).

[11]See Joel F. Handler, ed., *Family Law and the Poor, Essays by Jacobus tenBroek* (1971).

of judges in two cities, Minneapolis and Pittsburgh.[12] He also interviewed the judges. Levin found differences in behavior and in attitude. Pittsburgh judges gave lighter sentences than Minneapolis judges, for example. The Minneapolis judges were "more oriented toward 'society' and its needs for protection, and toward the goals of their professional peers, than toward the defendant." Their decision-making was "formalistic." The Pittsburgh judges, on the other hand, were "oriented toward the defendant rather than toward punishment or deterrence."[13]

These are attitudes, an aspect of culture, and they relate neatly to the behavior of the judges who expressed them. But Levin did not frame his study as a study of attitude. It was structure that fascinated him. Pittsburgh's judges were drawn from the ranks of active party workers. They ran for office in partisan elections. Minneapolis judges ran in nonpartisan elections. The local bar association in Minneapolis had a decisive voice in choosing judges; political parties did not. In Pittsburgh, the opposite situation obtained. Levin's research did suggest, therefore, a systematic relationship between structure and legal behavior. No one "intended" to produce different outcomes in the two cities. The culture of the judges was an intervening variable. But structural decisions led to recruitment of judges of materially different legal culture.

ON THE CLASSIFICATION OF LEGAL SYSTEMS

The concept of legal culture suggests that at least in some sense each country or society has a legal culture of its own and that no two are exactly alike, just as no two societies are exactly alike in politics, social structure, and general culture. Yet some societies are more closely related than others. Perhaps that is so of legal cultures too. Can we classify societies or countries, according to legal cultures? There have been, in fact, many attempts to classify legal systems. The results are not terribly useful from the point of view of social science. The problem is the basis for classification. Conventionally, jurists divide legal systems into families, circles, or groups.[14] Each family, circle, or

---

[12]Martin A. Levin, "Urban Politics and Judicial Behavior," 1 *J. Legal Studies* 193 (1972).

[13]Ibid., pp. 202–203.

[14]See, for example, René David and John E. C. Brierley, *Major Legal Systems in the World Today* (1968), pp. 9–20; Konrad Zweigert and Hein Kötz, *Einführung in die Rechtsvergleichung* (1971), vol. I; Ake Malmström, "The System of Legal Systems," 13 *Scandinavian Studies in Law* 127 (1969).

group contains those legal systems thought to be most closely related. Members of a "family" have a common "parent"; they have descended from this parent or borrowed its legal institutions. The model for this scheme, more or less, is the taxonomy of animals, languages, and plants.[15]

Comparative legal scholars agree that several "families" dominate the legal world. One huge group, the civil-law circle, has been strongly influenced by classical Roman law and has a penchant for codification. Western Europe, Latin America, and French-speaking Africa are assigned to this family. Many African countries have retained some of their customary law, but French influence is powerful in the former colonies; and the Ivory Coast, for one, is insisting on "new uniform civil legislation which is applicable to all persons regardless of status," which means the end of customary law, at least officially.[16] Scotland, Louisiana, and Quebec also have greater or lesser amounts of affinity with the civil-law world. Some scholars divide the civil-law world into French and German subfamilies. The Scandinavian legal systems stand somewhat apart from the others in this group, though they have many traits in common with the continental systems.[17]

The countries of the common-law family include Great Britain, its colonies, former colonies, and colonies of former colonies: the United States and Canada (except, in some regards, Louisiana and Quebec), Australia and New Zealand, Jamaica, Trinidad, Barbados, and the Bahamas, among others. The common law is an important element in Kenya, Ghana, and Nigeria, in other former colonies in Africa, and in Liberia. The influence of the common law is also strong in India, Pakistan, and Malaysia.

Some scholars treat the socialist law systems of Europe—the Soviet Union, and the people's democracies of Eastern Europe—as a separate family.[18] This group, however, has strong affinities with the civil-law world. The Moslem countries form another distinct family. The Far East stands more or less by itself. Japanese law is a unique

---

[15]See Lawrence M. Friedman, "Legal Culture and Social Development," 4 *Law and Society Rev.* 29 (1969).

[16]Jeswald D. Salacuse, *An Introduction to Law in French-Speaking Africa* (1969), vol. I, pp. 125–126.

[17]Zweigert and Kötz, *supra* note 14, pp. 339–349.

[18]E.g., David and Brierley, *supra* note 14, p. 17; Zweigert and Kötz, pp. 349ff. The division of Germany into a socialist and a non-socialist part provides an interesting "natural" experiment on the impact of East European socialism on received legal thought. See Inga Markovits, *Sozialistisches und Bürgerliches Zivilrechtsdenken in der DDR* (1969).

blend of civil law and native features with a dash of recent American influence.[19] Modern India and Israel have mixed systems of law in which elements of Hindu and Judaic law rub shoulders with overlays of modern Western law. Many systems are extinct and have left behind fossil remains—old books, inscriptions, papyri. The taxonomy of tribal systems is almost completely undeveloped.

To divide legal systems in this way, that is, into "families," assumes that a country's legal system is something more than the sum of its parts, that it has a definite character and style, that this character is long-lasting and is genetically derived from the "parent." What makes legal systems members of a single "family" are certain basic traits they hold in common. These are not isolated traits; they hang together and persist over time; they permeate the legal institutions of a country and give it its distinctive flavor or character.

What are these traits?[20] Classifiers, like taxonomists in other fields, look for a few core features which they can use for diagnosis and distinction. The traits used, on the whole, are those of lawyers' law. That is, they come from the branches of law which lawyers find most practical and interesting as lawyers and which are most impervious to outsiders and outside influence. Or they are pieces of the legal system which, for some historical or traditional reason, loom large in the minds of lawyers or are stressed in legal education regardless of their practical importance. To many legal scholars, common-law systems of Ontario or Pennsylvania, for example, are worlds apart from such civil-law systems as those of Bolivia or France. The doctrine of precedent, the civil jury, and certain concepts and institutions (the trust, the doctrine of consideration) are peculiar to the common law. Civil law, for its part, has its own armory of concepts, a Roman law base, and in most countries a comprehensive code.

But our imaginary scholars did not single out these traits, because they were especially vital parts of living law or had anything much to do with the impact of law. Indeed, in England the civil jury is almost extinct; the doctrine of consideration has little practical importance anywhere. A taxonomic philosophy that works for biology may not work for law. The theory of evolution gives a starting point and a

---

[19]Charles R. Stevens, "Modern Japanese Law as an Instrument of Comparison," 19 *Am. J. Comp. L.* 665 (1971).

[20]David and Brierley, *supra* note 14, ask, what makes a family a family? They suggest as one criterion "whether someone educated in the study and practice of one law," can "handle" another, "without much difficulty." Another criterion is whether the two laws compared "are founded on opposed philosophical, political or economic principles, and . . . seek to achieve two entirely different types of society" (p. 12).

framework for classification in biological science. There is no analogous theory for law.

Of course, it is true that American law "descends" from English law in one interesting sense, and the law of Louisiana does resemble in some ways the civil law of Spain or France. But these historic connections, in point of fact, may not amount to much. The classical typology explains very little *except* the formal sources of those traits selected as "basic." But the traits are singled out as basic traits precisely because they make a scheme of classification possible. If we know what "family" a country belongs to, what else do we know about the society? Can we predict anything about its politics, society, or economy? Its level of development?

It is fair to say that nothing has been proven. One problem is with the traits themselves. We do not know the impact, for example, of the jury. Does the jury system have political consequences? Does it foster democracy? It would be rash to say "yes." Many systems which lack a jury seem just as democratic as the common-law countries. Some countries with juries seem less "participatory" than countries without juries. No doubt, serving on a jury might affect a person's attitudes and behavior. But we do not know how important a place the jury occupies in the legal and social life of the community or what functional equivalents exist elsewhere. We could ask similar questions about other diagnostic traits and about the traits taken together. It is just not possible to say that the common-law system, as it developed in England, played a role in shaping the rise of representative government. Even less would one want to say that it had something to do with the outbreak of an industrial revolution. Could we say anything about the common law, as such, as a moving cause of economic or political change? What does the common law do for a country today? What would it do for Burma or Iran?

Notice that our skepticism is confined to the concept of the common-law "family." English *law* certainly influenced the history of England. English *society* produced English *law,* and English law fed back influence on English society. By English law, we mean all of it, including these rules and institutions which lawyers typically ignore in formal writing—especially, in modern law, rules of regulation and administration.

English law, too, was an important part of the background of American law. Englishmen brought it over, English magistrates imposed it, lawyers and judges who knew no other model copied and followed it. A good deal, of course, remains of this common-law substratum. American land law has a distinctly English flavor, especially in the vocabulary of estates, trusts, conveyancing, easements, and covenants. Commercial law too has close resemblances to English law.[21] Contract and tort law in the two countries closely interacted in the nineteenth century and retain some family resemblance.

It is, on the whole, easy to exaggerate the historical, i.e., English, element in American law,[22] easy also to exaggerate how much old English law is left in modern England. Since the two countries parted company politically, their law also diverged. In important areas of modern regulatory law—town and country planning, tax law, company law, social welfare law—the two have grown so far apart that they are almost like mutually unintelligible dialects. An American lawyer can barely understand English cases and statutes and vice versa. The English division between barristers and solicitors is unknown in the United States.

In law, form and phraseology are often fairly arbitrary. There has to be a name for an easement, but the name hardly matters so long as everyone relevant knows it. Obviously, then, law holds on to traditional words on strict cost-benefit grounds. American law speaks English. Why change the name of the *plaintiff* or call *torts* something else? Many minor substantive rules are like ancient names: They are convenient, arbitrary, basically English, and they stay.

Then, too, the two countries share a language and, to some extent, a culture. Both have experienced an industrial revolution along with other modern nations; both urbanized; both absorbed the gifts of science and technology. Both have given more and more of their people the vote. Both have suffered wars and depressions. Both have set about to regulate business; both extract from their citizens billions of dollars in taxes every year; both have established elaborate programs of social welfare, although the programs differ greatly in details. In short, one would expect a close connection between the law of these two countries even without common membership in a "family" of common law. Similar history and similar economic conditions should produce striking similarity in legal culture.

Why then is the French legal system so different? France has gone through similar modern experiences. In fact, French and English law

---

[21] In theory, commercial law was not the law of any nation but the international custom of merchants. In any case, mercantile doctrines and documents entered American law by way of England.

[22] The civil law also left traces on American law as well. Much of it, in the law of wills, for example, came by way of England. In the West and Southwest, Spanish-Mexican law left behind the community property system and the holographic will. The presumption is that these institutions were exceptionally functional and survived for that reason.

undoubtedly *have* converged quite a bit, if one looks at living law rather than diagnostic traits. Of course, no one could confuse the legal culture of an English barrister with that of a French *avocat*, but convergences are most striking precisely where national experiences have been most alike, in business law, for example. It is not surprising that the countries remain far apart in terminology and in many minor and marginal rules. These and the customs of jurists preserve a foreign appearance that may to some degree be deceiving.

THE CULTURE OF MODERNITY

One can speak about legal culture at many levels of abstraction. At a high level of abstraction, for example, there may be cultural traits common to all modern or industrial nations. (By modern, we mean nothing more than a system functioning in an industrial society.)

Some scholars believe they see such traits. Particularly, they see a general pattern of legal evolution from lower to higher stages, from pre-modern to modern. These theories will be discussed in Chapter X. For now, we note the general idea that modern law, say, since the Industrial Revolution, is quite special, quite unlike the systems in pre-modern and non-modern societies. The rules and institutions, of course, are different, but so are the underlying attitudes, in short, the culture.[23]

Traditional legal systems have distinctive theories of *legitimacy* that separate them from modern law. They do not readily accept the idea of legal change. In many traditional societies, law was divine or transcendental, part of a gift of God or God's command delivered in person or through vicars, prophets, and oracles. In others, law consisted of *custom*—traditional ways handed down from time immemorial, sacred because of their antiquity. Non-modern law, in short, did not consider law to be man-made and changeable. Of course, changes did occur. Some were gradual, subtle, unnoticed. Some legislative changes, as in medieval German law, were disguised as corrections or restorations of law that was essentially unchangeable.[24] In some traditional societies, kings and chiefs occasionally made new rules or laid down decrees with or without the concurrence of a senate or council of elders.[25] In some, charismatic leaders changed the law in dra-

---

[23]No one can really measure attitudes in whole societies—certainly not in dead ones. Statements about legal culture, then, rest on shaky evidence at best.

[24]Wilhelm Ebel, *Geschichte der Gesetzgebung in Deutschland* (2nd ed., 1958), pp. 15–20.

[25]T.O. Elias, *The Nature of African Customary Law* (1956), pp. 191–206.

matic strokes, often claiming direct revelation. Change, then, was possible; but change was extraordinary and marvelous, never part of the regular path of the law.

In the common law, a subtle form of tradition cast a glow of legitimacy over the law. According to Lord Coke, "reason" made legal principles valid: "For reason is the life of the law, nay the common law is nothing else but reason. . . . Law . . . is the perfection of reason."[26] By reason, he meant, more or less, long tradition and experience expressing the proper order of the world. In this system, law slowly evolved, except for the intrusions of king and parliament, which were never common. Modern law, however, turns the basic presumption about law upside down. Law is constantly in flux. Some parts of the law embody timeless values, but the bulk of the law changes and changes often, at least in its outer garments. People know that much or all of the law is neither eternal nor divine. Large parts of it are nothing more than morally neutral tools, means toward some end. Law is "good," if it advances a useful purpose and advances it well.[27]

The change from traditional to instrumental theories of law was fundamental and momentous. By *instrumental* theories, we mean theories that law is essentially man-made, is shaped by society to accomplish some purpose, and can be changed to fulfill its purpose better. The change was not an isolated change, reflected only in the law. Rather, it was the legal phase of a cultural revolution. Modern society differs from its past in many ways which Weber summed up in a single concept: the *rational*. Modern society is society in pursuit of the rational. Division of labor, "scientific specialization," and "technical differentiation" have utterly transformed the modern world; despite exceptions, enclaves, survivals, and counter trends, "efficiency and productivity" have become major values in society.[28]

Such a broad, fundamental change did not take place overnight, nor did a single man or a single school invent it. It is natural to look on the Industrial Revolution as the process which, more than any other, triggered the change; and the English Utilitarians naturally come to mind as thinkers who expressed most clearly the modern

---

[26]Sir Edward Coke, Commentaries on Littleton (1628), 97b.

[27]Legitimacy as we defined it, is a procedural idea: the *way* law is made validates *what* has been made. Legitimacy in this sense is itself somewhat intermediate and unstable, somewhat dependent on what we have called *trust*, in some societies. Majority rule, one of the favored procedural forms, is not an end in itself but a means. Other procedures, too, are means justified by their ends. "Due process" would be nothing, or nearly nothing, unless it produced due results.

[28]Julien Freund, *The Sociology of Max Weber* (1968), p. 18.

theory of law. Bentham began his "Principles of Legislation" with a bold statement: The "public good ought to be the object of the legislator; general utility ought to be the foundation of his reasoning. To know the true good of the community is what constitutes the science of legislation; the art consists in finding the means to realize that good."[29] Bentham, for all his genius, did not pull these ideas out of thin air. He and his school were probably more effect than cause; they summed up ideas that the new society churned up spontaneously, and they expressed these thoughts in fresh paradigms.

The great legal philosophers, in general, are those who expound ideas about law and legal process in an elegant, thoughtful, systematic way. But the *essential* theorems of jurisprudence probably come from looser, less systematic ideas, which are in the air during a particular time period. The needs of the legal profession are another stimulus for these theorems. At the same time, legal thought, however noble, stimulating, and ethically sound, is necessarily bound to its culture. The culture provides the limits within which legal thought can range. Culture also determines, in large part, which of the competing schools of thought is likely to command the most respect at any given time and by whom.

The instrumental theory of law doubtless had its basis in public opinion. By public opinion, of course, we do not mean a simple head count,[30] but rather "public opinion" in the sense of operating attitudes among those with power and influence—what opinion leaders thought and what the ordinary person accepted from them. The ordinary person of, for example, 1800 or 1820 or 1850 refers, in this context, to the ordinary merchant, landowner, or man of affairs.[31]

Did ideas about law shift decisively at the time of the Industrial Revolution? Legal thought itself, however untrustworthy, is evidence pointing in this direction. In Europe, this was the age of the great codifications. Country after country set about to draft new, systematic, "rational," and man-made codes. To be sure, there were strong intellectual movements behind the codes as well as stirrings in the econ-

[29]Jeremy Bentham, *Theory of Legislation* (4th ed., 1882), p. 1.
[30]See Chapter VI, pp. 162–165.
[31]This is the sense in which Albert V. Dicey used "public opinion," in his *Lectures on the Relation between Law and Public Opinion in England during the Nineteenth Century* (1905). For another view of the origin of the "instrumental theory," see Morton Horwitz, "The Emergence of an Instrumental Conception of American Law, 1780–1820," in Donald Fleming and Bernard Bailyn, eds., *Law in American History* (1971), p. 287. Compare the discussion of "positivism" in Niklas Luhmann, *Rechtssoziologie* (2 vols. 1972), vol. 2, pp. 207–217.

omy,[32] but whatever the cause, the shift in attitude seems unmistakable. With reference to the United States, William E. Nelson advances an interesting argument. He points out that, in the eighteenth century, preambles were usually attached to statutes. These explained the point or *purpose* of the statute. After about 1800, the practice of including preambles virtually ceased. When statutes were not yet "normal," changes in the body of law called for explanation and justification. The nineteenth century, however, expected a constant tinkering with law. Therefore, no excuses were needed or made.[33]

The new legal culture, though pervasive, has not driven out older attitudes entirely. (Old law, too, had pockets of rational and utilitarian thought.) Traditional and sacred theories still color the law—for example, in constitutional law and the law of "basic rights." It would not be fair to call every element of law that is not strictly instrumental a "survival" of the past. This would imply that these elements were doomed to die out or that progressive societies ought to get rid of them. Constitutional law in the United States is a dynamic field of law and a vehicle for dramatic social change. This branch of law has survived and flourished and been useful, even though (or perhaps because) its power depends, in part, on appeal to the timeless, the traditional, to morality and ideals.

MODERNITY IN LAW AND MODERNITY IN SOCIETY: CAUSE AND EFFECT

It is one thing to argue that modern attitudes about law are the children of industrial society or that modern legal thought and modern industrial society sprang into being at the same time, perhaps caused by some third, unknown factor. It is quite another to suggest that new forms of law or new ideas about law were themselves instrumental in ushering in the new world or were some sort of prerequisite for it. This, on a broad scale, is the question of the structural variable. It is also a question about the connection between "families" of law and economic development. The Industrial Revolution by conventional reckoning be-

---

[32]Franz Wieacker, *Privatrechtgeschichte der Neuzeit* (1952), pp. 197–216.

[33]William E. Nelson, "The Americanization of the Common Law" (Ph.D. thesis, Harvard University, 1971), a study of changes in the law of Massachusetts in the late eighteenth and early nineteenth centuries.

The preamble never entirely died out. Statutes today sometimes carry a preamble or at least a broad statement of purpose. In the United States, this sometimes happens when legislators want to make the validity of the law abundantly clear, because of possible constitutional doubts.

gan in England. It is natural to wonder what part the common law played.

Talcott Parsons takes one side of this question. The English legal system, he says, was "an integrated system of universalistic norms"; modern economy and society could not develop without such a system.[34] Max Weber took a rather different view. Industry and business do demand some level of rationality; but Weber was struck by the fact that the common law was and is less "rational" than other European systems. Capitalism, Weber felt, came to England almost in *spite* of its legal system. Indeed, "modern capitalism prospers equally and manifests essentially identical economic traits under legal systems containing rules and institutions which considerably differ from each other at least from a juridical point of view."[35]

The last phrase, however, is crucial: "from a juridical point of view." The "juridical point of view," as we have many times pointed out, is narrow and distorted. It refers, essentially, to lawyer's law. This part of the law may or may not be vital from the standpoint of economic development. As we argued, mere membership in a "family" of legal systems hardly advances or impedes capitalism (or socialism, for that matter). The members of great families are a most diverse lot: Haiti and France, for example, belong to the same "family" and are closely related at that. Each "family" seems adaptable to any level of culture, just as any language can adapt itself to discourse on any human topic, any science, any art.

This is not to say that there are no traits that a modern legal system, a system that functions in industrial society, must have. Certainly, a legal system which has no slack or give, which cannot change with changing times, which does not support reasonable certainty in business affairs, will not work in the twentieth century. These demands are not hard to meet; every legal system seems to meet them as the need arises.

Certainly, predictability and flexibility do not have to be features of the *formal* legal system. It would be a mistake to rank legal systems as more or less developed, more or less modern, more or less functional merely by looking at formal traits. The test is how the system works in life. This raises a question of cause and effect. Perhaps, at a certain stage of economic growth, social processes automatically produce the needed kind of law or try to. If the formal system will not meet the demands, the informal system will.

---

[34]Talcott Parsons, "Evolutionary Universals in Society," 29 *Am. Soc. Rev.* 339 (1964).
[35]Max Rheinstein, ed., *Max Weber on Law in Economy and Society* (1954), p. 315.

ON NATIONAL LEGAL CULTURE: WITH SPECIAL REFERENCE TO THE UNITED STATES AND BRITAIN

Each nation, we have said, has a distinctive legal culture. But legal culture is difficult to research, and there is little systematic data on comparative culture.[36] We are left, then, with little more than impressions. Is there a specifically American legal culture—attitudes and values common or reasonably common to the nation as a whole and distinct from attitudes and values of other countries? The answer is far from clear. National culture is a kind of aggregate, hard to compare with other aggregates. Comparisons of parts of a culture are also tricky. French and American farmers might have different attitudes about law; but if the two societies define "farmer" differently and if farmers occupy different social roles in the two countries, the comparison as such might be misleading.

Recent research has begun to explore differences in legal knowledge and attitudes toward law on the national level.[37] Attitudes, of course, are only part of the story. Legal culture is important, because attitudes help manufacture real *demands* on the legal system. What counts are attitudes that burst forth into behavior. Culture builds structures; structures in turn work on attitudes, because they define what is possible, establish what is usual, and describe the circle within which the mind in that culture must rotate. Moreover, structure is valuable evidence of attitude. A consistent structural pattern betrays and describes underlying attitudes, like clothing which follows the lines of the body. Attitudes and structures interact. For example, the law of wills and succession may tell a great deal about social attitudes toward property, family, and death. The *structure* of the law of succession, in turn, defines the way we dispose of our property at death; other ways become unthinkable. Where people are used to the *idea* of litigation, that is, the idea that one takes disputes to court, courts will be

---

[36]Some studies in history or sociology bear obliquely on comparative legal culture. An interesting body of literature, for example, has compared legal and social aspects of slavery in various countries of the Western hemisphere. The law of slavery has been used now as evidence of underlying attitudes, now as an independent variable. See Carl N. Degler, *Neither Black nor White, Slavery and Race Relations in Brazil and the United States* (1971); Herbert S. Klein, *Slavery in the Americas, a Comparative Study of Virginia and Cuba* (1967); Stanley M. Elkins, *Slavery, A Problem in American Institutional and Intellectual Life* (1959).

[37]See, for example, Adam Podgórecki et al., *Knowledge and Opinion About Law* (1973); for a description of other ongoing projects, see *Sociologie du Droit et de la Justice* (1970), a report of the 1969 meeting of the International Sociological Association, Research Committee on Sociology of Law.

busy and prestigious. People then see courts as busy and prestigious; this affects their own point of view. And so it goes.

Some features of American legal life have struck observers as unique or uniquely pervasive. One is *fragmentation of power*. The United States began with a revolution against the primacy of a distant monarchy. The Constitution of 1787 was obsessed with the idea of checks and balances; and the plan of government was federal. The states retained great power. Political thinkers of the late eighteenth century were fearful of concentrated power. Merchants, landowners, ministers, and lawyers agreed. The basic attitude seems to persist to this day. The Constitution was an effect, not a cause of this attitude; it may have helped, however, to keep it alive. We must remember, however, that other countries are equally insistent on checks and balances—on paper, while in practice the words are ignored.[38] In the United States the philosophy of checks and balances is so striking that one might call it a distinctive mark of legal culture.

The distrust of concentrated power among influential Americans is an attitude, not a "philosophy," not a systematic, consistent world view. The attitude has structural consequences: Americans tolerate or build political structures that allow for "pluralism," fragmented authority, multiple veto groups. Andrew Shonfield has referred to a "national instinct to break up government into many small parts"; Americans conceive of their government as a "loose confederation of more or less hostile bodies competing with one another for more money and more power."[39] This is true of local government as well as of the federal system, if not more so. Metropolitan areas—Boston, New York, Los Angeles—are governed by a patchwork of hundreds of overlapping jurisdictions. Political lines are drawn one way, school districts another way; sewer districts still differently. When a new need arises, cutting across old boundary lines, one more structure will be simply slapped on top of the others (for example, the New York Port Authority).

American government and law is organized on what might be called a warlord system.[40] Almost every stronghold of formal power is balanced by some counterpower.[41] Federalism itself is one manifesta-

---

[38]The Soviet Constitution, for example, gives every republic the right "freely to secede from the U.S.S.R." See Dieter Blumenwitz, "Das Sezessionsrecht Innerstaatlicher Rechtsgemeinschaften," 3 *Verfassung und Recht in Übersee* 429, 436–437 (1970).

[39]Andrew Shonfield, *Modern Capitalism, The Changing Balance of Public and Private Power* (1965), pp. 318–319.

[40]See Lawrence M. Friedman, "Law, Order and History," 16 *S.D. L. Rev.* 242 (1971).

[41]The president's virtual dictatorship in foreign policy is a sad and significant exception, and, under recent presidents, dangerously great power has flowed into the White House. It remains to be seen if this trend can be arrested.

tion of this culture. Even the judicial system demonstrates this trait and so do ordinary fields of law, for example, rules of evidence. Probably no country in the world has so complicated a law of evidence. Why do we not have simple, rational rules as European nations do? The finger of blame is commonly pointed at the jury. The jury is a precious institution, but, on the other hand, is not to be trusted too far. The rules keep from the jury's ears all evidence that is not predigested, perfect, free from prejudice. On the other hand, the jury's value lies precisely in the way it balances the power of the judge, and through him, the state. Hence, a network of rules, equally elaborate, muzzles the judge to the advantage of the jury. As one body of rules expands, so does the other. Judges are not allowed to comment on evidence, and the law strictly curbs their power to instruct and influence the jury. Meanwhile, higher court rules bear down hard on what judges and juries do below.[42]

What is the source of the attitudes underlying this hypertrophy of structure? Clearly, instrumentalism is an element. Law is a means to an end, a tool to be used; and people use it. In a purely instrumental world, tradition and habit do not keep one interest group from trying to gobble others up. There are cultural elements that help; some of these we have already discussed. But they may not go far enough. One way to avoid the law of the jungle is the constitutional solution: that is, to agree in advance on some rules of the game which will protect all against all. Many of these rules are procedural and structural. The Bill of Rights is one such agreement: the majority, presumably, cannot crush a minority through the use of majority rule. Other rules erect defensive structures, bailiwicks, enclaves where a group can build a fortress for itself, safe from incursions of the outside world. An incorporated suburb is a fortress, if it can control land use within its borders. Middle-class whites can in effect keep the central city out. In enclaves carved out inside a federal system, states can run their own show, free from the power of the national government and majority, i.e., national interests and ideals.

The underlying problem is common to all modern societies. It may be particularly virulent, however, in the United States. Relatively early in its history, the United States opted for equality and mobility. The "equality" was always a question of more or less and so was the mobility. There were rich and poor and even some who were forcibly kept in slavery, but compared to Europe, the country was open and free, a revolutionary country, where the middle-class masses shared in the wealth and the power. The American experiment set off a chain

---

[42]Lawrence M. Friedman, *A History of American Law* (1973), pp. 134–137.

reaction of incalculable consequence. The country had to face one basic problem: how to arrange government and law to accommodate so wide a dispersal of power within a culture that did not frown on the use of power for private purposes. The warlord system was one major response.

Claims-consciousness is another aspect of American legal culture. Some cultures are shy about litigation. On a scale of aggressive pursuit of legal rights, Americans seem to rank high at least among modern nations. Americans are not afraid or unwilling to press their rights in court. These are, at any rate, strong impressions.

Litigation in the United States is costly, which keeps the rate of litigation lower than it otherwise might be. However, one kind of litigation, judicial review of governmental action, although not common in absolute terms, is unusually important. Judges can and sometimes do overturn major political or economic arrangements. In 1857, the Supreme Court, in the *Dred Scott* case,[43] attacked the Missouri Compromise and created a political uproar. The United States Supreme Court recently destroyed all existing laws on the death penalty and then, a year later, wiped dozens of abortion laws off the books.[44] Litigants who are claims-conscious press cases before judges who are responsive and activist; the two groups reinforce each other. Even in closely related legal cultures, such as that of Great Britain, courts defer much more to the government.

The British citizen may be more deferential, less rights-conscious than his American counterpart,[45] but there are also important structural differences between the two legal systems. The British bar is small and elite; the judges come from a tiny in-group of barristers. Bench and bar are more of one piece than in the United States. Barristers almost never see a client except with a solicitor; they do not involve themselves in their client's affairs; barristers do not become "advocates" for clients and causes except in the narrowest technical sense. Their loyalty lies with the profession, yet they have the sole right to argue cases in the higher courts.[46] Judges have the same exaggerated

---

[43] *Dred Scott* v. *Sandford*, 19 How. 393 (1857); Stanley I. Kutler, *The Dred Scott Decision: Law or Politics?* (1967).

[44] *Furman* v. *Georgia*, 408 U.S. 238 (1972); *Roe* v. *Wade*, 410 U.S. 113 (1973).

[45] On this point, see W. G. Runciman, *Relative Deprivation and Social Justice: A Study of Attitudes to Social Inequality in Twentieth-Century England* (1966); Robert McKenzie and Allan Silver, *Angels in Marble, Working Class Conservatives in Urban England* (1968); a recent survey of British attitudes towards courts and law is in Brian Abel-Smith, Michael Zander, and Rosalind Brooke, *Legal Problems and the Citizen, A Study in Three London Boroughs* (1973), Appendix III, pp. 249–250.

[46] Michael Zander, *Lawyers and the Public Interest* (1968), ch. 12.

loyalty to the profession. Courts are hardly hotbeds of social change. The state, regulating with one hand and handing out welfare with the other, bypasses the courts; tribunals and agencies make and apply middle-range policy, free from judicial review. The courts sit proudly in their robes and wigs, but the real work of government ignores them almost completely. There is little "political" use of the courts.[47]

These remarks, we have said, hardly rise above suggestion and impression. Studies of comparative legal culture, however, are already in progress, using more rigorous methods, and the subject is bound to gain in knowledge in future years.

ASPECTS OF MODERN LEGAL CULTURE

Changes in *basic* theories of legitimacy have massive effects in any society. New attitudes and ideas about law, however interesting, are important only when they lead to different behavior. In an earlier chapter, we discussed legitimacy as one root of compliant behavior. A change in basic theories of legitimacy should change patterns of obedience and disobedience. In traditional societies, people follow rules more or less out of custom or faith. In modern societies, faith becomes attenuated. Sanctions must be invoked to ensure a satisfactory level of compliance. To run a modern state takes a heavy investment in enforcement and social control. Laws may have to be altered to induce more compliance. In either case, new opinion sets in motion a cycle of social change.

The instrumental theory has a devastating effect on the *making* of law. If law is man-made, a mere means to an end, there is little reason not to use it. Traditional theories of legitimacy shielded society from the naked play of interests. The modern state lacks this shield. Changes in theories of legitimacy of law also brought about striking changes in style—the decline in legal fictions and the rise and eclipse of "conceptual jurisprudence." These will be discussed in the next chapter.

The change in legitimacy shows itself also in a general decay of *authority*. Respect for status and authority were at the very heart of traditional society. A person who was born a peasant died a peasant. He never dreamt he might rise in society. Probably he accepted the social order, believed in it, and gave it his total obedience. At any rate, he had no choice in the matter.

---

[47]British courts, judges, and lawyers may in the 1970s be moving slowly in the American direction. On the general conservatism of British courts, see Fred L. Morrison, *Courts and the Political Process in England* (1973).

Authority, in the modern world, has a more difficult task; it must justify itself pragmatically, if not for all of the people all of the time, then for some of the people some of the time. Of course, every society has an authority structure and probably could not survive without one. And the authority depends on legitimacy and trust. But these are rebuttable presumptions today.

In modern times, political power has gradually spread downwards. A handful of nobles once ran society, then the nobles together with the rich. Next the middle classes stepped onto the stage. Each new group in power has refused to accept the role of mere subject or the label of an inferior caste. The bonds of faith between citizen and state gradually weaken. Groups strive for power and privilege for their own self-interest, as they see it. Ultimately, even the most disadvantaged join in the struggle—blacks, the poor, prisoners in jail, and leftist splinter groups along with such unlikely bedfellows as Catholic militants, women, and long-hidden sexual minorities. The process seems to go on in every modern nation, although at different rates and in different forms. Everywhere, interest groups multiply, and competition over scarce resources is sharp. Within limits, this state of affairs may be beneficial to society,[48] but in order for the interest-group society to work, losers must accept the rules of the game. Intense disappointment in outcomes, however, weakens legitimacy. In extreme cases, there can be violence or war.

Of course, violence, crime and disorder have many causes.[49] Crime correlates with high mobility and a transient population. A weakening of traditional bonds is part cause, part effect of the great, shifting movement of peoples. People move to the cities and become part of a rootless urban mass. Disorder breeds among the dislocated.

When traditional authority decays, the legal culture must discover some new principle of legitimacy. The overriding principle now is rationality: A law is valid that is validly produced and *which produces the*

---

[48]See, for example, V.O. Key: pressure groups may cause "decision-makers to attend to shades of opinion and preference relevant to decision though not necessarily of great electoral strength—a disposition of no mean importance in the promotion of the equitable treatment of people in a democratic order." *Public Opinion and American Democracy* (1965), p. 530.

[49]Unfortunately, crime statistics are not very reliable; the further back one goes, the shakier they get. See, in general, Nigel Walker, *Crimes, Courts and Figures* (1971). The rate of commission of classic crimes of violence may *not* have increased seriously, if one takes a long enough time span into account; see Roger Lane, "Urbanization and Criminal Violence in the Nineteenth Century: Massachusetts as a Test Case" and Fred P. Graham, "A Contemporary History of American Crime," in Hugh D. Graham and Ted R. Gurr, eds., *Violence in America: Historical and Comparative Perspectives* (1969) p. 359.

right results. A legal system cannot hang together on this basis without genuine consensus or community of interest. If there is none, other principles must deliver acquiescence—principles that validate actions at law, even when they do *not* produce "right" results. This is legitimacy, strictly speaking. But, in modern times, even procedural principles are valued instrumentally. Here, we suggest, lies one source of great instability.

The concept of *science* is pivotal in modern law. Since modern law is instrumental, it must use rational means to achieve its end. Science means reason. It means tested, empirical methods to find out the truth. Science validates the law. It is the bedrock in which *trust* rests. Modern law makes heavy use of experts and defers to their superior wit. Experts do most of the work of making and applying law. In the modern administrative state, doctors, engineers, economists, and other technicians decide thousands of matters which, if handled at all in the past, were within the sphere of lawyers, judges, or politicians. Sometimes, of course, experts are used merely as a screen, as a legitimating device. Psychiatrists play this dubious role, as we noted, in civil commitment cases.[50] On the whole, however, modern law accepts "science" as a touchstone of truth. It accepts blood tests, ballistics, and fingerprint evidence as conclusive and infallible. Even those who attack the experts presuppose a deep faith in science and limit their complaints to what they consider imposter sciences, such as sociology or psychiatry, or to experts who do the bidding of others.

The concept of "science" has another, special role in modern law. It helps protect the position of lawyers and judges in society. It is an open secret that judges do innovate, that is, they make law. Legal theory, however, vigorously denied this fact in the nineteenth century. Still, the power was there, and it was difficult to justify. The concept of legal science was one solution.[51] The judges needed a theory of law that validated change, yet justified their control over the law. The model of science, as popularly understood, did the job perfectly. Scien-

---

[50]Thomas Scheff, *Being Mentally Ill: A Sociological Theory* (1966), discussed earlier. This is apparently not only an American problem. In Switzerland a rather similar process takes place. Peter Aebersold, *Die Verwahrung und Versorgung vermindert Zurechnungsfähiger in der Schweiz* (1972).

The role of psychiatrists as experts in criminal trials has been severely criticized, notably by Dr. Thomas Szasz in such books as *Law, Liberty and Psychiatry* (1963).

[51]Another American solution was to make judgeships elective. If judges ran for office, they would reflect the will of the people. By the time of the Civil War, some judges were popularly elected in almost every state. See, in general, Evan Haynes, *The Selection and Tenure of Judges* (1944).

tific rules are truths of the real world. They describe an external reality. They are not subject to any individual's whim. But only the scientists have the skill to deal with science, to find new principles and handle old ones. A science of law, like natural science, would be cumulative and progressive, and it would be controlled by the jurists.[52]

Legal science, to be sure, is no science at all, merely an imitation of science. For one thing, it is not experimental or empirical but, if anything, deductive. Euclid has been more of a model than Galileo or Pasteur. But it was important for lawyers and judges to treat law as a genuine science. The concept of legal science promoted the prestige of law and legal learning; at the same time, it affirmed that law was an independent domain, distinct from politics, utilitarian policy, and the ideas of the man of the street.

Conceptual jurisprudence was another defense against the threat to legal independence. The typical legal opinion of the late nineteenth century was written in what Karl Llewellyn has called formal style[53] —dull, technical, impersonal, and addicted to *stare decisis*. These cases are boring to read, but this vice is a virtue. The cases made no dangerous claims to innovation. They treated law as a realm unto itself; the judges merely discovered and announced preexisting principles of law. Conceptualism, however, was in turn forced to retreat by the legal realist movement. Today, decisions must, to a greater extent than before, justify themselves on policy grounds. Simply to appeal to the past, to precedent, will not do for legitimation. What legitimates is rational policy—a legal act must serve the interests or ends of some individual, group, or society. This does not mean that appeals to the past are valueless or illegitimate. The doctrine of precedent is instrumentally useful. If issues were endlessly repeated, the legal system would lose all efficiency and sink into chaos. (At least, people might *think* this would happen.) The doctrine of precedent, honestly followed, limits the discretion of decision-makers. This too is functional. A system cannot tolerate more than a few philosopher-kings. For efficiency, and fairness, it is better if lower-order functionaries, including trial court judges, stick to old and well-worn paths. The clerk who sells

---

[52]C.C. Langdell, at Harvard, argued that law was a "science" and had to be studied as a science—through its primary sources, reported cases. C.C. Langdell, *Contracts* (1871), preface. This was the beginning of the revolution in legal education; see the comprehensive survey by Robert Stevens, "Two Cheers for 1870: The American Law School," in Donald Fleming and Bernard Bailyn, eds., *Law in American History* (1971) p. 405; Langdell's theories dominated legal education by 1900.

[53]Karl Llewellyn, "Remarks on the Theory of Appellate Decision," 3 *Vand. L. Rev.* 395 (1950).

marriage licenses is not supposed to invent new rules or to decide whether this man and that woman are suited for each other.

A doctrine of *stare decisis* that survives because it is useful is no longer a doctrine of blind adherence to the past. Old decisions fall, when they have outlived their usefulness. If a rule or doctrine comes under attack, it must be defended, not by citations alone but by appeal to some standard of value. A talented judge or lawyer will usually find a defense. Sometimes, however, if the job is hard enough or if external pressures are strong, courts will reverse or overrule. In modern times, particularly in the recent past, a judge will be somewhat more likely to kill a rule openly, rather than avoid it by fiction or distinguish it to a whisper.

This new technique is somewhat dangerous for judges. The doors of the system stand slightly ajar; judges can, at least sometimes, frankly decide a case by appeal to data outside formal legal sources— science, current ethics, ideas of the public interest, or common opinion. The problem is, if these cases are not purely "legal," why give them to *judges* to decide? Chemists decide which drugs carry danger of cancer. Economists, engineers, doctors, and soil specialists rule within their specialties. There are, of course, delicate decisions beyond any experts, decisions of values and policies; for these, the elected official is the proper authority, since he is accountable, in theory at least, to the people. What role is left for the judge?

There is no simple answer. Courts have indeed lost ground to the experts. Administrative agencies are frankly more instrumental and more expert than courts; they have taken over large areas of decision,[54] after a period in which courts showed considerable hostility to these rivals.[55]

Yet courts are not obsolete. Their decline is relative and has been partly hidden by a new and dramatic role: protecting individual rights and underprivileged minorities against big government and the callous majority. Here the courts confront few experts and fewer rivals. To some extent, American courts have had this powerful role since the early nineteenth century. It has been prominent on the docket of the United States Supreme Court. But it seems fair to say that the role has now taken on a greater importance, especially in appellate courts in the big industrial states, in criminal cases raising points of constitu-

---

[54]See, in general, James M. Landis, *The Administrative Process* (1938).

[55]See, in general, John Dickinson, *Administrative Justice and the Supremacy of Law* (1927); *Schechter Poultry Corp. v. U.S.*, 295 U.S. 495 (1935), holding void, as an improper delegation, the National Industrial Recovery Act of 1933.

tional law, and in judicial review of acts of government. Paradoxically, high courts in the states with the biggest economies and the most professionalized governments do not spend much time on business and contract cases; they specialize in civil liberties and civil rights.

In such cases, what criteria do courts use? Common sense, expert opinion, and the Constitution itself—a peculiar combination of a sacred, almost immutable text and "nonlegal" propositions. In the famous *Brown* case,[56] which outlawed segregation in the schools, the Court cited the work of sociologists and psychologists in a footnote. This set off a controversy which has not yet quieted down. Was it proper to go outside the "law" in this way? Were the cited studies any good? In any event, did the court use them as anything but make-weight?[57] American courts, in general, often cite law review articles. Once in a while, courts go even further afield. Since "outside" articles—even law reviews—sometimes mention what social science has to say, the larger society creeps into decisions through this back entrance.

American courts also make free use of "legislative history." To get at the meaning of a statute, courts can and do refer to committee reports, even arguments made by legislators in debate. British courts, by way of contrast, are much more conservative. The standard British doctrine is that commission reports, debates, and the like are not relevant evidence of what Parliament meant.[58] In the United States, since legislative "history" may include statements drawn from any field rather than merely "legal" ones, an open attitude toward legislative history is one more way to absorb nonlegal criteria into the formal operation of law.

PLURALISM AND THE MODERNIZATION OF LAW

Another characteristic of modern legal culture is its dislike of cultural pluralism, its commitment to uniformity. Why should accidents of birth or place determine which laws govern a person's life and affairs? Traditional society did not even ask the question; modern society asks and demands the right answer. Why should a man spend a longer time in jail because he robbed a house in Minneapolis, instead of Pittsburgh? Why should an act be legal for whites, illegal for blacks?

Discretion breeds pluralism, at least informally, and the resulting system seems to the modern mind unfair. Cultural pluralism is also in

[56]*Brown* v. *Board of Education*, 347 U.S. 483 (1954).
[57]See Edmond Cahn, "Jurisprudence," 30 *N.Y.U. L. Rev.* 150 (1955).
[58]Gerald Dworkin, *Odger's Construction of Deeds and Statutes* (5th ed., 1967), p. 326.

retreat. In one of the great secular trends in legal history, central governments have struggled to control and reduce legal pluralism of every kind. A modern nation-state feels it needs a single national law.

In its early phases, the movement to unify law was rational and, perhaps, inevitable. Medieval law was a hodgepodge. In many European countries, the law was split into dozens and dozens of local dialects. This was true even in England, where the royal common law was relevant to a tiny handful of people, the nobles and landed gentry. The mass of the population had little to do with it, and there were innumerable local customs, many of them with some official recognition.

After the Industrial Revolution, with the rise of a market economy, the number of consumers of commercial law, tort law, and even family law multiplied greatly. Law had to be recast to suit the needs of the rising middle class. In the United States, for example, hundreds of thousands of people were "in" the market in 1820 or 1850 in a way that had never been true in England. This vast army of legal customers owned land, dealt in land, bought land and sold land, wrote out promissory notes and received notes in return, put mortgages on their homes, made out wills, and entered into contracts. Old, slow, cumbersome institutions could not handle the volume of transactions. In the process of accommodation, land law and commercial law became more standard and routine; forms and formalities were simplified; old quirks, whims, and customs were ruthlessly pruned away. Differences in "custom" from place to place interfered with predictability and efficiency and had to be leveled. The process continues to this day. No one *designs* it; it simply happens, as socially significant groups put demands to the legal system, and these institutions react. The working class and, finally, the poor, have also been drawn further into the mainstream of the law—again as the result of concrete social pressures.

Reduction of pluralism, then, is a natural historical process. But reduction of pluralism is also part of the program of jurists. Jurists believe, in general, that a legal system ought to be uniform, orderly, and systematic; the more it attains these goals, the better it is, or the more modern, or the more developed, and presumably, the more useful for society as a whole. These assumptions about "legal" rationality are almost totally unexamined and in many respects cannot bear the weight of plain fact. After all, the law of the United States ranks low on the scale of jurists' rationality. Even after a century of law reform, it is unsystematic and disorderly, not much of it is codified, and, to the continental mind, the conceptual apparatus is primitive. But does the "irrationality" of American law, in the lawyers' sense, disturb the economy in any way? Does it make social life more difficult?

No doubt, modern society and the economy need legal order. A society of robber barons will not have a high GNP. In both capitalism and socialism, economic organizations have to plan ahead; they need reasonable certainty about the future course of law. But what is needed is real, not paper, order. A magnificent code can conceal a state of anarchy. An efficient working reality, on the other hand, can lie behind a complex, pluralistic order, even when it offends the sensibilities of professors. Reality, not form, is what matters.

Internationally, too, there has been some reduction of pluralistic disorder. The world economy, more and more of a unit, demands, as it always has, a certain amount of commercial lockstep. Overarching political structures, such as the Common Market, encourage uniformity of business law among the members.

Some scholars have noticed or thought they noticed that various legal systems are converging. Civil and common law draw closer together. Each is dropping some of its characteristics in favor of traits from the other "family." The common law codifies its commercial law; the civil jury is disappearing. German and Italy, on the other hand, have adopted a form of judicial review[59]; the civil law preference for written documents over oral testimony is weakening.[60] Updating and convergence are rampant in the third world nations, too.[61] Native systems of law fall into decay; non-Western countries borrow law from the West.[62]

Some of this convergence is mere form, some is substantial. A world legal culture would, quite naturally, produce wide convergence, and modern legal culture is conquering the world. Science and technology do not respect political boundaries. There is no room for local custom in airport control towers, and banking, vaccinations, and dam building are much the same the whole world over. Universal needs and institutions produce a certain uniformity of law.

---

[59]See, in general, Mauro Cappelletti, *Judicial Review in the Contemporary World* (1971).

[60]Mauro Cappelletti, *Procédure Orale et Procédure Ecrite* (1971).

[61]See Lawrence M. Friedman, "On Legal Development," 24 *Rutgers L. Rev.* 11 (1969); David M. Trubek, "Toward a Social Theory of Law: An Essay on the Study of Law and Development," 82 *Yale L.J.* 1 (1972).

[62]Turkey, under Ataturk, adopted a version of the Swiss Code; see Paul Stirling, "Land, Marriage and the Law in Turkish Villages," 9 *Int'l Social Sci. Bull.* 21 (1957); Paul J. Magnarella, "The Reception of Swiss Family Law in Turkey," 46 *Anthropological Q.* 100 (1973). Ethiopia commissioned a French legal scholar to draft a code based on European models; see René David, "A Civil Code for Ethiopia: Considerations on the Codification of the Civil Law in African Countries," 37 *Tul. L. Rev.* 187 (1963).

Other convergence, however, *is* merely formal, and hence, in its own way, false. The movement to modernize law in the third world nations and the law reform movement in the more developed nations run more or less parallel. Law reform, in the lawyer's sense, means tidying up the law—giving it order, consistency, system. Law reform of this sort has little or no social impact. It has, however, a certain symbolic value. Government, to keep itself in office, must be responsive to influential groups. Some governments and bureaus are ambitious; they are not content with self-defense but feel an imperial urge to expand. In many countries, the government is seized with a passion to centralize, to unify the country. A general demand for modernization is pressed by the educated elite. One cheap way to help satisfy this demand is to modernize and unify the law. A new French Code is far cheaper than a steel mill, a national airline, or any program that calls for taxes, and it is less disruptive than a program to redistribute power or wealth. As Antony Allott has written, "Whatever else African countries may lack in the way of modern armies, a literate population, an adequate infrastructure, large capital resources, and an experienced cadre of leaders at all levels, there is one thing they all have, which can be as rapidly and cheaply manufactured as paper money and which has the same tempting property of seeming to be available to solve all problems; that is the legislative power."[63] To be sure, *some* kinds of law reform or modernization would shake society to its roots; but "pure" law reform is innocent of direct impact, and as for side effects, externalities, mischievous latencies, these cannot be measured and are therefore ignored. The benefits, if any, are equally elusive,[64] but they have this virtue at least: The jurists believe in them strongly.

The idea of nation-building runs like a scarlet thread through the literature of political modernization. Undeniably, many new nations feel a crisis of political identity.[65] Their boundary lines have little or nothing to do with tribal, social, or language boundaries; they are simply left over from the squabbling of colonial powers. Many new nations, then, are hopelessly divided in language, culture, and religion. Their leaders feel they need unity and pride—nationalism, in short—to glue the fragments together.

[63]Antony Allott, "The Unification of Laws in Africa," 16 *Am. J. Comp. L.* 51 (1968).

[64]See Albert Hirschman, *Development Projects Observed* (1967), pp. 9–21.

[65]On the concept and importance of nation-building, see Sidney Verba, "Comparative Political Culture," in Lucian W. Pye and Sidney Verba, eds., *Political Culture and Political Development* (1965), pp. 512, 529–537; Lucian Pye, *Politics, Personality and Nation Building* (1962). See also Leonard Binder, "National Integration and Political Development," 58 *Am. Pol. Sci. Rev.* 622 (1964).

Logically, a single, uniform system of law should act as a tool of unification; like a common language or common flag, it should help weld a single nation out of the jumble of classes or tribes. What sort of law could this be? Borrowed modern law, usually inherited from the colonial period, seems rational, general, and scientific; it is certainly free of local or tribal influence. The new nation will have to be built from the center. The center will have to grow at the expense of provinces, local elites, and outlying cultures. Actually, a single legal system radiating out from the center would, in fact, revolutionize legal life, but not by virtue of the *content* of the law, nor even because of its structure or form. The revolution would consist in the *effect* of the law on the national catalogue of power. New law would replace old law; village chiefs and elders who knew and applied their law would be expropriated. Their knowledge would become useless; their authority undermined. Civil servants would now accede to their power.

René David, the French scholar who drafted a civil code for Ethiopia, felt that Ethiopia could not afford to "wait" for a law appropriate to its culture. It would take several hundred years, he believed, to "construct in an empirical fashion" a unique system of Ethiopian law. Better to adopt a ready-made system, which would "assure as quickly as possible a minimal security in legal relations."[66]

Professor David assumed, then, that Ethiopia could not guarantee "security" by using native materials. Third-world leaders, no matter how strong their national fervor, seem to agree. The more modern the law, that is, the more it conforms to European models, the better it must work for social and economic development. Hence, this paradox: Ardent nation-builders in Africa and Asia, anti-West in many regards, reject their own legal traditions and build up systems of law out of imported luxury goods.[67] These leaders accept the implicit theory of legal development which legal scholars hawk in the schools. That theory stresses uniformity, order, and system. Scholars and leaders absorb this theory—a theory that European law is superior!—in schools both at home and abroad. Whether a "highly developed" law, in the lawyerly sense, has anything to do with economic and social development is a question no one can answer. Not a shred of real evidence supports this theory on which the present course of action seems to rest.

---

[66]René David, "A Civil Code for Ethiopia: Considerations on the Codification of the Civil Law in African Countries," 37 *Tul. L. Rev.* 187, 188, 189. (1963).

[67]There have been some exceptions, for example, the Moslem reaction in Libya.

Chapter IX
On Internal Legal Culture

In an earlier chapter, we discussed the concept of a *demand* on the legal system in general terms. A writ of habeas corpus, a letter to a congressman, a scream for help from the police in a dark street at night —all these are demands on the legal system. Behind each demand is a concrete interest and a cultural proclivity to address such demands to some part of the system. People may have similar needs or interests, but because of cultural differences or differences in the structure of the legal system, they make different demands. Also, a person who writes every day to his congressman does not think of this as legal behavior in the same sense as filing a lawsuit. The same cultural attitude need not support both acts.

We can distinguish between an *external* and an *internal* legal culture. The external legal culture is the legal culture of the general population; the internal legal culture is the legal culture of those members of society who perform specialized legal tasks. Every society has a legal culture, but only societies with legal specialists have an internal legal culture. What sets legal process in motion is demand on the system. Interests must be converted into demands; attitudes and behaviors which are part of the external legal culture must be processed to fit the requirements of the internal legal culture. "Social pressure," in the air is not a demand on the legal system, except insofar as it is communicated to a legal actor—a judge, a legislator, a lawyer. Some demands can proceed quite informally (the letter to the congressman, the cry for help); others must be translated into the appropriate "legal" form (the writ of habeas corpus). In this chapter, we will discuss aspects of formal demands on the legal system, particularly as they are shaped by the internal legal culture.

In every society, some demands are *legitimate* and some *illegitimate*. Legitimacy can be either social or legal—that is, a matter of outside opinion, of attitudes within the legal system, or of external or internal culture. The ordinary lawsuit in the United States, Great Britain, and most Western countries is legitimate both internally and externally. It is acceptable to ask for a writ of habeas corpus or to sue a bus company for negligence. Neither the law nor the outside world disapproves of the demand (win or lose). Betraying a comrade to the police or informing are socially illegitimate, but the police themselves may approve. If a culture strongly disapproves of litigation, even an ordinary lawsuit may be socially illegitimate.

Also, some conduct may be formally illegal, but socially approved. This is even true of corruption—bribery and nepotism—in some societies. In other societies, Sweden, for example, bribery and corruption are illegal, socially illegitimate, and presumably disapproved of by the internal legal culture.

Corruption varies greatly from society to society and within a society. In the United States, corruption in the federal courts is rare,[1] but this cannot be said for some of the lower courts, particularly in the cities. Some state and federal agencies have long histories of corruption; others are traditionally clean. England and most European countries seem less corrupt than the United States. Many of the underdeveloped countries, on the other hand, are notoriously open to nepotism and worse.

What makes a difference is the social status of corruption. Corruption will appear where public opinion does not condemn it. James C. Scott has catalogued some social reasons for corruption in non-Western countries.[2] One is the tradition of gift-giving; another is the persistence of kinship loyalties. "When the brother of a personnel official asks his relative for a clerical post . . . the strength of kinship bonds makes it difficult to refuse. A refusal would be seen as a betrayal of family loyalty." Ties to the state, on the other hand, are weak: "Western standards of official conduct are . . . relatively recent imports . . . seldom held with strong personal conviction." Again, government in many

---

[1] For the few exceptions, see Joseph Borkin, *The Corrupt Judge* (1962).

[2] James C. Scott, *Comparative Political Corruption* (1972). Scott defines corruption as "behavior which deviates from the formal duties of a public role . . . because of private-regarding . . . wealth or status gains; or violates rules against the exercise of certain types of private-regarding influence" (p. 4).

new countries is one of the few sources of wealth; government service is one of the major ladders to success; and officials can make or break businesses or careers with their decisions. These facts create a situation in which temptation is almost irresistible. For this reason, too, building and housing inspectors in American cities are more corruptible than, for example, forest rangers.[3] So much more rides on the decisions of housing and building inspectors. If these low-paid officials are too zealous, they can ruin a landlord or building owner. The inspectors have a certain amount of formal discretion; the network of rules is so dense that it is almost impossible for landlords in "bad" neighborhoods to follow them all and still make money. This tempts the landlords to offer bribes.

Explanations of corruption, then, contain both structural and cultural elements. Where the legitimacy of the formal legal system is low, corruption will thrive. Corruption, once begun, is hard to root out; it becomes an accepted way of behaving. If a clerk in Chicago will always "lose" the files of a lawsuit unless the lawyer pays, lawyers who want to make a living will have to go along. The public sees the bribery and gets used to it. People do not even know that things happen differently in London or Milwaukee. They lose their desire and capacity for outrage.

Official law, internal culture, and public opinion can also differ about the substance of demands. All three agree that the wounded war veteran should apply for his pension. But in many situations, an individual or group will lack a "right" which some segment of the public feels is justified or the other way around (Shylock's demand for a pound of flesh). These mismatches come about for a variety of reasons. One is cultural pluralism. Sometimes the culture supports application of a general rule in the ordinary case, but the same rule seems "unjust" in an extraordinary one. How often this occurs is an open question. Modern legal systems, at least, provide themselves liberally with escape hatches. The general clauses of the continental codes allow judges to avoid "harsh" results; judges in common-law countries can distinguish, overrule, or fall back on general principle. The jury system too allows norms and rules to remain unchanged, while continuous, covert small adjustments are made.[4]

In an interesting essay,[5] Vilhelm Aubert distinguishes between

---

[3]Who, at least according to Herbert Kaufman, *The Forest Ranger: A Study in Administrative Behavior* (1960), are models of probity.

[4]See, on this point in general, Harry Kalven and Hans Zeisel, *The American Jury* (1966).

[5]"Competition and Dissensus: Two Types of Conflict and of Conflict Resolution," 7

two kinds of demand, *interests* and *claims of right*. Two people have a conflict of interest when they both want the same valuable object: two men in love with one woman; two politicians running for a single office; two cities vying for a convention. Conflicts of interest arise out of scarcity. In the examples given, both parties have a legitimate claim, and there is no conflict over values or principles. Indeed, conflict comes from a certain base of agreement. Both suitors love the woman, both candidates want the Senate seat. A *claim of right*, on the other hand, is couched in terms of right or wrong. In a lawsuit, two parties each claim title to a single tract of land. Each party will insist in the pleadings that his claim is right and the other party's wrong, that the opponent misconceives the facts or the rules. The argument will be couched in terms of rights, not interests—facts, norms, and "law."

The difference between claims of right and conflicts of interest has consequences. Parties can easily compromise conflicts of interest, less so conflicts of values or fact. In a sense, a contract is the resolution of a conflict of interest. One man wants to buy a horse for a low price; the other wants to sell but very high. The two sides bargain, and agree when they feel they have gotten all they could. Usually, neither one is "morally involved." Courts of law do not resolve conflicts of interest. A party would have to *convert* his claim into a conflict of value or fact, before he could go to law. In a land case, the plaintiff would be wasting his time if he stated that he needed the land for business or home or that he liked it. These statements of interest are irrelevant. He will have to refer to some value, rule, or norm to justify his claim.

A value or fact conflict, according to Aubert, must be resolved by some third party. A *mediator* is a third person who merely helps the parties reach an agreement; he does not decide the issue himself. A *judge* decides cases on a clear-cut, all-or-nothing basis; one side wins, the other loses. Partly, this is because the third party (the judge) needs to show that he is independent, morally superior to the parties, and that he is impartial, adhering to rules and norms that float high above the short-run, particular case.

Aubert sees a progression in the history of law. The main business of law once consisted of conflicts of interest; later, conflicts of value dominate; mediation evolves into adjudication. A third person cannot authoritatively resolve a conflict of interest. He cannot decide between

J. Conflict Resolution 26 (1963); see also Torstein Eckhoff, "The Mediator, the Judge and the Administrator in Conflict-Resolution," in Britt-Mari Blegvad, ed., *Contributions to The Sociology of Law* (1966), p. 148.

A and *B,* if each simply wants the same piece of land. Interests alone never yield a rule. The third party, then, must appeal to facts, norms, or standards. To bind the two parties, he must appear independent, impartial—and strong.

Aubert's analysis depends, it would seem, on characteristics of external and internal legal culture. One can approach a legislature frankly in interest terms, but to bring a lawsuit, a party must convert his interests into demands and phrase the demands in terms of claims of right or disputes of fact. This may be merely a formal step, but the culture demands it. Many claims before a court are merely claims of interest, transformed on paper into claims of right. The "real reasons" why a man wants Blackacre—it is rich land, produces a good income, is comfortable to live on—are not reasons a court is supposed to listen to.

Are claims of interest, as a rule, easier to compromise than claims of value? Some conflicts of interest cannot be compromised at all—two suitors; two candidates for senator. The good that these claimants want happens to be indivisible. Another factor is the subjective strength of the claim. If one claimant is more intense in his desire than the other, he might, in theory, buy the other one off. This holds for conflicts of all sorts, value or interest. The third factor is the objective strength of the claimants. If two parties at an auction bid on a painting, the one with less money will have to give up. Equally balanced claims of value will often be compromised.

Of course, it is generally true that the trial process does not, in Western law, envision compromise, only winners and losers. This fact may exacerbate conflict. Macaulay and Walster point out that tort law, for example, "gives the harmdoer an incentive to derogate his victim," and "the opportunity to escape legal liability by contesting his responsibility." The law thus "may encourage him to utilize denial and minimization techniques."[6] There is compromise all about and around the courtroom but rarely in it. Once the parties reach the stage of trial, they tend to define their issues in black-and-white. Mostly, this is sham or strategy. Still there *is* such a thing as a subjective sense of right, which is different from an interest or desire. The interior label is not necessarily the same as the exterior one. An underpaid worker may feel he has a "right" to more money; this may be vivid and real and make him militant, even though it is not a "legal" right.

---

[6]Stewart Macaulay and Elaine Walster, "Legal Structures and Restoring Equity," 27 *J. Soc. Issues,* no. 2, 173, 180 (1971).

ON LEGAL RIGHTS

But now we must stop and define our terms. What, after all, is a *right?* Rights are basic building blocks of law. A court processes claims of right. Legal doctrine, in the main, is made up of propositions about rights.

In everyday speech, the word "right" has a number of meanings.[7] To begin with, a right is a claim asserted through or against some public authority. A right is a claim against the state. People do talk, very often, of their rights against other people rather than against the state. A buyer has a claim for breach of contract; he considers this a right to collect damages from his seller, who delivered a carload of lumber two months late. Mrs. *X* has a claim for divorce "against" Mr. *X*. *P* was in an accident; now he has a claim in tort "against" the bus company, whose driver was careless. We can describe most rules of law this way—in dyadic (two-party) terms: a landlord's rights against a tenant, a tenant's against a landlord; a child's rights against his parent; a parent's against a child; a person's rights against his pawnbroker, employer, creditor, trustee; and vice versa. Some legal scholars, noting how many rules can be expressed in dyadic terms, came to feel that a right *always* implies a two-party relation; that any rule can be reduced to a statement about dyads. So, to say that you "own" a piece of property means that you have the right to exclude *A, B, C, D,* . . . *n,* that is, everybody in the world, considered one at a time, from possessing and enjoying it.[8]

One can, of course, describe rights in this way, but it is equally true that one can describe them in quite another way—not as claims against a second party at all but as claims against the state. A right "against" a particular person is a kind of ticket which entitles the holder to invoke the law, that is, the state, to protect him or advance his interests in some way. Mrs. *X*'s right to a divorce "against" Mr. *X* is, in this sense, a right to make courts perform certain acts at the completion of which she will be legally free of Mr. *X,* will be able to remarry, and will have some of his money besides. *P*'s right "against" the bus company invokes the power of a court to force the company to pay. "Ownership" is an owner's call on the state to protect his interests against rival claimants, trespassers, and others.

Clearly, rights have a public aspect. They do not vindicate or en-

---

[7] See, in general, Lawrence M. Friedman, "The Idea of Right as a Social and Legal Concept," 27 *J. Soc. Issues,* no. 2, 189 (1971).

[8] This view was expounded by Wesley N. Hohfeld in his "Some Fundamental Legal Conceptions as Applied in Judicial Reasoning," 23 *Yale L.J.* 16 (1913).

force themselves; they depend on public agencies. So, the bearer of a right must want to assert his rights. An abstract right, like an interest, is not an influence on the legal system; what matters are demands. The bearer of a right must want to assert it, to use the agencies of law. Often, we take this frame of mind for granted. When Mrs. *X* and her husband discussed a divorce, they may have discussed cost, what the neighbors would think, how Mrs. *X* would manage on her own, the fate of the children, but not willingness to use the law. Yet this element had to be there in the background.

This is one aspect, then, of a right: it is a claim against or through authority. In the second place, it is a claim which, if it is truly a right, *has* to be granted. Authorities must not deny the citizen his right. This is at the core of the meaning of the word. A right is, by definition, not a matter of discretion.

In economic terms, a free good is one whose production is costless; production and consumption of the good do not reduce the supply of it, or that of any other goods. A right is this kind of magic good. To put it another way, a right is a claim to a good which, in theory at least, or at any rate ethically, exists in unlimited supply. A *right* is not rationed. This is what we mean when we say that citizens, who are adults and have registered, have the *right* to vote for president. The law puts no ceiling on the number of voters. If more people come of age and register, more people may vote. The government can issue tickets to vote, so to speak, without limit. It prints more tickets as more are needed. Free speech and other "basic" rights have this same quality. If *A*, *B*, and *C* exercise their right to free speech, it in no way affects the rights of *D*, *E*, and *F* to do likewise. The same is true of "rights" to certain benefits or pensions. Under the Social Security Act, a person who has made past contributions and has reached retirement age has a right to his pension.[9] Each eligible person has a claim, independent of the claim of all other eligibles. In theory, it does not matter how many people demand the right. As many as become eligible, i.e., when their "rights" become ripe, that many will receive regular payments. It is not a matter of merit, not first-come, first-served; it is absolute— in short, a matter of right.

It is clear, then, how a claim of right differs from a claim based on an interest. When workers go on strike, they know they do not have an

[9]Actually, there are technical doubts about how "vested" this right is; see *Fleming v. Nestor*, 363 U.S. 603 (1960); Lawrence M. Friedman, "Social Welfare Legislation: An Introduction," 21 *Stan. L. Rev.* 217, 232 (1969); but practically speaking, the right is nearly absolute, and people think of it that way.

absolute claim, or "right" to more money, vacations, and fringe benefits. They must argue and struggle for their share; they know, too, that benefits will sometimes come out of someone else's hide—the consumer, perhaps, or stockholders, or management in some way. Farmers demand price supports on cotton and tobacco. They know they have no "right." They know, too, that their subsidies may bring higher taxes, or lower subsidies for somebody else. These demands in the short run at least are part of a zero-sum game. Of course, interest groups argue that they deserve what they demand, that their claims are just, that they have some sort of "right" to more money or power. But they understand this "right" as moral, not as a legal claim of right. The inner feeling that goes with a claim of right denies limits, denies that one man's claim is at another man's expense.

This subjective aspect of a right is, in a way, objectively false. There are no free goods, in fact, in the legal system. All things of value are in limited supply. What government can grant or allow is never absolute. This is even true of such basic rights as the right of free speech. One does not normally think of a "supply" of free speech. Theoretically, everyone can say what he pleases, whenever and wherever he pleases. In fact, the reality of the right depends on demand and supply. If five million people decided to do their free speech in Times Square on a Tuesday at noon, they would create an impossible situation, nor would New York City let them try. One *could* say that here one right—free speech—conflicts with other rights or with the demands of public safety and traffic control, so that some sort of balance is required. But this is indeed the normal situation. When rights are exercised beyond what the state or the public has expected and has planned for, the right is apt to conflict with other rights or with some policy or rule of law.[10] Subjectively, a right is absolute. Objectively, few if any rights can be absolute, not as matter of theory but as matter of fact.[11]

Ordinarily, no problem arises from the exercise of rights. People and governments come to know what quantity and pitch to expect. Supply is adjusted to probable demand. Changes in demand, if they are too sudden, are followed by changes in supply. The exercise of rights is like traffic flowing through a city's streets. Only a *sudden* increase makes a traffic jam. If traffic increases slowly, the city can hire more

---

[10]There are a few exceptions: a turnout of voters higher than expected creates few problems, although partly because the government prints extra ballots, etc.

[11]Even the heavy turnout of voters *may* mean lines so long the electoral system is disrupted.

policemen, change traffic laws, limit access to some streets, convert to one-way streets, ban parking, and, if time permits, build new or wider streets. The right to a day in court, too, creates traffic in the halls of justice. There is theoretically no limit. Causes of action are infinite. But the state provides only so many judges and lawyers and courtrooms. How many depends, among other things, on past experience or a guess as to future demand. Courts in the United States, in urban centers, tend to be crowded; there are long delays before cases come to trial. Of course, this affects the reality of the right to a day in court. The litigating public has, over the years, more or less adjusted itself to this supply, just as government, over the years, has adjusted the supply of courts to the level of tolerable demand. The situation is costly and unjust, but it is a *kind* of equilibrium. If the number of litigants rose suddenly, the system would be badly disrupted; the slow interaction of supply and demand would no longer work. Long lines and delay might bring about tension and complaints, perhaps even major reforms or adjustments. There might be a crisis, even though no one actually demanded any change in the system—only his time-honored "rights."

The level of demand for welfare rights, pensions, and other benefits also creates a pattern of expectations. The government appropriates money, not by computing *potential* beneficiaries but by looking at past experience. Not everyone eligible asks for his money. If suddenly everyone did, there would be serious upheaval. In fact, at one point, militants tried exactly this tactic: They sought to mobilize the poor to demand every penny of benefits, every scrap of right which the law on paper allowed. In this way, they hoped to bring the system tumbling down.[12]

When claims of right are asserted suddenly or with great intensity or volume, institutions may be simply unable to process the claims. They cannot afford to. A city collects its garbage twice a week. The Sanitation Department has adjusted itself to a certain budget; the city, as usual, is chronically short of cash. The "better" neighborhoods get the best service partly because the people who live there complain bitterly if the service falls off. The city collects garbage with less regularity and care in poor, black neighborhoods. But then the poor neighborhood organizes and demands its "right" to municipal services. In the short run, at least, the city will find it hard to respond. There are only so many garbage trucks, so many garbagemen, and so much money in the till for collecting garbage. The city cannot improve the situation, unless it cuts back on garbage collection in middle-class

---

[12]Professor Richard A. Cloward, of the Columbia University School of Social Work, was associated with this approach. *New York Times*, Aug. 1, 1968, p. 23, col. 4.

neighborhoods. In the short run, garbage collection is a zero-sum game. The city has a serious problem—politically speaking—on its hands. Whatever way it goes, some group will be intensely dissatisfied. Yet the poor have asked for nothing more than equality, nothing more than their rights.

At present, the United States seems to be passing through a time of accelerated demand, of volcanic eruption in claims of right. The demands come out of social conflict and produce social conflict as well. The movement has certainly affected at least the leaders of the traditional underdogs—a minority among the minorities. A stable society, however, depends on more than approval by a bare majority; it needs overwhelming acquiescence. Society can tolerate without disruption few active rebels, few enemy deviants, either in absolute numbers or percentages, particularly when the rebels attack important values or arrangements. The "rights explosion" or the "law explosion" is important, even if it is statistically small.

The "rights explosion" is revolutionary but in a peculiar way. Many of the "rebels" do not feel themselves rebellious at all. They ask only what is coming to them legally and ethically. The minorities demand mainly that society take down barriers which kept them from enjoying their rights. The claim is revolutionary only because a whole social system grew up on the assumption that they would not claim or demand certain rights.

Yet, a claim of right is nonviolent in at least one important sense. It is, indeed, an alternative to violence. American elites are constantly preaching that people should use established channels, that they should take their grievances to court, not to the streets. The *rights* movement does exactly this at least in its initial stage. A claim of right, moreover, wears a peculiarly ethical, even conservative, dress. A claim of interest is a claim for a new value: higher wages, tax relief, police protection, better schools. Claims of rights come clothed in old-fashioned phrases. They ask for what is already supposed to be or for restoration of rights unjustly taken away. Many American constitutional claims have this peculiar quality. The Constitution itself changes very slowly. A demand for "equality" under the Fourteenth Amendment is not, in theory, a demand for new norms and new arrangements. It is a demand against the majority for rights that ethically or legally were already there "inside" the Constitution.

This does not mean that a society where the dissatisfied use claims of right is safe from violent change. The American colonists demanded the ancient rights of Englishmen, which, they said, George III had taken away; dissatisfied, they went to war. Violence often follows, when a claim of right is refused or ignored. When rights fail, groups that feel intensely enough may choose a more lawless way. Their sense of the justice of the cause supports them in this path.

As we noted, there are rights which are not (morally) right to claim, but most rights are moral, and almost all are legitimate. This was the logical basis for Aubert's prediction that people are not prone to compromise values or rights as opposed to interests or desires. The matter, we said, is not so simple, but Aubert's hypothesis has a certain surface likelihood. Zealous pursuit of one's rights is, in a sense, aggressive behavior; and some types of personality may be more aggressive, more claims-conscious than others. Obviously, social factors influence claims-consciousness. A civil rights movement could hardly emerge from a passive, traditional people. On the other hand, claims of right are oddly ceremonial and legitimate *forms* of aggression, if they can be called aggression at all.[13] The language of a claim of right is often cold and impersonal. The opponent is the state, the government—an abstraction—rather than evil men. But this too varies.

Of course, we cannot always take a claim of right at face value. In a courtroom, a claim of right is above all a matter of pleading. It does not always reveal the plaintiff's true state of mind. The main motive is often an interest pure and simple—a crass and ordinary want. Lawyers turn these into claims of right to get the case properly to court.

Not all rights litigation is interest litigation in disguise. In the civil rights movement, for example, though the interest element is strong, so is the undercurrent of belief, the sense of moral and legal right. Unrest, of course, is common in the world and in all sorts of legal systems with or without any particular structure of rights. The exact form of social demand varies with the legal culture. Why, for example, must claims be converted into claims of right before the court can receive and process them?[14] There is no such requirement for pushing a claim before the legislature. The legitimate sphere of courts is narrower than that of legislatures. This narrowness is not inherent in courts; it follows from social concepts about the proper role of courts which serve as the basis of their legitimation.

---

[13]John Dollard et al., in the well-known study, *Frustration and Aggression* (1939), defined aggression as "an act whose goal-response is injury to an organism" (p. 11); the authors specifically mention the lawsuit as a kind of "change in the form of aggression" (p. 41).

Dollard's basic thesis is that "aggression is always a consequence of frustration" (p. 1). A disappointed claimant, then, might react aggressively.

[14]Of course, not all courts process claims, giving them legal form in the modern, Western sense.

The claim of right is an old idea, deeply imbedded in Western law. A high level of militance, however, upsets the balance of the legal system, in two ways: First, it produces an unexpected volume of business; second, and more important, groups now demand major changes in society and demand them as matters of right. The protesting groups may be poor or oppressed, but they need not be. Rich householders, for example, can become quite militant in battling against a new highway through their neighborhood. Middle-class and right-wing militance was an important factor in prewar Germany, in Chile before the coup of 1973, and in countless other societies.

The litigious militance of civil rights groups seems peculiar to Western society and to have its major focus in the United States. Clearly, historical experience has built up this special attitude toward rights: for example, the natural law tradition and the French and American revolutions. In the United States, strong rights movements would be unthinkable without the written Constitution, an active federal bench, and the doctrine of judicial review. There seems to be an ingrained American habit to take political and economic controversies to court. Americans specialize, in other words, in making claims of right out of interests. But rights movements can and do crop up in countries without written constitutions. Domestically, many strong claims—for improved civic services, for ending the war in Vietnam, for higher welfare rights—have had little or nothing to do with the Constitution. The American style of judicial review has made an appearance since the war in Germany and Italy.[15] In this development, the United States has been a model and an influence; yet, something must be stirring in the soil of world culture, conducive to the growth of claims of right.

Vindication of rights feeds on its own success. Success in one claim encourages and reinforces more claims and gives others a model and hope of success. Hence the process can be expected to continue and to grow, unless and until checked by some factor as yet unforeseen.

ON LEGAL REASONING

One can enter a court only in a special formal way, following rules of pleading and framing the issues as a claim of right. The response of the court also takes on a special and specialized form. Many courts, for example, small claims courts, are allowed to speak the colloquial

---

[15]John H. Merryman and V. Vigoriti, "When Courts Collide: Constitution and Cassation in Italy," 15 *Am. J. Comp. L.* 665 (1967).

tongue, but all institutions that possess the name and the style of a "court" will be bound by certain rules of jurisdiction and procedure and influenced by role-conceptions of the internal legal culture.

In many countries, a striking feature of appellate courts is their reasoned, written opinions. These courts issue decisions settling the controversy between the litigants, but they also produce and publish statements which justify the decision and purport to describe how the judges reached their conclusions.

We need not take these at face value, as many jurists do, but neither is it necessary to go to the other extreme, completely ignoring what judges *say* and emphasizing only how the cases come out. Legal reasoning and legal style are important social facts—whether these give any real clue to what judges think or not. Legal reasoning, in short, must be explained and accounted for. It is an element of the internal legal culture, and it has obvious significance, since reasoning is a type of legal act which produces rules and "interpretations" of statutes. Written opinions spread doctrine to lower courts, lawyers, and relevant members of the public, including the legislature.

Why do courts reason? And what is legal reasoning?[16] In Anglo-American law, legal reasoning refers chiefly to a single type of legal act: the reasoning of appellate courts. In this chapter, we will apply the term "legal reasoning" only to a formal, authoritative exposition, which purports to show how and why a decision-maker reached his particular conclusion. A lot of "reasoning" in the law does not meet this definition. Arguments of legal scholars in their treatises, though they influence judges, are not considered binding—are not, in short, authoritative. In a legal system that considered treatises "authority," reasoning in a treatise *would* be legal reasoning under our definition.

Formality is also part of the definition. Any human act or decision which is "voluntary" is in a sense produced through reasoning. A person's heart beats and his eyelids flutter without conscious mental process; but if a man crosses the street, he has to think about it in at least some rudimentary way. *Formal* legal reasoning—usually in writing—has no necessary connection with actual mental processes. A written opinion is not a photograph or X ray of a judge's mind. At one time, jurists perhaps took a form of X-ray theory seriously. This is no longer the case.

The question remains: What is the purpose of this formal outer husk? It is interesting, for a start, to note some legal actors who do *not*

---

[16]See Lawrence M. Friedman, "On Legalistic Reasoning: A Footnote to Weber," 1966 *Wis. L. Rev.* 148.

236 The Legal System: A Social Science Perspective

use formal reasoning. A legislature does not, for one. Statutes are a prime source of law, but they come into the world as naked fiat. They consist of propositions and conclusions, vague or detailed; a few may have an explanatory preamble. Some begin with a declaration of policy; others have no preamble, no declaration of policy at all. Often, of course, there are debates on the floor about the bill. Proponents and opponents give reasons on one side or the other, but this is not essential to the life cycle or a law; some laws are never debated. An "opinion" does not come attached to the statute.

Some legal actors, then, give reasons and others do not. The explanation must lie in the theories of *legitimacy* that support various institutions. We can distinguish two types of legitimacy within a legal system. *Primary legitimacy* is the legitimacy of ultimate authority. Every society will have some final authority. Some person, or institution, or process will have the power and right to make or change law on its own, and not by delegation from some other authority, institution, or process. In an absolute monarchy, the king's word is law; the king has primary legitimacy. In Great Britain, Parliament has primary power. In some societies, no purely human or worldly authority has primary legitimacy. The ultimate authority resides in a book, a code, God, or tradition.

Authority which has primary legitimacy does not need to give reasons. The king in an absolute monarchy may make law by decree; he need not attach any reasons to his acts. Statutes of Parliament do not need special justification. The Ten Commandments were naked fiat. Whatever the basis of primary legitimacy—charismatic, traditional, or rational authority, using Weber's terms[17]—some form of it will be present in every society.

All other legal actors have derivative power and *derivative legitimacy.* They may have to justify their acts or may have to show some link to higher authority or higher legitimacy. The links are of two kinds: general and specific. A policeman wears a uniform and a badge; when he makes an arrest, he carries a warrant. Badge, warrant, and uniform are all devices or signs of legitimate authority, whatever else they may be.[18] The badge and uniform express the policeman's *general* authority. The warrant is authority to do one *specific* act.

In a complex legal system, with many slots, niches, and offices,

---

[17]See p. 116.

[18]The uniform is a "certificate of legitimacy," a "symbolic statement that an individual will adhere to . . . standardized roles." Nathan Joseph and Nicholas Alex, "The Uniform; a Sociological Perspective," 77 *Am. J. Sociology* 719, 722–723 (1972).

there will also be many devices to link legal acts with higher authority. Legal reasoning is one of these devices—one of the most powerful and important. It is a device of *specific* legitimacy, that is, more like a warrant than a badge. Its purpose is to link the judge's conclusions and decisions with some higher body of principles or some agency or institution with primary legitimacy. Judges, like policemen, have derivative legitimacy. They have rarely, if ever, assumed authority to make law, fresh and whole, like a king or a Parliament. Whatever they do, then, requires some *linking* device. The opinion with its reason provides one such link.

Not everyone, of course, who has derivative authority uses legal reasoning. Lower court judges usually do not; and policemen do not hand out statements of reasons when they catch a burglar in the act. For one thing, the policeman's job is such that he must at times act quickly. Occasionally, the policeman *will* have to justify his acts. If someone challenges them, he will have to show, formally if need be, that he had proper authority to act. He will have to show a warrant. For arrests without warrant, there may be a further challenge in court. *Challenge* is a key concept in explaining legal reasoning. Only legal acts that are challenged, typically, will have to show how they link to higher authority. In every appellate case, the appellant has challenged some act taken by a court. Hence the prevalence of reasoning.[19]

Legal reasoning takes a logical form; it can be broken down into sentences or propositions of law and fact. Some propositions are used as premises, some as conclusions. The building blocks of legal reasoning are propositions which serve as premises. Where does the decision-maker get his premises? We will call a formal system *closed*, when its decision-makers, on the whole, believe that they must base their decisions only on "legal" premises. This means that they divide the universe of propositions into two parts. One part consists of "legal" propositions; only these can legitimately act as premises for legal reasoning. There are a limited number of these, and it is possible to tell which propositions are "legal" and which propositions are not. Any system which does not draw this line, which has no distinction between "legal" and other propositions, is an *open system.*

Again, some legal systems accept *innovation*—they expect new legal premises to arise. Some systems do not.[20] Combining these two distinctions, we isolate four ideal-typical legal systems. Since legal

---

[19]An appeal challenges the opinion of the lower court. The lower court decision, then, will have to be justified. But the upper court will do the justifying.

[20]Many of these do, however, accept the idea of occasional extraordinary change.

reasoning is a justifying device, a link between derivative and primary legitimacy, different attitudes about legitimacy in a society would produce specific and different styles of legal reasoning. The four types of system, then, correspond to four ideal types of legal reasoning, reflecting aspects of legal culture, in particular societies. The four types are shown schematically in Table II. Let us take a closer look at the four types.

1. First, some legal systems have a *closed* set of premises and deny any principle of innovation. A conservative book-religion with a single sacred text would come close to the ideal type, especially if there is no faith in new revelation. The society would have to squeeze all its law from one holy book; all decisions would have to be linked to the text. Classic Judaic and Muhammedan law have strong affinities with this type of system. Among post-biblical Jews, the Bible was the basic source of law. "Turn it, and turn it again," said a Talmudic scholar, referring to the *Torah*, "for everything can be found therein."[21] Answers to legal questions were hidden in the words of the Bible. In Islam, the Koran and the words of the Prophet were primary sources of law. In both systems, legitimacy was never so simple a matter; custom and legislation, for example, were supplementary sources of law; in Islam, traditional sayings of the Prophet and his companions, analogy, and the consensus of the community were also authoritative.[22] But both book-religions had many elements of a closed system of this first type.

The sacred books in these religions were pregnant with divine

Table II. Four Types of Legal System Classified by Forms of Reasoning

		Canon of Legal Propositions	
		Closed	Open
Innovation	Denied	Sacred	Customary
	· Accepted	Legal Science	Instrumental

---

[21]Michael L. Rodkinson, *The Babylonian Talmud* (1916), vol. 5, p. 133.

[22]On the legal theory of Islam, see Joseph Schacht, *The Origins of Muhammadan Jurisprudence* (1953); Ahmad Hasan, *The Early Development of Islamic Jurisprudence* (1970) pp. 33–56.

meaning; it was worthwhile, then, to extract the last drop of implication. Jewish sages endlessly debated points of law, haggling over every word of the text, making little distinction between real and imaginary cases. Scholars of the *Mishnah,* discussing the law of divorce, wondered if a husband could divorce his wife by writing the bill of divorce on a cow's horn and delivering the cow, or on the hand of the slave, if he gave her the slave. These, the sages decided, were valid means of delivering the bill of divorce; but one rabbi thought a bill of divorce could not be written on anything living.[23] Muhammedan scholars debated such questions as the "precise moment at which succession opens to the estate of a person turned to stone by the devil."[24]

In both Muhammedan and Judaic law, the sacred text was fixed and finished or became so at some point. Afterwards, there could be no new premises; "the gates of legislation" were "closed."[25] Of course, circumstances continued to change, and new social conditions constantly arose. The ancient texts became more and more out of date. This imposed a heavy burden on legal reasoning. Both systems ran heavily to casuistry, legalism, legal fiction, and a luxuriant growth of reasoning by analogy. The very word "Talmudic" has come to mean a certain pathology of reasoning. Talmudic reasoning was, at times, grotesque, but the sages faced the dilemma of a closed system of law. Actually, liberal use of analogy and fiction and the fortunate presence of certain vague, general clauses in the Bible, rather like the general clauses of the modern codes, mitigated Talmudic reasoning.

The classical common law, a curious hybrid, resembled a sacred law system in certain ways. To be sure, there was no sacred text. But the common law did, on the whole, deny innovation. The canon of premises was, on the whole, more closed than open. The only valid premises were common-law principles and doctrines, as found in reported cases. Of course, the canon changed slowly over time; so did the point of view of the judges. The common law was never as fixed or as closed as the sacred law systems. It did have dogmas of fixity; the doctrine of *stare decisis,* as it developed, became a notable pole of stability. At its prime, the doctrine insisted that relevant, legitimate premises were only to be found in prior cases.[26]

The doctrine did not become a dogma until about 1800. As John

---

[23]Herbert Danby, ed., *The Mishnah* (1933), p. 308.

[24]Noel James Coulson, *A History of Islamic Law* (1964), p. 81; see Max Rheinstein, ed., *Max Weber on Law in Economy and Society* (1954), p. 247.

[25]Haim H. Cohn, "Secularization of Divine Law," in Haim H. Cohn, ed., *Jewish Law in Ancient and Modern Israel* (1971), pp. 1, 32; David Bonderman, "Modernization and Changing Perceptions of Islamic Law," 81 *Harv. L. Rev.* 1169 (1968).

[26]Although cases of "first impression" might occasionally arise.

Dawson has pointed out, a "strict" theory of precedent was not possible "until reports became reliable."[27] Even then, courts retained the right to overrule cases based on "mistakes." Nineteenth-century courts, on the whole, were reluctant to use this power; and in England, the House of Lords, the highest English court, renounced the power completely in the late nineteenth century. Parliament alone could lawfully change legal premises, even judge-made ones. The Lords did not retreat from this dogma until 1966.[28]

Common lawyers have had, in general, little flair for legal philosophy and never worked out in detail a theory of legitimate decision. Two points were commonly understood before the twentieth century. First, judges and jurists strenuously denied that courts had the right to make law; second, jurists did not, on the whole, treat common-law rules as instrumental. Law, as a body of norms, claimed a legitimacy higher than that of mere technical tools. Common-law principles embodied justice and reason. They were the distillation of the wisdom of the people, sifted through time and perfected in the fires of experience. This was far less extravagant than the claims of a sacred law system, where God himself or his delegates were authors of law, but it was strong enough to give the canon a solid anchor. The judge was to find and apply the right norm, nothing more. The late nineteenth century was the high, or low, point of "mechanical" jurisprudence, both in the common- and civil-law system—the "deductive theory" of judicial decision-making in which, in Wasserstrom's terms: "all cases are decided by an appeal to rules that are certain and unchanging, whose application is completely predictable." In this theory, the "judge is peculiarly qualified to render decisions because he knows what many of the rules are, where the others may be readily located, and how to use the canons of logic to discern valid arguments."[29]

This may be a caricature, but it does capture something of an attitude toward judge-made law that is still quite vigorous. Because of this attitude, the judges sometimes faced problems not unlike those of the decision-maker in a sacred law system. To avoid the appearance of innovation, the judges had to turn to legalism, legal fictions, and strained analogies of all sorts.[30]

---

[27]John P. Dawson, *The Oracles of the Law* (1968), p. 80; see also Rupert Cross, *Precedent in English Law* (1961).

[28]Dawson, p. 94.

[29]Richard A. Wasserstrom, *The Judicial Decision, Toward a Theory of Legal Justification* (1961), p. 15.

[30]In modern times, because of the emphasis on "rationality," these habits have been modified, but courts remain very adroit at "distinguishing" cases.

2. In a sacred law system, the authority of a judge or sage was grounded in holiness, wisdom, and sacred institutions. But what was the source of authority for common-law judges? Blackstone called the judges, significantly, "living oracles" of the law.[31] As oracles, the judges "found" law through a process almost of divination. Blackstone's eighteenth-century idea, however, did not apply in the nineteenth century. The more modern idea was that judges were craftsmen of the law. Law was a science; judges were men trained in the science or art of "finding" and applying principles of law. This special skill set them apart from the laymen.

We have often referred to the idea of legal science. The theory in a sense was providential. "Science" was an appropriate model for law. In the popular mind, science is cumulative; it builds on its past—"on the shoulders of giants." It moves forward steadily, progressively, but what is new is not man-made. The new propositions exist outside, as rules that govern the real world; they only need to be "discovered."[32] If law were a science, then, the body of propositions would naturally change and grow, but the changes would not depend on politics or on the will or whim of the judge. Jurists would play a scientific role; they would discover, perfect, and analyze propositions of law. The man in the street—or the politician—would have no more say over legal science than he did over biology or physics.

Systems which fall under the second of our four ideal types can be called *legal science* systems, because legal systems, in which the idea of legal science is strong, come as close to it as any. In this type, the canon of premises is closed, yet the system accepts innovation. On the surface, this seems logically impossible. If the canon of premises is closed, how can there be innovation? The concept of legal science gives something of an answer: In the short run, the canon of premises is fixed, but the known canon of premises is not the same as the *potential* canon. Jurists can "discover" new propositions, improve old ones, and show fresh relationships.

The concept of legal science has been particularly evident in continental countries and colors their legal reasoning and scholarship.[33] In theory, the codes are the sole source of law; judges must link every decision to some concrete text of a code. The codes are not sacred and are frequently amended. Still, their language is fixed in the short run;

---

[31] 1 *Blackstone Commentaries*, 69.

[32] This concept of science, of course, is itself unscientific. See Thomas S. Kuhn, *The Structure of Scientific Revolutions* (1962).

[33] See John H. Merryman, *The Civil Law Tradition* (1969), pp. 65–72.

judges may have to stretch a point to connect their current case with a statutory norm. For this reason, common- and civil-law reasoning have some elements in common[34] and both, to some degree, have characteristics best described in terms of this second type.

3. The third category consists of systems where the canon of premises is open, but innovation is not really accepted. This is a common type which we can call *customary law*. Traditional or customary legal systems virtually all fall into this category.

We can take as one example the Lozi of Northern Rhodesia, whose highly developed legal system has been described by Max Gluckman.[35] Lozi judges were skillful at deciding cases and carefully explained their decisions.

But their reasons were hardly legalistic. The judges were not professionally trained. They were noblemen, counselors, wise men, elders, men of experience. They did not make new law.[36] The law was already there. Law was the way, the custom, the sense of the community. The Lozi believed that their kingdom was founded by a son of God, who gave the Lozi the law—"a whole body of rules defining rights and duties and of procedures for seeking justice from the king." The main body of law had thus "existed from time immemorial"[37]; the judges were only its spokesmen. Canons of reasoning were open. Judges drew on custom, experience, common sense, morality—any reasonable and fitting propositions. There was no text, no code, no fixity, no feeling that legal rules were separate from all other rules and unavailable except to trained minds. A similar system led Jan Vansina to the rather odd conclusion that the people he studied, the Kuba, had no legal norms. What he meant was that they had no specifically *legal* propositions. "Legal norms," he wrote, "are social norms, and nothing more."[38] This is merely another way of describing an open system, and it is generally true of the law of preliterate peoples.[39]

[34]See John P. Dawson, *The Oracles of the Law* (1968), an interesting comparative study of the treatment of case-law in Germany, France, and England.

[35]Max Gluckman, *The Judicial Process among the Barotse of Northern Rhodesia* (1955).

[36]There was some legislation among the Lozi—statutes of Lozi kings—but the Lozi did not believe that new rules came up out of case-law (ibid., pp. 246–252).

[37]Ibid., p. 1.

[38]Jan Vansina, "A Traditional Legal System: The Kuba," in Hilda Kuper and Leo Kuper, eds., *African Law: Adaptation and Development* (1965), pp. 97, 109.

[39]See Stuart Schlegel, *Tiruray Justice* (1970), p. 163; the Tiruray, who lived in the hills of Mindanao in the Philippines, lacked any institutionalized rules of law. "Legal recognition of validity is given to particular moral rules for the purpose of particular cases, but the moral rules remain only as moral rules."

4. The fourth type of system is one which accepts innovation and whose canon of premises is open. We can call these *instrumental* systems. In this type of system, some "judges" can make decisions without being bound by "legal" rules. These "judges" can invoke broad social standards, and they can change rules or their application as the standards dictate. The reasoning in such a system would resemble what Max Weber called "substantive rationality." In a substantively rational system, the judge decides on the basis of "ethical imperatives, utilitarian and other expediential rules, and political maxims," instead of "norms . . . obtained through logical generalization of abstract interpretations of meaning."[40]

Two rather different legal systems in the real world approximate this fourth ideal type. One of those subtypes we can call *revolutionary legality;* the other, *welfare legality.* In the early stages of a revolution —in Castro's Cuba or the Soviet Union in 1918—the new regime sometimes sweeps the old legal system away. The rulers institute revolutionary courts whose judges are zealous amateurs. These courts act swiftly and decisively. They may give reasons for their decisions, but the reasons do not come from the old codes of law. Rather, decisions are grounded on revolutionary principles and the expediency of the situation. The Peoples' Courts, in 1918, in the Soviet Union, were instructed to follow "revolutionary legal consciousness" in situations which were not covered by governmental decree. Special revolutionary tribunals handled sabotage and insurrection. These tribunals, according to Harold Berman, "enforced what was officially called the Red Terror. They were instructed to be guided 'exclusively by the circumstances of the case and by revolutionary conscience'." The old codes and courts and the old legal profession were abolished.[41] Soviet tribunals were to use law frankly as an instrument to build a new society. Nothing could be more ruthlessly modern, yet these tribunals shared with the Lozi the absence of a closed set of premises.

A court follows what we call *welfare legality,* when it holds itself open to change by the light of many criteria, not merely "legal" ones. Such a court would admit, as starting points for legal reasoning, policy

[40]Max Rheinstein, ed., *Max Weber on Law in Economy and Society,* pp. 63–64.
[41]Harold J. Berman, *Justice in the U.S.S.R.* (1963), pp. 31–32. For the similar period in Maoist China, see Jerome A. Cohen, *The Criminal Process in the People's Republic of China 1949–1963, An Introduction* (1968), pp. 9–10; Otto Ulç, in *The Judge in a Communist State, A View from Within* (1972), pp. 32–33, recounts how Czech judges were told to make their verdicts reflect the "class essence in each civil law case," a guideline difficult to follow. See also, Jesse Berman, "The Cuban Popular Tribunals," 69 *Colum. L. Rev.* 1317 (1969).

norms of all sorts, scientific truths, and statements of enlightened opinion—whatever would help guide the court to a better result, a result more in keeping with public policy, general welfare, or the social good. Each particular rule would have *its* goal or reason, fixing its place in the general web of social policy. Reasoning would be free, frank, and rational, never technical or legalistic.

This is the mode by which, ideally, governments in general decide what to do when framing policy and which enlightened arbitrators follow. Western courts are much more hamstrung by tradition. In the United States, a few courts, mostly appellate, *seem* to be moving slowly and slightly in this direction. A Swedish scholar also detects a movement toward "open" reasoning in the courts of his country.[42] In the United States, "open" courts are those that have less attachment to common-law precedent than courts of past generations. They give only limited deference to received propositions of law. Their judges feel free to use common sense as their touchstone, at least in some cases, to be guided by ethical or social norms, or to follow what they sense to be public opinion. A judge on such a court is therefore less scrupulous about the closed, finite set of legal propositions; "I need not affect not to know as a judge what I know as a man." In 1960 a New York appellate judge wrote these words in the course of an irate dissent; his opinion cited among other "authorities," *Commentary* magazine and a letter to the *New York Times*.[43] Neither of these is a canonical source, to say the least. Rigorous separation of judge and man was precisely what legal theory once called for. It was not the judge—as a man or a citizen—who would decide the case at hand; it was rather the *law*. Most American courts still make a sharp distinction between these two realms.[44]

We have talked about the four types at the level of whole systems of law. The classification fits as well, or better, when applied to *parts* of legal systems. The legalistic style found in sacred law systems is likely to occur in subsystems, too, when they have derivative legitimacy, a fixed canon of premises, and an obligation to decide and give reasons. These are common conditions of bureaucracy whatever the parent system. A civil servant has limited authority. He is supposed to decide "by the book." He must be able to link his decisions to prem-

---

[42]Per Olof Bolding, "Reliance on Authorities or Open Debate?: Two Models of Legal Argumentation," 13 *Scandinavian Studies in Law* 59 (1969).

[43]Hofstadter, J., dissenting in *New York City Housing Authority* v. *Watson*, 27 Misc. 3d 618, 620, 207 N.Y. S. 2d 920, 923 (Sup. Ct., 1960).

[44]Richard A. Daynard, "The Use of Social Policy in Judicial Decision-Making," 56 *Cornell L. Rev.* 919 (1971).

ises with higher legitimacy—some rule book, manual, regulations, orders, or governing statute. Consequently, bureaucrats will often
behave and write legalistically as befits a closed system.

Concepts of legitimacy determine styles of reasoning, and different
parts of the legal system depend on different theories of legitimacy.
Hence, a subsystem of one type can exist in a parent system of quite
another type. In Western nations generally in the late nineteenth
century, courts acted or pretended to act as if the system were closed.
At the same time, legislatures freely and openly made law. In the
Soviet Union during the turbulent period of "War Communism," immediately after the Revolution, courts had to follow government decrees to the letter; but popular tribunals had "open" authority in areas
not covered by decree. Juvenile courts, especially before *In re Gault*,[45]
were examples of free discretion, of welfare legality in a sense, inside
the more rigid framework of the common law.

American constitutional law is a somewhat closed subsystem but
with peculiar traits of its own. Every decision must be linked to the text
of the Constitution. No premises can be added to the Constitution,
except slowly and extraordinarily through amendment. The Constitution acts as the sole legitimate source for those propositions that give
federal courts their most dramatic power. An activist court "stretches"
the text with fictions and analogies. Not every problem *has* to find a
constitutional solution. A court can deny that there is a serious constitutional point and simply return an issue to the general body of law.
Traits of a closed system show up only when the court wants to decide
on constitutional grounds and cannot find an obvious text.

What lawyers call "legal reasoning," strictly speaking, is a trait of
closed systems from classical Roman law and the old book-religions to
the continental codes and the common law. The idea of *legal* reasoning
depends on a closed set of premises—the idea that some propositions
are *legal* propositions and others are not and that trained men can
winnow one from the other. In a purely open system, there are no legal
propositions as such, hence no such thing as a specialist in legal propositions—no lawyers or law-trained judges.

Revolutionary legalism, as an open system, does not want or need
lawyers; it needs revolutionaries. Some modern revolutionaries have
actually been lawyers, Fidel Castro, for example, but lawyers as a
whole make a living out of the law of a particular regime. In a revolution, they suffer the stigma of an overthrown order. A total revolution

---

[45]387 U.S. 1 (1967). For an interesting description of juvenile justice on the eve of
Gault, see David Matza, *Delinquency and Drift* (1964).

also makes lawyers unnecessary—at first. A lawyer is useful in a society, because he knows the canon of legal propositions. In an open system, he has no role. When a revolutionary regime "settles down" and develops its *own* canon of legal propositions, regardless of content, it tends to need lawyers again. This has happened, of course, in the Soviet Union.[46] Many premises of Soviet law are really old premises of civil law. Others are ossified bits of Marxist doctrine. Still others are precepts left over from the Revolution that turned into dogma. The source of the premises does not matter. *All* legal propositions ultimately come from the social world, just as all legal words were originally words of nonlegal speech, and *any* proposition can be a legal proposition, so long as it is bodily assumed into the corpus of norms. What is special about legal propositions is their claim to legitimacy, and the skill required to use them "properly." As the Soviet government codified its rules, its canon slowly closed. A new legal profession then sprang up. It did what lawyers had done before, using many of the old techniques,[47] but the premises and propositions had been recast, and, of course, the lawyers served new masters.

Only systems that are more or less closed need a professional class of law-men. Conversely, professionals have an economic and social interest in keeping a system closed. If common sense or native wit gives just as good answers as the lawyers do, then people with common sense or native wit might as well argue cases, and decide them. Revolutionaries handle revolutionary law even better than the lawyers. Or, if there are no specifically *legal* propositions, other professionals—doctors, engineers, economists, ballistics experts, even sociologists—might as well work on decisions within their field of competence. In a closed system, it is plausible to argue that no one without the proper skill, training, and mastery of the art can handle "legal" questions correctly and decide "legal" cases. In a secular system, this means lawyers, and law-trained judges; in a sacred law system, it means priests, rabbis, imams. For lawyers to flourish, however, the system must not only be closed, it must also be defined as *legal* and closed. Decision by experts means decision within a closed system, but that system need not be law. It can be medicine, biology, engineering, urban planning, or whatever.

The lawyer is such a familiar modern figure that one easily assumes he is universal. Law, arguably, is universal; lawyers are not. In fact, few societies in world history have had lawyers at all. Only com-

---

[46]See, in general, Harold J. Berman, *Justice in the U.S.S.R.* (1963).

[47]And, of course, they were organized and paid in a manner totally different from pre-1918 lawyers.

plex societies—literate, urbanized societies—have professional lawyers,[48] and even in these complex, urban societies, lawyers and law-trained judges work only on a small, limited range of social problems. They do *not* monopolize the interpretation of law. Specialists make and apply most rules of modern life, but not specialists in law. It is enough to point to the wild efflorescence of agencies, tribunals, boards, and commissions—all with power under and over law, all manned, by and large, by specialists in nonlegal disciplines or by lawyers not acting as such, or by outright amateurs. Vilhelm Aubert suggests that the lawyer's importance reached some sort of climax in the nineteenth century and, in advanced countries, has now entered a phase of slow decline.[49] Modern society believes in rational decision and experts—in closed systems, in short; but the experts are more specifically trained and need not be experts in law.

LEGALISM

Legalism, according to Judith Shklar, is "the ethical attitude that holds moral conduct to be a matter of rule following." Peter Blau speaks of legalism as "a form of displacement of the objectives of a law by the techniques designed to achieve them." Similarly, Philippe Nonet finds legalism where "insistence on legal rules or modes or reasoning tends to frustrate the purposes of public policy."[50]

In ordinary speech, the word has no precise, objective meaning. Rather, it is used loosely as a label of disdain or complaint. Basically, it refers to the slavish, literal worship of rules. Of course, everyone follows rules literally some of the time. The central meaning of legalism points to some sort of *misuse* of rules. This is a subjective judgment; one man's legalism is another man's idealism. When an appellate court sets a criminal defendant free "on a technicality," this is either "legalism" or strict justice, depending on one's point of view. Legalism, then, is a matter of values, but what people label legalistic is not random or unimportant.

Two distinct kinds of behavior are likely to be so labelled. The first is an exaggerated attention to some literal meaning of a word without regard to its context—in particular, when a court, interpreting a text,

---

[48]See Richard D. Schwartz and James C. Miller, "Legal Evolution and Societal Complexity," 70 *Am. J. Sociology* 159 (1964).

[49]See Vilhelm Aubert, "Law as a Way of Resolving Conflicts: The Case of a Small Industrialized Society," in Laura Nader, ed., *Law in Culture and Society* (1969), p. 282.

[50]Judith Shklar, *Legalism* (1964), p. 1; Peter Blau, The *Dynamics of Bureaucracy* (1963), p. 239; Philippe Nonet, *Administrative Justice* (1969), p. 265.

248 The Legal System: A Social Science Perspective

refuses to go beyond one of the dictionary meanings of the words and refuses to consider the policy, purpose, or context of the text. *Smith* v. *Hiatt,* a 1952 Massachusetts case,[51] is a well-known example. A Massachusetts law required an accident victim, if he wished to sue a city or town for injuries "caused by . . . snow or ice," to give prompt notice of his injury or lose his right to sue. Another section of the statute imposed the same requirement on victims suing private landowners for the same sort of injury. The Hiatt family hired Smith, a practical nurse, to take care of their newborn baby. Mrs. Hiatt defrosted the refrigerator, and apparently, some ice dropped to the floor. The nurse went into the kitchen, slipped on the ice, and was injured. The accident took place in July in Mrs. Hiatt's very presence. The nurse and her lawyer never gave the special notice required by the statute. When she did sue, the Hiatts, arguing that the injury was "caused by . . . ice," insisted that Smith had forfeited her rights. Amazingly, the Massachusetts courts agreed. Ice was ice.

Another type of legalism we might call the *legalism of evasion*. In a way, this is the opposite of *Smith* v. *Hiatt.* Here, the decision-maker twists the meaning of ordinary words like taffy, to reach some desired result, or avoid some painful outcome that the words seem clearly to point to. For example, the Statute of Frauds lists types of contracts that must be in writing. One type is contracts "not to be performed within a year." In *Joseph* v. *Sears Roebuck & Co.* (1953),[52] the plaintiff bought a pressure cooker from Sears. Supposedly, the saleswoman promised (verbally) that the cooker could not explode and that it would last from ten to fifteen years. A year and a half later, the pressure cooker blew up damaging the plaintiff's house. One might think that such a verbal guaranty (that the cooker would last from ten to fifteen years!) was a promise "not to be performed within a year," but the court felt otherwise. The cooker *could* have blown up within a day, a month, or a year. If so, Sears would have to make good the promise. Since it was *possible* that the agreement could be performed within a year, the statute did not apply. This twisting of the meaning of words occurs frequently in common-law cases, where judges feel bound by prior law (or bound to act bound) but do not like the results. They then "distinguish" away prior law through the legalism of evasion.

In either case, legalism is reasoning which offends some commu-

---

[51] 329 Mass. 488 (1952); the case was used by Henry Hart and Albert Sacks, in their book *The Legal Process* (tentative ed., 1958), vol. II, p. 1288, as a virulent example of literal interpretation of statutes.

[52] 224 S.C. 105, 77 S.E. 2d 583 (1953).

nity sense of the logic of meaning. In other words, legalism, whatever else it is, violates the standards of reasoning used outside the law. The word and the thing, then, are confined, practically speaking, to systems or subsystems with closed or partly closed legal premises. Hence legalism is inseparable from professional lawyers and judges. In a society with open premises, reasoning conforms to common sense, that is, to conventional ways of thinking, to ordinary language, to the habits of thought of everyday life. Sacred law systems are legalistic, for reasons we have noted. In sacred law systems religious leaders play the role that lawyers play in closed secular systems. The *responsa* of the rabbis on questions of religious law seem highly legalistic in our view. The community felt otherwise. The Jews accepted the reasoning of the rabbis, not as legalism but as truth, because they believed that the rabbis were wise men capable of piercing the veil of law and divine command.

It is clear, then, which legal systems support legalistic reasoning. *Within* those systems, what sorts of situation evoke it? Rules of law do not provide clear answers to all possible questions. This is especially the difficulty in a closed system where the old stock of norms may be inadequate for solving new practical problems. Yet problems have to be solved, and by the law, not by tossing a coin or by invoking "outside" principles.

This problem plagues the common law as well. Hence, "legalism" has appeared in the reasoning of many cases, even "leading" cases. Parties enter into a contract by mail. When does the contract become binding—when the offeree drops his letter of acceptance in the mailbox or when the offeror receives the acceptance?[53] Suppose a will, through mistake, leaves the same piece of land to two different people in different clauses of the will; if there is no other evidence to help us, does the first clause govern or the second?[54]

These questions, when they first arose, had no obvious solution. No rule, case, or doctrine plainly dictated a result or pointed logically toward one, nor was there any obvious policy. In some cases, good reasons for a decision are not "legal" enough to be openly cited. Or there may be no reasons at all—the matter must be decided and by a clear-cut rule, but it makes no difference what the rule is. Whether to

[53]*Adams* v. *Lindsell*, 1 B & L. 681 (1818); the contract is final upon mailing.
[54]*Paramour* v. *Yardley*, 2 Plow. 539, 541, 2 Eng. Rep. 794, 797 (K.B., 1580). The answer is, the first clause: "For as the last will repeals the first will, so by the same reason the last part of the will shall repeal the first part of the will, when they are contrary to each other."

drive on the right or the left side of the road would have presented this problem when it first arose, if no rule or custom bore on the point. If a *judge* had to decide this issue and write an opinion based only on principles of the common law—or worse yet, on the Koran—his decision could hardly fail to be "legalistic." The legislature might decide by fiat; an ordinary person in a similar dilemma might toss a coin. For such questions, legalistic decision, as a matter of fact, is as random a method as tossing a coin. The outcome depends on the unpredictable: the particular judge's intelligence, taste, or fancy. The randomness will not matter, if the outcome proves to be socially satisfactory or if the issue is one of those which must be settled, but the solutions are all equally good. In these situations, random choice is **perfectly functional**. The decision, then, will stand and be canonized into precedent.

LEGAL FICTIONS

The legal fiction is a well-known form of the legalism of evasion.[55] It is a proposition from the mouth of a judge or other legal actor that states as fact something which is not a fact at all—as he and everybody knows. It is, in short, a legal pretending. The medieval common law made heavy use of fictions. In the late Middle Ages, for example, common-law courts used a legal fiction to lay claim to jurisdiction over contracts executed overseas. Litigants would allege in their pleadings that the contract (actually drawn up in France or the low countries) had been made in England: "to wit, in the parish of St. Mary le Bow in the Ward of Cheap." The courts treated this allegation as nontraversable, that is, they refused to let the defendant deny that Paris was really in this ward in the city of London.[56]

Legal fictions seem strange and a trifle outrageous. The literature on legal fiction runs heavily to disapproval. Bentham defined a fiction as a "willful falsehood, having for its object the stealing of legislative power"[57]; and even more harshly as a "wart which . . . deforms the face of justice . . . a syphilis which runs in every vein."[58] Sir Henry Maine took a longer, more measured view. Every legal system, he felt, needed some device to keep it flexible, to bring law into harmony with current social needs. "Social necessities and social opinion," he wrote, "are

---

[55]See, in general, Lon L. Fuller, *Legal Fictions* (1967).

[56]William S. Holdsworth, *History of English Law* (1924), vol. V, p. 140.

[57]C. K. Ogden, *Bentham's Theory of Fictions* (1951), p. xviii.

[58]Quoted in Oliver R. Mitchell, "The Fictions of the Law: Have They Proved Useful or Detrimental to its Growth?" 7 *Harv. L. Rev.* 249, 250 (1893).

always more or less in advance of the law." He listed three harmonizing devices: fictions, equity, and legislation. A fiction was "any assumption which conceals, or affects to conceal, the fact that a rule of law has undergone alteration, its letter remaining unchanged, its operation being modified." Legal fictions, he felt, were the earliest, most primitive of the three devices—primitive, since fictions catered to a "superstitious disrelish for change." More mature legal systems used equity and legislation to bring society and law into harmony.[59]

Sir Henry's theory cannot be literally true. Ethnographic data, which he lacked, suggest that fictions, though found in customary law,[60] are far less common there than, for example, in medieval English law. Nor are they to be found in revolutionary law. Fictions are a form of legal reasoning in the strict sense; therefore, they are to be found in systems or subsystems which limit or deny innovation. These include traditional systems which deny innovation, but fictions flourish above all in closed systems where the need to stretch, pretend, and conceal change is at the highest. Fictions therefore do not belong to any specific state of legal evolution. Fictions may well appear whenever and wherever certain specific, concrete conditions come together—past, present, or future.

What function does the legal fiction serve? Clearly, it affects the distribution of power within a legal system. Many common-law fictions were jurisdictional. Courts used or responded to legal fictions to widen or narrow their own jurisdiction. In England, the Court of Exchequer originally heard cases in which someone owed a debt to the Crown. Later, the court extended its range to cases between ordinary litigants. Plaintiff would allege that he owed the king money and was less able to pay it, because defendant held back from plaintiff what he owed. The debt to the king was pure fiction; but Exchequer seized on it as early as the fourteenth century and successfully assumed jurisdiction over ordinary cases of debt.[61]

An extension of power is often a challenge to those authorities who are on the losing end. These may acquiesce or resist the "usurpation." The agency that uses a fiction wants to broaden its power, feels that normal legal reasoning will not or cannot help, and presumably senses that the use of the fiction will succeed. A fiction is phrased so as to *look*

---

[59]Sir Henry Maine, *Ancient Law* (1861), pp. 24, 26. See A.K.R. Kiralfy, "Law Reform by Legal Fictions, Equity and Legislation in English Legal History," 10 *Am. J. Legal Hist.* 3 (1966), critically examining Sir Henry's thesis on historical grounds.

[60]See T. O. Elias, *The Nature of African Customary Law* (1956), pp. 176–186.

[61]William S. Holdsworth, *History of English Law* (1922), vol. I, p. 240.

as if the court merely follows old and legitimate ways. The fiction assimilates the unusual to the usual, the new to the old. Disguising the change makes for a gentler transition. Most changes of this sort are small, but the cumulative effect may be substantial. The British government carries on business in the name of the queen, as if she wielded great power. The Crown in fact has no power at all; it lost it through a long series of small changes. Outward forms have politely survived.

In the long run in a society, ideology, including theories of legal legitimacy, probably tends to shift in such a way as to defend and support the social structure, that is, the real distribution of power. Legal fictions form a bridge between ideology and fact, when an institution asserts either that less change has taken place or more than is actually true.[62] If change is abrupt and is meant to be, fiction is not needed. Revolutionary ideology can be quite callous about old fictions and forms. The Soviets felt no need to keep the czar as a figurehead or to retain the trappings of the old legal system. Quite to the contrary, they were anxious to proclaim a total revolution. This was the first, most radical phase. Later they allowed or imposed on the law a new set of fictions. That the workers and peasants rule Russia is as much a fable as that Queen Elizabeth II governs the English.

Historically, many common-law fictions were jurisdictional but by no means all. A good example of a substantive fiction is the rule of *Jee* v. *Audley*.[63] This is part of the law restricting "perpetuities," that is, limiting how far in the future one can "tie up" interests in property—at what point all interests must "vest" in definite beneficiaries. In *Jee*, a man left £1,000 in trust for his niece Mary and her children, if any. If Mary died without children, the money would be divided among any daughters then living of John and Elizabeth Jee. When testator died, the Jees were about seventy years old. Under the rule, the gift to the Jees would be void if and only if the court held as a matter of law that Elizabeth Jee might have given birth to still another "daughter," who could share in the gift. Of course, biologically, it made no sense to suppose that she could, but the court did hold, as a matter of law, that a woman is able to bear children whatever her age.[64] The rule, despite its foolish form, could be defended as sensible in result, and it did not *need* to be stated as a fiction.[65] A substantive fiction, in other words,

---

[62]See Fuller, pp. 58–70, though laying rather heavy emphasis on the intellectual and cognitive purposes of fictions.

[63]*Jee* v. *Audley*, 1 Cox Eq. Cas. 324 (1787).

[64]See 1 *Blackstone's Commentaries*, 457.

[65]For example, it could have been phrased as a rule about interpretation of wills and deeds and the consequences of a certain kind of ambiguity.

is nothing but a rule of law expressed in the style of a fiction. Fictions of this sort are fast becoming obsolete. They can survive only as long as their style is tolerated; this is no longer the case. Yet as the fictions disappear, the rule they expressed may live on in more rational wording.

REASONING BY ANALOGY AND INCREMENTALISM

Reasoning by analogy[66] is a pervasive feature of common-law cases. Every volume of reports contains countless examples. This is not at all surprising. Analogy is an honorable, typical device of common sense reasoning, and many legal systems assign to analogy a formal place in their jurisprudence.[67] In the common law, analogy, essentially, gets small recognition; it even lacks an official name. Yet analogy is the very core or seed of common-law growth. Rules change slowly, as courts extend or contract them using analogy.

Edward Levi, in his valuable little book on legal reasoning,[68] has given some good illustrations of the common-law use of analogy. Among these is the development of the concept of the "inherently dangerous" object in tort law. The rule was that a person injured by some defect in a product might sue the person who sold him the product but not the original manufacturer. But if the product was "inherently dangerous," this limitation did not apply. In an early case, a loaded gun was held to be inherently dangerous, in another case, a defective gun. A defective coach was held *not* inherently dangerous. An exploding lamp, on the other hand, was. In still another case, plaintiff bought "belladonna, erroneously marked as extract of dandelion"; he sued the maker and won. Next came defective hair wash. A defective balance wheel on a circular saw, was not, however, imminently dangerous. And so it went, in and out, until the concept gained a decisive push forward in *MacPherson* v. *Buick* (1916), the famous case of a defective wheel.[69] Later, the case-law demolished most of the barriers against manufacturers' liability.

A common-law judge compares the cases before him with the facts of past cases that seem to fall under a similar principle or rule. Often enough, present and past, the paradigm case and the instant case, do not fit perfectly. Often enough, there are competing paradigms and

---

[66]See, in general, Edward H. Levi, *An Introduction to Legal Reasoning* (1949).

[67]Islam, for example. Joseph Schacht, *The Origins of Muhammadan Jurisprudence* (1953), pp. 98–99; in Jewish law, see H. L. Strack, *Introduction to the Talmud and Midrash* (1959).

[68]Edward H. Levi, *An Introduction to Legal Reasoning* (1949).

[69]217 N.Y. 382, 111 N.E. 1050 (1916).

rules. The courts must then decide which is the closer analogy. Was a defective wheel on a Buick as dangerous as poison or an exploding boiler? Could these comparisons outweigh the strong analogy to the wheel of a stagecoach? The maker of new rules, too, may use analogy to justify or explain the rule or to show how it relates to other principles and rules. These comparisons do not appear as formal reasoning unless the situation demands it. Congressmen argue from analogy as everyone else does, but their arguments do not appear in the texts of enacted law.

When courts change rules through the use of analogy, the changes tend to be small. Otherwise, the analogy would not fit. Reasoning by analogy is therefore incremental. A judge, who honestly believed he had no power to make law and who tried to hew as closely as he could to known rules and principles, would use analogy and creep forward incrementally, if at all. What American courts do today, in the main, is not *very* different from what they did in the late nineteenth century, when the idea of *stare decisis* and the principle of self-denial were even stronger. Then and now, courts moved incrementally and mostly by analogy. Then, as now, bold leaps forward were rare. Fictions once disguised some of the bolder leaps. Today, the leaps, when they occur, are more open.

In brief, courts as a rule move cautiously, in short steps. They adopt middling, short-run solutions; they change the status quo very little in their ordinary work.[70] Their caution is also a necessity, born from the political context in which they work. Bold leaps are dangerous to the court. When the court moves too fast, it becomes a hero to some; but it also runs the risk of resentment, controversy, loss of legitimacy —at least so judges think. Danger also comes from competitive institutions or from organized groups whose interests suffer from decisions of the court and who may turn against the court itself. Incrementalism, then, is not only a strategy or (as some legal thinkers believe) a virtue; the structure of the courts and the way courts are positioned in society incline them to incremental techniques.

Reasoning by analogy, we have said, is incremental. The prevailing attitude of judges favors judicial restraint, incrementalism, and reasoning by analogy, and behavior seems nearly as cautious as attitude. Theories come and go; the actual role of the courts within the legal system changes quite slowly. It has always been a limited role.[71] Some-

---

[70]On this point, see Martin Shapiro, "Stability and Change in Judicial Decision-Making: Incrementalism or Stare Decisis?" 2 *Law in Transition Q.* 134 (1964).

[71]It is often said that the common law is basically judge-made, that the judges

times, courts exert strong pressure in one field or a handful of fields. The main flow has been glacially careful. The United States Supreme Court is a dazzling exception. In most countries, if not all, courts cannot exert significant control over economic and political life and do not wish to. Characteristically, their role requires them to recast, not to seize the initiative; what they do, they do in response to litigant pressure. Analogy, then, is more or less a functional necessity for modern courts. To say that courts are cautious by "tradition" is to make a similar point. "Tradition" simply means strongly sensed jurisdictional limits that cannot easily be found in some formal document.

A system of reasoning has the best chance to survive, when the relevant public thinks it is useful and legitimate. Analogy, of course, is both, and it is persuasive and efficient. It relates the unknown to the known, new matters to old ones. It is comfortable; it stays within the safety zone of legitimacy. At the same time, it is a tremendous saver of time. It uses precedent as a base line, a point of departure. Adherence to the past is simpler, more efficient, than a fresh start. Stereotyped logic, stock reasons, shortcuts and analogies are valuable in any system of decision. *Stare decisis* is a form of stereotyped logic; it also supports the court's legitimacy, since it shows respect for the past rather than a lusting for power. When a court interprets a statute, it justifies its reasoning vertically, so to speak, linking its work upward to the governing statute. A decision based on precedent justifies itself horizontally; it refers back to some decision already justified and ultimately either to a statute or, if need be, to custom, the will of the people, natural justice, or some standard of unquestioned truth. Precedent is so valuable for judges and society that although *stare decisis* has been shorn of ridigity and magic, it survives as a habit and a need.[72]

RULES OF INTERPRETATION

Many legal systems have rules of *logic* and interpretation—rules for handling the premises of legal reasoning—as well as rules of procedure and law. Rules of interpretation, like the substantive premises, can be open or closed. A *closed* system of interpretation has special

---

developed the fundamental rules of law. That depends on what one thinks of as fundamental. Courts never invented the structure of the legal system or its essential procedures. At times, courts elaborated many of the principles of "private" law; whether that was fundamental or not is a matter of opinion. In any event, it was usually others who defined the work of the courts, who marked off the boundary lines. The advances made through jurisdictional fictions were exceptional.

[72]See Shapiro *supra* note 70.

rules of *legal* reasoning, rules not used outside the law. Open systems admit any form of reasoning, any logic current in the community whether specifically legal or not. Closed rules of reasoning occur only in closed systems, but even there rules of legal logic are never completely different from the ordinary canons of inference. All legal systems, open or closed, use ordinary logic in their work.

Nonetheless, special rules of *legal* logic have often appeared in various guises and forms. The Talmud records many rules for extracting meaning out of holy texts. At one stage, the sages listed seven rules, later thirteen, then thirty-two. Some of these were plain sense or folk wisdom—analogy, for example. Others had a more mystical nature and were more or less divining rods for unearthing textual secrets. *Gematria*, for example, one of these tools, depended on the fact that Hebrew letters serve as numbers, too. Every Hebrew word, then, has a numerical value. Through *gematria*, the sages inferred meaning from the number-value of biblical words.[73]

Nothing as dramatic as the Talmudic rules is found in more "rational" legal systems, ancient and modern, but special rules of logic are not uncommon. In a sense, the mere fact that a system is closed implies a special rule of logic. A closed system draws a noose about materials of inference in a way the common man finds foreign. Frequently, there are rules to decide what to do when rules themselves are in conflict. These rules put premises in rank-order—high, middle, and low. Rules may prescribe the authority of various authorities. The "law of citations" of imperial Rome (426 A.D.) named five jurists as primary legal authorities—Papinian, Paulus, Ulpian, Modestinus, and Gaius.[74] The doctrine of precedent, *stare decisis*, is itself a rule of this sort. The doctrine of legislative supremacy is another. There may be rules to resolve conflicts between other rules.

A whole body of law has grown up around the question of interpreting statutes. The rules include the so-called canons of construction— for example, the rule of *ejusdem generis* and the rule that "qualifying or limiting words or clauses are to be referred to the next preceding antecedent."[75] Some of these rules have been exceptionally important in legal history. One such is the canon that criminal statutes must be strictly, that is, narrowly, construed. In civil-law countries, because of

---

[73]Hermann L. Strack, *Introduction to the Talmud and Midrash* (1959), pp. 93–98.

[74]H. F. Jolowicz, *Historical Introduction to the Study of Roman Law* (1954), p. 472.

[75]See Karl N. Llewellyn, "Remarks on the Theory of Appellate Decision and the Rules or Canons about How Statutes are to be Construed," 3 *Vand. L. Rev.* 395 (1950), pointing out that for each rule there is a counterrule.

the primacy of the codes, jurists pay particular attention to rules of interpretation.[76] In the United States, special rules govern constitutional interpretation.[77]

Where do the special rules of legal logic come from, and what is the point of these rules? First of all, since these rules impose a special logic, they suggest that the lay mind and the legal mind work in different ways. This has some prestige value for lawyers in a secular country and for expositors of sacred law in a theocratic one. Second, the rules may help solve the problem of closed systems by adding to the small stock of premises. The sages of the Talmud, for example, had to resolve many issues of life, religion, and ethics with only a limited stock of premises on hand. Like the tones of Chinese words, which multiply the number of syllables by four, Talmudic rules of reasoning increased the range and number of inferences that sages could draw from the sacred texts. In the United States, "common sense" reading of the Constitution could not carry the law very far. Special rules, techniques, presumptions, and analogies permit the courts to build up a vast body of law over the years, case by case, even though the text stays exactly the same. Third, rules of reasoning serve as weapons in the struggle between institutions. Jurisdiction in a broad sense is dynamic. Active, ambitious agencies test the boundaries of neighboring agencies looking for soft spots, weaknesses through which power can ooze. In the common-law countries, the courts used rules of statutory construction to assert power over legislative bodies. Some of the rules were rules of deference, some were rules of aggression, such as the canon announcing a narrow construction of penal laws. Legislatures had to learn to draft laws to hold down the power of the courts.

It is, of course, not possible to draft a statute that can be applied to every relevant situation. Words do not have fixed meanings; unforeseen situations spring up. In fact, draftsmanship is often careless and imprecise. Mistakes creep in despite all precautions. Legal theo-

---

[76]See, for example, Karl Engisch, *Einführung in das Juristische Denken* (4th ed., 1956).

[77]See, for example, the rules laid down by Justice Brandeis in a concurring opinion in *Ashwander* v. *TVA*, 297 U.S. 288, 346–8 (1936). Actually, these were mostly rules of caution, rules to avoid constitutional issues, if possible. Brandeis gathered these rules out of prior cases. They have been often cited since. The rules are not exclusively rules of inference; they also concern standing to sue, that is, who may invoke legal process in a constitutional case. But there is a strong logical element in the *Ashwander* rules. The seventh rule, for example, states that when an act of Congress is challenged, the court must "first ascertain whether a construction of the statute is fairly possible by which the question may be avoided."

rists, especially in the common law, tend to exaggerate the uncertainties. For many statutes, there *is* a "plain meaning," and the statute's purpose is also reasonably plain. Someone can always dream up a doubtful situation, but in life, the scope of the statute may be free of doubt practically speaking. A court can honestly look for the plain meaning in a common sense way. To do so is to defer to the legislature —not to its "will," but to its power. Courts in the common-law world were not usually willing to defer. The courts used canons of construction to claim a kind of superiority. The rules of interpretation were not empirical rules, dictionary rules, rules about how people mostly use their words. They were rules which often twisted meaning. That criminal statutes should be strictly construed is not an observation about the way people use words, but a rule of policy and a rule about the relative power of institutions.[78]

Special rules of logic have still another use. The idea of an objective, impartial body of law is beneficial to judges. Judges can blame unpopular or difficult decisions on "the law" rather than on their own acts of will. No one blames a doctor for his patient's diseases. Scientific rules of legal logic would have the same value as a scientific concept of substantive law. Moreover, closed rules of logic, like closed premises in general, have a certain efficiency. They make the judge's task easier, and the law more predictable—in theory at least.

The common law was, on the whole, closed rather than open both as to premises and rules of interpretation. A common-law judge, deciding an ordinary case, did not feel entitled to make bold changes. In a statutory case, the words of the statute are the premises of legal reasoning. These words are fixed. The judge can "interpret" within broad, but definite, limits. He cannot legitimately go too far, or too boldly, or too often. The average civil servant has an even tighter role. Orders, manuals, rule books bind him strictly.[79] This is not only normal, it is indispensable in modern government. A complex society cannot allow everyone the freewheeling right to make up rules. It has to keep this vital

---

[78]The *Ashwander* rules were, on the contrary, mainly rules of deference. These rules must be understood against the backdrop of constitutional history. The federal Constitution contains some wonderfully prismatic phrases—for example, "due process of law." American courts in the late nineteenth and early twentieth century swelled the meaning of this phrase tremendously. They boldly used constitutional doctrine to strike down state laws and acts of Congress which they disapproved of. The impact of judicial review, up to 1930, was conservative; Brandeis was suspicious of it. Moreover, he felt that it lowered public confidence in the court. In the *Ashwander* rules, he meant to codify self-restraint and limit the scope of "government by judiciary."

[79]If he steps out of line, his superiors will reverse him and perhaps punish him. This, as much as any sense of role, reinforces his timidity.

but powerful weapon under control. The alternative verges on anarchy.

There is, then, a tension between "hard" cases, new cases, socially important cases (which push courts toward change), and the firm boundaries society places on legitimate jurisdiction. *Formal* jurisdiction is rather static. It moves in awkward fits and starts. Authority, actual government, is dynamic. It flows smoothly, responding to changes in demand and to real situations. How does it manage this paradox? One way, as we have seen, is through tricks of legal reasoning, analogy, legal fictions, legalism. Attitudes about legitimacy in the community and the legal culture in general determine when and how the various techniques can be used. The Court of Exchequer could not have openly seized new jurisdiction, but it did so under cover of a fiction. The fiction was transparent, and we must assume that, in some sense, other holders of power acquiesced in the result.

LANGUAGE AND STYLE

The legal culture—particularly theories of legitimacy—influences the *language* and *style* of the law as well as the forms of legal reasoning. A specifically "legal" style can hardly exist outside a closed system.

J. Gillis Wetter, in an interesting study, compared and contrasted the style of appellate courts in Sweden, Germany, two American states (Arkansas and California), England, Canada, and France.[80] The differences were striking. The French Cour de Cassation, for example, used an elliptical, technical, impersonal style. Opinions were extremely sparse, extremely economical. There was no statement of facts. Essentially, the opinion did little more than point out the precise links between sections of the code and the results of the cases. "The judgments are concentrated and almost abrupt in their strict brevity. They speak law to law's men—in no respect are they addressed to laymen or to the parties." This, Wetter feels, is characteristic of a "bureaucratically organized judiciary, or among law men trained in a rigorous, quasi-scientific legal atmosphere."[81] The style thus suits what seem to be the prevailing theories of legal legitimacy in France. There the codes are supreme, and judges are strictly subordinate, bureaucratic, and anonymous. Judges do not emerge as individuals (cases are not signed), and they abjure any right to make law.[82]

---

[80]J. Gillis Wetter, *The Styles of Appellate Judicial Opinions, a Case Study in Comparative Law* (1960).

[81]Ibid., pp. 30–31.

[82]See K. Zweigert and H. Kötz, *Einführung in die Rechtsvergleichung* (1971), vol. 1, pp. 140–141.

260 The Legal System: A Social Science Perspective

English courts have a very different style. Opinions are discursive; the tone is distinctly casual, almost conversational. Here "men, not courts, are at work." One gets the impression of a group of wise, cautious gentlemen discussing difficult problems among themselves. This distinctive style, Wetter feels, reflects the peculiar English structure of bench and bar and the place of lawyers and judges in society. Bench and bar are a tight-knit little group. "The law of the London courts is the law of a guild."[83] The English view, essentially, is that folk wisdom makes the common law—the tried and traditional experience of the better people. The judge is a craftsman. His special gift is to know just how to work the raw materials of law to reach wise, just, and correct results. Judges as a group are a dignified, learned elite; they discuss law in an orderly, civilized way, as men discuss matters of principle among themselves.

The American judicial style falls somewhere between the English and the French. It is less conversational than the English style, far more personal than the French. In France, opinions are unsigned; they simply state the law; there are no dissents. In the House of Lords, judges give their opinions *seriatim*, that is, one by one. The majority wins, but there is, strictly speaking, no majority opinion. In the United States, the high courts publish opinions of the majority and the minority. Typically the majority opinion is signed; it is also *the* opinion of the court. Dissents and concurrences are frequent in the Supreme Court and some state courts.[84]

Judicial style does not remain immobile. It changes with society and the legal culture. Karl Llewellyn was struck by differences in style in various periods of American history. The style of the Grand Tradition flourished before the Civil War. The Formal Style replaced it in the late nineteenth century. The third and most recent style has been more or less a return to the Grand Tradition. The grand manner was grand, in Llewellyn's view, because it rested decisions on principle rather than on precedents—each rule had a "singing reason apparent on its face."[85] Formal Style was crabbed and technical; it was legalistic, obsessed with precedent; it lacked majesty and breadth. Llewellyn admired the style of the Grand Tradition, disliked Formal Style, and regretted that it lasted so long and left so persistent a legacy. Indeed, historical differ-

---

[83]Wetter, *supra* note 80, p. 32.

[84]Dissent rates were lower in the past, see Karl ZoBell, "Division of Opinion in the United States Supreme Court: A History of Judicial Disintegration," 44 *Cornell L.Q.* 186, 205 (1959); for the variability of dissent rates, see Henry R. Glick and Kenneth N. Vines, *State Court Systems* (1973), p. 79.

[85]Karl N. Llewellyn, *The Bramble Bush: On Our Law and Its Study* (1951), p. 157.

ences in styles seem real enough; John Marshall, Lemuel Shaw, and other famous judges of the first half of the nineteenth century wrote in a style clearly different from that of later judges. A 1900 case tends to bristle with "authority." Judges enter into minute, boring analyses of prior cases. Marshall's opinions, on the other hand, swept boldly along; he rarely cited much authority but built up his case out of great blocks of fundamental principle. Reason, logic, and argument carried more weight than legal tradition as such.

Of course, many factors enter into a style. There are mundane technical factors: Who can assess what impact the typewriter had on the way judges worked? The number of clerks is another factor, as is the sheer amount of time the judges can spend on each case. Court dockets tended to get more crowded between 1820 and 1900. The amount of work increased faster than public willingness to spend money on judges and courts. Judges without leisure to polish and repolish do not use the style of the Grand Tradition. Perhaps, too, the appellate judge of 1800, 1820, and 1840 was more likely to be a cultured, cultivated gentleman than the judge of 1900, who was elected to office and had a background of local political experience.

Still, all in all, changes in style probably reflected changes in theories of legitimacy. If judges say or believe that the only valid premises of legal reasoning are prior cases, they will write in something like the Formal Style. Judges of the Grand Tradition did not take *stare decisis* quite so literally. For them, the common law was a body of basic principle. Broad, sweeping principles underlay the case-law and validated it. This point of view will produce the style of the Grand Tradition or something like it. The modern "return" to the Grand Tradition is not a return so much as the impact of rationalism and legal realism on the judge's conception of his role.

THE LANGUAGE OF THE LAW[86]

Lawyers talk and write in their own peculiar way. The language of law has inspired a literature of invective, but little systematic study. A few points, however, seem obvious. First, one cannot speak at all of legal language except in a closed system, that is, a system in which the phrase "legal proposition" has some special meaning. Only in a closed system is there a legal profession and technical, *legal* words.

Some laymen think that lawyers speak and write a jargon of ob-

---

[86]See David Mellinkoff, *The Language of the Law* (1963); Lawrence M. Friedman, "Law and Its Language," 33 *Geo. Wash. L. Rev.* 563 (1964).

solete words and Latin phrases. In fact, neither the living law nor its technical terms are particularly old. "Zoning" and "capital gains" are new expressions. American lawyers, as a group, do *not* prefer old or Latin or law-French terms. They do not know Latin, cannot pronounce it, and find its use embarrassing. When they have a choice, lawyers reject more exotic terms for easier ones. They now say "beneficiary" instead of "cestui que trust."

To be sure, many legal words and phrases are of ancient lineage. Some come from or have gone into popular speech: judge, jury, verdict, mortgage, will. Lawyers invent their vocabulary, by and large, by adapting ordinary words to special meanings: offer and acceptance, murder, negligence, arrest. A lawyer uses a phrase like "the silver platter doctrine,"[87] not because it is hard to explain to a layman, but as a kind of shorthand. Any occupational group uses shorthand—indeed, any group with shared experiences. Most legal terms are simple shortcuts. A technical language is efficient for professionals. This is as true of law as of other fields. It would be clumsy, indeed, if law had to give up terms like "spendthrift trust" or "last clear chance." Some of these terms, of course, are technical in a strict sense: They describe concepts and institutions that do not exist outside of law: easement, attestation clause, anomalous endorsement. Use of such terms is as natural and unavoidable as "sodium fluoride" or "monocotyledon" are in other fields.

Legal language serves other, less cold-blooded functions. When words, phrases, and expressions are current *within* a group but unknown outside, the special language helps define the boundaries of the group, marking the members off from the ordinary world. Legal language is special; thus the profession too is special. Training in a learned art turns an occupation into a "profession."[88] Technical language, then, has symbolic value. It is a mark of status as well as an aid to communication. Besides, the lawyer's special claims derive from his skill in handling words.

In earlier times and in other societies, lawyers learned as apprentices from other lawyers. Modern lawyers go to school. In either case, common training binds lawyers together. Like members of the same faith, lawyers can speak to each other not only in concepts but emotionally. Not one lawyer in fifty has use for the doctrine of consideration in his work or earns his bread with the rule against perpetuities. But

---

[87]Mellinkoff, *supra* note 86 at 441.

[88]A. M. Carr-Saunders and P. A. Wilson, "Professions," 12 *Encyc. Soc. Sci.* 476; Ernest Greenwood, "Attributes of a Profession," 2 *Soc. Work* no. 3, 45 (1957); Wilbert E. Moore, *The Professions: Roles and Rules* (1970), pp. 10–13.

these marvelous phrases evoke feelings of camaraderie and nostalgia. Lawyers have a culture and a style in common. Words and phrases—and memories—bind and unite the profession.

Legal style and vocabulary are therefore economic in a second sense; they protect professional cohesion and prestige. This second use, however, does little to explain *particular* elements of lawyers' style. Any jargon preempted by lawyers and unknown to the public would serve this purpose well. This second aspect of legal language neither creates legal terms nor a legal style. But it may, from time to time, keep words and habits alive even when they are no longer "functional" in the most cold-blooded sense.

Legal style has a ritual function too. Law has many ritual phrases —for example, the words of the oath: "the truth, the whole truth, and nothing but the truth." Any difference between a truth and a whole truth is forgotten now, but the resounding phrase lives on. It conveys something of the magic and grandeur of an oath.[89] Such phrases, beamed at the layman, do not convey information as much as fear, awe, and respect. Ritual phrases are effective; like nursery rhymes and proverbs, they are easy to memorize and repeat. Probably, older law made more use of ritual phrasing than the highly rational systems of today. Cultures without a written language transmit law orally and directly. "Mature" legal systems, by contrast, which have lawyers and technical terms, reduce the number of magical-poetic phrases; theories of legitimacy stress usefulness and reason. Ritual language survives in some corners of law, reserved for solemn acts, like the oath. The typical will is also solemn, ritualistic, and highly formal; it tends to use archaic, singsong phrasing—"give, devise, and bequeath"; "rest, residue, and remainder."

Legal writing has been severely criticized as vague and verbose. Of course, lawyers are not the only ones to write vague or pompous English; perhaps it is more forgivable in lawyers than in doctors, educators, or civil servants. Vagueness is not always a vice. In a statute, vague language delegates responsibility to some subordinate agency which will have to flesh out its meaning. This vagueness can be an instrument of delay. The Supreme Court used the expression "with all deliberate speed," in framing its decree in the school segregation cases.[90] This vague direction shifted the burden for working out details to lower

---

[89]The oath supposedly began as a conditional "self-curse." In modern law, it still carries a flavor of the threat of divine retribution but in a "subjective" manner. It addresses itself to the person taking the oath and plays on his religious beliefs. Helen Silving, "The Oath," 68 *Yale L.J.* 1329, 1337, 1371 (1959).

[90]*Brown* v. *Board of Education,* 349 U.S. 294, 301 (1955); see George Christie, "Vagueness and Legal Language," 48 *Minn. L. Rev.* 885 (1964).

federal courts and delayed implementation of the decision. Deliberate vagueness is quite common in law. Lawmakers often choose to grant an agency the broadest discretion. The Federal Communications Commission in awarding radio licenses is to be guided by "public convenience, interest or necessity"; and is told to provide for "fair, efficient, and equitable distribution of radio services."[91] The Sherman Act of 1890 made illegal "Every contract [or] combination . . . in restraint of trade or commerce among the several States," adding few details.[92] In both cases, the vagueness was no accident or mistake but a deliberate tactic of delegation and delay for political reasons. Lawyers who draft wills, deeds, trusts, and contracts also leave issues hanging on purpose through vague and ambiguous language. This gives an executor, trustee, or party power to fill in gaps, to make further arrangements, or to "administer" under the general framework of the document. Vague language in a contract may usefully postpone or evade some divisive issues which in practice might never come up.[93]

The opposite vice, verbosity, is also more than mere accident or mistake. Anglo-American statutes are very wordy. They never seem to use one word, when six can be strung in a row. It is as if the draftsman is seized with "anxiety" and loads his text with reservations and limitations.[94] Common-law courts, however, have been rather cavalier in interpreting statutes. In the Middle Ages, they "construed" with great freedom, adding and subtracting as they pleased. Indeed, the statutes were poorly drafted.[95] Later courts continued the practice. Courts, as we noted, read some statutes "strictly," which means they successfully asserted power to rework and reword what the British Parliament had done.[96] For example, the courts strictly interpreted any statute "in derogation of the common law"—that is, one which took away a "common-law right," or added to "common-law disabilities," or provided "for proceedings unknown or contrary to" common law.[97] The courts

---

[91]48 Stat. 1083, as amended, 47 U.S.C. § 307 (a), (b) (1936).

[92]26 Stat. 209 (1890); see William Letwin, *Law and Economic Policy in America, the Evolution of the Sherman Antitrust Act* (1965).

[93]Stewart Macaulay, "Non-Contractual Relations in Business: A Preliminary Study," 28 *Am. Soc. Rev.* 55 (1963).

[94]Henrich Triepel, *Vom Stil des Rechts* (1946), p. 90.

[95]See Theodore T. F. Plucknett, *Statutes and Their Interpretation in the First Half of the Fourteenth Century* (1922).

[96]See Henry C. Black, *Handbook on the Construction and Interpretation of the Laws* (2nd ed., 1911), pp. 367–77.

[97]J. G. Sutherland, *Statutes and Statutory Construction* (1891), p. 510; "remedial" laws were, however, to be liberally construed.

paid lip service to the duty to interpret, to bow to the legislative will. But they skewed "interpretation" in particular directions. If a statute could reasonably apply to three situations, but mentioned only one of them explicitly, a court, if so inclined, could limit the statute to that one case under cover of a canon of construction.

Still, this power was, in theory, merely a power to *interpret.* When the words were unusually explicit, it was hard for a court to twist its meaning. Draftsmen became well aware of the power of judges to "construe" in a highhanded way. They were also aware that if the net of words was drawn tightly enough, the court might be obliged to do as it was told. Draftsmen would be tempted, then, to pile synonym upon synonym, trying to plug every leak and bar every door. What results is this kind of statute:

> The Department shall ascertain, fix and order such reasonable standards, rules or regulations for the design, construction, location, installation, operation, repair and maintenance of equipment for storage, handling, use, and transportation by tank truck or tank trailer of liquefied petroleum gases for fuel purposes, and for the odorization of said gases used therewith, as shall render such equipment safe.[98]

These words boil down to a statement that the industrial commission should lay down rules to ensure the safe handling of gases. Term is heaped upon term out of fear that some reviewing body will hack away at the power of the commission or as a habit left over from days when such fear was more justified. The style of the civil-law codes is quite different from that of the common-law statutes. In civil-law countries, no one questions the primacy of the codes. They tend, therefore, to contain broad, sweeping propositions. The Napoleonic Code of 1804, we are told, aimed at general principles, "rich in consequences," and refused to "descend into detail."[99] Common-law statutes, on the other hand, are mosaics, patchworks, made up of dozens of niggling terms and phrases.[100]

What was true of statutes was true of other legal documents: wills,

---

[98]Wis. Stat. § 101.16 (2). Notice the vague word "safe" alongside the stupefying verbosity.

[99]This was the view of the draftsmen, quoted in P. A. Fenet, *Recueil Complet des Travaux Préparatoires du Code Civil* (1827), vol. 1, p. 470; see André Tunc, "The Grand Outlines of the Code," in Bernard Schwartz, ed., *The Code Napoleon and the Common Law World* (1956), pp. 19, 26–27.

[100]The comparison is not entirely fair. As we pointed out, there are many broad, vague statutes in the common-law world. Everywhere, real regulation, either in statutes or in rules made pursuant to them, will have to to be carefully detailed. How stylistically different are the income tax codes or parking rules of modern nations?

contracts, and trusts. Historically, courts construed the powers of trustees very narrowly, to protect the beneficiary's rights. Trustees could not profit from any transaction with the trust; they had to manage the trust carefully, invest trust funds safely, and keep trust property entirely separate from their own. These rules were most sensible when trustees were amateurs and needed paternal guidance. Today big banks and trust companies have a dominant share of the management of trusts. They do not want meddlesome courts and beneficiaries who sue at the drop of a hat. The companies control the drafting of their trusts. They use two drafting techniques to secure their interests— first, language of unbridled discretion and second, very prolix and particular language. The two techniques are frequently combined. The trust agreement will spell out total discretion to invest as the trustee sees fit. The document will then go on to list the allowable investments in great detail: stocks, bond, notes, real estate, mortgages, etc. The list would be unnecessary if one took the general clause at face value. Both the gaseous vagueness and the neurotic hypertrophy of synonyms are attempts to undo the history of trust law, hold off the power of the courts, and deter beneficiaries from lawsuits.[101]

Legal language, once fixed, is conservative. Common-law courts in the past emphasized texts, that is, actual written words, and did not allow outside evidence of purpose or meaning. In case after case about wills, trusts, deeds, statutes, or contracts they ignored the context—the behavior of the parties. In contract law, the parol evidence[102] rule expressed this tendency. In the law of wills, courts would not hear testimony of the dead man's words; the meaning of the will had to come out of the text, from the "four corners," as they put it, of the document. Perhaps these rules were supposed to make their job as decision-makers easier. At the same time, emphasis on the text had a business or economic purpose. Language could be stabilized and standardized. Standardized language, in turn, would lead to reliable, predictable— and standardized—interpretation.[103] Courts with this general philoso-

---

[101]These habits of drafting statutes and documents may be somewhat out-of-date. Courts would probably now construe a safety statute sensibly and respect a broad, simple statement of the trustee's power. Good draftsmen are now responding to their sense of twentieth-century legal culture.

[102]Lawrence M. Friedman, *Contract Law in America* (1965), p. 7. "The core of the rule is this: when negotiations have resulted in a written agreement which seems to cover the whole subject-matter of the bargaining, the court will treat the agreement as embodying the whole agreement of the parties, and it will not pay attention to evidence, oral or written, of what went on in the prior period of bargaining, if that evidence contradicts the written agreement."

[103]See Lawrence M. Friedman, "Law, Rules, and the Interpretation of Written Documents," 59 *Nw. U. L. Rev.* 751 (1965).

phy paid great attention to phrasing. If a draftsman deviated from the conventional words, the court might wonder why this was so. A lawyer then would think twice before abandoning the snugness of habit. Safety was worth an extra phrase or two.

The common law used form to channel behavior. It made use of "magic words." In the Middle Ages and well into modern times, if a man wanted to transfer a fee simple, his deed had to run to the grantee and his "heirs."[104] Even if he wrote: "I deed this land to Smith, to own absolutely, and forever, to do with as he wishes," Smith did not take a fee. The grantor *had* to say "to Smith and his heirs." This seems stubborn, even foolish. But there *was* a rational point: Absolute insistence on form would tend to standardize deeds, reducing the chaos of draftsmanship to manageable proportions. The general idea is still valid. A bank check, which *must* be standard, uses the "magic words" *order* or *bearer* and tolerates no deviation. Of course, extreme technicality and form will not work unless technicians, who know what they are doing, do the drafting. The magic words are *printed* on checks. Only lawyers and conveyancers draw up deeds. The lesson of legal history has seemed clear. Extra words cost nothing, but draftsmen courted disaster if they left words out. Where the lawyer knew the magic words, he used them, and a commendable brevity resulted. Where he was the least bit unsure which words were magic and which were only words, he might heap phrases helter-skelter, hoping by sheer chance to hit on Rumpelstiltskin's name.[105]

---

[104]2 *Blackstone's Commentaries,* 107.

[105]This attitude too is probably unnecessary now. "Magic words" are still useful, as the example of the check makes clear. But draftsmen of wills and trusts have a freer hand. Courts do not play much of a role in interpreting these documents, since the overwhelming majority never pass through litigation. And if they do, courts do not slavishly adhere to text as the only touchstone of meaning.

Chapter X
Social Change and Legal Change

The prior chapters, by and large, have examined legal systems statically, that is, in cross section, as one would see them at one particular point in time. Legal systems are of course not static. They are constantly in motion, constantly changing. It is necessary to look at social systems in equilibrium, but in fact they are also exposed to ceaseless conflict and change.[1] This chapter deals specifically with legal and social change.

One *general* proposition about legal change was implicit in the earlier chapters, that is, that major legal change follows and depends on social change. Not every change in a legal system is major change; most change is quite minor. Any alteration, even adding a comma to a statute, is an instance of change in the law. Consequently, some of these changes need not be considered products of outside social forces. They may be treated as purely internal—matters of the parochial, housekeeping interest of lawyers and judge.

We can distinguish theoretically *four* types of legal change, depending on the *point of origin* of the change and its final *point of impact.*[2]

---

[1]William J. Chambliss and Robert B. Seidman, *Law, Order and Power* (1971), p. 18.

[2]See Lawrence M. Friedman, "Law Reform in Historical Perspective," 13 *St. Louis U.L.J.* 351 (1969); Lawrence M. Friedman and Jack Ladinsky, "El Derecho como Instrumento de Cambio Social Incremental," *Derecho*, no. 27, 22 (Lima, 1969); see also Joel B. Grossman and Mary H. Grossman, eds., *Law and Change in Modern America* (1971), pp. 1–10; William M. Evan, "Law as an Instrument of Social Change," in Alvin W. Gouldner and S. M. Miller, eds., *Applied Sociology* (1965), p. 285.

1. Change originating *outside* the legal system, that is, in society, but affecting *only* the legal system and ending there like a spent bullet.

2. Change originating *outside* the legal system but moving *through* it (with or without some internal processing) to a point of impact *outside* the legal system, that is, in society.

3. Change that begins *inside* the legal system and which also spends whatever impact it might have *inside* the legal system.

4. Change originating *inside* the legal system, then moving through the system and ending with its impact *outside* in society.

We will begin with the third type—*formal, internal changes.* Many changes in law seem to belong to this category, that is, they begin and end in the law with no external impetus or impact. Every year, hundreds of new laws and legal acts in every legal system do little more than tinker with details of procedure or the housekeeping of the law. Legislatures pass "technical change" bills, some very minor: changing an "and" to an "or," correcting slips of the pen. Others, however, sport the grand name of "law reform" and claim a certain significance.

Law reform is a major preoccupation of jurists. Scholars compile, classify, and codify law. In the United States, bar associations, the American Law Institute, and legislative drafting committees all assume "law reform" as one of their jobs. So do the various "law revision commissions" in the states. In England, the Law Commission performs this task. Law reform organizations work to revise the statutes, achieving a better or more logical order. They codify obscure doctrines and bring scattered rules together into one package; they improve legal forms and formalities. They systematize the law usually without much substantive change. They worry about data retrieval for practicing lawyers and how to improve the efficiency of courts. There are even some instances of law reform, in the technical sense, through judicial decision. A court may summarize, classify, or improve doctrine, restate issues or revise a line of holdings.

As a general rule, revisers of law do not pay much attention to impact. They more or less assume that "better" laws will have serious results in the world of behavior. Practically every commercial law scholar in the United States had some hand or stake in the Uniform Commercial Code—drafting it, discussing it, criticizing it, writing about it, getting it enacted, chronicling the results. Yet for all they knew, few of its provisions would or did make much of a difference to the business world, or would change the behavior of bankers or consumers, or affect anyone at all outside the law schools. The code was in the main pure code—pure system, pure "reform."[3] Many "model" and uniform laws and many codes also have small effect on the larger society. That, for example, the German Civil Code (the *Bürgerliches Gesetzbuch*) could ride out the first years of the Hitler regime, a time of fundamental revolution in governmental structures, essentially unaltered is, in fact, an admission that the social consequences of the code as code were or had become exceedingly slight.[4]

Not all law reform, of course, is merely form. Riots have occurred over court organization. Codification, too, may have great political meaning. Codification can be a means of taming absolute power. Before the law of the Massachusetts Bay Colony was codified, there were few limits on the discretion of the magistrates. The colonial codes, flowing out of political struggle, acted more or less like treaties defining what magistrates could or could not do.[5] The Magna Carta, too, was this kind of treaty code. The Code Napoleon itself had a political aim: It was part of a movement to reduce the authority of judges while expanding the power of revolutionary lawmakers.[6] The criminal law was codified in many countries, including the United States, to prevent judges from inventing new crimes under cover of their common-law or discretionary power.

But modern law reform, on the whole, is "reform" only in the draftsman's narrow sense. The profession is, in a way, myopic. Jurists, who literally devote life and career to "reform," along with professional law reformers and revisers of statutes, will naturally overestimate the impact of their work. It *must* make a difference in how people behave. But even a lawyer who suspected that "reform" made little difference to the world might want to continue with the work. "Improving" the law, in an aesthetic or systematic sense, fills a professional need, whether or not it fills a *social* need. Professions must justify themselves, must strike a posture of concern for the public good. Undertaking law reform is like a doctor's work with charity patients. Besides, it disarms outside criticism, if lawyers admit there are flaws in the temple of justice and set about to make the repairs themselves. The profession "cleans its own house." Also, law reform is lawyer's

---

[3]It is virtually indisputable that the fact that the code is a *code* has no behavioral consequences, whatever one thinks of particular provisions.

[4]Hellmut G. Isele, "Ein Halbes Jahrhundert deutsches Bürgerliches Gesetzbuch," 150 *Archiv für die Civilistische Praxis* 1, 15–20 (1949).

[5]See George Haskins, *Law and Authority in Early Massachusetts* (1960), p. 123.

[6]John H. Merryman, *The Civil Law Tradition* (1969), pp. 29–31; Jacques Godechot, *Les Institutions de la France sous la Révolution et L'Empire* (2nd ed., 1968), pp. 691–696.

work; only lawyers can do it. Lawyers therefore assert through law reform their claim to a monopoly of practice.

One kind of purely formal change is worth further mention. Some legal acts put a formal stamp of approval on behavior previously performed or codify a new social state or rules of behavior or attitude that already exist. We can call these legal acts *ratification*. Repeal of a "dead letter statute" is an act of ratification. An unused statute or rule, whatever its history, is "in force" only in a technical sense. It is a purely formal change to remove its corpse from the law books.

The removal, of course, may serve a useful, although minor, function. Someone might accidentally trip on the corpse and hurt himself. Dead letter law also threatens the public relations of the legal system. This was the case with *wager of law,* a famous example of a living fossil. In medieval English law, defendants might bring in "oath-helpers," to swear that the defendant's oath was clean and true; in certain types of cases, this was enough to clear the defendant of liability. Wager of law, obsolete for centuries, was never formally abolished. Once in a great while lawyers, by mistake, would use language in their pleadings which gave the defendant the technical right to "wage his law." Such an accident happened in 1824, when a defendant claimed the right, produced his oath-helpers, and went free. The case was a link in the chain of events which finally led Parliament, in 1833, to rid the country of the corpse of wager of law.[7] This merely ratified a change that had occurred for all practical purposes many centuries before. Trial by battle, too, was abolished in 1819, after an 1818 case showed it "was still a legal method of proof in appeals of murder."[8]

These incidents suggest that much of what is "archaic" in the common law is stable and, except for occasional accidents, perfectly innocuous. The common law preserves certain fossils of substance or procedure. Common law moves ahead case by case, sometimes rather slowly; it tends to bypass outworn institutions rather than abolish them. The whole English government, on paper, is a relic left over from the days of absolute monarchy. The survivals, as a whole, have little effect on behavior. Legal training tends to ignore the living law and hence may exaggerate the survivals. Nobody cares enough about these relics to "reform" them—nobody, that is, except legal craftsmen, who probably spend more time on the subject than it deserves. In European law, the ideology of "legal science" gives jurists a tremendous incentive to work on similar "problems"; whole armies of professors can engage

---

[7]3 and 4 Will. IV, ch. 42 § 13.

[8]William S. Holdsworth, *History of English Law* (3rd ed., 1922), vol. I, p. 310. The case was *Ashford* v. *Thornton*, 1 B. and Ald. 457 (1818).

in battle over trivial conceptual flaws, or cracks in the architecture of the codes.

Law reform, then, may follow an *incident* which draws attention to a harmful or embarrassing survival. Or, legal craftsmen, on their own initiative, may act as scavengers in the name of efficiency or justice. The incident probably plays more of a part in common-law than in civil-law countries where jurists constantly analyze and reanalyze the body of formal law. In both realms, jurists take the initiative in law reform particularly since the rise of university law schools. They ferret out and correct archaic law. The codes, model acts, and restatements of the twentieth century are products of their zeal.

Another common phenomenon can be called *hidden ratification.* For the United States, we may use the Married Women's Property Acts as examples. At common law, when a woman married, her husband gained control of her property. She could not buy, sell, or trade on her own. Under the Married Women's Property Acts, she gained the right to manage her own property. In 1839, Mississippi, an unlikely pioneer, passed the first of these statutes covering only a few situations. In the next generation, other states enacted their own laws in broader versions. On the whole, these laws seemed to make basic changes in the legal, economic, and social status of women. One would guess that they had been the subject of thunderous debate.

Yet, careful study of their history turns up a deafening silence. The laws seemed to have come out of nowhere. They evoked no debate, no response, no uproar in the press. This odd fact suggests that the acts were not quite the abrupt change that they seemed. For a long time, married women had, in fact, dealt in property on their own.[9] Particularly in England, they bypassed the formal rules with arrangements which were, however, costly and technical. These arrangements were possible in the United States, but landowners were an immeasurably larger class than in England, and the legal skills needed were in short supply. The laws swept away these artifices; afterwards women could do simply and directly what before could be done in a complex and indirect way. The acts were not meaningless, but, socially speaking, they were more ratification than innovation.[10]

Legal change often comes midway in the course of a chain of events. The change ratifies steps already taken; for those not yet taken, it innovates or appears to. Exactly what role formal law plays in the

---

[9]On the law of married women during the American colonial period, see Richard Morris, *Studies in the History of American Law* (2nd ed., 1959), pp. 135–172.

[10]Kay Ellen Thurman, "The Married Women's Property Acts" (M.LL. thesis, University of Wisconsin Law School, 1966).

sequence is often hard to tell, both as to origin and impact. A court abolishes the death penalty, but for some time past the state had been mysteriously unwilling to use it. Another state abolishes its unused adultery laws. How much of these legal acts are innovation rather than ratification? Does repeal of a dead letter law have some catalytic or symbolic effect? Not enough is known about the impact of legal behavior, let alone long-term social change, to give confident answers about any particular case.

FORMAL CHANGES WITH EXTERNAL CONSEQUENCES

Can a purely formal change have important social consequences? Conventional wisdom would say yes. Congress amends some rule, "intending" only a minor clarification or rewording, but an "accident" of phrasing leads to tremendous consequences.

To be sure, this *seems* to happen: But what is the proof? The legal change may be simply a tool, an occasion. Some social change was already rumbling underground; its force would have found one outlet or another; it hardly matters which. If we assume to the contrary, we deny the basic premise of any social theory of law and give tremendous weight to abstract rules and concepts in themselves. To refer to a familiar example: American courts at the end of the nineteenth century used the due process clause to protect business interests. It strains credulity to assume that an "accident" in draftsmanship caused this to happen. Law is part of general culture, but it is not normally the leading sector. One need not stubbornly refuse to believe in such "accidents," when the evidence is strong, but, in theory, the "accident" hypothesis is wrong, and there has to be a heavy burden of proof before it is accepted for any historical instance.

Legal style muddies this issue. When a lawyer argues, he must find some legal hook to hang his arguments on. If his client wants to or has to base a claim on the Constitution, the lawyer must find some clause to support his case. The Constitution is obliging; it contains any number of vague and plastic phrases, such as "due process" or "equal protection of the laws." In the judicial phase of the battle over regulation of business in the late nineteenth century, arguments and decisions pivoted on the Fourteenth Amendment and its convenient, plausible words. As we have argued, it would be wrong to claim that the words "caused" judges to take a conservative stance, or "caused" the economic struggle in which they were used, or determined the outcome of cases. Words and doctrine may make a difference, of course. American history might have taken *something* of a different turn, if other legal arguments had been used, or if the cases had gone the other way. But how different? Chance phrases and doctrines are not likely to affect social policy. The legal world is full of devices and phrases. If one does not work, there is always another.

A similar point could be made about the rise of the fellow-servant rule. This nineteenth century rule was of first importance in industrial relations. The rule cut off an employee's right to sue his employer in tort, if the negligent cause of the accident was a "fellow-servant." The "leading case," and the earliest, was *Priestley* v. *Fowler,* decided in England in 1837.[11] The injured worker in *Priestley* v. *Fowler* was a butcher's helper. The judge, Lord Abinger, could hardly guess what his decision would mean in a factory setting. Lord Abinger used examples and analogies drawn mostly from the world of household servants. The opinion was both inept and inapt, yet the doctrine spread like wildfire on both sides of the Atlantic.

How can we explain this history? The most *plausible* way is to treat *Priestley* v. *Fowler* as a mere incident, a hook to hang the doctrine on, a convenient case to cite. The first two American cases were truly industrial; they grew out of railroad accidents.[12] Judges took the doctrine, shaped it, extended it, and strengthened it to serve the needs, as they saw them, of an industrial society. It does not seem likely that the law would have gone off in a different direction without *Priestley* v. *Fowler.* Courts would have fabricated the same or some similar doctrine out of other scraps of law. The fellow-servant rule was "right" for its time, for a society with a business outlook. Whatever Lord Abinger might have done, tort law in the first half of the nineteenth century was bound to favor owners over workers.

SOCIAL CHANGE WITH PURELY TECHNICAL RESULTS

Another type of legal change is also common. Outside forces press against the legal system but what comes out is purely formal legal change, making no difference to society. Raging storms produce only the merest whimper within the realm of law. The only question is why this should occur. The theoretical bent of this book rejects one possible explanation: that law is inherently unresponsive, cannot absorb demands made upon it, and revolves in its own quiet orbit. In fact, social theories of law predict this third type of legal change in an important set of circumstances. If two or more social forces, more or less balanced in strength, make irreconcilable demands on the legal system, the legal

---

[11]3 M & W. 1 (Ex., 1837).

[12] *Murray* v. *South Carolina RR. Co.,* 1 McM. 385 (S.C., 1841); *Farwell* v. *Boston and Worcester Railroad Corp.,* 4 Metc. 49 (Mass., 1842).

result will be zero. "Zero" in the legal system may mean literally zero (no change at all), or pointless, technical, or toothless change. "Spent bullets," then, indicate not that the system does not respond but the presence of stalemate: two teams of equal strength, both pulling on the rope.

LAW AND MAJOR SOCIAL CHANGE

One last type remains to be considered. Social demands produce legal change which leads in turn to major social change. In modern times, the main vehicle for this process is legislation, although once in a while a court decision (the abortion case, for example) may be equally weighty. In the United States, the fugitive slave laws, the Social Security Act, the income tax laws, and the Economic Opportunity Act appeared to lead to or channel social change. Even more significant are cumulations of statutes or rules—the New Deal, for example, or the group of laws that established the welfare state in England; perhaps, too, the network of tort rules, in the nineteenth century, dealing with industrial accidents. In some countries, executive decrees are a major vehicle of change. For any single instance, of course, one can argue endlessly whether change has been "major" or "minor." Normally, legal change, especially judge-made change, takes place in small doses.[13] Nevertheless, revolutionary change does occur—deliberate, massive, social engineering through law.

Revolutionary change in and through law is an enormous subject. We will merely make a few general points.

First, we can divide major change into two types, *planning* and *disruption*, that is, positive and negative change. By disruption, we mean change through destroying or dismantling an established legal order. Planning is change that institutes *new* legal order. In reality, the two are usually joined. "Revolution" commonly refers to both: destruction of the old and birth of the new. Legal revolutions have both aspects, too. The Soviet government, when it laid its hand on family life and law among the Moslems of Central Asia, tried both to smash the old Moslem traditions and, at the same time, to replace them with the Soviet codes.[14]

Planning, in the literal sense, is a ubiquitous feature of the modern

---

[13]See Martin Shapiro, "Stability and Change in Judicial Decision-Making: Incrementalism or Stare Decisis?" 2 *Law in Transition Q.* 134 (1964); Lawrence M. Friedman and Jack Ladinsky, "El Derecho como Instrumento de Cambio Social Incremental," *Derecho*, no. 27, 22 (Lima, 1969).

[14]Gregory Massell, "Law as an Instrument of Revolutionary Change in a Traditional Milieu: the Case of Soviet Central Asia," 2 *Law and Society Rev.* 179 (1968).

world—most obviously, of course, in socialist countries, but the Western industrial powers and the new nations are also committed to planning to a greater or lesser degree.[15] Every society today seems to believe in a massive infusion of law from the center. Attempted social change, through law, is a basic trait of the modern world.

"Revolution" in the literal sense is the most vivid and obvious form of disruption. But milder forms are everywhere. Judicial review is frequently disruptive. American courts have smashed programs and institutions from the Missouri Compromise to the Alaska pipeline. Activist reformers have played a sensational role in American life in the last decade. Ralph Nader is the most well-known example. Nader is basically an investigator and publicist, but he is also a lawyer by training and so are most of his "raiders." He stimulates use of legal process as a lever of social change. Much of his work is technically disruptive; it focusses on litigation and injunctions, on stopping government dead in its tracks, when it fails to meet his ethical and policy standards. Legal disruption can take illegal forms—blocking streets, pouring blood on draft board records, some forms of civil disobedience. Legal and legitimate means include lawsuits; particularly after *Brown v. Board of Education,*[16] reformers have frequently gone to court to upset many old and established arrangements. This use of litigation continues an earlier American pattern, discussed in the chapter on legal culture, but in an exaggerated form. The most notorious cases go before the federal courts and involve constitutional issues. But the movement spills over these borders. It is as good at blocking highways and airports as it is in attacking police brutality or racial segregation. Its danger comes from the very fact that it disrupts. Courts can stop processes well enough, but they are not good at replacing or restyling whatever process they hold back. To be sure, federal courts have drawn school district lines; they have told schools how to bus children from one place to another; they have reapportioned states; they have run bankrupt railroads. More important, they throw down a gauntlet which other agencies of government must pick up; in this way, disruption clears the way for planning. The California supreme court destroyed the legal basis for the system of financing schools in the state.[17] This was plainly disruption, but it may force California to plan some alternative.

Disruption, through courts, has been both praised and blamed. It

[15]See Robert B. Seidman, "Law and Economic Development in Independent, English-Speaking, Sub-Saharan Africa," 1966 *Wis. L. Rev.* 999.

[16]347 U.S. 483 (1954).

[17]*Serrano* v. *Priest,* 5 Cal. 3rd 584, 487 P.2d 1241 (1971).

seems likely to continue, whatever the political complexion of new judges. The activist self-image is not a mere whim of the Supreme Court. It goes deeper and broader. It is not the self-concept of most judges, but it is an important minority attitude, and so long as there are customers to take advantage of the mood, there will be occasions for more and more exercise.

Will this American phenomenon spread to other countries? Creative disruption of the judicial type presupposes a number of conditions which rarely coincide. These include, first, an activist legal profession. There have always been political lawyers in the United States, but their numbers increased in the 1960s, sponsored and financed by the federal government and by private foundations. The money was important; a young lawyer no longer had to choose a life of grubby poverty in order to act out his ideals. Public interest lawyers won some notable cases and gained some notable publicity. The news helped, in turn, to attract other socially minded people into the practice of law. As of 1974, the federal share of the money seems to be drying up. This puts the future of the movement in some doubt, but no one predicts that the clock will turn back completely.

Activist judges are the second prerequisite. Few countries, besides the United States, can meet this condition. An active judge is not necessarily a liberal judge. It is a judge who is not afraid to change a rule or overturn a system or who, blinded by mythology, unconsciously plays the revolutionary. Most American judges have no doubt been passive and at best incremental, but the minority can point to a rich history of judicial review. The judges who weakened the New Deal, who destroyed the first income tax law, who struck down child labor laws, and who ended the death penalty were activist judges.

A genuine social movement, whose values are shared by at least some judges, is a third condition. It is a weak condition, and most societies can meet it. The strongest condition, perhaps, is the last. Elites—the power holders—must accept the results of disruptive litigation, like it or not. Clearly, no socialist or authoritarian country will tolerate anything remotely like the American form of judicial review, let alone the grosser forms of disruption. Their legal structures are not built to accommodate these patterns of behavior. But the matter goes deeper than structure. In the Union of South Africa, when the high court showed signs of mild interference with the government's policies on race, the government stamped out its power to intervene.[18]

---

[18]In 1952, the Appellate Division of the South African Supreme Court declared unconstitutional a law restricting the franchise of the "Cape Coloureds." The South

Dominant majorities in the United States could also overturn the work of the courts, if they were enraged and aroused enough. Once in a while they have done so. What is amazing is how rarely such a counterrevolution succeeds. For the most part, the majority, which sometimes includes rich and powerful people, allows the courts to push it around. On balance most people feel that the courts benefit them or their group or society, or they have faith in the courts or believe in an independent judiciary, or they are unwilling to take risks, because the alternatives are unknown or unthinkable. In some sense, acquiescence may be against the interests of the majority. But interests, as we have often pointed out, are not demands. The decision to press an interest —to make it into a demand—depends on the legal culture, that is, on ideas about when it is useful and right to make demands on the law and what sort of demands. Liberal doctrines in the nineteenth century helped restrain the working class from using latent power to reform the state in their interests. Belief in a semi-welfare state may persuade the middle class or even the high and mighty to allow disruptive reforms to proceed through the courts.

Judicial power may be a transient glory. It will certainly not last forever. And there is always a limit beyond which courts will not go, or, if they went, dominant interests would no longer acquiesce. The issue would be something deeper than busing and broader than the location of new airports. Still, acquiescence is a major social fact, a prerequisite for social change through litigation, which few societies share or are likely to share. The courts in America have shown amazing strength in stirring up or channeling social change, using old and conservative forms. This revolution has been slow and costly in the making and would be very hard to sell abroad.

MACRO-LEGAL CHANGE: THEORIES OF LEGAL EVOLUTION[19]

The discussion so far has not touched on the *direction* in which legal changes go. Are there patterns of legal change? Can one speak of

---

African Parliament passed a law giving itself the right to sit as a high court and overruled the decision. Later laws further restricted judicial review. International Commission of Jurists, *South Africa and the Rule of Law* (1960), pp. 15–16.

[19]See Lawrence M. Friedman, "On Legal Development," 24 *Rutgers L. Rev.* 11, 16ff. (1969); Leopold Pospisil, *Anthropology of Law: A Comparative Theory* (1971), ch. 5, discussing the evolutionary theories of a number of thinkers from Montesquieu through Hoebel; David W. Trubek "Toward a Social Theory of Law: An Essay on the Study of Law and Development," 82 *Yale L.J.* 1 (1972); Geoffrey Sawer, *Law in Society* (1965), ch. IV; Niklas Luhmann, *Rechtssoziologie* (1972), vol I, pp. 132ff.

evolution of law—legal systems as a whole, individual rules or doctrines, or systems of rules? Are there "laws" of legal development?

On the question of *legal evolution,* there is a literature, some of it quite distinguished, stretching back more than a century. There is, however, some question whether the term "evolution" applies to law at all. Evolution means progress from some lower or less complex form to a higher or more complex form. In biology, evolution is a natural, automatic process. The road from protozoan to man was not "intended" by either party or by any links in between. Nor is biological "progress" inevitable. The amoeba survives alongside and sometimes inside man. In law, evolutionary theory would mean, first, that one can identify higher and lower stages in the growth of law—stages *A, B,* and *C,* and second, that one can say something empirically valid about the sequence or order of these stages. Not that all legal systems must reach the highest stage, stage *C,* but those that do must pass through *A* and *B* first.[20]

The search for such stages or patterns began before Darwin. Sir Henry Maine's *Ancient Law,* a landmark treatise, appeared in 1861. Maine felt that legal systems did change in a definite pattern or sequence; he traced it from the first Roman code, the Twelve Tables, to his own nineteenth-century law. The growth line, to be sure, was not uniform and relentless; it zigzagged somewhat, but the main contours were clear. Early law, Sir Henry felt, was patriarchal; the family, not the individual, was the legal unit to which rights and obligations inhered.[21] In early Roman law, as in biblical society, the father was monarch and head of the family, *de facto* and *de jure.* The state grew out of the family; the king or chief modeled his authority on patriarchal power. A person's duties and rights depended on his position in the family and his family's position in the social order. Birth decisively fixed one's legal and social position. Early society was a society of status.

This primitive condition did not last. "The movement of the progressive societies," Sir Henry wrote, in a famous passage, "has been uniform in one respect. Through all its course it has been distinguished by the gradual dissolution of family dependency, and the growth of individual obligation in its place. The Individual is steadily substituted for the Family, as the unit of which civil laws take account." What

---

[20]See Richard Schwartz and James C. Miller, "Legal Evolution and Societal Complexity," *70 Am. J. Sociology* 159 (1964).

[21]See, for example, Maine, *Ancient Law,* pp. 244–303.

principle replaced *status* as the basis for social organization? The new ruling principle was *contract*. "[W]e seem to have steadily moved towards a phase of social order in which all these [legal] relations arise from the free agreement of Individuals." Performance, not birth, ordered modern society; individual achievement, not status or ascription.[22] Stress on achievement, on contract, on the individual, was the result—indeed the point—of all those centuries of evolution. "[T]he movement of the progressive societies," in Sir Henry's grand dictum, "has hitherto been a movement from Status to Contract."[23]

Sir Henry was not the only social theorist to see a pattern more or less of this sort in the history of legal institutions; Émile Durkheim, in his famous work *The Division of Labor in Society*, set forth a theory of legal development. In primitive society, according to Durkheim, there was little or no division of labor. Rules and social norms were more or less common to all; they were "universal." Everyone shared them, and they acted as a kind of adhesive force in society. Durkheim called the principle of cohesion in these societies, "mechanical solidarity." Violation of norms threatened the very basis of social solidarity. Thus, early law was mostly penal. The law was simple and repressive; institutions were unspecialized. The whole community enforced the laws either directly or through institutions which "represented" the whole community.

Modern society, on the other hand, is bound together by "organic solidarity"—interdependence and division of labor flowing out of voluntary acts. Society is complex; its parts are highly specialized. The main concern of modern law is contract; through contract, people arrange their innumerable, complex relationships. Since contract and contract law are central to society, legal penalties are mostly civil and "restitutive." Their aim is not punishment but a "simple return to state." To adjust the many delicate relationships, society develops all sorts of agencies and tribunals, each one adapted to some special kind of transaction.[24]

---

[22]"A role is said to be 'ascribed' if its occupants acquire it automatically as a result of certain objective characteristics or relations to others which are beyond their control . . . birth into a particular family, birth order, sex, and age. . . . [A]ny role is said to be 'achieved' if it is not 'ascribed'." Harry M. Johnson, *Sociology: A Systematic Introduction* (1960), p. 140.

[23]Maine, *supra* note 21, p. 170.

[24]See Schwartz and Miller, *supra* note 20, pp. 159–169, especially p. 166, discussing the empirical validity of Durkheim's hypothesis. Students of legal process continue to draw on Durkheim for insights and hypotheses, particularly with regard to criminal justice. See, for example, Kai Erikson, *Wayward Puritans* (1966).

The sociologist Ferdinand Tönnies drew a distinction much like Durkheim's distinc-

Weber, too, dealt at length with legal development. He had no theory of legal evolution, strictly speaking, but he was intrigued by the chasm between the modern West and other and earlier societies. He set himself the lifelong task of unravelling the mystery of the Western world and its distinctive social and economic order. For Weber, rationality ruled modern, Western, capitalist society[25]; it pervaded religion, government, economic life, and law.

Weber divided legal systems into four basic types, according to whether lawmaking and law finding were *substantively* or *formally rational* or *substantively* or *formally irrational.* Legal process was "formally irrational" when its modes of decision could not be "controlled by the intellect." An oracle speaks, but does not give out reasons; it is unpredictable and uncontrollable. The Ten Commandments were enacted in a formally irrational way: Moses, claiming direct revelation, presented the tablets and announced: "This is the law." Trial by battle or the ordeal are irrational modes of settling disputes. There is no way to extract a general rule out of their results or to use reason to predict future outcomes. Even trial by jury, in English law, Weber noted, has an irrational flavor; like an oracle or an ordeal, it is uncontrollable by reason.[26]

"Rational" lawmaking and law finding, on the other hand, follow general principles and rules. The rational jurist or judge does not use or react to magic, nor is he swayed by concrete factors of the particular case. The theme of modern law is formal rationality—a "peculiarly professional, legalistic, and abstract approach to law." Modern law

---

tion between the two kinds of solidarity. *Gemeinschaft* meant a status community—the domain of "intimate, private, and exclusive living together. . . . In *Gemeinschaft* with one's family, one lives from birth on, bound to it in weal and woe." *Gesellschaft* meant "public life," an "imaginary and mechanical structure"—relationships of "business, travel or science." *Gemeinschaft* was "old"; *Gesellschaft* was "new as a name" and as a "phenomenon." Ferdinand Tönnies, *Community and Society (Gemeinschaft und Gesellschaft)*, ed. and trans. Charles P. Loomis (1957), pp. 33–34. The relationship of Tönnies' concepts to Maine's is also fairly obvious. Tönnies quotes Maine's passage on the "movement from Status to Contract" (ibid., pp. 182–183).

[25]See Chapter VIII, p. 208. On the concept of rationality in Weber's work, see Talcott Parsons' introduction to Max Weber, *The Theory of Social and Economic Organization* (1964), p. 80; on Weber's legal thought, see David Trubek, "Max Weber on Law and the Rise of Capitalism," 1972 *Wis. L.Rev.* 720.

[26]Max Rheinstein, ed., *Max Weber on Law in Economy and Society* (1954), pp. 63, 79. For Weber, lawmaking and law finding were "substantively irrational" when decision was "influenced by concrete factors of the particular case as evaluated upon an ethical, emotional or political basis rather than by general norms." Weber made a parallel distinction between formal and substantive rationality in economic process. See Max Weber, *The Theory of Social and Economic Organization* (1964), pp. 184–185.

takes into account "only unambiguous general characteristics of the facts of the case"; it is explicitly based on general principle. In formally rational law, "the legally relevant characteristics of the facts are disclosed through the logical analysis of meaning." Accordingly, "definitely fixed legal concepts in the form of highly abstract rules are formulated and applied."[27] The rational legal system is universalistic; the irrational is particularistic. The rational legal system looks towards contract, not toward status.[28] Weber does not state baldly that the rational is better than the irrational or that the irrational is a lower form of justice. However, the irrational, lacking conceptual vigor and principle, does not produce clear, predictable law; therefore, it may not suit the businesslike, bureaucratic, modern world. Modern law, then, is rational; ancient, pre-modern, and primitive law was irrational or at least stood lower on the scale of rationality.

There is wide agreement that, in some sense, modern law is more "rational" than older law. Talcott Parsons has gone one step further; he sees the rationality of law as a cause or prerequisite of modernization, not an effect. A universalistic legal system, Parsons argues, is tremendously "important to [the] further evolution" of society—an "evolutionary universal."[29] This means that "rather than emerging

---

[27]The formalism of law can be, according to Weber, of two types. In one, the "legally relevant characteristics are of a tangible nature," that is, are "sense-data," for example, a signature. Ibid., p. 63. The second is the type discussed in the text.

The reader will note that Weber's description of formal rationality fits continental law rather better than it does the common law. Indeed, the common law, as Weber recognized, is a bit wobbly in its rationality.

"Substantive rationality" accords predominance to "ethical imperatives, utilitarian and other expediential rules, and political maxims," which it uses as the source of norms. See p. 243; see also Trubek, *supra* note 25, pp. 746–748.

Other social scientists have found Weber's typology fruitful; see for example, Georges Gurvitch, *Sociology of Law* (1942), pp. 203–226.

[28]See Talcott Parsons, "Evolutionary Universals in Society," 29 *Am. Soc. Rev.* 339 (1964). Harry Johnson has explained the difference between universalism and particularism in this way:

[S]ome obligations derive from the fact that the other person has a certain social position. . . . For example, the obligations of a son toward his father depend upon the social position the father occupies in relation to the son; they do not depend to any great extent upon the kind of man the father is. Such obligations are "particularistic." . . . The role of judge in court, on the other hand, is strongly "universalistic." A judge is supposed to make decisions, not on the basis of the social position of the persons before the bench, but on the basis of strictly impersonal criteria of justice.

Johnson, *supra* note 22, p. 138. The relationship of these concepts to *status* and *contract* is obvious.

[29]Parsons, *supra* note 28, pp. 339, 340–341, 351.

only once," "various systems operating under different conditions," are likely to "hit upon" it, as they proceed from one stage to another. In another part of the same paper, Parsons defines a universal as a "complex of structures and associated processes the development of which so increases the long-run adaptive capacity of living systems in a given class that only systems that develop the complex can attain certain higher levels of general adaptive capacity." A "general legal system" is such a universal. Parsons defines a general legal system as an "integrated system of universalistic norms, applicable to the society as a whole rather than to a few functional or segmental sectors, highly generalized in terms of principles and standards, and relatively independent of both the religious agencies that legitimize the normative order of the society and vested interest groups in the operative sector, particularly in government." The traits implied by this definition are, on the whole, *formal* traits of law; for the most part too, they are variations on the theme of what Weber called *formal rationality*.

More recently, Marc Galanter tried to define what makes a legal system "modern."[30] He proposed eleven traits which, he felt, made up the "cluster of features that characterize, to a greater or lesser extent, the legal systems of the industrial societies of the last century."[31] Modern legal norms are "uniform and unvarying in their application"; the same rules apply to everyone in society. Modern law is also "transactional." Rights and duties flow out of "transactions"; they are not "aggregated in unchanging clusters" that attach to a person by birth or position. The legal system is hierarchic and bureaucratic; it has a regular chain of command. The system is "rational," meaning that it can be learned. Society values legal rules, because they are useful— "instrumental . . . in producing consciously chosen ends." Professionals run the law; lawyers replace "mere general agents," as the legal system grows more complex. The system is "amendable"; it does not have "sacred fixity." It is also "political," that is, connected to the state which holds a monopoly on law. Finally, legislative, judicial, and executive functions are "separate and distinct" in modern law.

Richard Schwartz and James C. Miller[32] used anthropological data

---

[30]Marc Galanter, "The Modernization of Law," in M. Weiner, ed., *Modernization* (1966), pp. 153, 154–156.

[31]Non-modern legal systems often show some of these traits, and advanced industrial societies might lack one or more to some degree. The traits then, are "not a description, but a model," useful to isolate the "common salient features" of legal systems of advanced industrial societies. Ibid., p. 154.

[32]"Legal Evolution and Societal Complexity," 70 *Am. J. Soc.* 159 (1964); their work has been extended by Howard Wimberley in "Legal Evolution: One Further Step," 79 *Am. J. Soc.* 78 (1973).

to try to draw a pattern of legal evolution. Taking materials from fifty-one societies, they showed that it was possible to "scale" the development of legal institutions. Some societies, in the lowest of four scale types, had no police, no lawyers (counsel), and no forms of mediation. The top group had all three. Societies seemed first to develop mediation, then police, and counsel last. No society had counsel, but not mediation and police; almost no society had police, but not mediation. Only seven societies in the sample (including Imperial Rome, Czechoslovakia, and Elizabethan England) had moved to the stage of "counsel." Most of the fifty-one societies were preliterate. The study, then, though interesting, tells little about legal evolution in historical periods. Basically, Sir Henry Maine picks up where Schwartz and Miller leave off.

Philip Selznick has advanced a theory of what one might call micro-evolution—how "law" develops in organizations rather than, or as well as, in society as a whole. For Selznick, the proper goal of a legal system or subsystem is "legality."[33] "Legality" is missing in a system if rules are made "arbitrarily," that is, without consulting "appropriate interests," where "no clear relation" exists "between the rule enunciated and the official end to be achieved," and where rules "reflect confused policies," are "based on ignorance or error," and "suggest no inherent principles of criticism." There is a higher stage, which Selznick calls "formal justice," where the system is bureaucratic and legalistic. "Formal justice" is an improvement but falls short of full legality. When that rare plane is reached, law is concerned with true "problem-solving"; and is "guided by a commitment to rationality, personal autonomy, and rather general social ideals."[34] A whole society can move up the scale of legality, so can its parts, and the same dynamic is or could be at work in the "legal system" of a factory, school, hospital, or prison, as well as in a country as a whole.

Selznick finds support for his theory, or at least analogy, in the literature on "moral progression" in children. Some researchers claim that children pass through definite stages in learning about rules. Each stage has its own style of argument and judgment about moral behavior.[35] Even very young children understand that if they do not behave they may be punished. Older children grasp a more sophisticated idea: the concept of law and order. Rules must be obeyed, not because of risk of punishment, but because society would fall apart without rules. Still

---

[33]Selznick's theory has a strong normative flavor as, indeed, do some of the other evolutionary theories. It is hard to resist the idea that what is modern and rational is better than what is old and irrational.

[34]Philip Selznick, *Law, Society and Industrial Justice* (1969), ch. 1, "Law, Society and Moral Evolution."

[35]The pioneer work was Jean Piaget, *The Moral Judgment of the Child* (1932).

later, some children learn and adopt more "autonomous moral princi-ples."[36] In a recent study, children of various ages were asked to com-ment on some laws proposed for an imaginary new community located on a far-off island: "that men over forty-five be required to have a yearly medical check-up"; and that "people [should] paint their houses at least once every five years." Only 4 percent of a group of eleven-year-olds thought that the medical examination might "infringe individual liber-ties"; this figure rose to 30 percent for eighteen-year-olds. Eighty-three percent of the eleven-year-olds, but only 41 percent of the eighteen-year-olds, uncritically accepted the laws.[37]

It is tempting to project these results onto a broader canvas. Cer-tain kinds of law and certain attitudes toward law are more "primi-tive," more "childish"; others are more "mature" or more "advanced." There is, then, a sort of natural progression or evolution in social life and in law.

But a few words of caution are in order. The evolution of moral *judgment* among children does not necessarily prove or predict legal *behavior* among adults. Moreover, the studies tested attitudes about a narrow band of propositions. How do we know that these are a good sample of the universe of legal propositions? Many norms, parking laws, for example, perhaps remain fixed at a "primitive" cost-benefit level; norms about murder, arson, and rape may become more heavily weighted with notions of morality and tradition in adult life.[38] A major argument of this book has been that norms and rules are very various. They come in different packages, supported by different brands of legitimacy, and are enforced by techniques used in different propor-tions.

Selznick apparently feels that there is a single best pattern of legality, which fits every institution, at least if it is big enough and sufficiently complex. This is an assumption, nothing more. Nor does it have an empirical base. Indeed, if the issue were not in doubt, if "legal-

---

[36]Lawrence Kohlberg, "Development of Moral Character and Moral Ideology," in M. Hoffman and L. Hoffman, eds., *Review of Child Development Research*, Vol. I (1964), p. 383; June L. Tapp and Lawrence Kohlberg, "Developing Senses of Law and Legal Jus-tice," 27 *J. Soc. Issues*, no. 2, 65 (1971); Joseph Adelson and Lynnette Beall, "Adolescent Perspectives on Law and Government," 4 *Law and Society Rev.* 495 (1970).

[37]Judith Gallatin and Joseph Adelson, "Legal Guarantees of Individual Freedom: A Cross-National Study of the Development of Political Thought," 27 *J. Soc. Issues*, no. 2, 93 (1971). The study found cross-national differences (among American, German, and British children), but these were not as vivid and clear-cut as developmental dif-ferences.

[38]See Chapter IV, pp. 68–69.

ity" were an automatic process rather than the result of continuous struggle, then there would be no point in exhorting men and institutions to move toward this goal; the theory would be descriptive rather than normative.

EVOLUTION THEORIES: SOME PROBLEMS

Evolutionary theories are plagued by a number of general and specific problems. One is the range of phenomena they consider. The theories lean on evidence drawn from the most formal parts of law. It is hard to do otherwise. Informal behavior is perishable, like the soft tissues of animals; historians, like paleontologists, have to rely on bones. Weber's typology is built chiefly out of formal legal thought. The traffic laws of London or Munich are surely part of the legal system of England or Germany. However, they are not "rational" in Weber's sense, nor did Weber pay much attention to them. If one looks at legal systems as a whole, the line between modern and non-modern law ceases to be so clear-cut. Modern law is certainly more bureaucratic, less inclined to magic and to ritual, but is it more "rational" than ancient law, in Weber's sense?

Sir Henry Maine's grand dictum about the movement from status to contract has a distinct aroma of nineteenth-century liberalism. In an age of active government, some have seen a "return to status." The century *since* Sir Henry's has hardly moved in the direction of free contract. Planned economies seem less "contractual" than Victorian England, at least less contractual than Victorian England fancied itself. Are the planned economies, then, the next step in legal evolution? In the modern welfare states, Scandinavia or England itself, there has been no return to status in the literal sense, yet the slogan "free contract" hardly does justice to the actual situation. Manfred Rehbinder suggests that the focal point of modern law is not status but *role.* The atomized individual whom the nineteenth century assumed has died; in his place is the role player, the man in social interaction.[39]

The scholars of the last century could not, of course, go beyond their data. *Ancient Law* begins with a discussion of the earliest Roman code. The Twelve Tables was a code, but it did not cover all of Roman law. There must have been other rules of law, nor were the Twelve Tables the true beginning; prior law is simply lost. New knowledge has cast doubt on the factual assumptions in Durkheim and Maine. Modern

---

[39]Manfred Rehbinder, "Status, Contract, and the Welfare State," 23 *Stan. L. Rev.* 941 (1971).

288 The Legal System: A Social Science Perspective

anthropologists have discarded the patriarchal theory,[40] and field studies do not support Durkheim's thesis that the law of simpler societies is mostly "penal."

The most general problem for evolutionary theorists is the problem of cause and effect. For example, how shall we look at Galanter's eleven traits? Are they causes or effects? If a legal system has these traits, or adopts them, or some combination, does the standard of living go up? Does industry develop, does the army modernize, does the polity become more democratic? What, if any, are the social consequences? There is no obvious answer, and it is entirely possible that the traits themselves are effects. As society modernizes, it tends to remake the law in these eleven ways. It is possible, too, that the traits have nothing to do with modernization, that the correlation is spurious. Countries where men wear neckties are richer on the whole than countries where men do not, but one could not modernize a country by changing its clothes.

The theorists, in the main, rarely meet the causal problem head on. Parsons, for example, insists that the English legal system was a "fundamental prerequisite" for modernization, that it was "no accident" that the Industrial Revolution started there.[41] But he brings no evidence forward.

The absence of general theory embarrasses virtually *all* schemes of legal evolution. This is a serious failing. What is the mechanism that generates legal development? Why should we expect development to move in a single direction? It is more reasonable to assume that types of legal systems vary according to the type of social system in which they are embedded. If factors *A*, *B*, and *C* create or imply a legal system of type *X*, then we will expect a legal system of type *X* whenever factors *A*, *B*, and *C* occur, whatever the period. In discussing legal reasoning, for example, we suggested that certain conditions would produce a closed system of reasoning whenever they occur. Legal reasoning did not, in short, "evolve." Closed and open systems appeared and disappeared in society as the generating factors themselves came and went.

Legal evolution assumes a kind of progress and in one line: orderly, sequential. There is no question that legal systems change and that the past never repeats itself. Legal history is not cyclical; the law of the Greeks and Romans is dead. Evolutionary theory, however, does not,

---

[40]See Robert Redfield, "Maine's *Ancient Law* in the Light of Primitive Societies," *3 Western Pol. Q.* 574 (1950).

[41]Talcott Parsons, "Evolutionary Universals in Society," 29 *Am. Soc. Rev.* 339, 353 (1964).

on the whole, bother with detail; it discusses change in terms of one, or two, or a few large, abstract features. The orderly, one-way sequence which so many theorists assume simply may not occur. Systems become more or less legalistic, more or less centralized, more or less litigious, swinging back and forth over the years. Complicated societies have complicated histories. Russian law, for example passed from czarist law through revolutionary legality, the legalism of the NEP (New Economic Policy) in the early 1920s, the lawlessness of the Stalinist terror, and then a partial rebirth of legal formalism. The history is instructive in may ways, but it gives no support to the idea of one single line of evolution. The same would, in fact, be true of lines of change in *any* national system or group of systems. Nor does it help to take a longer time period.   *must food for though*

Micro-evolution poses similar problems. The "law" of institutions does not move in one direction only. Systems shift from category to category, back and forth, in and out. If we look, not just at courts, but at the *whole* legal system, at all the laws, ordinances, and rules, at all the institutions that use them or carry them out, then the law of the United States and England and other nations, too, may well be *more* rigid, formal, and routine than two or three centuries ago. Legal systems today *must* be formal and routine. "Open" areas are important, but there cannot be too many of them. This is plain necessity in a modern society. The bank check must be standardized; there are too many of them to tolerate individuality. Parking violations cannot be mooted one by one. The future may continue down this road or veer off in some quite unforeseen direction. Who can say what type of arrangement is best for every conceivable society?

Even the normative assumptions of micro-evolution can be questioned. Handler and Hollingsworth write that the "discretionary distribution of benefits" is the "most serious and intractable problem in welfare administration."[42] One suggestion is to replace formlessness with form, to reduce freewheeling grace and discretion, to impose clear-cut rules. They feel, and many agree, that here a more mechanical system would be more just than a system in which social workers carefully and rationally assess each particular case.[43] This does not

---

[42]Joel F. Handler and Ellen Jane Hollingsworth, "Reforming Welfare: The Constraints of the Bureaucracy and the Clients," 118 *U. Pa. L. Rev.* 1167, 1184 (1970); see also Kenneth C. Davis, *Discretionary Justice* (1969).

[43]Liberals also generally approve the new developments in juvenile law. They feel judges should have less discretion and that stricter adherence to legal form will protect the juveniles better than the older system. Kenneth Davis wants more rules in general in the administrative process.

destroy Selznick's point, in itself. Selznick could argue that the old system of juvenile justice, despite its rhetoric, was a system low in legality. Judges and social workers acted arbitrarily; young defendants did not properly participate; rules were biased and confused. This is why formal legality was a definite advance. The trouble is, it is hard to tell the "arbitrary" stage from the stage of moral, informed, and autonomous legality. Sometimes the two look suspiciously alike. One man's "arbitrary" process may be another man's informed, autonomous problem-solving.

Is "legality," in Selznick's sense, always worth the price? The highest stage undoubtedly costs more than formalism—in money and time. Would it really be better than the slapdash way of handling parking fines? It *is* undoubtedly better for murder trials. Sometimes there are good reasons not to run a ship, a university, or even a country by strict "legality." No doubt there ought to be a heavy presumption in favor of legality, but the presumption can be, and often is, overcome.

If we abandon evolutionary theories of law, we need not stop drawing lines between different types of legal systems. No one could confuse the *content* of modern English law with the law of Edward I, or Augustus, or the Lozi. None of these had any railroad law or rules about wiretapping. Every new tool and technique, every new kind of social organization, drags along with it some change in legal norms. In law, despite Maitland's remark about the common law, substance is the leading sector; procedure and form follow substance and exist to serve its ends.

Is modern law also different in its *structure?* On the surface, this also seems true. Bureaucracy is characteristic of state and law today; government regulates business assiduously and gives out billions of dollars in welfare benefits. In modern, technological society, law has to be more definite, formal, and "legal" with less room for common sense norms than, for example, among the Lozi. Probably no structural aspect of modern law is absolutely new, but the mix is.

The biggest difference, perhaps, between modern and non-modern law is cultural. We have discussed the shift in theories of legitimacy from traditional to instrumental. Weber thought modern Western law was more rational than other systems. He used the word in a special sense. Whether modern law works better than ancient law depends on the goals of the legal system. It is possible that older systems held their societies together better than Mexican law or Swedish law does today or were just plain better at satisfying people. Whether modern law *is* rational or not, people think that it is or, more important, that it ought to be.

ON THE EVOLUTIONARY MOVEMENT OF RULES

Every legal change is a unique historical event. Social forces, history, and culture constantly work on the legal system, changing legal rules, or retarding, molding, and moderating change. Each legal change has its own life history. But there are certain typical patterns —paths which legal change tends to follow.[44]

Legal rules seem to be constantly changing. This comes as no surprise; social change itself is pervasive. Rule-makers work within institutions, they receive demands, and they respond. Moreover, institutions interact with each other. The people who work in them have superiors and inferiors. They want to do a good job; they have values; they wish to satisfy demands made upon them from inside and outside, to earn praise, and to avoid trouble and blame if at all possible. They want to protect their jobs; some too, will be eager to maintain or expand their power.

Legal institutions also have boundaries. Society places limits on their jurisdiction and authority. Sometimes these limits are vague; sometimes more definite. Most legal institutions, however, are subject to some sort of review, some sort of appeal, a limit of some kind on some area of work. The boundaries are fixed by law, by custom, by public opinion, sometimes even by physical necessity. There is likely to be some doubt about the exact location of the boundaries. Some institutions are less adaptable than others; some have less room to seek new power or to satisfy new demands. Adaptability can be a matter of personnel—people are rigid or flexible, risk-avoiders or risk-seekers. However, the concept of legitimate authority, socially defined for the agency, is more important; it surrounds every agency like an invisible, electrified fence. Some of these fences, to be sure, are more movable and flexible than others.

What bureaucrats and judges do are legal acts, and like other legal acts, they are responses to a mixture of motives. A lower court, deciding whether to change a rule or not, will consider the possibility of sanctions (the upper court may reverse with a reprimand, or there may be sanctions from other agencies of government); what various publics, including litigants, will think; and what its own training, conscience, sense of right conduct, or role dictates for the case. Each agency, whether a court, police force, or the Securities and Exchange Commission, will behave according to the pressure of these three groups of

---

[44]See Lawrence M. Friedman, "Legal Rules and the Process of Social Change," 19 *Stan. L. Rev.* 786 (1967).

factors. Jurisdictional rules do nothing more than express some of these in concrete form.

An agency puts out decisions and rules. Agencies which make rules tend to be more important than those which only make decisions. Where agencies do both, they are likely to think that their rules are more important than other outputs. Rules can be objective or discretionary.[45] A rule is objective when its terms are clear-cut and unambiguous. A discretionary rule cannot be carried into effect without the exercise of judgment. It is impossible to draw a hard and fast line between the two types of rule. A rule that a person may vote at age eighteen, we said, is relatively objective; a rule that the driver of a car is liable for damages "caused" by his "negligence" is, comparatively speaking, discretionary.

The legal system, at any given time, is generating new rules and changing the form and content of old rules. Some old rules are discretionary; some are not. The changes, too, go in both directions. Any living vital segment of the legal system moves to reduce uncertainty. Those who actually use the rules will want courts or other agencies to define the rules further, to make them more exact, and to lower the risks and costs of uncertainty. At the same time, new pressures crowd in on the legal system; these demands crack open well-settled rules and introduce uncertainty. Discretionary rules emerge where there were objective rules before. The discretionary rules are unstable. They will now be pushed toward further specificity. But a well-settled area of objective rules, if no one challenges it, may well remain stable.

Lawmakers and appliers spend much of their time making refinements, distinctions, and supplements to general rules. Partly, this is done on the flat surface of the rules (often statutes) themselves, partly by agencies which hold delegated power and make sub-rules. Factory regulation began in the nineteenth century with vague statutory rules; employers had to maintain "safe" places to work. A worker could presumably sue his employer, if the employer maintained an unsafe factory and the worker suffered an injury. But "safe" was a vague concept, and the process of finding out if a worker had a cause of action was therefore uncertain and expensive. Serious enforcement began only when states set up special agencies to regulate safety in factories.[46] The agencies promulgated rules. Some rules were discretionary; others were quite specific. The agency might specify that a factory was

---

[45]See Chapter II; Lawrence M. Friedman, "Law, Rules, and the Interpretation of Written Documents," 59 *Nw. U.L. Rev.* 751 (1965).

[46]E. g., Wis. Laws 1911, ch. 485, at 584.

"safe" only if it had a sprinkler system, a fire-retarding floor, windows of a certain kind and size, etc. The *statute* might remain highly discretionary so long as sub-rules were objective.

If *routine* is important, there is a great need for objective rules, and routine is important for volume. Transactions that must flow through a system in tremendous numbers will have to be standardized. Users of rules will be able to rely on objective rules and predict how the system will operate.

These are general conditions, and they suggest that living rules of law will *move toward objectivity* as part of their life cycle. A rule is living if consumers of law use it, if it is applied to or against real behavior by some agency, or if it is subject to challenge and controversy. Living rules tend toward mechanical, quantitative form. They have a theoretical resting point at which they are perfectly quantitative or mechanical. A rule reaches this point in one of two ways. Under pressure, the rule-makers may modify the rule itself into quantitative form, replacing all the empty, discretionary terms. Another way is to split a single, vague rule into a number of quantitative parts. So, the law can prismatically refract a rule about safe factories into sub-rules about window size, strength of floors, and so on.[47]

The more *quantitative* the rule, the more it lends itself to mechanical application or use. Objective rules are those which have numerical terms, by and large. There is no magic in numbers as numbers, but, in our society, number concepts are among the most mechanical and the most objective. A word has an objective meaning when everyone agrees on that meaning, when there is no controversy about its scope. People agree that twelve oranges make up a dozen, and they agree on how many oranges are twelve. They agree, too, about what an orange is. They might not agree about the taste, value, or beauty of the same dozen oranges; or on how many oranges are "a lot" or "enough." What eighteen-years-old means is much more definite than "old enough" or "mature" or "adult."

Many rules are quantitative, even though no obvious numbers appear in their texts. *Nothing* is also a quantitative term. A rule that includes a flat *no* is quantitative; the number term is zero. This is a common type of rule, which one might call a *rule of refusal*. The Supreme Court once held that it would hear no case which challenged the apportionment of electoral districts. This was a rule of refusal. It

---

[47]The term "rule-makers" here need not, of course, refer only to those at the statutory level; in other words, "living rule" must be understood to refer to a rule and all of its vertical sub-rules.

was objective and quantitative. The opposite of a rule of refusal is a *rule of reception*. A rule of reception is also quantitative. It contains or implies the word "all"; and a proposition with the word "all" can be turned upside down and rephrased as a rule with a "no." Thus, a rule that a court must hear appeals in *all* capital cases can be rephrased as a rule that the court can turn down *no* capital appeal.

A legal rule, of course, does not automatically change its form. The "tendency" of rules to move toward quantitative form is not a physical drift; nothing inherent in a rule pushes it in this direction. Everything depends on outside force. Except for purely technical changes or "law reform," only *challenges* produce changes in rules.[48] Many legal propositions, old rules, old statutes, and old doctrines never come before a court or any other body for challenge or interpretation. Some are dead rules; others are rules of high consensus. In court, the high cost of litigation puts a shield around many legal rules. The higher the costs of litigation, the less consensus is needed to protect a rule from challenge. More people will invest $100 to fight for a new rule than would invest $1,000. Sometimes, however, the state subsidizes challenge, and sometimes there are people who want or need to challenge a rule so intensely that they will overcome any obstacle. No rule is completely stable today, whatever its form, if public interest lawyers, or their clients, or the Sierra Club passionately want to overturn it. No tort rule is completely safe if millions and millions of dollars ride on overthrowing it, however unlikely.

In one sense, Jerome Frank was assuredly right. The results of a lawsuit are never certain. The outcome may *seem* foreordained in legal theory. But a litigant must always reckon with risks and intangibles which affect his actual chances. The risks are many: the judge and his personality; the jury, if any, and its quirks; the skill or ineptness of attorneys on both sides. It is always possible that someone will perjure himself in a persuasive way. There is always a chance of some accident or mistake at the trial. The facts and how to present them are always a problem; evidence which seemed solid as a rock can turn out to be inadmissible on technical grounds.

Very routine matters are the least uncertain—garnishments, parking cases, uncontested divorces. Any matter actually disputed car-

---

[48]Usually, in litigation, the plaintiff is the challenger, less commonly, the defendant. The rule stands or falls in the case the plaintiff brings or when the defendant challenges it in his defense. Once in a while, a court might change doctrine "on its own" or raise a point no litigant raised *in that case*. Here, however, someone had earlier presented the challenge, or the challenge was in the air so to speak.

ries a risk. The police will "win" all their parking cases, but not if a stubborn motorist comes to court. That changes the picture drastically. The riskless matters do not go to court, and anything that goes to court cannot be riskless. One speaks of the outcome of trials therefore in probability terms, like predictions of rain. When some person or group decides to challenge a rule, they make a guess about costs. A court challenge is bound to cost money. There is also an assessment of odds. If we challenge this rule, or its interpretation, trying to end it, or bend it, or open it up in some new way, how likely are we to win? Some rules are very clear-cut in the formal sense. Highway drivers must keep to the right. No one challenges this rule. The challenge is not worth the effort—there is no chance at all that a court can be persuaded to change it. Suppose a driver is arrested for driving, while intoxicated, on the left side of the road. His lawyer *could* theoretically build a defense by arguing that the rules of the road were invalid or that "right" in the wording of the law really means "left." These arguments have so microscopic a chance that one might as well assess them at zero. No one, then, will challenge the rule.

One can state, then, what kinds of rules are least subject to challenge and change. The answer is, on the surface, unexciting: the rules which would cost most to change. These are rules which are, first of all, formally clear-cut and secondly, buttressed by high social consensus. The two aspects are interrelated. Suppose it would cost $1,000,000 to mount a possible challenge, and the chances of winning would be one out of a thousand. This will deter everyone without the money or everyone who thinks the change is not worth the price. But *why* does the challenge cost so much? *Why* is the chance of winning so small? The sheer cost of *any* use of lawyers, courts, and legal process explains part, but only part. The rest comes from the toughness of the rule. The more social force supports a rule of law, the more costly and difficult to overturn it. A quantitative rule has an extra source of strength. It is supported by great consensus about what the rule should *mean*. If the rule is procedurally legitimate, it has still another pillar of support. If, in addition, some powerful group in society benefits from the rule as it is, it probably cannot be budged at all. No uncertainty exists in fact, and none can be fomented.

Quantitative rules, then, are only a special case of a larger category, that is, rules supported by one or another type of social consensus. If a statute sets the voting age at eighteen, it would be a waste of breath to argue in court that seventeen, nineteen, or twenty-five is a better age. No one would listen to the argument. The court would feel bound by the words of the statute. Courts are always "bound" by the law; what makes *this* language really binding is that the meaning is so plain. But a plain meaning is only a use of words about whose meaning people strongly agree, so that the judge cannot justify playing games with "interpretation." A court, then, would be a poor forum in which to try to change the voting age; the rules have great formal strength and great legitimacy. In fact, the United States did change the basic voting age from twenty-one to eighteen. Courts played no part in this change. There was no way to shift the voting age from twenty-one to eighteen, moving inch by inch, from case to case, and exploiting ambiguities in doctrine. It had to be done by fundamental attack, by a campaign for new laws and a constitutional amendment (the Twenty-sixth Amendment, ratified 1971). The process was costly and long-winded, but it worked.

A statute fixing the voting age benefits from a double consensus: first, as to the meaning of the words and second, about how judges should react to such words. For all we know, the substantive consensus may be shaky—some people may think eighteen is too old or too young; some may prefer a sliding scale; some might want to handle the question case by case. If so, the rule will be unstable, but not in court. This was precisely the case with the old rule, setting the age at twenty-one. The rule changed—but not in court.

Contrariwise, high consensus about a situation will protect a rule or doctrine even when the words are not objective. Oliver Wendell Holmes in a famous passage stated that the right of free speech did not mean the right to shout "fire" in a crowded theater. But why? The First Amendment, which sets out the right of free speech, says nothing about shouting, fires, or crowded theaters, nor do the cases. Holmes meant that general opinion would refuse to condone such an act or treat it as legitimate expression. In the nineteenth century, no one seriously argued that the right of free speech protected hard-core pornography. It was unthinkable that "freedom of speech" meant naked people doing their act on a stage.

To repeat: three kinds of consensus affect the stability of rules—consensus about words, about the role of institutions, and about outcomes. A rule heavily supported by all three would be hardest and most costly to change. Perhaps, of the three, the weakest and most vulnerable is consensus about the meaning of words, at least in the long run, and with regard to *some* words. Many rules which seem formally clear-cut are a mass of confusion in practice. Repeated litigation or challenge has generated complexity; the meaning of the words gets unstuck; doctrine comes to mirror the confusion and controversy raging in the outside world. Uncertainty encourages still further challenges, since experience shows that the rule has soft spots, that it bends like rubber. The fate of invented ambiguity has overtaken the Statute of Frauds, originally passed in England in the seventeenth century.[49] The text, which makes certain classes of contract unenforceable unless they are in writing, is reasonably straightforward. But business, the courts, and litigants apparently do not agree on the subject. The statute promotes formality; this is generally in harmony with commercial practice, but it is not the custom to write memos for *all* transactions. A literal reading of the statute, since it flaunts custom and refuses to enforce real agreements on technical grounds, sometimes leads to "unfair" results. Centuries of opinions have battered against the statute; whole treatises can be and have been written about its case law. The meaning of the words has been twisted radically out of shape.

Litigants usually do not challenge a clear-cut statute that has popular support. But sometimes, for whatever reason, litigants feel strongly enough about an issue to go against the averages, that is, they attack a rule which is *formally* clear-cut and institutionally stable as well. These are usually lost causes, but the very challenge introduces some uncertainty, some imbalance. The plaintiff may be an isolated eccentric throwing his money away. But if he represents some social force, his action may give the public a message, catalyze debate, begin a process. If enough people hammer away at a rule which, in theory, is well-settled, they stand a good chance of unsettling the rule. Here, however, we would always have to ask: *Why* are so many attacking this settled rule? They, or their lawyers, or both, sense some change in the wind, or else the matter is so vital to the litigants that they cannot or will not face "reality." The pioneers in civil rights cases showed something of this dogged intensity. High costs in court act as a conservative force or, more accurately, as a channeling force. They close off the courts to any but well-recognized causes of action. They reinforce the role of the courts in reflecting the way in which power actually lies. Unrecognized causes of action can burst through, but only if their adherents are very intense, or have become very numerous or extremely powerful or rich, or if the change is one which has subtly gained a general strength, so in hindsight one could say its time had come. The costs, in short, do not shut off all avenues of evolution, but they raise the threshold price of change.

When open-ended rules are repeatedly challenged, the natural response is to reframe the rules in the direction of the mechanical, that is, toward objective terms. We will take judge-made rules as an exam-

---

[49]28 Ch. II, ch. 3 (1677).

ple. How does a court react to unusual challenge? Every case is a challenge of sorts, but most of these are minimal. Litigation is the court's normal business. Requests for change mostly come disguised as no-change or small change. Ordinary cases do not threaten the court as an institution in any way.

Once in a while, however, a case arises which is exceptionally delicate or new. It may contain a serious challenge and provoke or threaten some crisis. It is useful, however, to draw a line between *recurrent* and *non-recurrent* crises. Two famous Supreme Court cases illustrate what makes a crisis *non-recurrent*. In *Wilson* v. *Girard*,[50] an American soldier stationed in Japan was guarding a machine gun. Nearby, in a field, Japanese civilians were gathering spent cartridge cases. Girard put a cartridge case into a grenade launcher, fired it, and killed a woman. A mammoth furor arose in Japan. By treaty, the United States could insist on trying Girard in American courts, but the government in response to Japanese pressure waived jurisdiction. Girard brought suit in federal court, claiming his rights to American justice. In a crisp, short decision, the Supreme Court denied him relief. The political point was obvious. Afterwards, the Japanese tried Girard, convicted him, and gave him a rather mild sentence. The incident died down into history. What was needed here was quick and decisive resolution, and the court obliged.

The great Steel Seizure Case of 1952[51] is another example of a non-recurrent crisis. The Korean War was on; a steel strike was brewing. To ward off the strike, President Truman seized the industry. This was bold, almost unprecedented action; it raised a storm of controversy. Had Truman exceeded the powers of the presidency? This was the basic issue in the case, which moved quickly to the Supreme Court for resolution. In one sense, the case went to the heart of presidential power. Yet realistically, this was a non-recurrent case. Some president might, in the future, indeed seize a major industry again. If so, he would surely cite the earlier case as precedent. But in the American system, a president does not seize a basic industry every day or for frivolous reasons. Each situation of seizure will be difficult, delicate, special; each will be uniquely time-bound; each will be politically volatile. These factors dilute the importance of precedent almost to the vanishing point.

A crisis is non-recurrent when some particular person or event

---

[50] 354 U.S. 524 (1957).

[51] *Youngstown Sheet and Tube Co.* v. *Sawyer*, 343 U.S. 579 (1952); the background and progress of the case are set out in Alan Westin, *The Anatomy of a Constitutional Law Case* (1958).

brings it on. Paradoxically, then, many crises are not crises for the court as an institution at all. The court decides them efficiently and in a rather satisfying way. Society wants and needs some legitimate, impartial tribunal to put non-recurrent crises to rest. The recurrent crisis is, institutionally, far more serious. A new problem or issue may have emerged from the social background. The courts may have given an encouraging response to some strong, new demand. Social forces, ranged on either side of the issue, clamor for definition and solution of the problem. This is a crisis which a single stroke does not banish. One case brings on another.

The rational court will try to reduce the crisis to easily managed proportions. It will try to develop a rule to get rid of the problem—a rule it can delegate to others. Of course, the solution must be "right." It must be lawful and correct, as the court sees it, and it must "solve" the problem for the outside world. But the rule should have the right *form* as well. The ideal rule should answer whatever questions people who use it might reasonably ask and end the constant probing lawsuits. The rule should be as objective, as quantitative as possible. Objective, quantitative rules are easy to apply in lower courts, other agencies, and among the public. Such rules invoke social consensus about the meaning of words and about the role of the court. Ideal rules, then, will be numerical rules, or rules of refusal, or rules with very clear-cut terms.[52]

The reapportionment cases of the 1960s illustrate the movement of doctrine toward quantitative form. In the United States, state legislatures draw boundary lines for electoral districts. Many legislatures, however, were reluctant to redraw lines despite population change. This froze district lines in such a way as to favor rural areas over cities and suburbs. State constitutions called for periodic reapportionment, but the legislatures, dominated by rural assemblymen, paid no attention. In many states—California, for example—the upper house of the legislature was even more distorted than the lower house. Six million people in Los Angeles County had one vote in the California senate; so too did three mountain counties which had a total population of only 14,000 people among them.[53]

Legislatures would not reform; reform would mean voting away

---

[52] A rule of refusal may seem too negative to solve pressing problems or to meet new social demands. In fact a rule of refusal may be innovative and dramatic; for example, a rule that no branch of government could censor any book, for any reason, including obscenity or that the court could not review any action of the president.

[53] *Silver* v. *Jordan*, 241 F.Supp. 576 (S.D. Cal., 1964), *aff'd per curiam*, 381 U.S. 415 (1965), put an end to this system.

their own jobs. Until 1960, the courts were almost equally discouraging. They answered requests for reform with a flat rule of refusal, the so-called "political question" doctrine.[54] Reapportionment was a "political thicket," not suited "for judicial determination."[55] The rule of refusal had all the *formal* requirements to lay the issue at rest. It was quantitative and clear. The trouble was it was wrong as a substantive solution. It was not a compromise rule, and those who demanded change simply would not accept it as final.

The rule *had* an effect, of course. It set up heavy odds against change, but the price was not high enough to keep litigants away. There was a further problem: In *Colegrove* v. *Green*, decided in 1960, the rule of refusal won only a bare majority. This close division was a sign of instability; it gave hope to those who wanted change. New justices and slight variations in facts encouraged fresh attacks. In *Gomillion* v. *Lightfoot* (1960),[56] plaintiffs complained that the boundaries of Tuskegee, Alabama, had been gerrymandered to keep blacks from voting in city elections. The Court agreed and voided the boundary lines. *Gomillion*, said the Court, was not the same at all as *Colegrove* v. *Green*, where there was no racial issue. Nonetheless, it was easy to read *Gomillion* as another sign of weakness in the rule of refusal. The rule of refusal, in other words, no longer seemed a flat *no*. It was a maybe, and a maybe, unlike a no, is not a quantitative term. A rule of refusal with this weakness loses even its formal claim to govern.

In *Baker* v. *Carr* (1962),[57] a majority of the Court abandoned the rule of refusal. Plaintiffs in this famous case attacked the apportionment of the Tennessee assembly. They claimed that many people in the state were underrepresented and thus were denied the "equal protection of the laws." The Supreme Court's actual holding was narrow: merely that plaintiffs had stated a valid complaint and were entitled to be heard. The case was sent back for full trial.

Baker v. *Carr* provoked much comment, some quite critical. The case undid the rule of refusal and paved the way for further evolution. Legislatures might have taken the hint and worked out their own solutions. The rule in *Baker* v. *Carr* was formally unstable. It lacked

---

[54] The "political question" doctrine had served the Court well on other occasions; it was a good rule of evasion to avoid conflict with the executive branch or to keep out of areas that might threaten the prestige of the Court. The leading case on the "political question" doctrine was *Luther* v. *Borden*, 17 U.S. (7 How.) 1 (1849), arising out of the so-called Dorr rebellion in Rhode Island.

[55] *Colegrove* v. *Green*, 328 U.S. 549 (1946).

[56] 364 U.S. 339 (1960).

[57] 369 U.S. 186 (1962).

objectivity; it could survive only if it led to out-of-court compromise or touched on some wellspring of consensus, or if the matter was so trivial that it ceased to agitate the law. *Baker* v. *Carr* moved toward a solution in the *substantive* sense, but in the formal sense, it was a step *away* from a stable solution. It overturned an objective rule and put a discretionary rule in its place. Within one year after *Baker* v. *Carr*, there were seventy-five cases on reapportionment pending in the federal courts.[58] Every legislative body was under a legal cloud. A few legislatures made minimal changes. Reform groups, who now smelled victory, refused to accept these. The Supreme Court felt forced to meet the ultimate question head on: What standards should guide reapportionment? In other words, the court was asked to frame the solution itself, then hand it on to lower courts and other agencies.

What happened next is well-known. Briefly, the Court moved toward a *formal* solution. Six cases, headed by *Reynolds* v. *Sims*[59] (1964), ruled, in essence, that states must apportion both houses on a strict population basis. The language of the case, to be sure, was cautious, stressing the need to handle each situation carefully and individually and conceding that states did not need to draw their lines with "mathematical" precision. Yet, on the whole, the Court did *not* frame a discretionary rule. The actual rule is often loosely referred to as "one man, one vote." This loses some of its subtleties but accurately reflects the central point. The Court drafted a rule that would solve the problem *formally*—in short, a quantitative rule.

Of course, a hard and fast rule is only an attempt to solve a problem. A rule must also "solve" the social and institutional problem. This it does if it wins enough acceptance so that the cost of challenge, measured against the likelihood of change, will deter those groups still opposed. If not, these groups will repeatedly challenge the rule, and the Court will have to retreat or suffer some loss in power or prestige. The Court cannot know in advance how the matter will end. In the reapportionment cases, the immediate reaction was ominous. There were angry cries from wounded politicians, a proposed constitutional amendment,[60] fulminations in the press, and waspish carping in the law reviews. But then these passed; now the decision seems firmly, even serenely, entrenched. Even during the period of protest, the opposition worked on Congress, not on the Court—a sign of hopelessness, vis-à-vis the Court, if not of acquiesence.

---

[58]R. Hanson, *The Political Thicket* (1966), p. 57.

[59]377 U.S. 533 (1964).

[60]See Alexander M. Bickel, *Politics and the Warren Court* (1965), pp. 148ff.

Many factors, then, determine when a rule will be stable. The first, and no doubt most important, is its level of support in society. This support cannot be measured by a head count of citizens.[61] The legal system has many facets, angles, and institutions. An institution often has its own special constituency; the support of this constituency is more important than that of the rest of the public. The federal courts, for example, have played a special role as guardians of the rights of minorities. Minority groups are significant customers for the courts. Rules unacceptable to them will tend to be unstable, that is, open to repeated challenge, even if a diffuse national majority (and an intense majority of the Jackson, Mississippi, city council) supports the rules.

The *form* of a rule also affects its stability. This counts less than the level of social support, but is not trivial. Objectivity is vital to the application of law. Ultimate use of a rule is always concrete. One either does or does not arrest Mr. Smith. A court either does or does not award Blackacre to the plaintiff. A jury awards a plaintiff $10,510.63 for his injury. A verdict of a "reasonable" amount would be absurd; the matter must end somewhere; anything else is delegation. Similarly, appellate decisions are binary; they take a simple yes-no form; they reverse or affirm.

Objectivity affects the cost of challenging a rule. A plain, straight rule, a mathematical rule, is safer from attack than a vague rule. As we pointed out, this is only a special case of a more general proposition: that what keeps a rule stable is its social support. Objectivity, in this society at least, affects social judgment about the legitimacy of judicial behavior. The plainer the meaning of the words in a law, the tighter the court is bound to follow them as written. Other agencies, of course, may have more freedom of action—the legislature, for example, which has primary legitimacy.

The reapportionment rule followed the path from discretionary to objective form. This path is typical, but by no means inevitable; it is not a "law." Nor does a rule move with any particular speed. Some rules take centuries to change to objective form. Everything depends on the strength and will of the litigants, that is, the moving social force. In the legal system, at any given time, many rules are in motion; others are stable and at rest. Many rules can be analyzed as moving toward the quantitative. At the same time, some rules, which represent old compromises and balances, are under attack. The attacks, if strong and frequent enough, may break open formally stable rules and start them on their travels in search of new, more acceptable solutions. Rules and

---

[61]See Chapter VI, pp. 162–165.

rule-makers, flushed out of one burrow, run about like frightened rabbits till they find another, hopefully one of more permanent repose.

At any given time, one finds some issues whose formal solution is hopelessly unpredictable. Forces are well balanced, the courts divided and confused, society torn apart over means and ends. Here all will be uncertainty and flux; litigants will constantly test the boundaries of doctrine. At present, obscenity law is in this position. The nineteenth-century consensus on the limits of sexual candor has completely broken down.[62] No new consensus has replaced it. It is easy to dream up a rule which would provide formal stability. The courts might end, once and for all, any censorship of books. But a large part of the articulate public is unwilling to accept this; and the court has never wanted to go so far. No objective test of obscenity has ever been acceptable to the court. Such a test would be hard to devise. Existing "tests" are empty formulae. There is no logical resting place. Public opinion is vigorous on all sides of the issue. No stable delegation is in sight; the issue is stalled at dead center. Courts rule on *particular* movies and books, one by one; they make feeble attempts to generalize, and doctrine wobbles back and forth.[63]

Common-law courts, by tradition, have denied that they made up new rules. Even today, judges change the law, by and large, in a gradual way, bit by bit. Judicial behavior is supposed to be slow, evolutionary, creeping along a continuum. Tradition favors clandestine change. Tradition supports vague, qualitative rules, rules rather empty of content, rules capable of expansion by small degrees, discretionary rules that conceal the fact of change. But these traditional ideas inhibit the courts when pressure seems to call for new rules. Stable rules, as we have seen, tend to be quantitative. How can a court reconcile its *institutional* need for stable rules with these cultural constraints? Courts have at their disposal a number of techniques. They can, for example, absorb some quantitative term which has independent meaning or legitimacy, either in the legal system or in the outside world. The rule against perpetuities which limits how long property can be "tied

---

[62]For background, see Norman St. John-Stevas, *Obscenity and the Law* (1956), pp. 100–171. The United States Supreme Court did not decide any important case on obscenity and free speech until *Roth* v. *U.S.*, 354 U.S. 476 (1957). The question, what *is* obscene, had been litigated from time to time beforehand. Judge Woolsey's decision, in *U.S.* v. *One Book Called "Ulysses,"* 5 F. Supp. 182 (S.D. N.Y. 1933), was a landmark case.

[63]See Raymond F. Sebastian, "Obscenity and the Supreme Court; Nine Years of Confusion," 19 *Stan. L. Rev.* 167 (1966). Lately the Supreme Court has tried to throw the whole matter back to the states. With what success, only time will tell. *Miller* v. *California*, 413 U.S. 15 (1973).

up" in a trust or some similar arrangement[64] illustrates this technique. The rule grew slowly and reached its quantitative stopping point around 1800. In its classical form, the rule invalidated any future interest unless it would vest within "lives in being," plus twenty-one years. Why twenty-one years? Twenty-one was the common-law age of majority, the age at which a minor left "the empire of the father," and entered "the empire of reason."[65] There was some point in framing the rule, partly in terms of the distance from birth to legal majority. But the number twenty-one had special virtue for the rule; that is, it already had a legal meaning. Thus the courts could import it into a newly shaped rule without seeming to pass beyond institutional limits.

RULE-SYSTEMS

So far, we have discussed patterns of change in individual rules. But the same logic applies to rule-*systems,* networks of interrelated rules. Rule-makers will move systems of rules toward objective, quantitative form for much the same reasons and under much the same conditions as single rules. The key concept, once more, is challenge. A person in authority prefers, no doubt, to have a free hand. A teacher likes to run his own classroom, a judge his own juvenile court. Authority does not like binding rules. But when challenged, authority will retreat toward greater specificity. We earlier pointed out that codification often served as a kind of treaty limiting the power of magistrates. Moreover, we saw that society needs formal "law" when consensus breaks down. Specificity is a higher degree of formalization than non-specificity. The less trust, the less acquiescence in discretion, the greater the need for hard-and-fast rules. Hence, areas of living law struggle toward acceptable compromises between opposing sides; these take quantitative form. This observation applies to whole "fields" of law, to codes and statutes, as well as to judicial rules. It even applies to movement across institutions, for example, *from* judge-made law to code law.

One common and illuminating pattern goes as follows: First, an authority enunciates a rule. The rule applies to a life-situation which is or becomes the subject of conflict. In the process of pulling and hauling, the single rule splits under pressure. Courts and other bodies develop a whole system of more and more complicated rules. Finally

---

[64]The classic American formulation of the rule is in John Chipman Gray, *The Rule Against Perpetuities* (1886).

[65]1 *Blackstone's Commentaries,* 453.

the groups on various sides of the issue work out a new legal solution in compromise form. This will probably be more mathematical, more objective than the prior state of the law.

We will use the law of industrial accidents as a convenient example.[66] We can take the fellow-servant rule as our starting point. This was a simple rule of refusal. An injured workman could not sue his employer, if the negligence of a fellow-servant, that is, another workman, was the cause of the accident. In modern industrial society, the rule took from the workman *any* practical remedy for injury. "Employers" were mostly corporations or absent entrepreneurs. Negligence on the job had to be the negligence of a fellow-servant. The injured workman could, of course, sue his co-worker, but workers had no money and did not carry insurance.

As we noted, the fellow-servant rule can be conventionally traced to an English case *Priestley* v. *Fowler* decided in 1837.[67] Four years later, an American court adopted the rule in a railroad case.[68] By the 1860s, the rule was universally in force. It was not finally abolished until the states adopted workmen's compensation systems; this they did one by one between 1911 and 1948.

The fellow-servant rule was harsh, but formally speaking, it was stable. Still, after one generation of enthusiasm, it began to lose its political strength. When the rule was first adopted, it fit what influential people thought was needed to help the economy grow. Transport and manufacture had to be coddled.[69] This stage of great popularity did not last. Once the railroads were built, for example, there was less passion for encouraging them at any cost. The rise of labor unions added a powerful adversary. In court cases, judges were not immune to feelings of sympathy. The rule was strong medicine; men were crippled or killed in industrial accidents, leaving families in need. It was hard to refuse some relief for the victims. Judges and juries began to manipulate the rule. Some litigants won.

This weakened the rule, however; and the weakness had an inevitable effect: It encouraged more litigation. The courts developed "exceptions." Soon the rule was no longer clear-cut; it no longer solved the

---

[66]See Lawrence M. Friedman and Jack Ladinsky, "Social Change and the Law of Industrial Accidents," 67 *Colum. L. Rev.* 50 (1967).

[67]150 Eng. R. 1030 (Ex. 1837), but see Chapter VII, p. 171.

[68]*Murray* v. *South Carolina RR.*, 26 S.C.L. (1 McMul.) 385 (1841); followed soon by the influential case of *Farwell* v. *Boston & W. RR.*, 45 Mass. (4 Metc.) 49 (1842).

[69]See J. Willard Hurst, *Law and the Conditions of Freedom in the Nineteenth Century United States* (1956); Stanley I. Kutler, *Privilege and Creative Destruction, the Charles River Bridge Case* (1971).

problem even *formally*. Only continued loyalty could guarantee efficiency for such a rule. It did not get or keep this loyalty. No doubt, the rule prevented thousands of lawsuits, but it did not choke off *all* industrial accident actions. The weaker it got, the less it achieved its purpose. Litigants and lawyers saw the weakness and brought more cases. At the height, or depth, of its amazing career, the simple rule had spawned an incredible complex of sub-rules, exceptions, and exceptions to exceptions. Whole treatises were written on the subject. A text on the law of master and servant, published in 1913 on the eve of abolition, spent no less than 524 pages discussing the ins and outs of *one* of the sub-rules.[70] There were literally thousands of reported cases on the fellow-servant rule and uncounted numbers of lower court decisions.

The system of rules now included statutes and pieces of statutes. These too showed how far consensus about the doctrine had broken down and the growing strength of opposing pressure groups. As early as 1855, a Georgia law sharply cut back the rule for railroad cases.[71] Twenty-five states tampered with the rule, as regards railroads, before 1911, yet railroad accidents had once been the prime source of accident litigation. Every year legislatures bit deeper and deeper into the rule.

In this middle period, the rule was so complex and so costly that it benefited no one, not industry, not labor. Most workmen did not recover any damages; yet industry spent vast sums on insurance, lawyers' fees, and other frictional costs. The stage was set for a compromise. This was workmen's compensation, which put an end to the fellow-servant rule once and for all.[72] Compensation laws made the employer liable without fault for any industrial accident. But the law also placed strict limits on the *amount* of recovery. Under the old tort system, the jury was free to award whatever it liked in damages. But in Wisconsin, for example, under the 1911 law, if an accident caused "partial disability," the worker could not receive payments of more than 65 percent of his wages while disabled. The total recovery could be no more than four times his average annual earnings.[73] The new

---

[70]This was the so-called vice-principal rule, the rule that an employee could sue, if the negligence was that of a supervisory employee, a "vice-principal." The text is C. Labatt, *Commentaries on the Law of Master and Servant,* 4 vols. (1913).

[71]Ga. Acts 1855, No. 103. Railroad workers could recover for injuries caused by fellow-servants, so long as they themselves were free of negligence.

[72]The first statute to survive a court test was Wisconsin's, upheld in *Borgnis* v. *Falk Co.,* 147 Wis. 227, 133 N.W. 209 (1911); an earlier New York law had fallen, *Ives* v. *South Buffalo Ry.,* 201 N.Y. 271, 94 N.E. 431 (1911). Mississippi was the last state to enact a compensation law, Miss. Laws 1948, ch. 354.

[73]Wis. Laws 1911, ch. 50, § 2394–9(d).

system in short was precise, objective, actuarial. It was meant to be quantitative and clear—a new and hopefully stable resting point, like the rule against perpetuities or the rule of one-man, one-vote. And the law was a substantive compromise. It captured the huge frictional cost of the old system. It compromised the issues, gave both sides some advantages, made litigation less likely, and divided the savings between capital and labor.

Industrial accident law thus developed in three stages. In the first stage, the rule appeared—simple, objective, clear-cut. In the second stage the rule broke down; it became "riddled with exceptions." In the third stage, the legal system started afresh. It codified a new rule-system, made up, for the most part, of clear-cut rules. There is an obvious resemblance to the reapportionment story. There too a mechanical rule, a rule of refusal, broke down; a complex period of unsettlement followed; then came a stable resting point, once more quantitative and mechanical. In one case, a single rule changed form; in the other, a rule split up into a whole set of rules and ended up as a major codification.

Social theories of law suggest that at any given time existing rules reflect with rough accuracy those social forces actually bearing on the subject of the rules. Sometimes, one interest group is clearly dominant. In court cases, one party wins and one party loses. Compromise is not uncommon, but it is not in any event the norm. In whole *systems* of rules, judicial, or legislative, or both, it is much less likely that one side totally prevails and another loses out. The legal system will probably reflect *all* social forces in proportion to their influence and power. Yet no interest group has absolute power and none absolute zero, at least in theory.[74]

The problem of legal change is a little like Zeno's paradox, the race between the tortoise and the hare. Any given state of law is a kind of equilibrium. Everybody's interest is reflected in proportion to his power. How then is it possible to change? The simplest explanation is that the outside context changes. The map of power shifts. Wars, acts of God, new technology, or development or decay of the economy alter social relations, and legal change follows rapidly, obediently, thereafter.

Change in attitude or perception can also be the spur, altering in kind or amount the pressure of the social world on the legal system.

---

[74]In practice, some groups have their way, for all intents and purposes, in particular sub-areas which society concedes to them; and some groups are such pariahs that they gain little or nothing of value.

As we have noted, *interests* in the abstract do not make law. What makes law are *demands*—social force actually applied. An "interest" of an "interest group" is not a fact of the real world like a horse or a hurricane; it is merely a perception. Perceptions come and go. People who felt that Los Angeles needed more highways turn into people who feel that highways are ruining the city. Reformers argue, persuade, mobilize, mold, and manipulate opinion. They persuade, in the main, by bending perceptions of interest. A successful reformer affects the amount of force that will bear against legal institutions. He persuades people to write their congressmen or bring lawsuits—even to riot in the street. Equally important, people must believe or be persuaded that it is practical and right for them to demand from the law what they see as their interests or needs.

At any given time, many rules and rule-systems are stuck in the middle stage of their three-stage development.[75] This stage is unstable and inefficient. It is costly in dollars spent on litigation, not to mention the many other costs of uncertainty. Sometimes a point is reached at which battling interest groups finally realize how much they all suffer from this lack of efficiency; they discover that they can move without loss to a new and better stage of law. They can expropriate the friction costs and divide them among themselves. This too is a source of legal change. One way to look at workmen's compensation, for example, is as an implicit agreement between business and labor that they would come out ahead if they abolished the old tort rules, swept lawyers, insurance, and litigation away, captured these costs, and redivided them among themselves.

In the first stage, in other words, a dominant interest or some popular viewpoint gets a rule enacted or adopted in its favor. The rule will usually be clear-cut; it will distribute rights, goods, or power as the dominant interest wishes. The fellow-servant rule served business and the railroads; people of influence probably generally supported it.

The second stage may follow exogenous changes in power. By 1880, labor had gained muscle; railroads were no longer the darlings of public opinion. But business in general, and the railroads in particular, still remained strong. This was a stage of conflict, struggle, and adjustment —therefore, of legal complexity. Formal efficiency gave way to inefficiency. The law became "confused," muddled, difficult. Frictions produced a multitude of rules and counter-rules. The rule-system repre-

---

[75]See, for one example out of many, the description of the law and practice relating to imprisonment for debt in New York in Peter J. Coleman, *Debtors and Creditors in America: Insolvency, Imprisonment for Debt, and Bankruptcy, 1607–1900* (1974), p. 121.

sented more or less accurately the balance of forces. Society was hope-lessly divided over industrial accidents. The rule-system mirrored these divisions. The inefficiencies, however, did not in themselves benefit the contending forces. They benefited only the middlemen—lawyers and insurance adjusters among others.

Before stage three, the inefficiency became gross and manifest. It became rational then to capture the costs and redivide them by some formula of compromise. Such an outbreak of rationality is not inevitable; it may come slow or fast; frequently reformers help it along; ideological disputes, hatred between groups, may delay it. The fresh start will be a new, clear-cut rule or system of rules; it will reflect relationships of power but more efficiently than the rules in the second stage. Stage three was the stage of workmen's compensation.

What has been described is a model, a picture, a pattern, not a theory. It is a model that fits reality at many points. It helps explain why some areas of law are "muddled" or "confused" and others clear-cut. There is no way to predict how long a rule or rule-system will stay in one stage. That depends upon interests, perceptions, and events. Some rule-systems are mired so deeply in stage two that one wonders if they will ever emerge. The legal profession, one must remember, has a pocketbook interest in stage two, the stage of complexity, and will fight to maintain it, tooth and nail. The struggle for "no-fault" in auto accident law is a struggle for stage three over the dead bodies (so to speak) of lawyers who make money out of accident litigation.

Of course, there are other patterns of legal change. The starting point (stage one) may be a *vague* rule, a rule of total delegation. This too may flow from a situation of dominant power. Before *Gault*, a vague rule of broad delegation gave utter dominance to judges in juvenile courts.[76] Right now, the system is rapidly moving, but to what destination is unclear. Different social situations require different starting points.[77] A rule of private entitlement must be clear-cut; a rule under which the state exerts dominance, like the teacher in an old-time class-room or the Puritan magistrate, can be vague and broad, delegating enormous power to itself or to others. In any case, rules flow from the social setting. They change as it changes. They rise and fall with these forces, like a tide, obeying the pull of a power that cannot be seen.

---

[76] In one sense, however, the power of juvenile judges depended on a rule that upper courts would not tamper with the holdings of the juvenile judge. This was, of course, a rule of refusal.

[77] It is worth repeating that each rule is a "starting point" only for analytical purposes. In the real life of the law, one does not find neat "stages." Each rule is a beginning, middle, and end in itself.

takes on all
comers but is
remarkably free
of contentious

two levels
for approach p.289.
the bittering
process
high-power
intellectual
achievement

Bibliography

Abington School District v. *Schempp*, 374 U.S. 203 (1963)

Adams v. *Lindsell*, 1 B & L. 681 (1818)

Ashford v. *Thornton*, 1 B. and Ald. 457 (1818)

Ashwander v. *TVA*, 297 U.S. 288 (1936)

Baker v. *Carr*, 369 U.S. 186 (1962)

Borgnis v. *Falk Co.*, 147 Wis. 227, 133 N.W. 209 (1911)

Brown v. *Board of Education*, 347 U.S. 483 (1954); 349 U.S. 294 (1955)

Chicago, Milwaukee & St. Paul Ry. Co. v. *Minnesota*, 134 U.S. 418 (1890)

Colegrove v. *Green*, 328 U.S. 549 (1946)

Doubleday & Co. v. *New York*, 335 U.S. 848 (1948)

Dred Scott v. *Sandford*, 19 How. 393 (1857)

Furman v. *Georgia*, 408 U.S. 238 (1972)

Gideon v. *Wainwright*, 372 U.S. 335 (1963)

Engel v. *Vitale*, 370 U.S. 421 (1962)

Farwell v. *Boston and Worcester Railroad Corp.*, 45 Mass. (4 Metc.) 49 (1842)

Fleming v. *Nestor*, 363 U.S. 603 (1960)

Gomillion v. *Lightfoot*, 364 U.S. 339 (1960)

In re Gault, 387 U.S. 1 (1967)

Ives v. *South Buffalo Ry.*, 201 N.Y. 271, 94 N.E. 431 (1911)

Jee v. *Audley*, 1 Cox Eq. Cas. 324 (1787)

Joseph v. *Sears Roebuck & Co.*, 224 S.C. 105, 77 S.E. 2d 583 (1953)

Lochner v. *New York*, 198 U.S. 45 (1905)

Luther v. *Borden*, 17 U.S. (7 How.) 1 (1849)

MacPherson v. *Buick Motor Co.*, 217 N.Y. 382, 111 N.E. 1050 (1916)

Miller v. *California*, 413 U.S. 15 (1973)

Murray v. *South Carolina RR. Co.*, 26 S.C.L. (1 McMul.) 385 (1841)

New York City Housing Authority v. *Watson*, 27 Misc. 3d 618, 207 N.Y. 2d 920
    (Sup. Ct. 1960)

Paramour v. *Yardley*, 2 Plow. 539, 2 Eng. Rep. 794 (K.B., 1580)

People v. *Doubleday & Co.*, 297 N.Y. 687, 77 N.E. 296 (1947)

Priestley v. *Fowler*, 3 M&W. 1; 150 Eng. Rep. 1030 (Ex., 1837)

Reynolds v. *Sims*, 377 U.S. 533 (1964)

Riggs v. *Palmer*, 115 N.Y. 506, 22 N.E. 188 (1889)

Roe v. *Wade*, 410 U.S. 113 (1973)

Roth v. *United States*, 354 U.S. 476 (1957)

Schechter Poultry Corp. v. *U.S.*, 295 U.S. 495 (1935)

Serrano v. *Priest*, 5 Cal. 3rd 584, 487 P. 2d 1241 (1971)

Silver v. *Jordan*, 241 F. Supp. 576 (S.D. Cal., 1964), *aff'd per curiam*, 381 U.S.
    415 (1965)

Smith v. *Hiatt,* 329 Mass. 488 (1952)

Wilson v. *Girard,* 354 U.S. 524 (1957)

Youngstown Sheet and Tube Co. v. *Sawyer,* 343 U.S. 579 (1952)

U.S. v. *Butler,* 297 U.S. 1, 62 (1936)

U.S. v. *O'Brien,* 391 U.S. 367 (1968)

U.S. v. *One Book Called "Ulysses,"* 5 F. Supp. 182 (S.D.N.Y. 1933)

Abel-Smith, Brian, Michael Zander, and Rosalind Brooke, *Legal Problems and the Citizen, A Study in Three London Boroughs* (1973)

Adamany, David W., "Legitimacy, Realigning Elections, and the Supreme Court," 1973 *Wis. L. Rev.* 790

—————, "The Party Variable in Judges' Voting: Conceptual Notes and a Case Study," 63 *Am. Pol. Sci. Rev.* 57 (1969)

Adelson, Joseph, and Lynnette Beall, "Adolescent Perspectives on Law and Government," 4 *Law and Society Rev.* 495 (1970)

Aebersold, Peter, *Die Verwahrung und Versorgung Vermindert Zurechnungs-fähiger in der Schweiz* (1972)

Alford, Robert, *Bureaucracy and Participation: Political Cultures in Four Wisconsin Cities* (1969)

Allott, Antony, "The Unification of Laws in Africa," 16 *Am. J. Comp. L.* 51 (1963)

Almond, Gabriel, and G. Bingham Powell, Jr., *Comparative Politics, a Developmental Approach* (1966)

—————, and Sidney Verba, *The Civic Culture* (1963)

Andenaes, Johannes, "Deterrence and Specific Offenses," 38 *U. Chi. L. Rev.* 538 (1971)

—————, "The General Preventive Effects of Punishment," 114 *U. Pa. L. Rev.* 962 (1966)

Antunes, George, and A. Lee Hunt, "The Impact of Certainty and Severity of Punishment on Levels of Crime in American States: An Extended Analysis," 64 *J. Crim. L. and Criminology* 486 (1973)

Arnold, William R., "Race and Ethnicity Relative to Other Factors in Juvenile Court Dispositions," 77 *Am. J. Sociology* 211 (1971)

Asbury, Herbert, *The Great Illusion* (1950)

Atkinson, David N., and Dale A. Neuman, "Judicial Attitudes and Defendant Attributes: Some Consequences for Municipal Court Decision-Making," 19 *J. Public L.* 69 (1970)

Aubert, Vilhelm, "Competition and Dissensus: Two Types of Conflict and Conflict Resolution," 7 *J. Conflict Resolution* 26 (1963)

—————, *Elements of Sociology* (1967)

—————, "Law as a Way of Resolving Conflicts: The Case of a Small Industrialized Society," in Laura Nader, ed., *Law in Culture and Society* (1969)

—————, ed., *Sociology of Law* (1969)

—————, "Some Social Functions of Legislation," 10 *Acta Sociologica* 98 (1967)

Austin, John, *The Province of Jurisprudence Determined,* originally published in 1832 (1954)

Ball, Harry V., "Social Structure and Rent-Control Violations," 65 *Am. J. Sociology* 598 (1960)
_____, et al., "Law and Social Change: Sumner Reconsidered," 67 *Am. J. Sociology* 532 (1962)
_____, and Lawrence M. Friedman, "The Use of Criminal Sanctions in the Enforcement of Economic Legislation: A Sociological View," 17 *Stan. L. Rev.* 197 (1965)
Bandura, Albert, *Aggression, A Social Learning Analysis* (1973)
Banfield, Edward C., *Political Influence* (1961)
Banton, Michael, *The Policeman in the Community* (1964)
Barch, A. M., D. Trumbo, and J. Nangle, "Social Setting and Conformity to a Legal Requirement," 55 *J. Abnormal and Soc. Psychology* 396 (1957)
Barkun, Michael, *Law Without Sanctions* (1968)
Bean, Frank D., and Robert G. Cushing, "Criminal Homicide, Punishment, and Deterrence: Methodological and Substantive Reconsiderations," 52 *Soc. Sci. Q.* 277 (1971)
Beaney, William M., and Edward N. Beiser, "Prayer and Politics: The Impact of *Engel* and *Schempp* on the Political Process," 13 *J. Pub. L.* 475 (1964)
Becker, Howard S., *Outsiders, Studies in the Sociology of Deviance* (1963)
Becker, Theodore L., *Comparative Judicial Politics, the Political Functionings of Courts* (1970)
_____, ed., *The Impact of Supreme Court Decisions* (1969)
_____, *Political Behavioralism and Modern Jurisprudence* (1964)
Beiser, Edward N., "Lawyers Judge the Warren Court," 7 *Law and Society Rev.* 139 (1972)
Bentham, Jeremy, *Theory of Legislation* (4th ed., 1882)
Berkowitz, Leonard, and Nigel Walker, "Laws and Moral Judgments," 30 *Sociometry* 410 (1967)
Berman, Harold J., *Justice in the U.S.S.R.* (1963)
Berman, Jesse, "The Cuban Popular Tribunals," 69 *Colum. L. Rev.* 1317 (1969)
Bernstein, Marver H., *Regulating Business by Independent Commission* (1955)
Bickel, Alexander M., "Mr. Taft Rehabilitates the Court," 79 *Yale L. J.* 1 (1969)
_____, *Politics and the Warren Court* (1965)
Binder, Leonard, "National Integration and Political Development," 58 *Am. Pol. Sci. Rev.* 622 (1964)
Black, Donald J., "The Social Organization of Arrest," 23 *Stan. L. Rev.* 1087 (1971)
_____, "The Boundaries of Legal Sociology," 81 *Yale L. J.* 1086 (1972)
Black, Henry C., *Handbook on the Construction and Interpretation of the Laws* (2nd ed., 1911)
Blackstone, Sir William, *Commentaries on the Laws of England* (1765–69)
Blankenburg, Erhard, "Die Selektivität Rechtlicher Sanktionen," 21 *Kölner*

Zeitschrift für Soziologie und Sozialpsychologie, 805 (1969)

Blau, Peter, *The Dynamics of Bureaucracy* (1963)

Blegrad, Britt-Mari P., Ed., *Contributions to the Sociology of Law* (1966)

————, and Jette Moller Nielsen, "Recht als Mittel des socialen Wandels," in *Zur Effektivität des Rechts,* vol. 3, *Jahrbuch für Rechtssoziologie und Rechtstheorie* (1972)

Blum, Walter J., and Harry Kalven, Jr., "The Art of Opinion Research: A Lawyer's Appraisal of an Emerging Science," 24 *U. Chi. L. Rev.* 1 (1956)

Blumberg, Abraham, "The Practice of Law as Confidence Game: Organizational Cooptation of a Profession," 1 *Law and Society Rev.* no. 2, 15 (1967)

Blumenwitz, Dieter, "Das Sezessionsrecht Innerstaatlicher Rechtsgemeinschaften," 3 *Verfassung und Recht in Übersee* 429 (1970)

Bohannon, Paul, "The Differing Realms of the Law," in Laura Nader, ed., *The Ethnography of Law,* 67 *Am. Anthropologist,* special publication, no. 6, part 2, 33 (1965)

Bolding, Per Olof, "Reliance on Authorities or Open Debate?: Two Models of Legal Argumentation," 13 *Scandinavian Studies in Law* 59 (1969)

Bonderman, David, "Modernization and Changing Perceptions of Islamic Law," 81 *Harv. L. Rev.* 1169 (1968)

Bonn, Robert L., "The Predictability of Nonlegalistic Adjudication," 6 *Law and Society Rev.* 563 (1972)

Bordua, David J., and Edward W. Haurek, "The Police Budget's Lot," 13 *Am. Behav. Scientist* 667 (1970)

Borkin, Joseph, *The Corrupt Judge* (1962)

Box, Steven, and Julienne Ford, "The Facts Don't Fit: On the Relationship between Social Class and Criminal Behaviour," 19 *Soc. Rev.* 31 (1971)

Brinkmann, Gerhard, "Die Diskriminierung der Nicht-Juristen in allgemeinen höheren Verwaltungsdiensten der Bundesrepublik Deutschland," 129 *Zeitschrift für die Gesamte Staatswissenschaft,* no. 1, 150 (1973)

Brooker, Frank, "The Deterrent Effect of Punishment," 9 *Criminology* 469 (1972)

Broom, L., and P. Selznick, *Sociology* (4th ed., 1968)

Buchanan, James, and Gordon Tullock, *The Calculus of Consent* (1962)

Cahn, Edward, "Jurisprudence," 30 *N.Y.U. L. Rev.* 150 (1955)

Calabresi, Guido, *The Costs of Accidents* (1970)

Campbell, Donald T., and H. Laurence Ross, "The Connecticut Crackdown on Speeding: Time-Series Data in Quasi-Experimental Analysis," 3 *Law and Society Rev.* 33 (1968)

Cappelletti, Mauro, *Procédure Orale et Procédure Écrite* (1971)

————, *Judicial Review in the Contemporary World* (1971)

Carbonnier, Jean, *Sociologie Juridique* (1972)

Carlin, Jerome E., *Lawyers on Their Own, A Study of Individual Practitioners in Chicago* (1962)

_____, Jan Howard, and Sheldon L. Messinger, *Civil Justice and the Poor, Issues for Sociological Research* (1967)

Carr-Saunders, A. M., and P. A. Wilson, "Professions," 12 *Encyc. Soc. Sci.* 476

Carter, James C., *Law, Its Origin, Growth and Function* (1907)

Casper, Jonathan D., *American Criminal Justice, the Defendant's Perspective* (1972)

Chaiken, Jan M., Michael W. Lawless, and Keith A. Stevenson, *The Impact of Police Activity on Crime: Robberies on the New York City Subway System* (1974)

Chambliss, William J., "Types of Deviance and the Effectiveness of Legal Sanctions," 1967 *Wis. L. Rev.* 703

_____, and Robert B. Seidman, *Law, Order and Power* (1971)

Chevigny, Paul, *Police Power: Police Abuses in New York City* (1969)

Chiricos, Theodore G., and Gordon P. Waldo, "Punishment and Crime: An Examination of Some Empirical Evidence," 18 *Social Problems* 200 (1970)

Christie, George, "Vagueness and Legal Language," 48 *Minn. L. Rev.* 885 (1964)

Christie, Nils, "Temperance Boards and Interinstitutional Dilemmas: A Case Study of a Welfare Law," 12 *Social Problems* 415 (1965)

"Civil Commitment of the Mentally Ill," 14 *U.C.L.A. L. Rev.* 823 (1967)

Claster, Daniel S., "Comparison of Risk Perception between Delinquents and Nondelinquents," 58 *J. Crim. L. C. & P. S.* 80 (1967)

Cloward, Richard A., and Lloyd Ohlin, *Delinquency and Opportunity* (1960)

Cohen, Jerome A., *The Criminal Process in the People's Republic of China 1949–1963, An Introduction* (1968)

Cohen, Julius, Reginald A. Robson, and Alan P. Bates, *Parental Authority: The Community and the Law* (1958)

Cohn, Bernard S., "Some Notes on Law and Change in North India," in Paul Bohannon, ed., *Law and Warfare, Studies in the Anthropology of Conflict* (1967)

Cohn, Haim H., "Secularization of Divine Law," in Haim H. Cohn, ed., *Jewish Law in Ancient and Modern Israel* (1971)

Coke, Sir Edward, *Commentaries on Littleton* (1628)

Cole, George F., "The Decision to Prosecute," 4 *Law and Society Rev.* 331 (1970)

Coleman, Peter J., *Debtors and Creditors in America: Insolvency, Imprisonment for Debt, and Bankruptcy, 1607–1900* (1974)

Collier, Jane F., *Law and Social Change in Zinacantan* (1973)

Colombotos, John, "Physicians and Medicare: A Before-After Study of the Effects of Legislation on Attitudes," 34 *Am. Soc. Rev.* 318 (1969)

Conard, Alfred, et al., *Automobile Accident Costs and Payments* (1964)

Conklin, John E., "Criminal Environment and Support for the Law," 6 *Law and Society Rev.* 247 (1971)

Cooperrider, Luke, review of Cohen, Robson, and Bates, 57 *Mich. L. Rev.* 1119 (1959)

Coulson, Noel James, *A History of Islamic Law* (1964)

Cramton, Roger C., "Driver Behavior and Legal Sanctions: A Study of Deterrence," 67 *Mich. L. Rev.* 421 (1969)

Cross, Rupert, *Precedent in English Law* (1961)

Currie, Elliott P., "Crimes Without Criminals: Witchcraft and its Control in Renaissance Europe," 3 *Law and Society Rev.* 7 (1968)

Curtis, Charles R., "A Better Theory of Legal Interpretation," 3 *Vand. L. Rev.* 407 (1950)

Dahl, Robert A., *Pluralist Democracy in the United States: Conflict and Consent* (1967)

——————, *Who Governs? Democracy and Power in an American City* (1961)

——————, and Charles E. Lindblom, *Politics, Economics and Welfare* (1953)

Danby, Herbert, ed., *The Mishnah* (1933)

Danelski, David J., "Conflict and Its Resolution in the Supreme Court," 11 *J. Conflict Resolution* 71, (1967)

——————, *A Supreme Court Justice Is Appointed* (1964)

——————, "Values as Variables in Judicial Decision-Making: Notes Toward a Theory," 19 *Vand. L. Rev.* 721 (1966)

Dannick, Lionel I., "Influence of an Anonymous Stranger on a Routine Decision to Act or Not to Act: An Experiment in Conformity," 14 *Sociological Q.* 127 (1973)

David, René, "A Civil Code for Ethiopia: Considerations on the Codification of the Civil Law in African Countries," 37 *Tul. L. Rev.* 187 (1963)

——————, and John E. C. Brierley, *Major Legal Systems in the World Today* (1968)

Davis, Kenneth C., *Discretionary Justice: A Preliminary Inquiry* (1969)

Dawson, John P., *The Oracles of the Law* (1968)

Daynard, Richard A., "The Use of Social Policy in Judicial Decision-Making," 56 *Cornell L. Rev.* 919 (1971)

Degler, Carl N., *Neither Black nor White, Slavery and Race Relations in Brazil and the United States* (1971)

Dershowitz, Alan M., "Increasing Community Control over Corporate Crime: A Problem in the Law of Sanctions," 71 *Yale L. J.* 280 (1961)

Dicey, A. V., *Lectures on the Relation between the Law and Public Opinion in England, during the Nineteenth Century* (1905).

Dickinson, John, *Administrative Justice and the Supremacy of Law* (1927)

Dolbeare, Kenneth M., *Trial Courts in Urban Politics* (1967)

——————, and Phillip E. Hammond, *The School Prayer Decisions, from Court Policy to Local Practice* (1971)

Dollard, John, et al., *Frustration and Aggression* (1939)

Dror, Yehezkel, "Law and Social Change," 33 *Tulane L. Rev.* 787 (1959)

Durkheim, Emile, *The Division of Labor in Society* (1933)

Duster, Troy, *The Legislation of Morality: Laws, Drugs, and Moral Judgment* (1970)

Dworkin, Gerald, *Odger's Construction of Deeds and Statutes* (5th ed., 1967)

Dworkin, Ronald, "The Model of Rules," 35 *U. Chi. L. Rev.* 14 (1967)

Dye, Thomas R., *Politics, Economics, and the Public: Policy Outcomes in the American States* (1966)

Easton, David, *A Framework for Political Analysis* (1965)

_____, *A Systems Analysis of Political Life* (1965)

Ebel, Wilhelm, *Geschichte der Gesetzgebung in Deutschland* (2nd ed., 1958)

Eckhoff, Torstein, "Impartiality, Separation of Powers, and Judicial Independence," 9 *Scandinavian Studies in Law* 9 (1965)

_____, "The Mediator, the Judge and the Administrator in Conflict-Resolution," in Britt-Mari Blegvad, ed., *Contributions to the Sociology of Law* (1966)

Ehrenzweig, Albert A., "Reimbursement of Counsel Fees and the Great Society," in Jacobus tenBroek, ed., *The Law of the Poor* (1966)

Ehrlich, Eugen, *Fundamental Principles of the Sociology of Law* (1936)

Ehrlich, Isaac, "The Deterrent Effect of Criminal Law Enforcement," 1 *J. Legal Studies* 259 (1972)

Eley, Lynn W., and Thomas W. Casstevens, *The Politics of Fair-Housing Legislation* (1968)

Elias, T. O., *The Nature of African Customary Law* (1956)

Elkins, Stanley M., *Slavery, A Problem in American Institutional and Intellectual Life* (1959)

Elms, Alan C., ed., *Role Playing, Reward, and Attitude Change* (1969)

Engisch, Karl, *Einführung in das Juristische Denken* (3rd ed., 1964)

Engstrom, Richard L., and Micheal W. Giles, "Expectations and Images: A Note on Diffuse Support for Legal Institutions," 6 *Law and Society Rev.* 631 (1972)

Erickson, Maynard L., and Jack P. Gibbs, "The Deterrence Question: Some Alternative Methods of Analysis," 54 *Soc. Sci. Q.* 534 (1973)

Erikson, Kai T., *Wayward Puritans, a Study in the Sociology of Deviance* (1966)

Erskine, Hazel, "The Polls: Capital Punishment," 34 *Public Opinion Q.* 290 (1970)

Eulau, Heinz, and John D. Sprague, *Lawyers in Politics, A Study in Professional Convergence* (1964)

Evan, William M., "Law as an Instrument of Social Change," in Alvin W. Gouldner and S. M. Miller, eds., *Applied Psychology* (1965)

_____, "Public and Private Legal Systems," in William M. Evan, ed., *Law and Sociology* (1962)

Fagen, Richard, *Politics and Communication* (1966)

Fair, Daryl R., "An Experimental Application of Scalogram Analysis to State Supreme Court Decisions," 1967 *Wis. L. Rev.* 449

Fallers, Lloyd A., *Law Without Precedent* (1969)

Farrand, Max, ed., *Laws and Liberties of Massachusetts, 1648* (1929)

Feeley, Malcolm, "Coercion and Compliance, a New Look at an Old Problem," 4 *Law and Society Rev.* 505 (1970)

Feest, Johannes, "Compliance with Legal Regulations: Observation of Stop Sign Behavior," 2 *Law and Society Rev.* 447 (1968)

—————, and Erhard Blankenburg, *Die Definitionsmacht der Polizei* (1972)

Fenet, P. A., *Receuil Complet des Travaux Préparatoires du Code Civil* (1827), vol. I

Ferrari, Vincenzo, *Successione per Testamento e Trasformazioni Sociali* (1972)

Festinger, Leon, and James C. Carlsmith, "Cognitive Consequences of Forced Compliance," 58 *J. Abnormal & Soc. Psychology* 203 (1959)

Finman, Ted, and Stewart Macaulay, "Freedom to Dissent: The Vietnam Protests and the Words of Public Officials," 1966 *Wis. L. Rev.* 632

Fox, Sanford J., "Juvenile Justice Reform: An Historical Perspective," 22 *Stan. L. Rev.* 1187 (1970)

Frank, Jerome, *Law and the Modern Mind* (1930)

Freund, Julien, *The Sociology of Max Weber* (1968)

Friedenberg, Edgar Z., "The Side Effects of the Legal Process," in Robert Paul Wolff, ed., *The Rule of Law* (1971)

Friedland, N., J. Thibaut, and L. Walker, "Some Determinants of the Violation of Rules," 3 *J. Applied Soc. Psychology* 103 (1973)

Friedman, Lawrence M., *Contract Law in America* (1965)

—————, "Freedom of Contract and Occupational Licensing, 1890–1910: A Legal and Social Study," 53 *Calif. L. Rev.* 487 (1965)

—————, *Government and Slum Housing: A Century of Frustration* (1968)

—————, *A History of American Law* (1973)

—————, "The Idea of Right as a Social and Legal Concept," 27 *J. Soc. Issues*, no. 2, 189 (1971)

—————, "Law and Its Language," 33 *Geo. Wash. L. Rev.* 563 (1964)

—————, "Law, Order and History," 16 *S.D. L. Rev.* 242 (1971)

—————, "Law Reform in Historical Perspective," 13 *St. Louis U. L. J.* 351 (1969)

—————, "Law, Rules, and the Interpretation of Written Documents," 59 *Nw. U. L. Rev.* 751 (1965)

—————, "Legal Culture and Social Development," 4 *Law and Society Rev.* 29 (1969)

—————, "On Legal Development," 24 *Rutgers L. Rev.* 11 (1969)

—————, "Legal Rules and the Process of Social Change," 19 *Stan. L. Rev.* 786 (1967)

—————, "On Legalistic Reasoning: A Footnote to Weber," 1966 *Wis. L. Rev.* 148

—————, "Social Welfare Legislation: An Introduction," 21 *Stan. L. Rev.* 217 (1969)

—————, and Jack Ladinsky, "El Derecho como Instrumento de Cambio

Social Incremental," *Derecho,* no. 27, 22 (Lima, 1969)

_____, _____, "Social Change and the Law of Industrial Accidents," 67 *Colum. L. Rev.* 50 (1967)

_____, and Stewart Macaulay, *Law and the Behavioral Sciences* (1969)

Fromkin, Howard L., and Timothy C. Brock, "Erotic Materials: A Commodity Theory Analysis of the Enhanced Desirability that May Accompany Their Unavailability," 3 *J. Applied Soc. Psychology* 219 (1973)

Fuller, Lon L., *Legal Fictions* (1967)

_____, *The Morality of Law* (1964)

Galanter, Marc, "The Modernization of Law," in M. Weiner, ed., *Modernization* (1966)

Gallatin, Judith, and Joseph Adelson, "Legal Guarantees of Individual Freedom: A Cross-National Study of the Development of Political Thought," 27 *J. Soc. Issues,* no. 2, 93 (1971)

Gans, Herbert J., *The Levittowners, Ways of Life and Politics in a New Suburban Community* (1967)

_____, *The Urban Villagers* (1962)

Gardiner, John A., *Traffic and Police, Variations in Law Enforcement Policy* (1969)

Garfinkel, Harold, "Conditions of Successful Degradation Ceremonies," 61 *Am. J. Sociology* 420 (1956)

Geis, Gilbert, "The Heavy Electrical Equipment Antitrust Cases of 1961," in Gilbert Geis, ed., *White Collar Criminal* (1968)

Gelfand, Donna M., Donald P. Hartmann, Patrice Walker, and Brent Page, "Who Reports Shoplifters? A Field-Experimental Study," 25 *J. Personality and Soc. Psychology* 276 (1973)

Gény, François, *Méthode d'Interprétation et Sources en Droit Privé Positif,* trans. Jaro Mayda (1963)

Gibbs, Jack P., "Crime, Punishment and Deterrence," 48 *Southwestern Soc. Sci. Q.* 515 (1968)

_____, "Definitions of Law and Empirical Questions," 2 *Law and Society Rev.* 429 (1968)

Gifford, Daniel J., "Communication of Legal Standards, Policy Development, and Effective Conduct Regulation," 56 *Cornell L. Rev.* 409 (1971)

Glaser, Daniel, *The Effectiveness of a Prison and Parole System,* abridged ed. (1969)

Glass, Gene V., George C. Tiao, and Thomas O. Maguire, "The 1900 Revision of German Divorce Laws: Analysis of Data as a Time-Series Quasi-Experiment," 5 *Law and Society Rev.* 539 (1971)

Glick, Henry R., *Supreme Courts in State Politics, an Investigation of the Judicial Role* (1971)

_____, and Kenneth M. Vines, *State Court Systems* (1973)

Gluckman, Max, *The Ideas in Barotse Jurisprudence* (1965)

——————, *The Judicial Process among the Barotse of Northern Rhodesia* (1955)

Godechot, Jacques, *Les Institutions de la France sous la Révolution et L'Empire* (2nd ed., 1968)

Goffman, Erving, *Stigma, Notes on the Management of Spoiled Identity* (1963)

Goldman, Sheldon, and Thomas P. Jahnige, "Eastonian Systems Analysis and Legal Research," 2 *Rutgers-Camden L. Rev.* 285 (1970)

Goldstein, Stephen R., "The Scope and Sources of School Board Authority to Regulate Student Conduct and Status: A Nonconstitutional Analysis," 117 *U. Pa. L. Rev.* 373 (1969)

Golunski, S. A., and M. S. Strogovich, "The Theory of the State and Law," in *Soviet Legal Philosophy*, trans. Hugh W. Babb (1951)

Goodhart, Arthur L., "Determining the Ratio Decidendi of a Case," 40 *Yale L. J.* 161 (1930)

Graham, Fred P., "A Contemporary History of American Crime," in Hugh D. Graham and Ted R. Gurr, eds., *Violence in America: Historical and Comparative Perspectives* (1969)

Graham, Howard Jay, *Everyman's Constitution* (1968)

Gray, John Chipman, *The Nature and Sources of the Law* (1909)

——————, *The Rule Against Perpetuities* (1886)

Green, Christopher, *Negative Taxes and the Poverty Problem* (1967)

Green, Edward, "Inter- and Intra-Racial Crime Relative to Sentencing," 55 *J. Crim. L., C. & P.S.* 348 (1964)

Green, Justin J., John R. Schmidhauser, Larry L. Berg, and David Brady, "Lawyers in Congress: A New Look at Some Old Assumptions," 26 *Western Pol. Q.* 440 (1973)

Greenwood, Ernest, "Attributes of a Profession," 2 *Soc. Work* no. 3, 45 (1957)

Greer, Scott, *Urban Renewal and American Cities* (1965)

Grosman, Brian A., *The Prosecutor, An Inquiry into the Exercise of Discretion* (1969)

Grossman, Joel B., "Role Playing and the Analysis of Judicial Behavior: The Case of Mr. Justice Frankfurter," 11 *J. Pub. L.* 285 (1962)

——————, "Social Backgrounds and Judicial Decision-Making," 79 *Harv. L. Rev.* 1551 (1966)

——————, and Mary H. Grossman, eds., *Law and Change in Modern America* (1971)

Grupp, Stanley E., and Warren C. Lucas, "The 'Marihuana Muddle' as Reflected in California Arrest Statistics and Dispositions," 5 *Law and Society Rev.* 251 (1970)

Gurr, Ted Robert, *Why Men Rebel* (1970)

Gurvitch, Georges, *Sociology of Law* (1942)

Gusfield, Joseph, "Moral Passage: The Symbolic Process in Public Designations of Deviance," 15 *Social Problems* 175 (1967)

——————, *Symbolic Crusade, Status Politics and the American Temperance Movement* (1963)

Hahm, Pyong-Choon, "The Decision Process in Korea," in G. Schubert and D. Danelski, eds., *Comparative Judicial Behavior* (1969)

Hakman, Nathan, "The Supreme Court's Political Environment: the Processing of Noncommercial Litigation," in Joel B. Grossman and Joseph Tanenhaus, eds., *Frontiers of Judicial Research* (1969)

Hamer, John H., "Dispute Settlement and Sanctity: an Ethiopian Example," 45 *Anthropological Q.* 232 (1972)

Handler, Joel F., "Controlling Official Behavior in Welfare Administration," in Jacobus tenBroek, ed., *The Law of the Poor* (1966)

——————, ed., *Family Law and the Poor, Essays by Jacobus tenBroek* (1971)

——————, *The Lawyer and His Community, The Practicing Bar in a Middle-Sized City* (1967)

——————, and Ellen Jane Hollingsworth, *The "Deserving Poor," A Study of Welfare Administration* (1971)

——————, ——————, "Reforming Welfare: The Constraints of the Bureaucracy and the Clients," 118 *U. Pa. L. Rev.* 1167 (1970)

Hanson, R., *The Political Thicket* (1966)

Harris, Richard, *A Sacred Trust* (1966)

Hart, H. L. A., *The Concept of Law* (1961)

Hart, Henry, and Albert Sacks, *The Legal Process* (tentative ed., 1958), vol. II

Hasan, Ahmad, *The Early Development of Islamic Jurisprudence* (1970)

Haskins, George, *Law and Authority in Early Massachusetts* (1960)

Haynes, Evan, *The Selection and Tenure of Judges* (1944)

Heldrich, Andreas, "Sozialwissenschaftliche Aspekte der Rechtsvergleichung," 34 *Rabels Zeitschrift für ausländisches und internationales Privatrecht* 427 (1970)

Hines, N. William, "Personal Property Joint Tenancies: More Law, Fact and Fancy," 54 *Minn. L. Rev.* 509 (1970)

Hirschman, Albert, *Development Projects Observed* (1967)

Hoebel, E. Adamson, *The Law of Primitive Man, A Study in Comparative Legal Dynamics* (1954)

Hohfeld, Wesley N., "Some Fundamental Legal Conceptions as Applied in Judicial Reasoning," 23 *Yale L. J.* 16 (1913)

Holdsworth, William S., *History of English Law* (3rd ed., 1922), vol. I; (1924) vol. V

Holmes, Oliver W., Jr., "The Path of the Law," 10 *Harv. L. Rev.* 457 (1897)

Horwitz, Morton, "The Emergence of an Instrumental Conception of American Law, 1780–1820," in Donald Fleming and Bernard Bailyn, eds., *Law in American History* (1971)

Hunter, Floyd, *Community Power Structure* (1953)

Huntington, Samuel P., "The Marasmus of the ICC: The Commission, the Railroads and the Public Interest," 61 *Yale L. J.* 467 (1952)

Hurst, J. Willard, *The Growth of American Law: The Lawmakers* (1950)

——————, *Law and the Conditions of Freedom in the Nineteenth Century United States* (1956)

International Commission of Jurists, *South Africa and the Rule of Law* (1960)
Isaac, Paul E., *Prohibition and Politics: Turbulent Decades in Tennessee 1885–1920* (1965)
Isele, Hellmut G., "Ein Halbes Jahrhundert deutsches Bürgerliches Gesetzbuch," 150 *Archiv für die Civilistische Praxis* 1 (1949)
Ishwaran, K., "Customary Law in Village India," 5 *Int'l J. Comp. Sociology* 228 (1964)

Jacob, Herbert, "Black and White Perceptions of Justice in the City," 6 *Law and Society Rev.* 69 (1971)
——————, *Debtors in Court, the Consumption of Government Services* (1969)
James, Dorothy B., "Role Theory and the Supreme Court," 30 *J. Politics* 160 (1968)
Jaros, Dean, and Robert I. Mendelsohn, "The Judicial Role and Sentencing Behavior," 11 *Midwest J. Pol. Sci.* 471 (1967)
Jeffrey, C. Ray, "Social Change and Criminal Law," 13 *Am. Behav. Scientist* 523 (1970)
Johnson, Harry M., *Sociology: A Systematic Introduction* (1960)
Johnson, Richard M., *The Dynamics of Compliance* (1967)
Jolowicz, H. F., *Historical Introduction to the Study of Roman Law* (1954)
Jones, Harry, *The Efficacy of Law* (1969)
Joseph, Nathan, and Nicholas Alex, "The Uniform: a Sociological Perspective," 77 *Am. J. Sociology* 719 (1972)

Kalven, Harry, Jr., " 'Please Morris, Don't Make Trouble': Two Lessons in Courtroom Confrontation," 27 *J. Soc. Issues,* no. 2, 219 (1971)
——————, and Hans Zeisel, *The American Jury* (1966)
Kaplan, John, *Marijuana, the New Prohibition* (1970)
——————, "The Prosecutional Discretion: A Comment," 60 *Nw. U. L. Rev.* 174 (1965)
Kaufman, Harry, "Legality and Harmfulness of a Bystander's Failure to Intervene as Determinants of Moral Judgment," in J. Macaulay and L. Berkowitz, eds., *Altruism and Helping Behavior* (1970)
Kaufman, Herbert, *Administrative Feedback* (1973)
——————, *The Forest Ranger: A Study in Administrative Behavior* (1960)
Kaupen, Wolfgang, *Die Hüter von Recht und Ordnung* (1969)
——————, "Public Opinion of the Law in a Democratic Society," in Adam Podgórecki et al., *Knowledge and Opinion about Law* (1973)
Kelsen, Hans, *Pure Theory of Law,* trans. Max Knight (2nd ed., 1967)
Key, V. O., *Public Opinion and American Democracy* (1965)
King, Harry, as told to William J. Chambliss, *Box Man, a Professional Thief's Journey* (1972)
Kiralfy, A. K. R., "Law Reform by Legal Fictions, Equity and Legislation in

English Legal History," 10 *Am. J. Legal Hist.* 3 (1966)

Klein, Herbert S., *Slavery in the Americas, a Comparative Study of Virginia and Cuba* (1967)

Koch, Hartmut, and Gisela Zenz, "Erfahrungen und Einstellungen von Klägern in Mietprozessen," in Manfred Rehbinder and Helmut Schelsky, eds., *Zur Effectivität des Rechts,* vol. 3, *Jahrbuch für Rechtssoziologie und Rechtstheorie* (1972)

Kohlberg, Lawrence, "Development of Moral Character and Moral Ideology," in M. Hoffman and L. Hoffman, eds., *Review of Child Development Research,* vol. I (1964)

Kolko, Gabriel, *Railroads and Regulation, 1877–1916* (1965)

Krislov, Samuel, "The Amicus Curiae Brief: from Friendship to Advocacy," 72 *Yale L. J.* 694 (1963)

Kuhn, Thomas S., *The Structure of Scientific Revolutions* (1962)

Kutler, Stanley I., *The Dred Scott Decision: Law or Politics?* (1967)

_____, *Privilege and Creative Destruction, the Charles River Bridge Case* (1971)

Kwasniewski, Jerzy, "Motivation of Declared Conformity to a Legal Norm," *Polish Soc. Bull.* no. 1, 74 (1969)

La Fave, Wayne R., *Arrest: The Decision to Take a Suspect Into Custody* (1965)

Labatt, C., *Commentaries on the Law of Master and Servant,* 4 vols. (1913)

Lander, Byron G., "Group Theory and Individuals: The Origin of Poverty as a Political Issue in 1964," 24 *Western Pol. Q.* 514 (1971)

Landis, James M., *The Administrative Process* (1938)

Lane, Roger, "Urbanization and Criminal Violence in the Nineteenth Century: Massachusetts as a Test Case," in Hugh D. Graham and Ted R. Gurr, eds., *Violence in America: Historical and Comparative Perspectives* (1969)

Langdell, C. C., *Contracts* (1871)

Larson, Gustive O., *The "Americanization" of Utah for Statehood* (1971)

LaVoie, Joseph C., "Type of Punishment as a Determinant of Resistance to Deviation," 10 *Developmental Psychology* 181 (1974)

Lefkowitz, M., R. R. Blake, and J. S. Mouton, "Status Factors in Pedestrian Violation of Traffic Signals," 51 *J. Abnormal and Soc. Psychology* 704 (1955)

Lefstein, Norman, Vaughan Stapleton, and Lee Teitelbaum, "In Search of Juvenile Justice: *Gault* and Its Implementation," 3 *Law and Society Rev.* 491 (1969)

Lemert, Edwin M., *Social Action and Legal Change: Revolution Within the Juvenile Court* (1970)

Lempert, Richard, "Strategies of Research Design in the Legal Impact Study," 1 *Law and Society Rev.* 111 (1966)

Letwin, William, *Law and Economic Policy in America, the Evolution of the Sherman Antitrust Act* (1965)

Lev, Daniel S., *Islamic Courts in Indonesia* (1972)

Levi, Edward H., *An Introduction to Legal Reasoning* (1949)

Levin, Martin A., "Policy Evaluation and Recidivism," 6 *Law and Society Rev.* 17 (1971)

—————, "Urban Politics and Judicial Behavior," 1 *J. Legal Studies* 193 (1972)

Levine, James P., "Implementing Legal Policies through Operant Conditioning: The Case of Police Practices," 6 *Law and Society Rev.* 195 (1971)

—————, "Methodological Concerns in Studying Supreme Court Efficacy," 4 *Law and Society Rev.* 583 (1970)

Levine, Michael, "Is Regulation Necessary? California Air Transportation and National Regulatory Policy," 74 *Yale L. J.* 1416 (1965)

Lévy-Bruhl, Henri, *Sociologie du Droit* (1961)

Lewis, W. David, *From Newgate to Dannemora, the Rise of the Penitentiary in New York, 1796–1848* (1965)

Lipsky, Michael, *Protest in City Politics: Rent Strikes, Housing and the Power of the Poor* (1970)

Litwak, Eugene, and Henry J. Meyer, "A Balance Theory of Coordination between Bureaucratic Organizations and Community Primary Groups," 11 *Admin. Sci. Q.* 31 (1966)

Llewellyn, Karl, *The Bramble Bush: On Our Law and Its Study* (1951)

—————, "A Realistic Jurisprudence—the Next Step," 30 *Colum. L. Rev.* 431 (1930)

—————, "Remarks on the Theory of Appellate Decision and the Rules or Canons about how the Statutes are to be Construed," 3 *Vand. L. Rev.* 395 (1950)

—————, "Some Realism about Realism," 44 *Harv. L. Rev.* 1222 (1931)

Lowi, Theodore J., "American Business, Public Policy, Case-Studies, and Political Theory," 16 *World Politics* 677 (1964)

—————, *The End of Liberalism: Ideology, Policy, and the Crisis of Public Authority* (1969)

Luhmann, Niklas, *Legitimation durch Verfahren* (1969)

—————, *Rechtssoziologie* (2 vols., 1972)

Macaulay, Stewart, "Non-Contractual Relations in Business: A Preliminary Study," 28 *Am. Soc. Rev.* 55 (1963)

—————, and Elaine Walster, "Legal Structures and Restoring Equity," 27 *J. Soc. Issues*, no. 2, 173 (1971)

MacCallum, Spencer, "Dispute Settlement in an American Supermarket, a Preliminary View," in Paul Bohannon, ed., *Law and Warfare, Studies in the Anthropology of Conflict* (1967)

McEntire, Davis, *Residence and Race* (1960)

McKenzie, Robert, and Allan Silver, *Angels in Marble, Working Class Conservatives in Urban England* (1968)

MacKinnon, F. B., *Contingent Fees for Legal Services* (1964)

Magnarella, Paul J., "The Reception of Swiss Family Law in Turkey," 46 *Anthropological Q.* 100 (1973)

Main, Eleanor C., and Thomas G. Walker, "Choice Shifts and Extreme Behavior: Judicial Review in the Federal Courts," 91 *J. Soc. Psychology* 215 (1973)

Maine, Sir Henry, *Ancient Law* (1861)

Malinowski, Bronislaw, *Crime and Custom in Savage Society* (1926)

Malmström, Ake, "The System of Legal Systems," 13 *Scandinavian Studies in Law* 127 (1969)

Manne, Henry G., *Insider Trading and the Stock Market* (1966)

Markovits, Inga, *Sozialistisches und Bürgerliches Zivilrechtsdenken in der DDR* (1969)

"Marx et le Droit Moderne," Vol. 12, *Archives de Philosophie du Droit* (1967)

Massell, Gregory J., "Law as an Instrument of Revolutionary Change in a Traditional Milieu, the Case of Soviet Central Asia," 2 *Law and Society Rev.* 179 (1968)

Matza, David, *Delinquency and Drift* (1964)

Mayhew, Leon, *Law and Equal Opportunity* (1968)

Mellinkoff, David, *The Language of the Law* (1963)

Meltsner, Michael, "Litigating against the Death Penalty: The Strategy behind *Furman*," 82 *Yale L. J.* 1111 (1973)

Merelman, Richard M., "Learning and Legitimacy," 60 *Am. Pol. Sci. Rev.* 548 (1966)

Merryman, John H., *The Civil Law Tradition* (1969)

_____, and V. Vigoriti, "When Courts Collide: Constitution and Cassation in Italy," 15 *Am. J. Comp. L.* 665 (1967)

Merton, Robert K., *Social Theory and Social Structure* (1968)

Mileski, Maureen, "Courtroom Encounters: An Observation Study of a Lower Criminal Court," 5 *Law and Society Rev.* 473 (1971)

Milgram, Stanley, "Liberating Effects of Group Pressure," 1 *J. Personality and Soc. Psychology* 127 (1965)

Miller, Loren, *The Petitioners. The Story of the Supreme Court of the United States and the Negro* (1966)

Mills, C. Wright, *The Power Elite* (1956)

Milner, Alan, review of Cohen, Robson, and Bates, 21 *U. Pitt. L. Rev.* 147 (1957)

Milner, Neal, "Comparative Analysis of Patterns of Compliance with Supreme Court Decisions," 5 *Law and Society Rev.* 119 (1970)

Mitchell, Oliver R., "The Fictions of the Law: Have They Proved Useful or Detrimental to its Growth?," 7 *Harv. L. Rev.* 249 (1893)

Moore, Wilbert E., *The Professions: Roles and Rules* (1970)

Morris, Richard, *Studies in the History of American Law* (2nd ed., 1959)

Morrison, Fred L., *Courts and the Political Process in England* (1973)

Moynihan, Daniel Patrick, *Maximum Feasible Misunderstanding: Community Action in the War on Poverty* (1969)

Muir, William K., Jr., *Prayer in the Public Schools: Law and Attitude Change* (1967)

Murphy, Walter, *Elements of Judicial Strategy* (1964)

Myers, D. G., F. B. Schreiber, and D. J. Viel, "Effects of Discussion on Opinions Concerning Illegal Behavior," 92 *J. Soc. Psychology* 77 (1974)

Nader, Laura, "An Analysis of Zapotec Law Cases," 3 *Ethnology* 404 (1964)

Nagel, Stuart, "Political Party Affiliation and Judges' Decisions," 55 *Am. Pol. Sci. Rev.* 843 (1961)

──────, and Felix V. Gagliano, "Attorney Characteristics and Courtroom Results," 44 *Neb. L. Rev.* 599 (1965)

Nelson, William E., "The Americanization of the Common Law," (Ph.D. thesis, Harvard University, 1971)

Nemeth, Charlan, and Ruth H. Sosis, "A Simulated Jury Study: Characteristics of the Defendant and the Jurors," 90 *J. Soc. Psychology* 221 (1973)

Nonet, Philippe, *Administrative Justice* (1969)

Oaks, Dallin H., and Warren Lehman, *A Criminal Justice System and the Indigent* (1968)

Ogburn, William F., *Social Change with Respect to Culture and Original Nature* (1950)

Ogden, C. K., *Bentham's Theory of Fictions* (1951)

Otte, George, "Role Theory and the Judicial Process: a Critical Analysis," 16 *St. Louis U. L. J.* 420 (1972)

Packer, Herbert L., *The Limits of the Criminal Sanctions* (1968)

Parsons, Talcott, "Evolutionary Universals in Society," 29 *Am. Soc. Rev.* 339 (1964)

──────, *The System of Modern Societies* (1971)

Paul, Arnold M., *Conservative Crisis and the Rule of Law: Attitudes of Bar and Bench, 1887–1895* (1960)

Petrick, Michael J., "The Supreme Court and Authority Acceptance," 21 *Western Pol. Q.* 5 (1968)

Piaget, Jean, *The Moral Judgment of the Child* (1932)

Platt, Anthony M., *The Child Savers: The Invention of Delinquency* (1969)

Plucknett, Theodore T. F., *A Concise History of the Common Law* (5th ed., 1956)

──────, *Statutes and Their Interpretation in the First Half of the Fourteenth Century* (1922)

Podgórecki, Adam, "Public Opinion on Law," in Adam Podgórecki et al., *Knowledge and Opinion about Law* (1973)

──────, et al., *Knowledge and Opinion about Law* (1973)

Pospisil, Leopold, *Anthropology of Law: A Comparative Theory* (1971)

Pound, Roscoe, "The Economic Interpretation and the Law of Torts," 53 *Harv. L. Rev.* 365 (1940)

_____, *Interpretations of Legal History* (1923)

Powers, Edwin, *Crime and Punishment in Early Massachusetts, 1620–1692, a Documentary History* (1966)

Pritchett, C. Herman, *The Roosevelt Court: A Study in Judicial Politics and Values, 1937–1947* (1948)

Prosser, William L., *Handbook of the Law of Torts* (4th ed., 1971)

Pye, Lucian, *Politics, Personality and Nation Building* (1962)

Rabin, Robert L., "Agency Criminal Referrals in the Federal System: An Empirical Study of Prosecutorial Discretion," 24 *Stan. L. Rev.* 1036 (1972)

Raz, Joseph, "Legal Principles and the Limits of Law," 81 *Yale L. J.* 823 (1972)

Redfield, Robert, "Maine's *Ancient Law* in the Light of Primitive Societies," 3 *Western Pol. Q.* 574 (1950)

Rehbinder, Manfred, "Status, Contract and the Welfare State," 23 *Stan. L. Rev.* 941 (1971)

Reich, Donald R., "Schoolhouse Religion and the Supreme Court: A Report on Attitudes of Teachers and Principals and on School Practices in Wisconsin and Ohio," 23 *J. Legal Ed.* 123 (1971)

Reik, Theodore, *The Compulsion to Confess, On the Psychoanalysis of Crime and Punishment* (1959)

Rheinstein, Max, ed., *Max Weber on Law in Economy and Society* (1954)

Riebschläger, Klaus, *Die Freirechtsbewegung* (1968)

Robertson, John A., and Phyllis Teitelbaum, "Optimizing Legal Impact: A Case Study in Search of a Theory," 1973 *Wis. L. Rev.* 665

Robertson, Leon S., Robert F. Rich, and H. Laurence Ross, "Jail Sentences for Driving While Intoxicated in Chicago: A Judicial Policy that Failed," 8 *Law and Society Rev.* 55 (1973)

Rodgers, Harrell R., Jr., *Community Conflict, Public Opinion and the Law: The Amish Dispute in Iowa* (1969)

_____, "Law as an Instrument of Public Policy," 17 *Am. J. Poli. Sci.* 638 (1973)

_____, and Edward B. Lewis, "Political Support and Compliance Attitudes: A Study of Adolescents," 2 *Am. Pol. Q.* 61 (1974)

Rodkinson, Michael L., *The Babylonian Talmud* (1916), vol. 5

Romans, J. T., "Moral Suasion as an Instrument of Economic Policy," 56 *Am. Econ. Rev.* 1220 (1966)

Rosenberg, Maurice, *The Pretrial Conference and Effective Justice* (1964)

Rosenn, Keith S., "The Jeito, Brazil's Institutional Bypass of the Formal Legal System and Its Developmental Implications," 19 *Am. J. Comp. L.* 514 (1971)

Ross, H. Laurence, "Law, Science, and Accidents: the British Road Safety Act of 1967," 2 *J. Legal Studies* 1 (1973)

——————, *Settled Out of Court: the Social Process of Insurance Claims Adjustments* (1970)

Rothman, David, *The Discovery of the Asylum, Social Order and Disorder in the New Republic* (1971)

Rubin, Jeffrey I., and Roy J. Lewicki, "A Three-Factor Experimental Analysis of Promises and Threats," 3 *J. Applied Social Psychology* 240 (1973)

Rubinstein, Amnon, "Law and Religion in Israel," in Haim H. Cohn, ed., *Jewish Law in Ancient and Modern Israel* (1971)

Rumble, Wilfrid E., Jr., *American Legal Realism, Skepticism, Reform, and the Judicial Process* (1968)

Runciman, W. G., *Relative Deprivation and Social Justice: A Study of Attitudes to Social Inequality in Twentieth-Century England* (1966)

Rushing, William A., "Organizational Rules and Surveillance: Propositions in Comparative Organizational Analysis," 10 *Admin. Sci. Q.* 423 (1966)

St. John-Stevas, Norman, *Obscenity and the Law* (1956)

Salacuse, Jeswald D., *An Introduction to Law in French-Speaking Africa* (1969), vol. I

Salem, Richard G., and William J. Bowers, "Severity of Formal Sanctions as a Deterrent to Deviant Behavior," 5 *Law and Society Rev.* 21 (1970)

Sawer, Geoffrey, *Law in Society* (1965)

Schacht, Joseph, *The Origins of Muhammadan Jurisprudence* (1953)

Schafer, Jeffrey A., "Prosecution for Selective Service Offenses: A Field Study," 22 *Stan. L. Rev.* 356 (1970)

Scheff, Thomas, *Being Mentally Ill: A Sociological Theory* (1966)

Schlegel, Stuart A., *Tiruray Justice* (1970)

Schubert, Glendon, *Judicial Decision-Making* (1963)

——————, *The Judicial Mind* (1965)

——————, *Quantitative Analysis of Judicial Behavior* (1959)

Schumann, Karl F., and Gerd Winter, "Zur Analyse des Strafverfahrens," 3 *Kriminologisches Journal* 136 (1971)

Schur, Edwin M., *Crimes without Victims* (1965)

——————, *Labeling Deviant Behavior, Its Sociological Implications* (1971)

Schuyt, C. J. M., *Rechtssociologie, een Terreinverkenning* (1971)

——————, and Joop C. M. Ruys, "Die Einstellung gegenüber neuen sozialökonomischen Gesetzen," in *Zur Effektivität des Rechts*, vol. 3, *Jahrbuch für Rechtssoziologie und Rechtstheorie* (1972)

Schwartz, Richard D., "A Learning Theory of Law," 41 *So. Cal. L. Rev.* 548 (1968)

——————, "Social Factors in the Development of Legal Control: A Case Study of Two Israeli Settlements," 63 *Yale L. J.* 471 (1954)

——————, and James C. Miller, "Legal Evolution and Societal Complexity," 70 *Am. J. Sociology* 159 (1964)

——————, and Sonya Orleans, "On Legal Sanctions," 34 *U. Chi. L. Rev.* 274 (1967)

_____, and Jerome H. Skolnick, "Two Studies of Legal Stigma," 10 *Social Problems* 133 (1962)

Schwitzgebel, Ralph K., "Issues in the Use of an Electronic Rehabilitation System with Chronic Recidivists," 3 *Law and Society Rev.* 597 (1969)

Scott, James C., *Comparative Political Corruption* (1972)

Sebastian, Raymond F., "Obscenity and the Supreme Court; Nine Years of Confusion," 19 *Stan. L. Rev.* 167 (1966)

Segal, Ronald, *The Race War* (1967)

Seidman, Robert B., "Administrative Law and Legitimacy in Anglophonic Africa: A Problem in the Reception of Foreign Law," 5 *Law and Society Rev.* 161 (1970)

_____, "Law and Economic Development in Independent, English-Speaking, Sub-Saharan Africa," 1966 *Wis. L. Rev.* 999

Sellin, Thorsten, *The Death Penalty* (1959)

Selznick, Philip, *Law, Society and Industrial Justice* (1969)

Shapiro, Martin, "The Impact of the Supreme Court," 23 *J. Legal Ed.* 77 (1970)

_____, "Stability and Change in Judicial Decision-Making: Incrementalism or Stare Decisis?" 2 *Law in Transition Q.* 134 (1964)

_____, "Toward a Theory of *Stare Decisis,*" 1 *J. Legal Studies* 125 (1972)

Shklar, Judith, *Legalism* (1964)

Shonfield, Andrew, *Modern Capitalism, The Changing Balance of Public and Private Power* (1965)

Silving, Helen, "The Oath," 68 *Yale L. J.* 1329 (1959)

Simon, Rita J., *The Jury and the Defense of Insanity* (1967)

_____, "Murder, Juries, and the Press," 3 *Transaction* 40 (1966)

Sinclair, Andrew, *Prohibition, The Era of Excess* (1962)

Sinclair, Upton, *The Jungle* (1906)

Singer, Barry F., "Psychological Studies of Punishment," 58 *Calif. L. Rev.* 405 (1970)

Skidmore, Max J., *Medicare and the American Rhetoric of Reconciliation* (1970)

Skolnick, Jerome, "Social Research on Legality: a Reply to Auerbach," 1 *Law and Society Rev.* 105 (1966)

Smigel, Erwin O., *The Wall Street Lawyer* (1964)

Sociologie du Droit et de la Justice (1970)

Sofaer, Abraham D., "The Change of Status Adjudication: A Case Study of the Informal Agency Process," 1 *J. Legal Studies* 349 (1972)

Spradley, James P., *You Owe Yourself a Drunk* (1970)

Sprague, John D., *Voting Patterns of the United States Supreme Court* (1968)

Staff, Ilse, ed., *Justiz im Dritten Reich* (1964)

Stebbins, Robert A., *Commitment to Deviance, The Nonprofessional Criminal in the Community* (1971)

Stevens, Charles R., "Modern Japanese Law as an Instrument of Comparison," 19 *Am. J. Comp. L.* 665 (1971)

Stevens, Robert, "Two Cheers for 1870: The American Law School," in Donald Fleming and Bernard Bailyn, eds., *Law in American History* (1971)

Stirling, Paul, "Land, Marriage and the Law in Turkish Villages," 9 *Int'l Social Sci. Bull.* 21 (1957)

Stone, Julius, *Human Law and Human Justice* (1965)

―――――, *Legal System and Lawyers' Reasonings* (1964)

―――――, *Social Dimensions of Law and Justice* (1966)

Stouffer, Samuel A., *Communism, Conformity, and Civil Liberties* (1955)

Strack, Hermann L., *Introduction to the Talmud and Midrash* (1959)

Sussman, M. B., J. N. Cates, and D. T. Smith, *The Family and Inheritance* (1970)

Sutherland, Edwin H., "The Diffusion of Sexual Psychopath Laws," 56 *Am. J. Sociology* 142 (1950)

―――――, *White Collar Crime* (1949)

―――――, "White-Collar Criminality," in Gilbert Geis, ed., *White Collar Criminal* (1968)

Sutherland, J. G., *Statutes and Statutory Construction* (1891)

Sykes, Gresham, *The Society of Captives: A Study of a Maximum Security Prison* (1958)

Szasz, Thomas, *Law, Liberty and Psychiatry* (1963)

Tanenhaus, Joseph, "The Cumulative Scaling of Judicial Decisions," 79 *Harv. L. Rev.* 1583 (1966)

Tapp, June L., and Lawrence Kohlberg, "Developing Senses of Law and Legal Justice," 27 *J. Social Issues,* no. 2, 65 (1971)

―――――, and Felice J. Levine, "Persuasion to Virtue, A Preliminary Statement," 4 *Law and Society Rev.* 565 (1970)

Tedeschi, James T., et al., "Power, Influence and Behavioral Compliance," 4 *Law and Society Rev.* 521 (1970)

Teeven, James J., Jr., "Deterrent Effects of Punishment: the Canadian Case," 14 *Canadian J. Criminology and Corrections,* no. 1, 68 (1972)

Teubner, Gunther, *Standards und Direktiven in Generalklauseln* (1971)

Thibaut, John, Laurens Walker, and E. Allan Lind, "Adversary Presentation and Bias in Legal Decisionmaking," 86 *Harv. L. Rev.* 386 (1972)

Thompson, Victor, *The Regulatory Process in OPA Rationing* (1950)

Thorsell, Bernard A., and Lloyd W. Klemke, "The Labeling Process: Reinforcement and Deterrent?" 6 *Law and Society Rev.* 393 (1972)

Thurman, Kay Ellen, "The Married Women's Property Acts" (M.LL. thesis, University of Wisconsin Law School, 1966)

Timasheff, Nicholas S., *An Introduction to the Sociology of Law* (1939)

―――――, *Law and Morality: Leon Petrazycki* (1955)

Tittle, Charles R., "Crime Rates and Legal Sanctions," 16 *Social Problems* 409 (1969)

Tobias, J. J., *Crime and Industrial Society in the Nineteenth Century* (1972)

Tönnies, Ferdinand, *Community and Society (Gemeinschaft und Gesellschaft),* ed. and trans. Charles P. Loomis (1957)

Treves, Renato, *Giustizia e Giudici nella Società Italiana* (1972)

Triepel, Henrich, *Vom Stil des Rechts* (1946)

Trubek, David M., "Max Weber on Law and the Rise of Capitalism," 1972 *Wis. L. Rev.* 720

——————, "Toward a Social Theory of Law: An Essay on the Study of Law and Development," 82 *Yale L. J.* 1 (1972)

Tunc, André, "The Grand Outlines of the Code," in Bernard Schwartz, ed., *The Code of Napoleon and the Common Law World* (1956)

Turk, Austin T., *Legal Sanctioning and Social Control* (1972)

Twining, William, *Karl Llewellyn and the Realist Movement* (1973)

Twiss, Benjamin, *Lawyers and the Constitution* (1942)

Ulç, Otto, *The Judge in a Communist State, A View from Within* (1972)

Ulmer, S. Sidney, "The Political Party Variable in the Michigan Supreme Court," 11 *J. Public L.* 352 (1962)

——————, "Social Background as an Indicator to the Votes of Supreme Court Justices in Criminal Cases: 1947–1956 Terms," 17 *Am. J. Pol. Sci.* 622 (1973)

Urofsky, Melvin I., and David W. Levy, eds., *Letters of Louis D. Brandeis* (1972), vol. II

Vansina, Jan, "A Traditional Legal System: The Kuba," in Hilda Kuper and Leo Kuper, eds., *African Law: Adaptation and Development* (1965)

Verba, Sidney, "Comparative Political Culture," in Lucian W. Pye and Sidney Verba, eds., *Political Culture and Political Development* (1965)

Vines, Kenneth N., "Federal District Judges and Race Relations Cases in the South," 26 *J. Politics* 337 (1964)

Vose, Clement E., "Litigation as a Form of Pressure Group Activity," 319 *Annals* 20 (1958)

Waldo, Gordon P., and Theodore G. Chiricos, "Perceived Penal Sanction and Self-Reported Criminality: A Neglected Approach to Deterrence Research," 19 *Social Problems* 522 (1972)

Walker, Nigel, *Crimes, Courts and Figures* (1971)

Walker, Thomas G., "A Note Concerning Partisan Influences in Trial-Judge Decision Making," 6 *Law and Society Rev.* 645 (1972)

Walker, William L., and John W. Thibaut, "An Experimental Examination of Pretrial Conference Techniques," 55 *Minn. L. Rev.* 1113 (1971)

Wasby, Stephen L., *The Impact of the United States Supreme Court, Some Perspectives* (1970)

Wasserstrom, Richard A., *The Judicial Decision, Toward a Theory of Legal Justification* (1961)

Way, H. Frank, Jr., "Survey Research on Judicial Decisions: The Prayer and Bible Reading Cases," 21 *Western Pol. Q.* 189 (1968)

Weber, Max, *The Theory of Social and Economic Organization,* ed. Talcott Parsons (1964)

Wenger, Dennis E., and C. Richard Fletcher, "The Effect of Legal Counsel on Admissions to a State Mental Hospital: A Confrontation of Professions," 10 *J. Health and Soc. Behavior* 66 (1969)

Westin, Alan, *The Anatomy of a Constitutional Law Case* (1958)

Wetter, J. Gillis, *The Styles of Appellate Judicial Opinions, a Case Study in Comparative Law* (1960)

Wettick, R. Stanton, Jr., "A Study of the Assignment of Judges to Criminal Cases in Allegheny County—the Poor Fare Worse," 9 *Duquesne L. Rev.* 51 (1970)

Weyrauch, Walter O., "The 'Basic Law' or 'Constitution' of a Small Group," 27 *J. Social Issues,* no. 2, 49 (1971)

_____, *The Personality of Lawyers* (1964)

Wheeler, Stanton, "Socialization in Correctional Communities," 26 *Am. Soc. Rev.* 697 (1961)

Wieacker, Franz, *Privatrechtsgeschichte der Neuzeit* (1952)

Wilensky, Harold L., and Charles N. Lebeaux, *Industrial Society and Social Welfare* (1958)

Wilson, James Q., *Varieties of Police Behavior* (1968)

Wimberley, Howard, "Legal Evolution: One Further Step," 79 *Am. J. Soc.* 78 (1973)

Woodward, C. Vann, *The Strange Career of Jim Crow* (2nd rev. ed., 1966)

Zander, Michael, *Lawyers and the Public Interest* (1968)

Zeisel, Hans, "Reflections on Experimental Techniques in the Law," 2 *J. Legal Studies* 107 (1973)

Zimring, Franklin E., *Perspectives on Deterrence* (1971)

_____, and Gordon J. Hawkins, *Deterrence, The Legal Threat in Crime Control* (1973)

ZoBell, Karl, "Division of Opinion in the Supreme Court: A History of Judicial Disintegration," 44 *Cornell L. Q.* 186 (1959)

Zweigert, Konrad, and Hein Kötz, *Einführung in die Rechtsvergleichung* (1971), vol. I

Index

Acts, legal, 4; definition of, 25, 44; effectiveness of, 45, 67–136; impact of, 45–66
Aggression, 233
American Law Institute, 270
Analogy, reasoning by, 253–255
Andenaes, Johannes, 64
Ascription, as mode of allocation, 22
Aubert, Vilhelm, 59–60, 145, 225–227, 247
Authority, decay of, 213–214; theories of, 114
Authorizations, 32, 39–40

Baker v. *Carr*, 300–301
Ball, Harry V., 119
Banfield, Edward, 168
Bargaining, 93, 105, 127–130
Bentham, Jeremy, 206, 250
Behavior, characteristics of, as affecting control, 86–91; judicial, 170–171, 180–187, 303 (*see also* Courts; Judges); legal, 4–5, 16, 67–104, and *passim;* theories of, 62–66
Bohannon, Paul, 7
Borrowing, of legal institutions, 194
Brown v. *Board of Education,* 47, 263–264, 277

Calabresi, Guido, 49
Capitalism, 208
"Capture" of regulatory agencies, 128
Cardozo, Benjamin, 2, 170–171
Carter, James C., 141
Challenge, concept of, 237
Chambliss, William, 64–65, 87–88
Chance, as allocative criterion, 22–23

Change, social and legal, 204–208, 269–309
Charisma, as source of authority, 114
Children, development of legal thought, 285–286; and obedience, 117
Civil commitment, 183–184
Civil law family, 200–201; convergence with common law, 220
Civil litigation, benefits and costs, 133–136; *see also* Damages, civil.
Claims-consciousness, 212
Claims of right, 226, 228–234
Class structure, and law, 178–187
Classification of legal systems, 199–204
Codification, 271
Common law, 200, 201, 203, 205, 220, 241, 254n–255n, 258, 261, 265, 266, 267, 272
Compliance, 46–48, 52–53; and legitimacy, 115–120
Communication, of legal acts, 56–62, 93
Competition, and conflict, 145–146
Colonial legal systems, 196–197
Conceptualism, 216
Conflict, 145–146, of interests, 226–227
Conscience, as element in legal behavior, 64–66, 69, 111–113, 120–121
Consensus, and formality of legal systems, 144–148
Conspiracy theory, of 14th amendment, 139–140
Contract, breach of, 39–40
Corruption, 126, 128, 224–225
Costs, of litigation, 133–135, 297